Nat Jackson
zweebex@gmail.com
617.960.7001

Prayer Has Spoiled Everything

BODY, COMMODITY, TEXT

Studies of Objectifying Practice

A series edited by

Arjun Appadurai,

Jean Comaroff, and

Judith Farquhar

Prayer Has Spoiled

Everything POSSESSION, POWER, AND

IDENTITY IN AN ISLAMIC TOWN OF NIGER

Adeline Masquelier

DUKE UNIVERSITY PRESS   DURHAM & LONDON   2001

All rights reserved Printed in the United States of America
on acid-free paper ∞ Designed by C. H. Westmoreland
Typeset in Bembo by Tseng Information Systems, Inc.
Library of Congress Cataloging-in-Publication Data
appear on the last printed page of this book.

For Margaux, Eléonore, and Julia

In the hope that it will inspire them to do their best
while always keeping a sense of humor and perspective,
I dedicate this book to them.

There is no place that is not haunted by many different spirits hidden there in silence, spirits one can "invoke" or not. Haunted places are the only ones people can live in.

Michel de Certeau, *The Practice of Everyday Life*

Contents

List of Illustrations   xi
Acknowledgments   xiii
List of Terms   xvii

Introduction   1

1   *Bori,* Power, and Identity in Dogondoutchi   7

2   Lost Rituals: Changing Topographies of Spirit/Human
    Interactions   49

3   Socializing the Spirits   77

4   The Everyday Life of *Bori:* Knowledge, Embodiment, and
    Quotidian Practice   120

5   Kinesthetic Appropriation and Embodied Knowledge:
    Baboule Spirits and the Making of Value   159

6   Taking Hold of the *Kasuwa:* The Ritual Economy of *Bori* in
    the Market   192

7   The Mirrors of Maria: Sweetness, Sexuality, and Dangerous
    Consumption   227

8   Lightning, Death, and the Politics of Truth:
    The Spirits of Rain   262

Conclusion: Continuities and Discontinuities in *Bori*   291

Notes   301
Bibliography   321
Index   341

List of Illustrations

Maps (facing page 1)

1. Niger.
2. *Arrondissement* of Dogondoutchi.

Photographs

1. The rocky peak after which the town of Dogondoutchi was named stands against the late afternoon sky.   2
2. A sprawling Dogondoutchi neighborhood with its mud homes and clusters of trees.   2
3. An unused stone altar (*hango*) stands as a reminder of a time when people regularly shed sacrificial blood to feed the spirits.   54
4. A stone is erected for the spirit of a newly initiated medium.   66
5. During a wasa, the calabash players and violinists play the spirits' songs while women dance.   98
6. Two mediums possessed by Adama and her sister lie on the ground, embodying the paralysis the spirits cause in their victims.   106
7. Folded wrappers and robes are placed next to the hatchets of the spirits of lightning in preparation for a wasa.   108
8. Four mediums of Gurmunya, the lame spirit, wear their bori attire, including a hat sewn with cowrie shells and antelope horns decorated with strips of leather.   108
9. Hamissou is a bori devotee and a leather worker.   109
10. A bori devotee wearing the striped wrappers of Zanzana dances gracefully to the music of bori.   109
11. A bori healer sacrifices a white chicken at the onset of a wasa to insure the protection of the participants.   113
12. The *jima* (bori specialist) and three assistants prepare a calabash of medicated henna with which the amarya will be washed.   113
13. A senior bori medium (assistant to the jima) washes the *amarya*'s body with medicated henna.   115
14. While the amarya, covered with a white wrapper, holds on to the spear planted in the anthill, the ritual supervisor brushes a white chicken against her body to induce possession.   115
15. A house built for a spirit.   223

16. Mosque built by a bori medium who claimed that his spirit, a Muslim scholar, requested such a structure.   223

17. In the house he built for his spirit, Kirai, a bori healer, has assembled a variety of enamel bowls and calabashes in which he stores the medicines he provides to his patients.   224

18. Food is a crucial dimension of bori. Here millet and corn paste await guests.   242

19. A young medium posessed by Maria is offered a bowl filled with candy, money, and perfume as she straightens her head scarf to express vanity.   245

20. Maria devotees possessed by their spirits are offered an assortment of candy, perfume, and sugar cubes during a *wasa*.   251

21. All three bori leaders, who are erecting a stone altar for a spirit in someone's compound, wear Muslim attire.   264

22. This tree was struck by lightning in 1994. A wasa was held soon after to beg the spirits' forgiveness.   267

23. During a wasa held for the spirits of rain and lightning, two possessed mediums dispense advice to members of the audience.   277

24. A possessed bori devotee dressed in the costume of Kirai's brother, Souleymane, helps hold a goat that is about to be sacrificed.   280

25. Two assistants dress a devotee possessed by Kirai during a wasa held for the spirits of rain and lightning.   297

Acknowledgments

WHILE I ALONE AM RESPONSIBLE for the flaws that may appear in this study, I cannot take full credit for the book's strengths. There are numerous people I must thank for the guidance, support, encouragement, and friendship they have offered over the past thirteen years. This book owes a primary debt to the people of Dogondoutchi for their hospitality and assistance in documenting possession practices. At this time, I can only imperfectly repay this debt of kindness by expressing my gratitude in general and impersonal terms. To Rabi, Ibro, Tahirou, Houre, Mamou, Amadou, Baidou, Kyakai, Bagoudou, Zoumbaye, Rakwas, Bilen, Agabo, 'Dan Juma, Neni, and the many others who have enriched my life, I say: "*Na gode, Allah ya ba da sa'a!*" My friend Iyale patiently and generously guided my interest in possession and prostitution and helped me make sense of the world of the spirits. Her friendship sustained me throughout my stay in Dogondoutchi. Dije shared her home, humor, and knowledge of *bori* spirit possession and Islam. Besides providing me with her enjoyable company, she made sure I was apprised of any gossip that circulated around town. Ta'amadou's complex and troubled relationship with marriage and possession, which she freely discussed with me, provided a valuable vantage point from which to assess the challenges faced by young female *bori* devotees. Her kindness and understanding also helped me keep things in perspective during difficult times. I would like to thank the late *sarkin bori* Yenge for his support and his appreciation of my research. Though he will never browse through a copy of this book, I know he would have been tolerant of this attempt to inscribe the *tarihin* (history of) *bori* for younger generations. Mahammadou and Yahaya, each in their own ways, contributed a great deal to this study by assisting with interviews and transcriptions and by sharing their own views on Mawri society.

My warmest appreciation also goes to the government of Niger for granting me permission to do research in Niger and to Boube Gado, the director of the Institut de Recherches en Sciences Humaines in Niamey, for putting the resources of his institution at my disposal. I owe a huge debt to Boube Mahamane, librarian at the Institut, for his generous assistance and for letting me work after hours at the library.

The *sous-préfet* of Dogondoutchi and local authorities, including *sarkin* Amadou Gao, gave me a warm welcome and were helpful during my research. I must also acknowledge the assistance I received from the staff at the Archives Nationales in Niamey and at the Archives d'Outre-Mer in Aix-en-Provence, France. I am forever indebted to the Mayaki family, who offered me a home when I needed one and provided me with friendship, advice, and encouragement. A special thanks to Henriette for her generous attention and unfailing support. Knowing she was there for me in times of crisis made all the difference. The Catholic mission in Dogondoutchi was another safe haven to which I sometimes retreated when I needed solace or companionship. My heartfelt thanks, then, to Benito, Jimi, Yahaya, Isabelle, Thérèse, and everyone else. I am grateful to Yaji Dogo, who encouraged me initially to focus on Dogondoutchi and who helped me find a house and get situated in the community. Many thanks also to Jennifer Yanco, Tina and Pascal da Campo, Ahmed Zayan, and Barbara Cooper for their friendship and support. The Delmotte family provided valuable logistical assistance during my first visit to Niamey.

Financial support for this project was initially provided by a research fellowship from the National Institute of Mental Health, a grant from the Wenner-Gren Foundation for Anthropological Research, and a research grant from the National Science Foundation. These institutions are heartily thanked for their assistance. The vast majority of field and archival research contained in this book was carried out during 1988 and 1989. Two additional months of field research carried out in the summer of 1994 were made possible by a summer fellowship from Tulane University's Committee on Research.

This book is a revised and shortened version of my doctoral dissertation submitted to the University of Chicago in 1993. I am greatly indebted to the members of my dissertation committee at Chicago: Jean Comaroff, James Fernandez, and Nancy Munn, for sharing their insight and wisdom. I am particularly grateful to my committee chair, Jean Comaroff, for her close and constructive engagement in this project. Our conversations about my work were always such a precious source of insight and energy that I always left feeling invigorated and somehow "brighter." In addition to enriching the manuscript with her masterly, selfless efforts, she provided unfailing kindness, warmth, and support every step of the way. Also thanks to John Comaroff for offering assistance and encouragement when I needed them the most; and to Ralph Austen for his helpful suggestions. I must also signal my gratitude to my fellow students at the University of Chicago. Their questions, interest, and inspiration have been central to my intellectual development. In particular, my appreciation goes to Mark Auslander, Misty Bastian, Debra Spitulnik, and Brad Weiss for their careful and critical reading of some chapters of the dissertation version of this study. To Misty, I am deeply grateful for all the countless and varied ways—her critical insights, her suggestions for further reading, her nurturing hospitality—in which she demonstrated her enduring support and interest in this project. Brad was also a wonderful source of inspiration during the various phases of the writing. Chapters 4 and 7, especially, would not be what they are without his tremendous help. I thank them both for sharing so much of this intellectual journey with me.

I benefited greatly from the generous assistance and support of a number of colleagues, mentors, and friends—in particular, Janice Boddy, Tim Burke, Allan Darrah, the late Nicole Échard, Alma Gottlieb, Michael Lambek, Ute Luig, Jean Rahier, Pamela Schmoll, Rosalind Shaw, Paul Stoller, Dick Werbner, and Luise White. I am particularly indebted to Barbara Cooper, Nicole Échard, Murray Last, Éliane de Latour, Guy Nicolas, Marc-Henri Piault, and other scholars of Hausaland on whose work I have relied heavily. My debt to them will be obvious in what follows. Questions raised by Rosalind Shaw sharpened the conceptualization of chapters 5 and 8. Alma Gottlieb offered helpful criticism and corrections to chapter 1. Michael Lambek greatly assisted in the process of revision by providing pertinent but constructive criticism of the whole manuscript. He as well as Janice Boddy have influenced my thinking more than they realize. I must thank my editor Ken Wissoker for his supportive suggestions and his patient understanding, as well as Leigh Ann Couch and Patricia Mickelberry. The anonymous reviewers for Duke University Press also left their imprint on this work and improved it enormously. William Fisher was an invaluable source of support in the early phases of this project. Gaurav Desai, Christopher Dunn, and Roseanne Adderley, all three members of the exclusive "First Book Write-Up Club for Untenured Faculty at Tulane," made useful suggestions. If they ever read this book, they will find out I have not necessarily followed their advice, but I am nonetheless immensely grateful for their pointing out key issues that needed to be clarified and for helping me see both the trees and the forest during a critical phase of the rewriting. Our "dinner with a dissertation" sessions provided a much needed and invigorating intellectual experience. My colleagues in the department of anthropology at Tulane provided a collegial and caring environment that has sustained me for the last eight years. I am especially grateful to Victoria Bricker for her careful editing of chapter 3. Kay Marden and Sarah Rennard, both graduate students in the department, provided valuable research and editorial assistance.

Portions of the manuscript were published or given as papers elsewhere, and journal editors, anonymous reviewers, discussants, and audiences contributed to the revision process. A briefer version of chapter 6 appeared as "Narratives of Power, Images of Wealth: the Ritual Economy of *Bori* in the Market" in Jean and John Comaroff's edited volume *Modernity and Its Malcontents* (1993). Chapter 7 appeared in a condensed version as "Consumption, Prostitution, and Reproduction: The Poetics and Power of Sweetness in *Bori*" in *American Ethnologist* 22(4): 883–906 (1995). An expanded version of chapter 8 was published as "Lightning, Death, and the Avenging Spirits: *Bori* Values in a Muslim World" in the *Journal of Religion in Africa* (1994). Permission to publish these chapters here is gratefully acknowledged.

As much as I appreciate the assistance I received and the interest many friends and teachers expressed in my work, little could have been accomplished without the help of my family. My parents gave me financial and emotional support in the early phase of this endeavor, helping me with the purchase of my Peugeot 504, which took me to so many bori ceremonies in the bush. To both my mother and my father, I am grateful for intentionally—and, at times, unintentionally—fostering in me an interest in other cultures. Grace and Bill Fisher were also helpful in more ways than I can describe. Bill More demonstrated more forbearance, patience, and understanding than I could ever have asked for. He was a tremendous source of practical and emotional support in the last phase of this project. Finally, I thank my daughters, Margaux, Eléonore, and Julia, who have, since birth, participated in this lengthy authorial adventure and showed a healthy mixture of enthusiasm and skepticism toward "mom's book." It is their inexhaustible affection, endurance, energy, and optimism that kept me both human and cheerful during the difficult times.

Terms

al'ada	custom
alhaji	man who has accomplished the pilgrimage to Mecca
alhazai	the merchant class, most of whom have accomplished the pilgrimage to Mecca (plural of *alhaji*)
aljanu	jinn, spirits (plural of *aljani*, m., and *aljana*, f.)
amarya	bride; *bori* initiate
arme	marriage
arziki	good fortune; prosperity; well-being
Azna	non-Muslim Mawri who worship indigenous spirits under the leadership of the *'yan kasa*, or local priestly elders
biki	ceremony; celebration for a marriage or a naming ceremony
boka	healer; native doctor (*bokaye*, plural)
bori	a type of spirit; the practices surrounding possession by such spirits; more generally, the worship of these spirits
budurwa	unmarried girl
ci	to eat; to win over someone; to have sex
ciki	belly, stomach, insides; pregnancy
daji	bush; wilderness
'dan bori	"son of the *bori*"; *bori* spirit medium
'dan 'kasa	"son of the earth"; Azna priest
doki	horse; spirit medium
fura	millet porridge
gado	heritage
gargajiya	olden times; tradition
gari	town
garka	fenced plot, open space in front of compound, area where *bori* possession ritual is held
gida	house; household
goro	cola nut
gumba	raw millet paste
gyara	arrangement; *bori* initiation
gyaran gari	seasonal ritual performed to protect a town or village

hajiya	woman who has accomplished the pilgrimage to Mecca
hango	altar for local spirit
hau	to ride; to possess
hauka	crazy; family of military spirits also known as the Baboule
iska	wind; spirit (*iskoki,* plural)
'karfi	strength
karuwa	prostitute
karuwanci	prostitution
'kasa	earth, land, ground; country
kashin 'kwarya	"breaking of the calabash"; *bori* mortuary ritual
kasuwa	market
kumya	shame, embarrassment; respect; avoidance relationship
kunu	sweet millet gruel consumed by new mothers during the postpartum period
kurwa	soul; vital essence
lahiya	health
likita	practitioner of biomedicine
magani	medicine, remedy
mai goge	violinist
mai 'kwarya	calabash player
mai yanka	spirit devotee appointed to perform sacrifice
malam	male Koranic scholar; cleric (*malamai,* plural)
malama	female Koranic scholar
maroka	musicians (plural of *maroki*)
mata	woman; wife
maye	sorcerer; witch (*mayu,* plural)
miya	spicy sauce served to accompany *tuwo*
mutanen daji	"people of the bush"; spirits (*mutun daji,* singular)
namiji	husband
sa'a	luck
sadaki	bridewealth
salla	prayer, often synonymous with "Islam"
sana'a	trade; craft; any income–generating activity
sarauniya	queen
sarauta	ruling elite; aristocracy; official position held by members of the aristocracy
sarki	chief or traditional ruler

sarkin bori   chief of *bori*

saurayi   young unmarried man; youth

sha   to drink; to have sex

shan ice   *bori* initiatory ceremony

shari'a   Koranic law

takarda   paper; divorce papers; certificate

talakawa   commoners; peasants; the poor

tarkama   judgment by ordeal during which the corpse of the deceased Azna priest designates his successor

tuwo   staple food of millet or guinea corn grits served with *miya*

ulema   learned Muslim men

umma   worldwide community of Muslim believers

wasa   play; entertainment; joking; *bori* ceremony (*wasani,* plural)

wasam bori   bori ceremony

yanka   to cut, to slaughter, to sacrifice

'yan bori   "children of the bori"; *bori* devotees (plural of *'dan bori*)

'yan 'kasa   "children of the earth"; Azna priestly elders (plural of *'dan 'kasa*)

zaure   entrance room to a compound

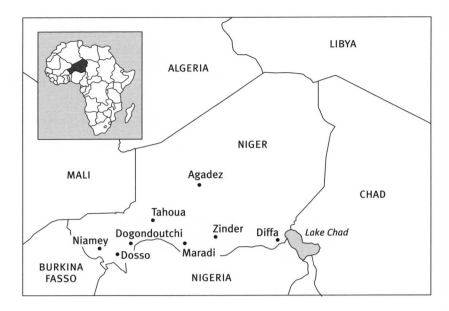

Niger.

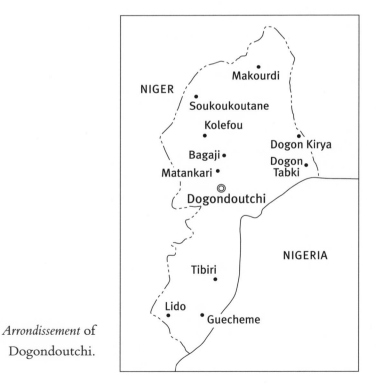

Arrondissement of
Dogondoutchi.

Introduction

DOGONDOUTCHI. The name variously evokes a haven for ancestral traditions, a center of anti-Islamic resistance, or a place filled with spirits dangerous for most Nigeriens, be they Zarma, Hausa, Fulani, or Tuareg. With a population of over 30,000, this Hausaphone Mawri community of northern Arewa is the size of a small regional "urban" center. Yet the collection of earthen homesteads clustered along a grid of unpaved streets that dwindle into footpaths gives it more the appearance of a large village huddling at the foot of the *dogon doutchi*— the "long stone," a rocky peak that towers over the nearly treeless savanna like a giant termite hill visible from miles away. Originally composed of a village core surrounded by small hamlets, Dogondoutchi has grown and progressively absorbed these neighboring communities. The overall town now counts fifteen *quartiers* (neighborhoods) and is the administrative seat of the *arrondissement* (district) bearing its name. It is a magnet for people who live in scattered hamlets throughout the district. They come to visit the weekly market, seek treatment at the dispensary, attend Sunday service at the Catholic mission, register their children in school, or mail a letter from the post office.

Save for a few dozen Fulani and Tuareg families who make a living herding their neighbors' cattle and sheep, villagers are sedentary farmers. They cultivate millet, sorghum, beans, and groundnut, the soil for which they till exclusively by hoe. Rainfall is highly variable, however, and the intensification of cash cropping has impoverished the soil and made good farmland scarce. The overharvesting of firewood has further hastened the process of desertification already under way. Over 140 years ago, the German explorer Barth described Arewa as rugged but "mostly covered with dense forest only now and then broken by a small tract of cultivated ground" (1857, 122). Later, the French geographer Élisé Reclus wrote of a region endowed with thick soils and "palm trees, bushy trees growing in picturesque clusters" (1887, 582). Today, northern Arewa is a dry savanna

The rocky peak after which the town of Dogondoutchi was named stands against the late afternoon sky. All photos by Adeline Masquelier.

A sprawling Dogondoutchi neighborhood with its mud homes and clusters of trees. In the background, the town mosque where Muslims gather for the Friday afternoon prayer.

where large trees remain few and far. While old men recall dreamily a time when Dogondoutchi was surrounded by a thick forest filled with wild animals of all sorts, many, among the younger generation, complain about land shortage. Faced with dwindling opportunities and resources, many of them have had to migrate to the city on a seasonal or even, sometimes, permanent basis.

Despite the unforgiving environment, the cycles of hunger and poverty, and the failure of successive development projects, Dogondoutchi is a bustling community. At sunrise, the soft, rhythmic clunks of pestles meeting the bottoms of mortars signal women's first involvement in the daily culinary preparations. The smoke of cooking fires soon rises in the misty air. As Fulani herders gather everyone's cows, sheep, and goats to lead them to the bush, petty traders are setting up tables covered with various small items they sell by the unit—candy, soap, perfume, medicine, batteries, matches, cassettes. Women sweep their courtyards with brooms without handles made of dried grass while old men, sitting in their doorways, survey the neighborhood. When the heat of midday becomes too oppressive, traffic in the sandy streets slows down to a trickle as villagers cling to the shade provided by acacias, baobabs, or mango trees. In their sun-drenched compounds, women seek shelter against the walls, away from the blistering heat, as they braid a neighbors' hair, roast peanuts, or fry bean cakes. As dusk approaches, the rhythmic thumping of pestles and mortars intensifies. The rising smoke of cooking fires mixes with the thick dust kicked up by the cattle returning from pasture. As men return home for a dinner of spicy millet or rice dishes, kerosene lamps are lit everywhere, their dim and quivering glows breaking the thick night to reveal the outlines of walls and doorways.

On certain nights, the sharp clatter of calabash drums bursts from the mud walls of a compound, drowning out the sound of sun-powered televisions that draw daily crowds of spectators in every neighborhood. People slowly gather in a circle as the musicians sing praise songs. These gatherings are public performances held for the mischievous and invisible beings that populate the bush. Frightening but also comforting, destructive yet, paradoxically, supportive of human projects, the wild forces that are tamed in the context of possession ceremonies are often called *mutanen daji* ("people of the bush") or simply *bori*. This book is an account of how they intervene—sometimes subtly, sometimes dramatically—in human lives to provide a constantly renewed source of meaning for Mawri peasants confronted with cultural contradictions and socioeconomic marginalization. In exploring the role of bori possession in local definitions of history, power, and identity, I have focused on the diverse ways in which spirit mediums share, transform, and contest a rapidly changing reality, threatened by Muslim hegemony and financial hardship.

For spirit devotees, the spread of Islam in Arewa has provoked unfortunate and irremediable changes. Prayer, a conspicuous element of daily life that has become virtually synonymous with Islamic practice in this region of west Africa, is thus equated with the loss of tradition and what was once "authentic" value. Hence, the title of this book, *Prayer Has Spoiled Everything,* is drawn from the disabused testimony of Adamou, a fifty-year-old spirit medium who routinely illuminated my understanding of things Mawri with his insightful commentaries on the costs and challenges of modernity. Adamou's disenchantment notwithstanding, the followers of the spirits are hardly powerless or "dispossessed" (Sharp 1993) in this region of Niger (see Map 1). The analyses in this book constitute an attempt to demonstrate how possession is implicated in the *making* of the Mawri lived world by focusing on some of the creative and complex ways that bori at once competes with and borrows from Islam and other wider processes of social transformation to mediate what many perceive as a widening gap between former ways of life and the contradictions of the present.

Prayer Has Spoiled Everything opens in chapter 1 with a discussion of the various theoretical perspectives on spirit possession around or against which I situate my own approach to bori. This review of the literature, which focuses primarily on the issues of meaning and marginality, power and resistance, is followed by a brief history of Arewa. The chapter then ends with a description of some of the orientations, strategies, and limitations of my ethnographic research.

In chapter 2, I lay out the background against which bori has emerged and describe the role played by the spirits in charting the land on which the first occupants established their settlements. I discuss the disappearance of pre-Islamic communal rituals and the sense of loss currently felt by spirit devotees in the wake of Islam's progressive erasure of the moral geography in which non-Muslim Mawri traditionally anchored their history and identity. In chapter 3, I provide a general overview of bori and those who have committed themselves to serving the spirits as musicians, mediums, or healers. In chapter 4,

I trace the significance of bori meanings in quotidian discourse and practice to emphasize the contextual dimension of the possession experience and to concretize the tacit and latent communication that exists between spirits and hosts on a daily basis.

I got to know certain spirits quite well during my fieldwork. The fickle Maria admiring her lovely reflection in a looking glass, the fearful Zarma siblings who control rain and lightning, and the fierce Baboule, immune to the effects of fire, have all captured my own imagination. In the process of writing their story, I found myself struggling with the problem of how to translate in anthropological language the rich, vibrant, and multilayered texture of bori experiences when much of the content of these experiences remained unarticulated. Rather than providing an objective—and therefore necessarily incomplete—listing of bori spirits with their basic characteristics,[1] I have opted for a narrower focus on selected members of the local pantheon who typify bori's potential for concretizing many of the elusive processes of transformation that have impacted Mawri society. Such an intimate discussion of the creative or, conversely, destructive role spirits play in orchestrating people's lives allows me to locate bori within the context of quotidian meanings shaping the cultural understandings through which 'yan bori share, mediate, or contest a constantly evolving reality. In chapter 5, I examine the Baboule spirits, focusing on their emergence in the 1920s. I explore how spirit mediums crafted an alternative economy in their creative efforts to rebel against the French colonial state while paradoxically appropriating its emblems of power and its techniques for producing wealth. The themes of chapter 6 resonate with those of chapter 5: they center around what I call the ritual economy of bori in contemporary Dogondoutchi. Here the contested authority is no longer a colonial administration but the rapidly growing body of Muslims who have taken control of the networks of trade. There again, protest goes hand in hand with compliance in the 'yan bori's response to Muslim ascendancy over local commerce. As we shall see, the mediums' efforts to appropriate new modes of generating value are motivated by an urgency to reclaim the partially effaced map of the moral landscape onto which, as seen in chapter 2, people inscribed their mythical connections to the spirits in pre-Islamic times.

The recent encroachment of Muslim practices in Arewa has impacted Mawri society well beyond the domain of marketing. Among other things, the progressive adoption of Islamic norms has altered local perceptions of femininity, reinforcing the need to harness female sexuality through the institutions of marriage, seclusion, and mother-hood. Mawri women's tendency to embody evil and contradiction is explored in chapter 7 through a discussion of the relationship between female sexuality, power, and possession. Focusing on the semantics of sweetness, I explore how the concept of things sweet meaningfully ties together the contexts of prostitution, alimentation, and obstetrics. As an icon of luxury, pleasure, and eroticism, sweetness in its many forms addresses the threats of uncontrolled consumption through its personification as the enigmatic and perverse Maria spirit. In chapter 8, I discuss yet another dimension of the 'yan bori's ongoing efforts to rework the terms of their authority in communities that have witnessed the growing control of Muslims in village affairs, this time by focusing on resistance to rather than complicity with Islam. I examine bori interpretations of lightning to illuminate how such dis-course can become an instrument of coercive power in the hands of a minority seeking both to reassert its indispensability and to redefine the parameters of superhuman justice. By branding on the minds of their opponents an alternative moral order, bori devotees provide a conceptual framework for understanding sudden tragedies while at the same time contesting hegemonic Muslim values. In the conclu-sion, I reflect upon the seemingly paradoxical implications of change and continuity for spirit mediums who have consistently used the bori both as a form of anchorage into the past and as a locus for the me-diation of historical transformations. Since both the spirits and their devotees can be either male or female, the pronouns "he" and "she" will be used interchangeably. Unless otherwise noted, all translations throughout the text are my own.

Chapter 1

Bori, Power, and Identity

in Dogondoutchi

The traffic in spirits is almost as widespread and intensive as
the teaching of Islam.—I. M. Lewis, *Religion in Context*

IN ONE OF HER PRAISE SONGS for the spirits, the nationally known
Mawri singer Tagimba declares that "those who say they have no
spirits are liars." There is much truth in the *griotte*'s (praise singer) statement for Dogondoutchi residents who take the presence of spirits in
people's existence to be a self-evident fact of life. There are spirits in
many—some would say, all—Mawri households who attend to the
needs of their human counterparts or who, conversely, inflict end-
less torments on them. The powers of these superhuman forces are
sometimes denied by the very people in whose lives they interfere for
better or for worse. Yet even those Muslims who most vehemently
castigate bori devotees for their "sinful" practices cannot deny ever
witnessing in their childhood a grandfather or father's sacrificial offering to the tutelary spirits. While such memories may have become
part of the dead stuff of *gargajiya* (tradition) for those who have opted
to follow the teachings of the Koran, they remain an important source
of meaning for bori mediums who have chosen to serve the spirits.
As these mediums eventually age and die, spirits must look for other
suitable, yet equally transient, vessels to possess. That these spirits may
find no adequate hosts in whose body to incarnate themselves, or that
they make no immediate demands on the descendants of their former
devotees, rarely means that they are gone forever, as some, who today
profess skepticism or indifference, may find out sooner or later. Spirits
come and go, but as bori devotees like to forcefully remind their Muslim foes, they are always nearby, waiting perhaps for the right occasion
to reinsert themselves in a human frame.

   Besides pointing to the inescapable contiguity between the world of
humans and the world of spirits, Tagimba's ironic statement also highlights the complex patterns of secrecy, complicity, and competition

that characterize relations between members of the bori, who call themselves 'yan bori ("children of the bori," or devotees of the bori), and Muslims. In their eagerness to demarcate themselves from bori identity, most Muslims will confidently declare that they want nothing to do with fetishes, spirits, or sacrifices. Yet every one of them, bori devotees will tell you, has had recourse to the services of bori healers, and may have even sacrificed to a spirit to insure a son's academic success or a daughter's recovery from illness. In the cautionary message she delivers to her Hausa-speaking audience, Tagimba seems to imply that many Muslims are acting like hypocrites by choosing to ignore, and even disparage, the spirits when they no longer need them.

At another level, the singer's denunciation of Muslim shallowness and duplicity partly illustrates the extent to which Islamic and bori identities overlap despite concerted efforts, on both sides, to reaffirm distinctive forms of knowledge, practice, and morality. The interaction between Islamic and indigenous world views has been extensive and complex; when 'yan bori choose to go on the hajj (pilgrimage to Mecca) or when Muslims turn up at possession ceremonies, the difficulties one faces in trying to pinpoint what distinguishes a follower of the Prophet from a spirit medium are further compounded.

The problem of analyzing bori in light of prevailing Muslim discourse is a complex one because bori has always maintained an ambiguous relationship with Islam: as will become clear, members of the bori tend to protest the hegemony of Islam while paradoxically borrowing from the Muslim repertoire of signifiers that they see as a reservoir of power ready to be tapped. In so doing, spirit devotees appear to revise the script of Islamic domination at the same time that they reassert the viability and centrality of indigenous values. The fact that those who seek the assistance of the spirits sometimes do so indirectly or secretly so as not to tarnish their Muslim identity only renders more problematic any attempt to locate bori within local networks of power relations, and to assess its continued influence in the lives of Dogondoutchi residents.

Bori is not a refuge from the inequities of modern life. It does not solely address the plight of divorced or childless women — as is mostly the case in the ethnographic realities described by Monfouga-Nicolas (1972) and Schmoll (1991); nor does it exclusively cater to the needs of those who identify themselves as devotees of the spirits. Bori, and this is where its strength resides, knows no boundaries and has no set territory because it often operates through the deployment of powerful tropes that touch the core of Mawri experience. In short, the strength of bori lies more in the grasp spirits have on the collective imagination than in the size of its visible membership. Through its broad concerns with the articulation of conflict-laden experience, bori speaks to a host of issues that transcend the confines of individual afflictions or personal crises to address the problems of entire communities variously confronted with such disruptive circumstances as the impact of colonial rule, the emergence of novel forms of production, or the raw reality of lightning—to cite some of the themes discussed at length in the following chapters.

Despite its centrality in the life of numerous communities, households, and families, in the last forty years bori has lost much ground to Islam on the visible terrain of religious practice. As more youths embrace Islam, and as bori devotees become increasingly pressured by local Muslim elites to abandon "traditional" rituals that, by official Islamic standards, are simply backward and sinful, it becomes relevant to ask whether bori will remain a significant force in Mawri history and society. Despite the fact that the recently adopted Charte nationale of Niger constitutionally guarantees the right of "Islam, animism, Christianity and all other forms of belief [to] coexist to answer the spiritual and social needs of Nigerien populations" (République du Niger 1987, 37), in Dogondoutchi and elsewhere bori is not awarded the same consideration as Islam.

In the face of Muslims' growing control over the nexus of trade, administration, and political leadership, some scholars have expressed the opinion that belief in spirits will fade over time as orthodox Islam becomes more firmly entrenched in rural communities. Guy Nicolas (1975) has suggested, for instance, that pre-Islamic signs and practices, which were intimately linked to a subsistence economy, have been weakened by the arrival of money and the shift to commercial agricultural production. Arguing that commodity capitalism and its socioeconomic impacts cannot be accounted for in the "traditional" system, he noted, for instance, the deleterious effects of the 1968–74 drought on bori: because they were not powerful enough to avert the climatic catastrophe, spirits have lost some of their prestige in the eyes of people. Such interpretation is contradicted by the studies of Échard (1992), who found that the massive hunger of the seventies provided renewed impetus for representing and acting upon historical forces via spirit possession: in the neighboring region of Ader, east of Dogondoutchi, a new female spirit associated with crickets made her appearance on the bori arena in 1973. She went by the name of Bobo, a term that refers to one of the twenty different species of crickets found in Ader. She had come from the west with the crickets, she said, to devastate the country. Other spirits of Zarma origin also appeared at that time to destroy Ader communities by throwing lightning. These dangerous figures symbolized Zarma political and economic domination: at independence, the numerically dominant Hausa—of which the Mawri are a subgroup—became politically controlled by the Zarma minority. Through their possession by violent and destructive spirits who caused hunger and harm, villagers expressed their sense that the famine was caused by the government's mismanagement of the national economy (Échard 1992).

I never heard of Bobo in Dogondoutchi but found numerous expressions of the bori's creative potential for mediating the shift to an increasingly monetarized economy. As will become apparent, bori provides a crucial medium for representing the unseen, interpreting the novel, and mediating the foreign. This ability to explain and act upon the puzzles, paradoxes, and disruptions of Mawri society by investing seemingly unambiguous media—the marketplace, a lightning bolt, or the sweetness of sugar—with newly relevant significations is what makes bori a productive, practical, and viable alternative to Islam for those who experience an increasing loss of control over the forces that give their lives meaning.

This book is an attempt to situate bori at the intersection of local experience and wider, encompassing processes in order to trace the transformations of Mawri symbols and values that, despite predictions of their impending obsoleteness in the face of Islamic expansion, have remained relevant and meaningful for many of those who seek to assert their own agency in contemporary Arewa. In my discussion of Mawri people's engagement with the spirit world, I treat possession as a dynamic force of history and analyze the idioms and tropes of bori as an expression of social consciousness. While bori often provides a lens through which to remember an idealized past, it also serves as an important arena in which to articulate the problems of contemporary life. Such capacity to simultaneously manage the forces of tradition and innovation is what enables bori to transform the experience of novel, ambiguous, or threatening realities into symbols of a shared consciousness. In drawing particular attention to the imaginative and agentive dimensions of possession, one may describe bori as a force in constant flux, whose representations remain perpetually shifting, often contested, and rarely totally articulated. It will be seen that the potency of bori in changing contexts of engagement between the local and the global is intimately tied to the historical circumstances in which its images and practices acquire their meanings.

Anthropological Approaches to Possession

Possession in its various cultural forms has long been an object of fascination for social scientists and psychiatrists attempting to interpret the nature of this profound religious drama. For early anthropologists intent upon classifying the alien and the exotic, possession was a theatrical form of hysteria, a disease that, as its name indicates (*hystera* means "womb" in Greek) prevailed among women. Following Plato ([1929],1981) who diagnosed trance as symptomatic of a distressed womb unable to generate children, researchers insisted on the pathological dimension of spirit possession. Frazer (Beattie and Middleton 1969, xxiv), for instance, wrote that in "savage" societies, possession was:

> commonly invoked to explain all abnormal mental states, particularly insanity or conditions of mind bordering on it. So these persons more or less crazed in their wits, and particularly hysterical or epileptic patients, are for that very reason thought to be peculiarly favoured by the spirits and are therefore consulted as oracles, their wild and whirling words passing for the revelations of a higher power, whether a god or a ghost, who considerably screens his too dazzling light under a thick veil of dark sayings and mysterious ejaculations.

Several decades later, the association between madness and possession remained the operating paradigm. Devereux wrote that shamans should be seen as "suffering from serious neurosis, or even as a psychotic in a state of temporary remission" (1970, 15). Bastide also took for granted the pathological dimension of possession, entitling one of his works *Le rêve, la transe, et la folie* (1972). In an essay on mediumship, de Heusch wrote that "trance can be seen as the cultural aspect of mental illness or as the 'madness of the gods'" (1971, 256). And Jean Rouch gave to his famous film on spirit possession among Nigerien migrants in Ghana the title of *Les maîtres fous* (The Mad Masters) (1956).

With the debate still raging over whether or not religious trance should be explained in pathological terms, anthropologists began to adopt a functionalist framework in their analyses of possession based upon an increasing concern with healing as a concept with the potential to resolve social contradictions. Such efforts were part of a widespread current of change in Anglo-American anthropology as functionalism took over the discipline. In the field of religious studies, such a move was heralded by Ioan Lewis's claim that possession—as a universal category of behavior that, together with shamanism, could fall under the rubric *ecstatic religion*—must be studied as a social phenomenon having to do with power and marginality (1966). Lewis's cross-cultural characterization of the powerless predictably spawned further studies of possession as viable strategies of redress for marginalized, deprived, or subordinate individuals in male-centered cultures or competitive contexts (Besmer 1983; Gomm 1975; Gussler 1973; Onwuejeogwu 1969; Wilson 1967). A parallel focus on possession as problem-solving process led other analysts to privilege the therapeutic dimensions of possession at the expense of its religious, aesthetic, and historical significance (Crapanzano 1973; Field 1960; Kennedy 1967; Messing 1958; Prince 1968; Ward 1980). Similarly eschewing the embededness of trance phenomena in a system of cultural meanings, Kehoe and Giletti have proposed a biological model that links women's participation in possession to calcium deficiency (1981; see also Raybeck, Shoobe, and Grauberg 1989).

The medicalization of possession in the Anglo-American literature can be contrasted with the more meaning-centered approach that has prevailed in French anthropology (see Boddy 1994; Csordas 1987). In the latter, the symbolic and aesthetic dimensions are often the focus of the study (Bastide 1978; Métraux 1958; Rouch 1989; Rouget 1985). Rather than casting ritual in a rationalist framework, some of these approaches have hovered between ethnographic analysis and literary account to become poetic testimonies to the complex reality of possession (Balandier 1957; Gibbal 1994; Leiris 1958; Rosenthal 1998). Such attention to aesthetic issues has led to an increased focus on the theatricality of possession (Leiris 1958; Métraux 1958; Schaeffner 1965). From this perspective, the possessed mediums are cultural actors who enact a play in front of an audience that shares with the performers an understanding of the staged sequence of events. Like a theater play, the ritual drama always reaches a denouement; categories, feelings, and relationships are expressed in an exaggerated manner, and the social processes of everyday life are epitomized in a stereotypical fashion (see Turner 1968).

Yet, as Kapferer notes in his ethnography of Sri Lankan demonic exorcism, performance is not merely the enactment of a text "reducible to terms independent of its formation as a structure of practice" (1983, 7). It is rather the union of text and performance in the sense that a text takes its shape and becomes experienced through performance. In short, the text constitutes the performance as much as it is constituted by the performance. This notion of a dialectical interplay between text and performance has important implications for the way one conceptualizes change and creativity in possession. The case of *vodou* in Haiti is a perfect example of how action as text shapes and is shaped by the actors' experience (Brown 1991). Yet when early anthropologists, who had come to take for granted the precise and rigidly orchestrated performances of Brazilian or Dahomean possession, observed the apparently chaotic displays of Haitian vodou, they saw in them a sign of degeneration. For Métraux, the frantic pace, the violent motions, and the frequent outbursts of passion and frenzy—which were only found in Haitian vodou—were a manifestation of anarchy, an indication that Haitian actors did not "follow the text" (1958). Other scholars interpreted them as a sign that old African ways were progressively being forgotten (Larose 1977).

Fortunately, more contemporary works have demonstrated how a revised concept of possession as a ritually enacted text can shape interpretive analyses of such practices both as lived-in experience and as rich and complex cultural statements (Boddy 1989; Lambek 1981; Rasmussen 1995; Rosenthal 1998). For Boddy, the aesthetic and therapeutic power of a *zar* (indigenous spirit "cults" found primarily in East Africa) possession ritual lies precisely in the fact that when it is enacted, the text takes on a life of its own and is open to multiple readings and interpretations (1989, 150). Stoller put a different spin on the theatrical metaphor to suggest that the sounds of *holey* ceremonies are the voices of the ancestors whose dramatic message is amplified through the musicians' instruments and the mediums' screams (1989a).

Recent ethnographies that explore how possession enables devotees to articulate a wide range of social, historical, and moral experiences have been influential to my thinking about the role and significance of bori in Mawri society. Whether they focus on the performative qualities of possession, its historical significance, or its embededness in quotidian contexts, these studies are largely concerned with the province of meaning. Replacing earlier models that sought to explain encounters between humans and spirits in universally valid terms, they explore the cultural logic of possession in terms of local definitions of identity, morality, knowledge, power, or memory, without losing sight of wider political and historical contexts (Boddy 1989; Comaroff 1985; Janzen 1992; Kapferer 1983; Kramer 1993; Lambek 1981, 1993; Lan 1985; Matory 1994a; Ong 1987; Rosenthal 1998; Sharp 1993; Wafer 1991). Drawing upon Ricoeur's notion of the text—which, once "written," takes a life of its own and opens itself up to the interpretation of cultural actors, audiences, ethnographers, and readers—Lambek argues that possession must be situated "within the wider system of meaning" in which it emerges (1981, 60). This is precisely what is attempted here by taking possession to be a culturally constituted, shared, but also contested idiom for the expression of affliction in its multiple guises. Interpreting possession (see Rabinow and Sullivan 1987) rather than explaining it—in terms of its function—makes it possible to show how its practices are grounded in the encompassing cultural logic that shapes people's quotidian efforts to act upon the world. On the other hand, such an approach has the distinct disadvantage of allowing one to ignore just how important possession "really" is to those who experience it. The symptoms of possession are not free-floating signifiers; they are anchored in an "organic" medium that partly controls their generation, emergence, and proliferation. At the same time, they cannot be isolated and extracted from the social reality through which they are experienced. The challenge, then, is to explain the "real" of possession without explaining it away through a singular focus on the "meaningfulness" of the phenomenon. While this book offers little in the way of a model on how to face this challenge, it nonetheless tries to convey the importance of possession and the reality of its effects through analyses of *specific* situations, particularly as they pertain to the Muslim/bori debate on what possession is and does.

Returning to a discussion of the approaches that have shaped this work, it should be noted how essential to the following ethnographic analysis is Boddy's notion that it is the mundane environment of possession that "empowers it to convey a range of meaning" (1989, 8). In her richly nuanced ethnography of zar in a Sudanese village, Boddy draws on the work of Bourdieu and Foucault to argue that spirit possession in Hofriyat is a meaningful discourse—inspired by a largely implicit cultural scheme—upon which women draw to articulate their experience of everyday life. By carefully locating zar in relation to local constructions of gender, fertility, and morality, she conveys possession as a palpable reality and as a multifaceted phenomenon whose richness and complexity can be uncovered only through a culturally sensitive analysis. In her own words, "Possession is a holistic reality. It penetrates all facets and levels of human life. . . . Possession has numerous significances and countless implications: it defies simple explanation. It has no necessary cause, no necessary outcome. Its province is meaning, and it is best addressed in that light" (Boddy 1989, 136). By focusing on the symbols and images that inform possession practices, and allowing ambiguity to emerge out of their polysemantic nature, Boddy vividly captures the essence of zar's social vitality as well as its ideological power. Just as zar provides an arena in which Hofriyati women can recognize that Islamic values are "cultural constructs, not immutable truths" (Boddy 1989, 1), this ethnography offers analyses of bori's capacity to open conceptual spaces where the givenness of Muslim values and conventions can be substantially undermined.

Marginality Reconsidered

This chapter opened with Tagimba's observation that in Arewa there are spirits everywhere, in order to convey the limitations of classic models of possession that take for granted the liminality of spirits, the polarization of gender-distinct domains of knowledge and power, and the homogeneity of Islamic (or elsewhere Christian) experiences. Before describing how power and peripherality figure in my analysis of bori, a brief review of the literature on gender and subordination is in order. The assumption that going into trance enables the powerless to symbolically express their predicament has long dominated the field of possession studies. It originated in the work of I. M. Lewis (1966, 1967, 1986, 1989, 1991), who, as noted above, argued that possession functioned as the dispossessed and the marginal's thinly disguised means of protest against the powerful. Those who were possessed were by and large women who used spirits as "oblique strategies of attack" when no other means to express frustration or exact concessions were available (Lewis 1967, 626). From this perspective, marginality is the common denominator of spirit possession phenomena. It also the prime explanation for women's involvement in these activities. Marginality thus becomes a sex-specific trait that is found universally rather than being the product of particular social or historical circumstances.

While possession that emerges from the tensions of marital life allows for the expression of social contradiction, such contradiction is never resolved by the staging of a possession ceremony. Nor is the woman's status modified by her momentary display of power. Like rituals of status reversal that "reaffirm the order of structure" (Turner 1969, 177), possession reinforces a wife's subaltern status because as a "mock" rebellion, it only serves to insure that the structures of male authority are preserved from a "real" rebellion. This model of female oppression has been criticized from a variety of perspectives. In her perceptive study of mediumship and migration in a Madagascar town, Sharp provides convincing evidence that *tromba* (possession by spirits of dead Sakalawa royalty) constitutes a central—rather than peripheral—aspect of Sakalava society that permanently empowers its participants (1993). Giles similarly shows that female mediums in Mombasa, Kenya, are not marginal members of their society and that possession is an important component of Swahili society (1987).

Giles further points out that the very idea of marginality often originates from highly subjective and ideological assessments made about the possession group and its members by nonmembers (235). Regardless of women's contributions to their society and of their own vision of morality, their official status is what determines the peripheral status of their possession activities. Lewis, himself, recognized that "the moral status of the spirits is by no means absolute, but *depends upon the position from which they are viewed*" (1989, 115, emphasis added). As I hope to demonstrate in the case of bori, the "liminal" and the "central" are largely imaginative categories of the cultural landscape that shift according to historical, social, and personal circumstances. Whether or not mediums succeed in negotiating their displacement

(Comaroff 1985) or in turning peripheral values into key tenets of morality (Boddy 1989), it remains that the "liminal" often plays a critical role in constituting the conceptual boundaries of the "central"—in our case, Islam.

From this perspective, the point is no longer to assume the irrelevance of possession for the society at large but precisely to locate the terms of its engagement with a wider—even dominant—culture. The issue of what might be termed *syncretism* has been cogently discussed by Boddy, who shows how Sudanese Islam has adapted itself to local conditions while indigenous elements have been reconciled and integrated with Muslim ideologies (1989). Women from the village of Hofriyat do not think of zar practices as being antithetical to the principles taught by the Koran. Nor do they think of themselves as peripheral to the moral core of their society. It is they, in fact, who reproduce village cosmology and morality, since men have moved away from their homestead to find work in the large urban centers (109, 113). In their bodies—loci of fertility—are vested the salient values of Hofriyati culture.

Brown has developed a parallel argument on the vodou of Haiti, claiming that people who serve the cult's spirits consider themselves good Catholics and see no contradictions between their obligations to the church and their ties to the spirits (1991, 111). Vodou is the religion of the oppressed and the impoverished, but that does not imply that it stands outside of Haitian society's moral nucleus, as Lewis would have us believe. It itself constitutes a moral core, even if "vodou morality is not a morality of rule or law but a contextual one. It is tailored not only to the situation but also to the specific person or group involved." (Brown 1991, 241). In his account of medicine and morality in Haiti, Brodwin similarly argues that Haitian villagers are not bound by immutable moral codes because Catholic, Protestant, and vodou identities are always negotiable (1996). Thus we see how morality and the relevance of one's involvement with the spirits are largely a matter of perspective, especially if, as is often the case, membership happens to be defined along gender lines (see Crapanzano for a rare example of male deviancy associated with possession [1973]).

To deal with the notion of women's marginality more adequately, feminist scholars put forth the concepts of "domestic" versus "public" social spheres. According to this model, women generally lead con-

fined lives centered around domestic tasks and gain power only insofar as they are able to transcend the private sphere and penetrate the
public arena of predominantly male activities (Rosaldo 1974). Using
the distinction between private and public worlds, some anthropologists have offered new definitions of power to account for the way
women derive authority from their secluded or separate positions in
society (Reiter 1975; Rogers 1975).

From yet another perspective, Edwin Ardener suggested that wom-
en constituted a "muted group" whose cognitive models contradicted
significantly the dominant male model (1972; see also Ardener 1975).
Women may appear relatively inarticulate, even silent, in relation to
men, but within their own world and in their own ways, they find the
means to be independent and self-assertive. Callaway has drawn upon
Shirley Ardener's work to explore the paradoxical nature of Hausa
women's seclusion in Kano, Nigeria (1984). She sees bori as part of
women's efforts toward autonomy and self-determination but asserts
that such involvement in possession offers no challenge to the Muslim model of male supremacy. Hausa women have a dual status that is
reinforced by the spatial polarity of male and female spheres: strong-
willed and independent within the confines of their households, they
become humble and subservient in the presence of men and seemingly conform to Muslim dictates.

The "muted group" theory is attractive because unlike the "deprivation" model, it allows for ambiguity and plurality of expression in
addition to acknowledging that "women can conduct their lives with
an independence for which there is no recognition in the 'dominant
model'" (Callaway 1984, 433). Mawri women, like Callaway's secluded
wives in Kano, compose their own meaningful version of what the
world is like, a version that differs significantly from their husbands',
sons', or fathers'. Though only a small minority lives in kubli (seclusion), most of them generally have little contact with their husbands.
They may not speak to them, or be spoken to, at all except when
given the daily rations of grain, meat, and spices they need to prepare
meals for the household. They remain shy and compliant when in the
presence of male kin or acquaintances but behave in a dramatically
different manner when in the company of their co-wives, female kin,
and women friends. In the latter context, they become outspoken and
self-assured, impulsive and opinionated. Within the walls of the compound, when they are not expected to acknowledge the supremacy

of a male presence, they lead lives whose values do not require male control or sanction.[1]

But though it may provide hints of what goes on in Mawri women's daily lives, the "muted group" model is not helpful in understanding the role and meaning of spirit possession, because bori is precisely the arena of Mawri life where, to a large extent, men and women socially and casually interact on an almost equal footing. They may sit, eat, and dance together, something that they do not do under normal circumstances. And they share the same values and principles relating to bori. One could adjust the model to consider that bori members, regardless of their sex, constitute a "muted group" in relation to the dominant body of Muslims. Yet, like Lewis's model, the perspective articulated by Ardener makes too neat a separation between orthodox and marginal forms of authority, as well as between implicit and manifest power. According to Callaway:

> The "muted group" construct implies that the seeds for total independence exist within the women's experience of apparently total suppression. With this extension it is possible to hypothesize that women in these societies may accept with apparent contentment a degree of suppression that to the outsider might appear unbearable, only because their own sense of value derives from, and contributes to, a muted counterpart of model behaviour of which they themselves may or may not be consciously aware, but which nonetheless stimulates and sanctions an assertiveness which could ultimately be the foundation for political efficacy. (1984, 430–31)

From this viewpoint, the "seeds for total independence" may exist, but women's practices as mediums are not in and of themselves a source of power that has ramifications outside the "muted group." Callaway's perspective limits the scope of her analysis to the domain of micro-politics. It shows how women's peripheral world can only perpetually reinforce the male structures of domination, not transform them. Not unlike Turner's concept of "permanent liminality" (1969, 145), an antistructural pattern that serves only to preserve the structure it ostensibly contradicts, the "muted group" theory reifies and isolates possession instead of seeing it in the context of the wider constellation of power relations.

Peripherality does not necessarily imply powerlessness: bori may no longer constitute the dominant voice in Dogondoutchi and the surrounding communities, but it has nevertheless retained the capacity to make a difference in many contexts. Often, the power to create an alternative reality that resonates in the audience's imagination is what makes a performance unconventional or different. For Bauman, the persistent association between performers and marginality lies in the performances' potential for transforming social structures. "If change is conceived of in opposition to the conventionality of the community at large, then it is only appropriate that the agents of that change be placed away from the center of that conventionality, on the margins of society" (1977, 45). Thus marginality is not simply a given; rather it emerges out of, and is constituted by, the ritual manipulation of words, images, and substances through which some individuals forcefully act upon, and reconstruct, the world. Though a bori identity carries less prestige than a Muslim one, it implies a certain form of power, the ability to manage, transform, even conceal reality through one's alliance with the spirits, one's iconoclasm, and the exercise of knowledge.

To return briefly to Lewis's argument, there are various forms and degrees of peripherality that cannot be easily encompassed by a model claiming to be cross-culturally valid. Marginality need not be a negative quality that refers to a lack or a want. It need not be passively experienced but may be actively constructed by individuals seeking to demarcate themselves from the cultural, political, or religious order they reject (Turner 1969). Jean Comaroff has eloquently demonstrated how Zionist practice allows marginalized South Africans to separate themselves from neocolonial culture, thereby empowering them (1985). When adroitly negotiated, marginality can thus become a source of empowerment and a means of self-assertion.

A Few Considerations on Power

In an article outlining the various forms that power may take among Bedouin women, Abu-Lughod noted that the relationship between resistance and power has been one of the central problematics in the human sciences in recent years (1990). This widespread concern for the complex dynamics of domination and subordination can perhaps be traced back to Weber's recognition that "power is the probability that one actor within a social relationship will be in the position to carry out his own will despite resistance, regardless of the basis on which this probability rests" (1964, 152). From this perspective, both power and authority—as legitimized power—were secular and independent of cultural meaning and experience. Based on nineteenth-century mechanistic theories concerning the dynamics of force and resistance, Weber's definition remained influential for a long time among analysts whose intent was to locate power as a discrete quantum of energy and circumscribe the way it was exercised (Arens and Karp 1989, xxv n).

The recent disaffection with mechanistic views of power has led to an understanding that power may not be easily situated as a concrete and concentrated force, the exercise and effects of which remain limited within the secular realms of society and polity. Following Gramsci, Bourdieu, and Foucault, students of resistance have paid increasing attention to the subtle and diffuse forms in which power is exercised (Abu-Lughod 1990; Comaroff 1985; Lan 1985; Ong 1987; Pratt 1992; Ranger 1977; Scott 1985, 1990; Vail and White 1978; van Binsbergen 1976). Circumscribing mechanistic and reductionist theories of power involves recognizing the artificiality of such distinctions as politics/ritual, mind/matter, symbolic/instrumental. It is only by disrupting such dichotomies that the many expressions power takes might be apprehended without unduly freezing them in the shape of our own preconceived categories.

In addition to the "obvious" forms of power—such as control over productive resources—that one may describe in Bedouin society, Abu-Lughod has analyzed other expressions of potency such as restrictions on movement and everyday activities, control over marriage, official ideologies of male superiority, and poetry (1986, 1990). Boddy has shown how rural Sudanese women wield appreciable measures of power by judiciously leaving the appearance of power to men (1989, 185). It is through the exercise of such implicit power—where compliance alternates with resistance—that Hofriyati women strategically renegotiate their subordination. In her historical analysis of marriage, identity, and domesticity in a Hausa town, Cooper describes the increasingly complex—and sometimes contradictory—strategies women have recourse to in order to secure status and social capital (1997). Through careful investments in dress and decor, ritual and pilgrimage, they slowly earn the symbolic capital necessary to enhance their identities as wives, mothers, or *hajiya* (honorific for a female pilgrim upon her return from Mecca). Bori, too, seeks to extend its power through the accumulation of cultural capital deemed vital to the preservation of central moral values.

Power has also been described as a facet of human creativity that is grounded in a culturally and historically specific context (Arens and Karp 1989). From this perspective, the focus is no longer on the locus, legitimate basis, and exercise of power but on its many and shifting expressions. Comaroff and Comaroff speak of a "non-agentive" form of power—which is contrasted to its "agentive" counterpart—to account for the influences that subtly and silently shape our social reality even though they are rarely experienced as power (1991, 22). There are three points to be made about the idea of power. First of all, power should not be defined as a distinction between explicit and implicit, or between material and ideational, forces, so much as taking a variety of shapes that may work simultaneously, together or against one another, often doing so in spite of their apparent mutual exclusivity. Often, power lies in signs, relations, and distinctions that are "naturalized" and become taken for granted. Internalized, embodied, and shared, these forms of power take on the status of cultural restrictions, norms, or values (Bourdieu 1977; Comaroff and Comaroff 1991, 22). Power, therefore, can no longer be located in the sphere of institutional politics but must be traced in mundane practices and everyday representations. Thus, the domination of Islam in Dogondoutchi must be interpreted not simply in terms of economic superiority or political advantage but also, and perhaps more important, through the habits and conventions, values and constraints that shape the moral and material reality of Mawri people. As Boddy, following Foucault, has put it, "Power is vested less in agents of hegemony than in the practices whereby it produces its effects" (1989, 185).

Second, it is important to underscore the transformative capacity of power that is crucial to analyses of bori as a dynamic force of Mawri society and history (Arens and Karp 1989, 185; Comaroff and Comaroff 1993). Throughout the book, the focus is on the imaginative and meaningful ways in which cultural categories, relations, and distinctions are manipulated and reshaped through bori practice, and how, in the process, both subject and context are implicitly transformed. These transformations are often subtle, yet their impact is usually far-reaching. They are realized not simply in the course of momentous events but also within the vaster yet more humble terrain of everyday practice and quotidian discourse. In the arena of possession, the human frame is often the privileged medium for the objectification of novel experiences having to do with the transgression of boundaries, the creation of new geographies and identities, or the commoditization of previously unmarketable goods or qualities. Habitual tasks such as writing at a desk or feeding one's husband, to cite two examples discussed below, may become vital media of the subversive imagination. Bori has the capacity to transform because it captures the imagination in the resonances of an alternate reality, a different world view created through a reworking of the old and the new, the foreign and the familiar. However, bori does not simply transform. It also articulates or deconstructs, clarifies or obfuscates, promotes or subverts particular visions, identities, or histories, and these various, sometimes contradictory, messages are themselves sources of empowerment and creativity.

Finally, power is not necessarily a negative, repressive force that excludes, denies, represses, restricts, and subjugates, as Foucault has pointed out: "What makes power hold good, what makes it accepted, is simply the fact that it doesn't weigh on us as a force that says no, but that it traverses and produces things, it induces pleasure, forms of knowledge, produces discourse" (1980: 119). The productive dimension of power is nowhere more apparent than in healing, where knowledge is put to use to cure the afflicted body. Though bori healers are feared for their ability to cause harm,[2] much of their power resides in the wisdom and experience they have acquired to heal afflictions. By demonstrating that they can diagnose illnesses, by finding appropriate cures, and by impressing upon their patients their understanding of what ails them, they establish their own authority. Of course, legitimation of the interpretations that emerge as authorized versions of "what really happened" or "what must be done" originates in the nexus of privileged relations bori healers nurture with the spirits.

Resistance, Ritual, and History

Returning to the issue of resistance that is so central to how bori must be understood as historical force and as everyday practice, one is led to ask what is meant by resistance and what the definition of resistance implies for the way intention, domination, consciousness, and, of course, power are perceived. In this respect, African studies have made valuable contributions to understandings of social dynamics. In Manchester, long before anthropologists rediscovered Marxism, Gluckman was refining the notion of resistance to include humbler and ritualized forms of collective defiance (1970) in his dynamic model of culture. In Kapferer's words, Gluckman "saw conflict and dispute as being founded upon contradictions located at the heart of cultural/social orders" (in Manning and Philibert 1990, 3). His investigations of "rituals of rebellion," in turn, paved the way for subtler accounts of conflicts and encouraged methodologies that brought to light the hitherto ignored conducts and techniques through which the oppressed and the marginalized resist their predicament (Turner 1957; Cohen 1969b).

While it is perhaps unfair to characterize Fanon as representative of the "resistance studies" paradigm emerging in the postindependence era, given the complexity of his writing, a brief mention of his work will nonetheless help contextualize some of the issues that have surfaced in more recent scholarship. For Fanon, one of the leading spokespersons of African liberation, resistance meant only armed struggle (1963). If victory over an oppressing colonial system was to be achieved, colonized subjects needed first to get rid of "the frightening enemy created by myth" and to focus on the "concrete" tasks awaiting them in the fight for freedom (56). In this mechanical model of history, there was no place for spirits and shades, no recognition of the power of images, and no concern for the semantics of resistance. Dreams, cosmologies, and ritual action stood outside of "reality" and therefore:

> During the struggle for freedom, a marked alienation from these practices is observed. The native's back is to the wall, the knife is at his throat (or more precisely, the electrode at his genitals): he will have no more calls for his fancies. After centuries of *unreality,* after having wallowed in the most outlandish phantoms, at long last the native, gun in hand, stands face to face with the only forces which contend for his life — the forces of colonialism. And the youth of a colonized country, growing up in an atmosphere of shot and fire, may well make a mock of, and does not hesitate to pour scorn upon the zombies of his ancestors, the horses with two heads, the dead who rise again, and the djinns who rush into your body while you yawn. The native discovers *reality* and transforms

it into the pattern of his customs, into the practice of violence and into his plan for freedom. (1963, 56, emphasis added)

Despite its formalized division between "political" and "symbolic" resistance, Fanon's work nonetheless already contained the seeds of more nuanced understandings of the concept and clearly anticipated later developments. Yet, despite their impact, his writings were hardly the first to focus on the plight of the colonized. Eight years before *The Wretched of the Earth* came out, Maya Deren, writing of Haiti, boldly asserted that the forces born out of rituals could successfully guide an oppressed people in its efforts to cast off the shackles of slavery ([1953] 1991). Eager to rehabilitate a religious form that had been largely misrepresented and denounced as immoral or evil, she unearthed not simply the poetic vision and imagistic expression of vodou but also its aggressiveness and potency. For Deren, vodou, and the Petro cult in particular, had been both the inspiration and the technique that Haitian slaves needed to fight for their freedom. Petro was, Deren explains:

the raging revolt of the slaves against the Napoleonic forces. And it [was] the delirium of their triumph. For it was the Petro cult, born in the hills, nurtured in secret, which gave both the moral force and the actual organization to the escaped slaves who plotted and trained, swooped down upon the plantations and led the rest of the slaves in the revolt that, by 1804, had made Haiti the second free colony in the western hemisphere, following the United States. (62)

Despite having been long recognized for its contributions to the field of ritual and religion, Deren's provocative study did not appear to provoke a reassessment of the political role of spirit possession. Fanon's influential "Handbook for Black Revolution," on the other hand, spawned numerous studies of resistance ranging from national rebellions guided by explicit ideologies of emancipation to other, humbler acts of defiance.

In an effort to transcend the conventional binary categories on which earlier scholarship was based, contemporary students of religion have pointed to the political role and historical impact of ritual practice (Comaroff 1985; Fry 1976; Lan 1985; Ranger 1977; van Binsbergen 1981), while others have focused on the more humble forms of everyday resistance (Abu-Lughod 1990; Comaroff 1985; Ong 1987;

Scott 1985; Van Onselin 1973). They have amply demonstrated that however frail and marginalized, these creative projects are important whether or not they succeed in overthrowing the system they oppose. Like any other human project, their importance for those who are involved, as well as for the social scientist, lies not in some preconceived utilitarian value but in the meaningful way they produce, reproduce, or transform the world.

Bori presents a case in point. Because possession has often been reduced to ritualized practice (Besmer 1983), treated as a marginal institution (Lewis 1989; Onwuejeogwu 1969), or analyzed as a form of subculture (Callaway 1984), leadership and involvement in bori have been interpreted as purely symbolic and limited to specific ritual and social contexts. Except for Échard's (1991a; 1992) studies, no attempt has been made to explore contemporary bori practices as a product of colonial history and as an implicit, yet cogent, protest to colonization and Islamization. Little consideration has been given to bori's significance in the wider context of Mawri society because its practices, like Bourdieu's "mechanisms capable of reproducing the political order, independently of any deliberate intervention" (1977, 189), are not *overtly* political. Yet the spirits played an important role in mediating the Mawri experience of the French conquest and the colonial structures of domination.

Bori's current attempts to reinsert itself in local networks of power relations further demonstrate the futility of analyses that categorize ritual rebellion as apolitical. Resistance, it has been amply illustrated, does not necessarily lie in the overt confrontation of tangible force but may find cogent expression in the more subtle language of symbolic activity (Comaroff 1985; Kramer 1993; Scott 1985; Shaw 1985; Ranger 1975; van Binsbergen 1981). It is part of a continuous process of adjustment to, and rejection of, the dominant culture, whose signs and values, in effect, frequently provide the terms for indigenous discourses of protest. Though immersed in a world that speaks mainly to indigenous practices, bori devotees nevertheless draw their imagery from a larger stock of cultural meanings. Indeed, the potential of bori seems to lie precisely in its ability to merge and symbolize the complex mixture of indigenous, Western, and Islamic signs in ways that distinguish its practice from both the Westernized practices of the educated elite and the cosmopolitan orientations of Muslims.

Resistance in bori may take the form of minor defiances enacted daily against the Muslim establishment and its many representatives. The potent and colorful figures of the bori pantheon, who are familiar to, and often feared by, Muslims and 'yan bori alike, are convenient vehicles of collective representation. And they are used as such by bori adepts, who deftly manipulate new and old signs, welding indigenous techniques and emblems of modernity to negotiate and, at times, impose upon others their own version of a shared reality. Dramatic and potent as bori representations may be, however, they are not routinely promoted to undermine Islam. Bori, after all, is as much a means of negotiating the complexities arising out of its coexistence with Islam as a means of protesting Islamic values. If chapter 8 (in which bori is shown as an arena for threatening and resisting Islam) thus appears disjoined from chapters 4 and 6, which emphasize the mediating capacities of possession, it is largely to remind us of the availability and convertibility of bori signs. Bori is, first of all, a cultural resource that people appropriate with differing degrees of enthusiasm and approval to satisfy a variety of needs in a variety of contexts. Viewed as such, it consists of a multiplicity of symbols and practices, the manipulation and performance of which may produce conflicting outcomes and promote contradictory interests. This book is an attempt to address the diversity—sometimes dissonant, sometimes harmonious—of meanings and motivations that emerge out of quotidian encounters between spirits and humans. Bori can provide spirit mediums with the tools they need to resist Islam, but, paradoxically, it also has the potential to "domesticate" Islam for those who long for the social and material benefits associated with Koranic orientations. Because it arises from a variety of perspectives and for diverse reasons, bori resistance—against the postcolonial state, Islamic institutions, or an authoritative husband—cannot ever be described as monolithic or unidirectional—an all-or-nothing phenomenon. Nor can it be conceived independently of the multiple and complex ways in which bori has insinuated itself in the very ideologies it sometimes ostensibly condemns. From this perspective, measuring the effectiveness of bori's resistance to Islam is sometimes as much a matter of figuring out the extent to which Islamic signs and values have been actively appropriated by "opponents" of Islam as it is a matter of assessing the persistence of bori elements in an Islamicized society. For by redefining the terms and boundaries of their own "tradition," bori mediums also redefine their role in the moral community, the nature of their relations to the spirit world, and their claims to a range of social and material resources. Moreover, because possession provides an arena for the negotiation of meanings that are often themselves constitutive of different, even competing, interests within the community, it is difficult to determine objectively whether bori "wins" or "loses" in its resistance to Islam and modernity: in a world increasingly run by rational individualism, the misfortune of one healer becomes the good fortune of another. In addition, while 'yan bori in Dogondoutchi and elsewhere have suffered serious setbacks since the spread of Islam, the prayer that has "spoiled everything" sometimes provides the spirit mediums' very means of ascendancy as bori redefines itself as a means of "fixing" the problems introduced by a widespread reliance on the Koran.

While summoning images of fearful spirits occasionally provides the basis for effectively subverting Muslim hegemonies, bori statements of resistance more often consist in defying daily the restrictions enforced by Muslim elders, scholars, or husbands. Both Muslim and non-Muslim women are known to sneak out of their compounds to attend bori ceremonies even though such escapades are strictly forbidden by their husbands. Co-wives often protect each other by providing alibis for the devious spouse who dared to go against her husband's will. Such silent conspiracy and fierce determination to protect the integrity and inviolability of their female world against men's intrusive control attest to the subtle forms defiance may take in quotidian contexts. Resistance in domestic settings takes on more threateningly subversive overtones when, as it happens sometimes, a woman overtly disregards her husband's ban on involvement in bori to disappear for several hours or days without warning. Hadiza, my next-door neighbor, regularly took off to attend bori rituals despite the fact that her new husband, a devout Muslim and brother to the *chef de quartier* (neighborhood chief), expressly forbid her to participate in *wasani* (possession ceremonies). By deserting the house for several days at a time without even giving him a clue as to her whereabouts, this once divorced mother of three was not only ignoring her domestic duties and mocking her husband's authority; she was also humiliating him in front of the entire Muslim community by setting her own rules and schedule in his household. Despite being repeatedly warned that she was "no good"—hadn't she had a child out of wedlock with a bori musician of questionable morality?—Amadou had stubbornly followed his heart and married Hadiza, hoping to make her his favorite and much loved third wife. But she was rarely home, and soon it was obvious to everyone around him that his dream of domestic felicity would never live up to his own expectations. After several unsuccessful attempts on his part to regain control over the terms of their marriage, and while the whole neighborhood speculated over the future of their troubled union, Hadiza's husband finally gave up the struggle and divorced her, thus ending months of heartache and embarrassment over his marital predicament.

However, it is not simply that bori devotees and sympathizers use bori as a source and means of resistance. Bori *is* resistance in a fundamental way. Though it has lost much ground in relation to Islam, it has defied predictions of its gradual disappearance in the face of social transformations. It has resisted the Muslim holy wars of the nineteenth century, the colonial push toward a capitalist economy, the tide of nationalism, and the recent waves of Islamization. Despite, or perhaps because of, repeated attempts to discredit and even suppress it, bori survives in what is now a predominantly Muslim society. If the message of bori remains successful—even in its most silent and subdued forms—it is because it provides an organizational framework grounded in the implicit logic of local Mawri culture. Bori signs, symbols, and practices aptly capture the Mawri predicament in postcolonial Niger at the same time that they effectively guide devotees' ritualized efforts to negotiate a place in the world.

If these attempts to act upon the world can often be interpreted as statements of protest or acts of defiance, they are not, however, part of an explicit philosophy of resistance. In the 1920s, angry spirit mediums gave coherence to the Baboule movement by merging independent grievances into a collective consciousness, but today, bori expressions of protest rarely take the form of coherent political messages. In 1989, when the appointed bori representative came back from the regional conference he was invited to attend with all the other dignitaries of the *département* of Dosso (town chiefs, Muslim representatives, chiefs of cultivators, etc.), he was criticized for not having secured more financial assistance from the conference delegates and for not speaking more forcefully on behalf of the bori community. Though his lack of aggressiveness partly reflected his own shyness and inexperience, it also became painfully obvious to many 'yan bori that there had been no concerted efforts to spell out complaints and come up with specific demands before the conference. While they take pride in the selfless accomplishments of their forefathers, the 'yan bori of today are mainly interested in being awarded recognition for their contribution to communal protection—through *gyaran gari,* for instance—and in receiving funding to subsidize public ceremonies. Because they have no explicitly stated agenda, they have no dealings with the *sous-préfet,* who only receives Muslim representatives. "Those of the Islamic Association are better organized," the sous-préfet once admitted to a reporter of the Nigerien periodical *Sahel Dimanche* (Ousmane 1985).

Unlike zar, which has been portrayed as an antisociety and a counter-hegemonic discourse (Boddy 1989), bori is not a conscious alternative to a hegemonic model. Though it certainly helps the Mawri to articulate an awareness of their history and of their modern-day predicament, it does so in ways that are only partially subject to explicit reflection. Rural Mawri are painfully aware of their continually worsening impoverishment, but they do not necessarily trace the cultural, economic, and political forces impinging upon their local world. Their efforts to mediate the contradictions of their postcolonial society may appear more poetic than political, like the healer I once met who chose to anthropomorphize the dangers of modern roads and travel in the figure of a seductive female spirit preying upon innocent travelers (Masquelier 1992). When bori devotees try to siphon off some of the wealth and fortune controlled by Muslims, their efforts to make sense of changing realities occasionally become more concretely formalized.

Yet whatever form or process they take, these imaginative renderings of social realities do not strictly and securely belong to the conscious or the unconscious. Rather, as Jean and John Comaroff (1991, 29) have pointed out, the unseen and the inchoate may rise to a level of explicit awareness, while the discernible and explicitly articulated may fall back into the unconscious to become invisible or taken for granted. Since what was once obvious can become obscure and what was once hidden can reemerge in full light, it is crucial to direct one's analysis of resistance to an oppressive reality toward "that liminal space of human experience in which people discern acts and facts but cannot and do not order them into narrative descriptions or even into articulate conceptions of the world; in which signs and events are observed, but in a hazy, translucent light; in which individuals or groups know that something is happening to them but find it difficult to put their fingers on quite what it is" (29). Thus if, at times, I have focused on the exotic or the horrible, it is not to "exoticize" the subject of my inquiry. Rather, by "unpacking" these poetic forms, I gain insight into the experience of Mawri peasants who consistently deploy vivid images and metaphorical language to deal with the multiple discordances arising between an idealized past and a morose present.

The heroic struggles, poignant dramas, and tragic encounters recounted in this book are the stuff Mawri history is made of; for history lies as much in representations as in actions. Or rather, it lies in both: in signifying practices whose role in the shaping of bori identity is explored in this study. The actors of Mawri history are not only the warriors who fought the French or the rulers who determined the economic fate of an entire region. Other participants include the mediums who dance out fights and protests, the healers who re-map the world onto afflicted bodies, and the *bricoleurs* who combine foreign signs with familiar symbols to articulate their experience of modernity. Poetic, yet hardly simplistic, their various renderings of human experience point to the complex dialectic of transmission and innovation, consensus and contestation that makes up cultural encounters. People do not passively absorb the values, categories, and practices of a foreign hegemony or a dominant culture. Rather, they creatively reshape and discerningly interpret foreign elements and novel techniques to fashion their own visions of an evolving world. Examining what bori has become in late-twentieth-century Arewa thus presupposes understanding how spirit mediums have variously dealt with the multiple challenges of colonization, commoditization, Islamic proselytism, literacy, and monetization. My aim is not to reduce bori to a response to contemporary political and economic forces but rather to stress the creative, at times subversive, but always practical potentialities that emerge out of bori for those who enlist the help of the spirits to navigate a changing socioeconomic landscape.

Mawri Society: Origins and Early History

The northern region of Arewa that provides the setting for this study and coincides with the arrondissement of Dogondoutchi (see map on p. xxx) is home to some 250,000 Hausa speaking Mawri, living for the most part in small villages or semipermanent settlements scattered in the savanna. In terms of conventional linguistic and sociocultural classification, this largely heterogeneous population is part of the more inclusive Hausa ethnic group that makes up more than half of the total population of Niger. Because it borders Zarma-Songhay country to the west, the Hausa states to the east and the south, and Tuareg territories to the north, Arewa has often provided asylum to those who wanted to escape the traumas of war, conquest, and enslavement in precolonial times. Whether they sought relief or adventure, newcomers generally found rich lands and plenty of water. Moreover, the rocky formations that make up the last remnants of a now fossilized valley known as Dallol Mawri offered secure protection from thieves and conquerors (Piault 1970, 44). As more people settled in the area from the sixteenth century onward, political, religious, and cultural differences gave way to a more unified society, though subgroups kept their distinct identities and territories.

After the French conquest in 1898 and the subsequent colonization of what is now the Republic of Niger, the last distinctions among the population subgroups were progressively abolished. The first half of the twentieth century witnessed heavy dispersions and migrations of people within the Dallol as villagers regularly tried to escape harsh living conditions imposed by an exacting colonial administration. Though many villages were far from ethnically homogeneous, Arewa's inhabitants came to be referred to as Mawri regardless of their origin. The only exception to this pattern applies to the descendants of the first inhabitants, who, because they still claim ritual ties to the land through the propitiation of ancestral and nature spirits, are known as *Azna* (or *Arna*). Some fifty years ago, the category *Azna* was often applied indiscriminately to any Mawri by a colonial administration more eager to distinguish the inhabitants of Arewa from their Islamicized Hausa-speaking neighbors than to establish separate local religious identities (Sérée de Rivière 1946). Today the term is used mainly to differentiate what has become a tenuous religious minority from the pockets of 'yan bori and the fast-growing community of Muslims who occupy Arewa. Throughout the area, the number of Azna has been rapidly dwindling in the face of Islamic expansion. Where they remain, their role as ritual experts and guardians of local "heritage" (*gado*) has often been eclipsed by the part 'yan bori play in the religious affairs of Arewa communities.

The Arewa region was first occupied in the sixteenth century by the Gubawa (plural of Ba'gube), who came from the east and allegedly found an empty territory upon their arrival. They were led in their quest for suitable land by a queen-priestess, Sarauniya, who had fled her country of origin, the Hausa state of Daura (de Latour 1984, 276). The newcomers founded the village of Lougou as their first settlement. The original Sarauniya and all those who succeeded her became the leading priestesses of a nature cult devoted to land spirits. As more populations settled in the region, these priestesses eventually relinquished direct control over politico-religious life to simply become the living embodiment of a general principle of fertility (Piault 1970, 114).

The Gubawa hunted and gathered, moving about in small groups (De Latour Dejean 1980). After they gradually became sedentary, they continued to hunt and gather but drew their chief subsistence from agriculture, leaving pastoral pursuits in the hands of their cattle-raising Fulani neighbors. They lacked a centralized political organization and followed the rules of clan organization, under the leadership of priestly elders, the 'yan 'kasa (Piault 1975). Gubawa patrilineage organization was centered around the ritual propitiation of land spirits. The gida (extended patrilineal household) was the primary socioeconomic unit. Several clans (dangi) formed a community under the ritual authority of the member of one of the village's founding lineages. As 'dan 'kasa ("son of the earth," singular form of 'yan 'kasa), this individual was responsible for maintaining the initial pact established between a local spirit and the ancestors through the performance of sacrifice, so that villagers could continue to enjoy the usufructuary rights to the land, which, in effect, had been handed to them by that spirit.

The notion of heritage was (and to some extent, often remains) a basic feature articulating a clan's relations to its ancestors through the transmission of knowledge and practices (de Latour 1984, 278). Each heritage is constituted by "a fan of activities, customs, rituals, objects, attributes and even psychological traits which are transmitted through blood" (Nicolas 1975, 73). Now an important component of bori identity, heritage once distinguished one clan from the next and provided clan members with a notion of tradition and continuity. Through membership in a clan, a villager had access to a particular activity or craft (smithing, dyeing, hunting, etc.) that could not be performed by any clan outsider. Each clan possessed sacred grounds, or sanctuaries, where a sacrifice was regularly performed to propitiate the clan's protective spirits and communicate with them. These sanctuaries also had a role as "anchorage points" (Nicolas 1975, 75) through which clans objectified their unity.

In the sixteenth century, not too long after the Gubawa founded their first communities in and around Lougou, a small group of warriors, the Arewa, conquered the area. With horses and swords, they soon imposed their military protection on the Gubawa, who fought with simple bows and arrows. Though they had to acknowledge the political suzerainty of the newcomers, the 'yan 'kasa retained control over the land. Religious power thus remained in the hands of the 'yan 'kasa, while defense and political management were entrusted to the Arewa chief and his entourage of warriors, who established a polity modeled after their state of origin, the Hausa state of Bornu (de Latour 1982, 1984; Piault 1975). Political power was concentrated in the royal house of Matankari—a village situated twenty miles southeast of Lougou. The *sarki* (chief) became the epicenter of Mawri social, political, and natural worlds and a central element of articulation between sacred authority and political power (de Latour 1984, 284). Every one of his actions had considerable cosmic consequences. This meant not only that the country's fate was tied to his but also that he was responsible for such things as rain and wind, global fecundity and sterility, peace and war, as well as prosperity and poverty throughout the land (Piault 1970, 173; see also Nicolas 1969, 224). If he did not fulfill his sacred obligations toward his subjects, he could be banished. Thus, while military victory or abundant harvests could reinforce a ruler's authority, repeated misfortunes affecting the kingdom could provoke his downfall (Nicolas 1969, 228).

After the Bornuan warriors settled in the Gubawa area, war, more than any other activity, became the test through which the power of the spirits and the viability of their initial alliance with Gubawa settlers were measured. Until the French took control of the region at the turn of the century, war was the essential driving force behind the structures of competition and domination laid by the emergent Arewa polity. It was the basic source of wealth and power for the aristocracy as well as an economic necessity for commoners forced to rely on insufficient harvests (de Latour 1984). War thus provided the potential for quick accumulation of riches, but it also implied constant insecurity. The dislocations war provoked upset the agricultural cycle and the organization of labor, thus forcing the peasants to find some external means of compensating for the resulting shortfalls. During the rainy season, farmers working in their fields were often attacked and captured while their harvest was stolen. Hence, the spatial and temporal organization of agricultural activities was shaped by a defensive awareness of the potential for ambush (de Latour 1982, 252). Insofar as harvests were unpredictable and famine was a constant threat, hunting and gathering activities provided a substantial share of people's subsistence (de Latour 1982, 252). In a society where political instability and economic inconsistencies were the norm, war was a game of chance in which every man participated according to his means and capacities.

   Military preparations and wars also brought together the Azna and the sarki's warriors as they renewed their ancestors' allegiance to the spirits. Yet relations between the two groups were far from peaceful. Mawri oral tradition is replete with references to disputes and battles between the people of Lougou—the seat of Gubawa power— and the people of Matankari, subjects of the *sarkin* Arewa.[3] Such quasi-permanent instability preserved Gubawa autonomy while enabling the Arewa to freely compete for power (de Latour 1982). So strongly established was the division of power between Arauci political supremacy and Gubance religious authority that the cults devoted to local spirits were never subsumed under, or integrated into, the Arauci system (de Latour 1982). Today the ethnic heterogeneity of the region often renders categories such as Azna, Arewa, and Mawri inappropriate and difficult to apply. Nevertheless, for the sake of simplicity and comprehension, I use these terms in the way people use them in Arewa. Though they do not express the complex history of invasion, migration, and intermarriage that resulted in the present composition of the population of Arewa, they do express the historical understanding of the people among whom I lived.

The Colonial Period

The imposition of peace, the abolition of slavery,[4] and the introduction of a market economy by French colonial forces all contributed to the erosion and reshaping of the political, economic, and religious institutions of Mawri society. The colonial administration not only imposed a heavy burden through taxes, forced production, forced labor, and military enrollment, but by ruining the political and economic bases of the ruling aristocracy, it profoundly upset the elaborate alliances and rivalries, exchanges and redistributions that constituted the Mawri social order (de Latour 1982, 259). In the realm of religious practice, the ignorance, incompetence, and limited means of the French administration often led to a complete realignment of power in Niger.[5] Although official policies toward Islam vacillated considerably according to politico-historical circumstances as well as the motivations and assumptions of individual administrators, they did not often have the effect intended (Clarke 1982; Cohen 1980; Oloruntemehin 1972). Hostile measures taken against Islam often proved beneficial to the Muslim cause because they fostered a resurgence of reformist movements and stimulated religious conversion throughout the colony. Similarly, but for different reasons, tolerance of Islam, and cooperation with Muslim leaders, encouraged adherence to Islam. In Arewa, the French administration, which distrusted Islam and applauded animist resistance to Islamic proselytism, eventually succeeded where commerce and religious imperialism had both failed previously: by upsetting the generative dynamics of the politico-religious order and breaking down local economic structures, colonial powers helped, to some extent, propagate the Koranic message among a people who had until then staunchly resisted conversion to Islam.[6]

Faced with the necessity to minimize administrative costs and to generate revenues from a territory that offered scarce resources, the French introduced policies that were purely exploitative. The objective was to break the circuits of subsistence in the rural economy in order to restructure the production toward fulfilling the needs of an expanding capitalist economy in France (Collion 1982, 2). Instructed to extract as much of the local material and human resources as possible, French officers often left the population impoverished and vulnerable to epidemics and hunger (Fuglestad 1983). In addition to having to pay the head tax in cash, taxable individuals were required to plant a minimum area (0.6 hectare in 1943) in groundnuts (Collion 1982). Such measures would have unforeseen consequences for the viability of the household as an economic unit. When the drought of 1913–15 and the locust invasion of 1931 produced famines of massive proportion (Egg et al. 1975), the breakdown of indigenous economic structures was highlighted by massive population migration to Nigeria.

As a result of its inability to financially provide for all its members, the extended family fragmented into smaller economic units. In tandem with the contraction of the farming unit, the organization of the sacred evolved to address and cope with the complexity of emerging identities and relations of power. Bori spirits became more personalized as religious practice evolved toward a greater individualization (Piault 1970, 59). Simultaneously, the bori pantheon expanded to include a diverse array of Mawri and non-Mawri spirits whose appearance expressed and mediated the Mawri's experience of political domination and drastic social transformations. While bori practices were progressively evolving to accommodate the changing needs of Mawri villagers, Islam was making timid progress in the area. In the 1910s, the few Muslims who could be spotted in Arewa were foreign merchants from Nigeria (Belle 1913). Thirty years later, the number of Muslims had risen to 3,000 in a total population of 72,400, but these new converts were either of Zarma or Fulani origin. No one, not even the local *malam* (Muslim scholar), who enjoyed a certain degree of prestige in Dogondoutchi, had yet allegedly managed to make converts among the local population. Yet even before Islam started slowly spreading in the colony of Niger, colonial administrators feared the emergence of revivalist holy wars and their redirection against Christian colonizers. French attitudes toward Mawri subjects reflected this anti-Muslim stance: "The Mawri are very attached to their customs and they, with the Azna, form the only population [of the district]. The animosity of Mawri-Azna for Muslims is real and it is in our utmost interest to capitalize on this feeling" (République du Niger 1912, 3).

Since Muslim proselytism was intimately associated with anti-French propaganda, in the eyes of the French administration, all Muslim preachers were inherently suspect — especially when they demonstrated connections to Egypt or Nigeria. In a letter addressed to all the *commandants de cercle* of the colony, Gov. William Ponty had already stressed the dangers of Muslim propaganda for the establishment of French domination (1906). Urging administrators to enforce a rigor-

ous surveillance of itinerant Muslim clerics, he insisted that "our administrative policy should not permit these individuals to continue,
on the one hand, their anti-French and anti-European propaganda,
and on the other, their swindles and blackmail of our indigenous
population. Urgent measures must therefore be taken against them"
(Ponty 1906, 3). French administrators in Niger knew very little about
Islam as a system of beliefs and practices and its relation to other African religions (see Labouret 1931, 69–71). What chiefly struck the colo-
nists on their arrival was the incidence of Islam in one area and "animism" in another. Africa seemed to be divided between two religions,
although a closer look would often reveal the tight interconnections
between Islam and indigenous traditions. If French attitudes toward
Islam oscillated substantially within the colonial period, it is in great
part because the French often perceived and judged African subjects
in terms of whether they were a help or a hindrance (Cohen 1980).

Hence the *marabouts* (Muslim scholar; from the Arabic word *mara-
bit,* a holy man), whose proselytizing efforts sometimes led to unrest,
were a threat to colonial peace and order (Arnaud 1912; Johnson 1978;
O'Brien 1967). The advent of World War II, during which colonial
subjects fought to defend the "free world," helped Islam to become
less threatening as the interests of colonial France appeared to co-
incide with Islamic aspirations (de Latour 1987; Triaud 1974). If local
colonial administrators eventually tolerated Islam because they believed that in spreading among Azna populations, it "degenerated"
and lost its bellicose character, they nonetheless continued to promote
and defend indigenous religious practices. After the war, the spread
of Islam in Mawri country became even more noticeable when local
elites converted massively to the religion of the Prophet in the hope
of gaining the status afforded high dignitaries in the rest of Hausaland (de Latour 1987, 161). Yet it was not until after independence that
conversion to Islam intensified dramatically.

Contemporary Perspectives

At independence in 1960, the French political withdrawal left Niger
with a depleted economy and a bitter struggle for power between
the two major ethnic groups, the Zarma and the Hausa—the latter

being the group with whom the Mawri identify. As memories of former colonial exactions faded, the Hausa, who constituted the largest ethnic group in the country, fell under the domination of the mostly Islamic Zarma, who took the reins of government when the French departed in 1960 (Nicolas 1971). Once resistance by the political party representing Hausa interests was suppressed with the help of the French, any opposition was systematically crushed, any change that would have widened the power base of the governing party was rigidly opposed, and no democratic elections were ever held (Higgott and Fuglestad 1975, 386). Legitimated only by the French military presence and supported by merchants and notables, the PPN,[7] as the ruling party was known, retained the socioeconomic and political structures laid out by the colonial administration (de Latour Dejean 1980, 113). Despite its apparent reliance on the masses and its egalitarian ideology, the PPN was nevertheless a party of cadres seeking to increase the latter's economic and political control.

The newly elected president, Hamani Diori, at first enjoyed a period of relative tranquillity and success despite mutinies and threats of "foreign invasion" orchestrated by opponents to the regime. This was a favorable period for Nigerien agriculture, the groundnut-based export economy was expanding, and, as a result, rural discontent was minimal (Charlick 1991, 57). Soon, however, a severe drought that began in 1968 forced the government to abandon a previously initiated drive for broad-based rural development. At the same time, nothing was done to alleviate the heavy tax burden on rural producers faced with repeated agricultural failures (60). Despite obvious signs of economic distress and impending famine, Diori lent a deaf ear to the growing protests of students and intellectuals, choosing instead to jail the leaders and punish those who could not pay their taxes. His cynical and corrupt management of food relief prompted a coup d'état in 1974. The subsequent beginning of Kountché's regime coincided with a short-lived prosperity brought by uranium revenues at a time when prices were high. The state invested heavily in agriculture and health care and expanded the size of its administrative sector (Cooper 1997). For a brief period, literate Hausa speakers could obtain jobs as state functionaries in the newly expanding bureaucracy. With the 1985 collapse of uranium prices on the world market, however, prosperity ended as the state found itself increasingly unable to meet its obligations. Upon Kountché's death in 1987, his successor, Ali Saibou, was faced with an increasingly weak economy, rising unemployment, and growing dissatisfaction among certain segments of the population. Subsequent governments inherited further crises that have plunged the nation deeper into chaos and poverty despite international aid and an aggressive structural-adjustment program. While the Tuareg militia that waged a war against an unyielding government to obtain autonomy has since agreed to a peaceful reconciliation, unrest generated by students in the capital remains a constant threat, inflation keeps rising, and the deficit shows no sign of diminishing, despite the severe austerity measures the state has adopted in response to pressure from international lenders. In addition, soil degradation, persistent drought, high import prices, and political instability have further weakened the already troubled economy, forcing many Nigeriens to migrate yearly to west African metropolises in search of poorly paid, unskilled jobs (Masquelier 2000). In tandem with declining living standards, the human rights record worsened, especially after the 1996 coup, the ousting of the first democratically elected president, and the establishment of a military regime. In July 1996, the coup leader, General Maïnassara, became the new president of Niger as a result of elections that several foreign governments condemned as fraudulent. The April 1999 coup, in which President Maïnassara—who had remained under a cloud of suspicion since his election—was assassinated, dealt yet another blow to the virtually bankrupt country by forcing international donors like France and the United States to pull their financial aid once again to protest this new abuse of power. In November 1999, presidential and parliamentary elections were held and Tandja Mamadou became the second democratically chosen president of Niger. Four days later, Mamadou called on the international community to resume aid to Niger following the successful completion of the elections that both he and his defeated rival, Mahamadou Issoufou, termed a "victory for democracy" (Mayer 1999). Most aid to Niger that had not already been cut off after General Maïnassara's coup d'état in 1996 was frozen following the general's death last April. Sadly, while this return to democracy has been hailed by all as a great victory for the people of Niger, the rapid resumption of foreign aid will most likely not bring long-term solutions to the country's most acute financial problems.[8]

Religious Practices in Modern Niger

When Hamani Diori was elected president of Niger at independence, he followed in the footsteps of the colonial regime when it came to the treatment of Islam. The country was officially run as a secular state—whose civil code did not directly mention *shari'a* (Koranic law) as such even as it acknowledged customary law—and religious education was co-opted through the establishment of state-run *médersa* schools (French–Arabic schools in which French language and culture are taught alongside Arabic and Islamic sciences) (Miles 1994, 251). While Diori publicly and regularly demonstrated his Muslim faith, he did so more to sustain his own legitimacy than to promote Islamic institutions (Triaud 1981). It was only after Col. Seyni Kountché seized the reins of government in a 1974 coup that Islam was officially recognized by the state and used to forge a nationalistic consciousness among the disparate ethnic elements (Nicolas 1987). Four months after the coup that put him in power, Kountché created the Association Islamique du Niger to promote communication between the central administration and the population as much as to legitimize the power structure of his government (Triaud 1982, 35). It soon became, in Nicolas's words, "one of the pillars of the regime" (1979, 105).

Even if Diori did not promote Islam as a central component of Nigerien nationhood, the religion of the Prophet nonetheless was making rapid progress. In fact, Islam was already solidly entrenched among the indigenous elite, the *évolués* (colonial subjects who, because they had acquired the accoutrements of French culture—language, dress, education—could petition for French citizenship and were exempt from *corvée*—labor) even before independence. As more educated Nigeriens turned to Muslim faith and culture to reaffirm their own identity vis-à-vis the Europeans, Islam came to be associated with power and *arziki* (a complex word bundle that signifies good fortune, prosperity, and well-being). In Dogondoutchi, conversion to Islam has intensified in the last few decades to the extent that the followers of the Prophet now outnumber the Azna and the members of bori. The spots where Muslim scholars used to pray are no longer burned by bori devotees eager to purify the land from what they saw as corrupt and polluting practices. On these very sites, a small mosque often stands, testifying to the vast expansion of a faith that counted few Mawri adherents some fifty years ago. Besides visibly anchoring themselves in the local landscape through the erection of places of worship, Muslims have successfully monopolized trading networks. Today they also hold most of the important positions in the administration of rural towns and villages (Nicolas 1975, 56). The large mosque built in 1975 in Dogondoutchi to accommodate the fervor of Islamic devotees can no longer contain the crowds who attend the Friday prayer led by the imam. Many of the residents thus pray outside.

Christianity, on the other hand, has made little progress in this region of west Africa. The Catholic mission that was established in 1947 had, from the beginning, a far greater educational than religious impact on local Mawri villagers. Years after independence, the mission school of Dogondoutchi was still known for providing the best French education available in Niger (Kotoudi 1988a, 51). Today, only a handful of families attend Sunday mass in the little mission church that overlooks the encampment set up during the 1984 drought by Tuareg refugees, who have since opted for sedentary life and become permanent Dogondoutchi residents. Because many of their flock, pressured by Muslim peers, have converted back to Islam, the missionaries rarely perform baptisms anymore. The local Protestant mission has an equally limited membership and makes no attempts to convert people, knowing all too well the pressures that Christians, who are teasingly referred to as "pork eaters" in Muslim households, face in this west African country.

Islam has thus practically experienced no competition from Christian proselytism on the local terrain. Yet, despite repeated efforts on the part of successive postcolonial regimes to promote Islam as *the* religion of the Nigerien people in an effort to encourage a nationalistic consciousness among disparate ethnic elements, one cannot speak of a unified Islam in Niger. Wherever the Muslim faith has taken root in Niger, it has drawn on a variety of indigenous traditions and resources to adapt itself to the local cultural landscape. The absence of *ulema* (learned Muslim men, initiated into sacred knowledge) in Mawri communities and the reworking of indigenous elements into Muslim epistemologies have greatly contributed to the richness of Islam as a localized practice. Through the use of magic, divination, and amulets, for instance, Islam fully participates in local efforts to cure diseases, ward off misfortune, and insure prosperity.

In the last few years, however, these syncretized practices have be-

come the target of 'yan Izala, a reformist group intent upon eradi-
cating all the innovations that are allegedly tainting the religion of
the Prophet in this part of the continent.[9] Concerned by the threatening onslaught of Westernization and secularization in local Islamic
communities, these zealots are urging all Muslims to return to a more
"authentic" Islam, devoid of heathenism and innovations (Grégoire
1993; Isichei 1987; Masquelier 1996b, 1999b; Umar 1993). Through the
implementation of sweeping reforms, which they argue will establish
moral traditions more in accordance with Koranic injunctions, they
have rallied a growing number of malcontents eager to contest previously unquestioned issues ranging from matters of dress, consumption, and commensality to problems of Islamic knowledge, piety, and
authority.

Against this local background of Islamic discord, a small minority,
unconvinced that Muslim identity is an indispensable element of
social and economic success, insists that the recent popularity of Islam
and the severance of people's ties with spirits underlie many problems people are currently facing in Arewa. Priding themselves in not
having strayed from the path of their ancestors like so many of their
neighbors who now follow the message of the Koran, the 'yan bori are
constantly struggling to reassert the centrality of their authority and
the viability of their practices in the face of religious opposition, social
marginalization, and economic pressure. It is these struggles that I explore here in order to document the central role and significance of
bori in local definitions of identity, power, and history.

Aims, Conundrums, and Strategies

Discussing bori as a means of mediating conflicts, disjunctures, or uncertainties also implies examining how its meanings and values are
grounded in an encompassing order of cultural practices. That is what
is attempted in this work, through focusing on the contexts, themes,
and images that best illuminate how bori appropriates, comments
upon, or refashions quotidian signifiers, thereby unmasking latent
ambiguities and addressing emerging contradictions. Whether in discussions of prostitution or soldiering, maternity or money, the aim is
to demonstrate the relevance of bori meanings to an understanding
of the contemporary world as it is experienced by the Mawri.

For the people among whom I lived, the complex reality of bori could not be easily translated into objective descriptions of "customs," inventories of spirits, or listings of calendrical rites. Nor could it be reduced to an abstract set of conventions. Rather, it had to be extracted from the incidents and arguments, songs and gestures, puns, proverbs, and insults that 'yan bori drew upon to capture the experience they were trying to relive or relate. As a result, some of my most important insights into local dynamics came accidentally rather than through systematic interviewing. I also found that a large amount of what I learned occurred through speechless but significant encounters as I slowly became attuned to the various forms that embodied knowledge takes in Mawri society. In his discussion of the divinatory and sensory nature of ethnographic inquiry, Desjarlais (1992, 30) notes the difficulty of objectifying through writing the largely tacit knowledge that the ethnographer's body has soaked up as a sponge soaks up water. Asking how to "translate the complexities of everyday life into the fixity of a few words," he answers his own question by suggesting that "the task is to pack the noise of the world into the words of a page so that a reader can hear it anew" (30). This is what I have tried to achieve through an exploration of the imaginative, vibrant, and moving ways in which some Mawri experience and act upon the world through the medium of bori.

Most of my fieldwork was spent attending wasani (possession ceremonies) and hanging out with bori mediums. Though I actually lived in a Muslim household[10] — becoming privy to much of what goes on between Muslim family members behind closed doors — my thinking about local truths, traditions, and values was powerfully shaped by what the 'yan bori themselves wanted me to learn about their world. After telling people in Dogondoutchi that I had come to write a history of bori so that their grandchildren could reflect on the place of gargajiya (tradition) in the world they would inherit, I became a valuable anasara (Christian foreigner) in the 'yan bori's struggle to regain visibility on the local terrain of religious politics. My presence at bori ceremonies, I soon realized, lent a much needed aura of legitimacy and prominence to the non-Muslim activities of this religious minority. "If bori was not important stuff, why would she come from so far away to study us?" I once overheard a young medium provocatively ask her Muslim neighbor. The question was, of course, purely rhetorical; more to the point were its implications: there was no ana-sara studying Muslims in Dogondoutchi.

Speculation about my motivations may have abounded in bori circles—after all, I was a Christian, I spoke Hausa very improperly, I was a poor dancer, and I showed little talent for mediumship—but one thing was clear: I was here to learn about the spirits, *not* Islam. This soon meant that my presence at wasani was invariably requested, regardless of whether my own plans could be accommodated by bori schedules. I thus attended close to a hundred ceremonies over the course of my research. As a result of my friends' own investment in what they took to be a project to rehabilitate bori in the eyes of local Muslim as well Western communities, my analysis of the politics of religious identity in Arewa is a bit one-sided. I did not work equally with Muslims and non-Muslims, and many of the "facts" I report here reflect bori rather than Muslim sensibilities.

Because this book speaks largely from a bori perspective, the por-trait I have painted of Muslim residents may, at times, be unflattering, even denigrating. This is not to suggest that Mawri Muslims are, by nature, callous, greedy, or selfish, even if they are perceived that way by non-Muslims. I have tried to capture the complex and, often, bit-ter negotiations for the control of identity that mold bori-Muslim relations in a rural Nigerien community. Such an agenda has meant reproducing as faithfully as possible bori stereotypical constructions of Muslim character. Hopefully, the generous individuals who, with-out a second thought for my bori leanings, gave freely of their time to teach me about the Koran will see their efforts rewarded, one day, in the form of another book—this time about Islam.

I conducted research in Arewa from January 1988 to June 1989. I then spent the months of July and August 1989 doing archival research, first at the Archives Nationales du Niger in Niamey and then at the Archives d'Outre Mer in Aix-en-Provence, France. Thus the ethno-graphic present refers to the years 1988 and 1989. During that time I lived in Dogondoutchi, a midsized rural town located in south central Niger, some forty kilometers from the Nigerian border. By working in Dogondoutchi proper as well as in several of the surrounding vil-lages, I was able to broaden my understanding of possession, especially with respect to the kinds of social networks spirit mediums progres-sively weave across communities as they gain experience in the ways of bori. Except when noted otherwise, however, the present discussion of bori is based on my research in Dogondoutchi. While a comparison of bori practices in and out of Dogondoutchi might shed light on bori's potential for the creation of close-knit groups in predominantly Islamic communities, it is not the aim of my study. Many mediums who lived in nearby villages came to Dogondoutchi regularly to attend wasani, meet acquaintances, and occasionally go to the local market held every Friday. I had an opportunity to observe and interview some of them both in Dogondoutchi and at home. Bori healers based in small communities often uniformly loathed the 'yan bori of Dogondoutchi for their alleged callous and competitive business practices, but Dogondoutchi mediums—ranging from ambitious young healers to shy elderly widows to spirited young prostitutes—constituted nevertheless a fairly typical sample of the rural bori population. In what has become a predominantly Islamic population, those who have officialized their ties to the spirits through their involvement in bori make up less than two percent of the total Dogondoutchi population. But as I have already noted, such an "objective" assessment of the popularity of possession in a Mawri community does not give us an adequate sense of how bori figures in local attempts to mediate the perception of a widening gap between an idealized tradition and a deceptively manageable modernity.

I conducted interviews with about a hundred bori mediums, following more closely the lives of about twenty of these through additional interviews and informal conversations.[11] I learned a great deal through my encounters with seven other individuals (five older male healers and two young female mediums) with whom I developed special ties. I also gleaned substantial information from the many hours spent watching mediums dance to the compulsive rhythms of the drums. Each *wasa* (bori ceremony, singular of wasani) was an occasion to identify the various spirits who, upon being summoned by the musicians, came to possess their hosts. I learned to recognize the screeching sounds of the Doguwa spirits, and to differentiate the stuttering speech of the Zarma spirits from the pidgin muttering of the Baboule. The signs of imminent possession, the characteristic motions of possessed mediums, and the personalities of the incarnated spirits became progressively more familiar as I sat, time after time, near 'yan bori who prided themselves on interpreting the content of wasani for the uninitiated bori sympathizer that I was.

Two assistants helped me throughout the course of this research. The first one was a thirty-eight-year-old man who claimed no specific religious identity but knew most of the mediums in the area. Through his mother, who had been a bori adept, Yahaya had gained a solid appreciation of local bori history and a healthy respect for the powers attributed to spirits. His own interest in bori matters combined with his knowledge of local politics greatly facilitated the initial stages of my research. Yahaya was smart, articulate, and naturally curious. Regrettably, he also had a propensity to convert every franc he earned into beer. After I paid him at the end of every month, I knew he would not show up for work again until he had sobered up. As the research progressed and I relied less and less on his "expertise," he also became withdrawn, resentful, and aggressive. When it became clear to me that Yahaya was hindering more than assisting my research, I decided to end our "partnership." In March 1989, he was replaced by a young Muslim man whose own father was a bori healer. Mahammadou was eager to please, conscientious, and hardworking. He enjoyed the visibility afforded by his new position and, unlike Yahaya, felt no compunction about working for a woman. Although he was not a "regular" in bori circles due to his Muslim leanings, Mahammadou had no difficulty fitting in. His sense of humor and his talent as a storyteller routinely enhanced our transcription sessions. Through our daily conversations, I learned a great deal about the dreams, frustrations, and anxieties of twenty-year-old males who aspire to become good Muslims but cannot ever definitively turn their backs on the spirits.

A final point: because my portrayal of bori often pits spirit mediums against Muslims, it may mislead the reader into thinking that bori—and perhaps Islam as well—is a uniformly monolithic institution whose values are shared unanimously by all its members. This is unintentional and only due to the shortcomings of my approach. Neither bori nor Islam should be perceived as distinct and homogeneous entities; they are both part of a larger set of intersecting, often dissonant, and rarely totally consistent discourses whose broad outlines I have tried to sketch in my analysis of bori meanings. While bori mediums often stand united against what they see as the dominant Muslim Other, they occasionally confront each other, questioning each other's motives or even nurturing long-standing feuds. What should emerge from the multiplicity of spirit and human voices whose specificities I struggled to discern is a picture of Mawri culture as a fluid, contested, and shifting field of interactions whose contours and contrasts are often best highlighted by those mysterious beings whom the Mawri knowingly refer to as mutanen daji ("people of bush").

Chapter 2

Lost Rituals CHANGING TOPOGRAPHIES

OF SPIRIT/HUMAN INTERACTIONS

It is not the boundary that defines the village but the village that engenders . . . the boundary. — Michel Cartry, *From the Village to the Bush*

The bush is always elsewhere, external to the town, outside of the village, at a distance from the hamlet. . . . Those who occupy this *beyond* hardly belong to the human world, they are closer to the wandering spirits. — Éliane de Latour, *Les temps du pouvoir*

"No wonder there is so much sickness in this village, they don't do the gyaran gari anymore." Such observations are frequently heard from bori adepts who disapprove of the recent abandonment of certain pre-Islamic traditions, or *al'ada* deemed essential to village prosperity. Given the widespread connection between health and ritual efficacy observed in this and other parts of Africa (Devisch 1993; de Heusch 1980; Janzen 1992; Kratz 1994; Last 1976; Muller 1999; Monfouga-Nicolas 1972; Sindzingre 1985; Taylor 1988; Turner 1968; Wall 1988; Weiss 1996), it comes as no surprise that the frustration generated by the progressive disappearance of indigenous rituals aimed at communal protection should find expression in growing concern about the resurgence of seasonal epidemics. When the harmattan, the dust-laden wind of the dry season, blows from November through May, communities are thought to become especially vulnerable to airborne diseases. As a result, a number of young children die of pneumonia and respiratory infections. By performing a gyaran gari (literally, arrangement of the town/village), members of a human settlement reinforce the impermeability of their community to various external influences, in particular spirit-caused afflictions or the disease-carrying dust that causes meningitis during the hot-dry season, in March and April. The keeping at bay of evil forces that threaten to impinge upon the *gari* (town) was traditionally accomplished by ritually delineating the boundaries of this social space at the time of its foundation as a human settlement. Once established, these boundaries were regularly resketched and reinforced through the periodic enactment of the gyaran gari during which sacrificial blood was shed by Azna priestly elders (*'yan 'kasa*) at strategic points along the village borders.

In contemporary Arewa, growing Muslim factions have sometimes put a stop to the performance of pre-Islamic communal rituals originally aimed at purging the village from pestilence. Because they reassert the symbiotic character of spirit-human relations, indigenous practices such as the gyaran gari are deemed sinful and contrary to Islamic standards. By thus stressing the alleged vulnerability of communities to dreadful epidemics, villagers who decry the absence of proper preventive rituals are also indirectly lamenting the lack of bori involvement in communal affairs. Disputes over whether or not to maintain *al'ada* are only too common in Dogondoutchi, where those who have secured wealth and respectability through their membership in the *umma* (worldwide community of Muslim believers) like to point out the backwardness of practices that encourage reliance on multiple spiritual forces rather than total subservience to Allah.

The following discussion highlights some of the media through which an idealized past—peopled by powerful spiritual creatures— is summoned as background against which spirit mediums who have witnessed the impact of Westernization and the rapid progress of Islam can assess how things have irremediably changed. Rather than providing a semblance of continuity with the past, these representations of pre-Islamic times invite reflections on the fast pace of the transformations that have taken place locally. The discussion of how contemporary people describe early Mawri interactions with indigenous spirits supplies some context for a subsequent examination of more recent attempts to mediate the impact of modernity through the intercession of spirits. Because they continuously recast prior meanings with new signs and symbols to produce innovative semantic configurations, spirits confidently address the current concerns of local populations. At the same time, they are so inescapably rooted in past representations that their present dispositions and interventions in human lives can rarely be understood outside of the context of how they came to be here in the first place.

Alluding to indigenous religious forms in the neighboring region of Ader, Échard (1991a) notes that evidence points to close links between the bori and Azna worship of land spirits in precolonial times. In Arewa, oral tradition also implies that close connections have long existed between the 'yan 'kasa devoted to land spirits and the members of the bori who become hosts to a diverse array of more personalized spirits. Historical evidence also suggests that the organization of the sacred evolved from communal propitiation of nature and clan spirits to more individualized relationships between people and mutanen daji ("people of the bush"). As Piault describes it, the different orders of spirit worship were structured like a set of Russian dolls; the further one went from a religious center, the more differentiated the identity and role of the spirits (1970, 58). At the center of this religious topography were relatively undifferentiated forces that were revered and placated by special individuals on behalf of the entire Gubawa population (58). Among them was Sarauniya, the spirit who guided the creation of Lougou, the first human settlement in Arewa (58). Her human receptacle also bore the name of Sarauniya. This priestess was invested with specific powers that translated into the ability to mediate communication between Sarauniya and the local population. From a centrifugal perspective, the next order of mediumship involved a number of spirits who manifested themselves to humans by riding "on the heads" of their priests during possession ceremonies (58). These spirits, such as Douna, who was revered in the village of Zakuda, had better defined personalities and attributes, and were each placated on behalf of a specific Gubawa subgroup (58). Furthest removed from the center, there existed yet another level of relationship between spirits and humans. The objects of this particular form of devotion were not propitiated during cyclical rites performed by 'yan 'kasa on behalf of a whole group. Rather, they were honored on an individual basis by villagers who acted on their own behalf and did not necessarily rely on the mediating powers of priests (58). Spirits belonging to this latter category have almost all been incorporated into the bori pantheon. This is why so many of the bori spirits of indigenous origin bear the same name as Azna spirits, most of whom have now become the stuff of memory. For the sake of clarity, I will refer to the spirits propitiated by the 'yan 'kasa ("sons of the earth") as *iskoki* (plural of *iska*) and speak of bori or mutanen daji ("people of the bush") when I am dealing with those spirits who possess their mounts during institutionalized rituals commonly referred to as wasani.

This chapter focuses, then, almost exclusively on the iskoki (the mystical forces belonging to the first two categories of spirit worship outlined above) to illuminate the centrality of unitary cults and their role in the shaping of precolonial notions of locality, power, and history among the various segments of the local population. The preservation of Mawri history and identity is inseparable from a mystic context out of which contemporary bori forms have emerged. The spirits who lived on the land upon which several groups of people successively settled played major roles in charting, apportioning, and protecting the spatial and cosmological space of these populations. This mythic landscape provides an idealized model of "moral geography" that spirit devotees occasionally deploy against the current backdrop of social, moral, and economic transformations to measure the complex and contradictory implications of modernity in communities where *neman ku'di* (the search for money) has progressively become the dominant preoccupation.

The Mythical Twins

Who are these spirits who regularly intervene in human affairs to upset the course of social or natural events or, conversely, to restore order where there was once havoc? What makes them so powerful yet so dependent upon human support? Why are they at once elusive and ubiquitous? The answer to such questions is rooted in a widely known myth that chronicles the origin of the mutual engagement between humans and spirits. According to this myth, the emergence of spirits must be credited to the first woman on earth, Hawa (Eve in Hausa) — whose own identity betrays the far-reaching influence of Islam on indigenous cosmology. Hawa (also known as Adama) and her husband, Adamu, produced fifty sets of twins. One day Uban Duniya ("father of the world"), the creator god, asked to be shown the twins. Thinking that Uban Duniya wanted to take them with him, Hawa told Adamu to hide in a cave the most beautiful child from each set of twins. The creator god, who knew and saw everything, was angered by Adama's attempt at deceiving him. To punish the parents for their deception, he condemned the hidden twins to remain forever invisible and to harm their human brothers and sisters. These ethereal beings would be dependent on their visible siblings for sustenance; people, on the other hand, would have to keep on begging their "hidden" twins for benevolence and protection.[1] This is why the Mawri must appease, satisfy, and even flatter those they call "mutanen daji."

Invisible, yet powerful, the hidden children of Hawa and Adamu married and had children themselves. Ever since they were punished for their parents' deed, they have caught (*kama*, i.e., seized hold of) their human counterparts and possessed them when the need to communicate arose. It is thus because of Hawa's deceitful behavior that spirits came to be what they are today, regardless of their degree of cooperation with human populations. Hawa's trickery also led to the emergence of sacrifice—an act that humans must regularly perform to prevent these invisible powers from becoming a source of torment. Besides being invisible, the hidden twins and their descendants are associated with the wild. Having been temporarily sent to a distant cave for the purpose of hiding, they became permanently exiled from the domesticated world of humans.

It is precisely because spirits belong to the bush and represent forces of the wild that their relations with humans must be carefully monitored. While the inherent difference between spiritual and carnal bodies is regularly transcended during the act of possession, the fundamental opposition between *gari* (town), as the domesticated space of humans, and *daji* (bush), as the domain of spirits, must be preserved if order is to be maintained.[2] This is why it is so important to regularly reinforce the spatial boundaries of human settlements through the periodic orchestration of the gyaran gari to prevent the daji from impinging on domesticated space. Before turning to the significance of gyaran gari, however, a further discussion of the terms of people's relationships to the spirits in precolonial times is in order and, more specifically, how these terms were inscribed onto the physical landscape.

The Village in the Bush: Anchoring Space

Prior to the establishment of ethnically heterogeneous villages and the introduction of land tenure based on private ownership, local populations nurtured tight bonds with various spirits who were the first occupants of the region. Each mountain, each cave, each tree

An unused stone altar (*hango*) stands as a reminder of a time when people regularly shed sacrificial blood to feed the spirits.

was the abode of a spirit and, as such, a crucial landmark for objectifying the interconnection between human space and spirit locales. Though 'kasa (land) could not be owned by individuals and had no intrinsic value unless it yielded a crop, sites known to be occupied by a certain spirit were entrusted to the care of the clan propitiating this particular iska. It is there, on a large stone marking the exact spot, that sacrifices were offered to the spiritual dweller in order to renew the arrangement that was concluded at the beginning of time between spirits and people. While circular stone altars were often erected in the compound of the clan's priest, it was not uncommon for a clan to present offerings to its protective iska at the foot of a tree located in someone's field or in the bush. Regardless of the way that it was physically delimited, or inscribed onto the landscape, the apportioned space was a sanctuary where the clan's members periodically united to meet with their spirits and share with them the sacrificial offerings.

Land for the Mawri was not a neutral, inert, and unified patch of villages and fields broken only by rivers or rocky mounds. It constituted a complex phenomenal reality grounded in the villagers' active involvement with the invisible forces that surrounded them. These "sacred" sites or landmarks that objectified one's ties to land spirits "structure[d] a ritual space specific to each clan and . . . transfigure[d] the landscape for the members of this clan. They [were] the anchorage points thanks to which members [became] conscious of their autonomy and unity through . . . the sharing of the same foods around the sacrificer" (Nicolas 1975, 75). By thus rooting their alliance with spirits in the physical reality of a tree or an anthill, Mawri appropriated the "natural" signs of the landscape as signifiers of their cultural order's interpenetration with a world of elusive forces. Yet there was never any sense that a tree or a patch of land *belonged* to those who had thus appropriated it. "Attachment" to a site did not translate into economic benefits for clan members. Anyone was free to forage or hunt in the vicinity, or even to harvest the fruits of one's agricultural labor, should the sanctuary happen to be located on the site where someone had sown sorghum, for instance. More often than not, an iska's altar would be located in the millet field of a villager who had no connections to the clan propitiating this particular spirit.

The local topography of sacred sites was thus superimposed on the physical map of hamlets, paths, and fields. As such it constituted what Munn (1970, 143), referring to Australian aborigines' construction of the land, described as a "fundamental object system external to the conscious subject within which . . . consciousness and identity [were] anchored." Put another way, if the land and its physical features were appropriated by settlers, the spatiotemporal contexts that emerged out of the process themselves appropriated human subjects by silently tuning them to their inner structural logic (Bourdieu 1977, 89). This is why the vitality and persistence of spirit-oriented practices demonstrating local residents' commitment to the bori depend so much on the 'yan bori's control of socio-spatial configurations, which, like the marketplace, have long concretized a community or a clan's reliance on mutanen daji.

Because their foundation was rooted in the settlers' mythic encounters with local iskoki, Mawri villages were—and, for some, still are— more than simple anchor points in the physical and temporal realms. As durable embodiments of the reciprocal ties forged long ago between people and spirits, they were part of the phenomenal topography in which villagers' sense of history, community, and selfhood was grounded. Once a village was erected, maintaining good relations with the community's protective spirit was essential to the survival of the population. War constantly menaced the fragile socioeconomic stability of local communities, and precautions were required to ward off the threat of sudden attacks by neighboring chiefdoms. It was in times of deep insecurity that Doguwa spirits would prove most useful in protecting human settlements from potential destruction and pillage at the hands of the enemy. The heroic role once played by local spirits is gladly evoked by bori elders, who like to reminisce about the particular "tricks" each iska employed to deceive would-be assailants. Ungurnu, the guardian spirit of Dogondoutchi, would transform what was at the time only a small village into patches of grass to trick the enemy. Upon approaching the location of the hamlet, the enemy would only be greeted by a few lonely bushes that showed no sign of having ever been disturbed by a human presence. A black ox would be (and still is) sacrificed to the spirit every year to insure that she would promote the arziki (good fortune) of all villagers and the sa'a (luck) of the warriors. Legend has it that Ungurnu would warn the local chief of any imminent danger. From the dogon doutchi (long rock) where she resided, she would emit a long, ululating sound that the chief would recognize as a warning signal that enemy troops were approaching or that another kind of peril was threatening the village.

The Knife of Sacrifice

In exchange for the protection they afforded local communities, spirits requested one or several annual sacrifices. The sacrificial animal, a goat or an ox, was usually provided by the village chief and put to death by the 'dan 'kasa who had been designated through a ritual procedure known as tarkama. The tarkama also referred to the spiritual force that vested a chosen individual with the knife of sacrifice. The knife bestowed upon a male member of the priestly lineage gave him the power to shed blood for that spirit so as to renew the original covenant between spirits and humans that formed the basis of Azna religious practice. It officialized his ritual role in the preservation of the community's heritage and the maintenance of the precarious balance of power between human and spiritual realms. When a priest died, his corpse would be carried through the village until the tarkama spirit took control of the procession to choose a successor. The men who carried the corpse on a bed of millet stalks would be led by an invisible and irresistible force to the house of the man whom the spirit had elected to carry out sacrifices in his or her honor. Though perhaps not the head of a lineage the individual thereby designated to succeed the deceased priest always belonged to one of the founding lineages of the community and would from then on be known as Magaji (heir).

Once chosen through the tarkama, the newly invested priest could not ignore his current responsibilities because the spirit who had chosen him to hold the "sacrificial knife"—the emblem of his new position that was kept in the thatched roof of the priest's home—would have been quick to remind him of his duty by sending some form of punishment. Regardless of his personal aspirations or affinities, he was now heir to a long tradition of priesthood and would, until his death, be considered by his fellow villagers as the guardian of a collective heritage. Some of his tasks included invoking the spirit's intervention for those who suffered a crisis. Unlike the more personal form of Azna mediumship out of which bori emerged, spirit possession was here confined to an exclusive body of priests, the 'yan 'kasa, who operated as mediators between people and their invisible counterparts. Conflicts that could not be solved at the level of the household were arbitrated by a council of elders, but when disputes and crimes involved individuals belonging to separate groups, they were brought to the attention of the spirits.

Over the last decades, many of the 'yan 'kasa designated through tarkama have relinquished their obligations to the spirits in order to follow divergent paths, despite being warned that their actions would have ominous consequences. Because no one would periodically renew the original bond contracted between the mythical settlers and the invisible residents of the land, some protective spirits progressively sunk into anonymity. Their altars became neglected as more mosques were built to accommodate the rapid expansion of Islam. Yet, despite indications that the weakening of people's ties to the mutanen daji has intensified since independence, the abandonment of spirit-centered practices is not a new trend. It originated in the French conquest of Niger and is rooted in the deep sociopolitical and economic transformations of the colonial period. To make sense of the bori practices examined in this work, it is therefore useful to focus for a moment on the Mawri's perception of how local forms of devotion to the spirits were progressively weakened by the advent of peace and commoditization. From this perspective, a number of interrelated themes emerge that will have particular relevance to the discussion of how 'yan bori interpret modern realities: the neglect of gado (heritage), the widespread hunger for wealth, and the worsening shortage of resources.

Lost Spirits, Fragmented Communities: Changing Religious Practices

Half a kilometer south of the dogon doutchi, another rocky mound raises its massive silhouette against an otherwise flat horizon. Known as *tozon bijini* ("the big bull's hump"), the rocky landmark is the abode of a Doguwa named Tarwa. Until recently, a goat was slaughtered annually on tozon bijini as an offering to the resident spirit. On the night following the sacrifice, it would invariably rain because Tarwa liked to wash her altar stone right after blood had sullied it. In 1989, Baidou, the 'dan 'kasa who had been chosen fifteen years earlier to carry the sacrificial knife for Tarwa, died unexpectedly. Baidou was crazy, people said. He had long suffered from violent and unexpected fits of insanity and had been known to harm children who came to set up bird traps in his fields. What was more, he had never sacrificed to the spirit because he wanted nothing to do with Azna practices. Many believed he had started losing his mind soon after he became *mai yuka* (owner of sacrificial knife) and neglected his ritual responsibilities. Because he had continued to ignore Tarwa, she had eventually killed him. No one could refuse to satisfy a spirit's request without suffering the consequences. Baidou had paid a heavy price for declining to serve the spirit. After his death, no tarkama had been held to designate the new mai yuka.

Besides angering the small minority of Dogondoutchi residents still committed to serving the land spirits, such blatant neglect of Azna tradition only served to confirm once more what many in town already knew: namely, that most Mawri no longer felt the need to ensure their security and prosperity through offerings to the invisible forces of the land. What made the realization so painful, this time, is that no one — not even zealous Muslims — had forced the 'yan 'kasa to forgo the performance of tarkama. If there was no mai yuka currently serving

Tarwa, a friend of mine had philosophically noted, the 'yan 'kasa could only blame themselves for their own lack of commitment to the spirit.

The progressive disengagement from local spiritual powers has affected many communities of Arewa. Today, people no longer fear the threat of impending attacks at the hands of enemy chiefdoms. The exploits of Doguwa spirits who emitted warning and protected local residents against external competitors have become the stuff of memory. When the past is brought up in conversations, there is often a tendency to romanticize precolonial warfare as an era of heroic deeds and glorious achievements. Discussions I had with older 'yan bori would thus largely focus on the momentous battles fought by arrow- or bullet-proof Mawri warriors made invincible by powerful spirits (Masquelier 1993). Pacification, on the other hand, is often experienced as a form of loss: with the progressive disappearance of military threat, people no longer felt the need for a protective presence and many spirits lost their raison d'être. Because they ceased to be vital to the Mawri's economic survival and moral stamina, they slowly fell into oblivion. Bori mediums who lament the current lack of commitment to local tradition thus perceive the advent of peace as a mixed blessing: if the pax colonial appeared to minimize the threat of famine and slavery, it also brought about the breakdown of socio-religious mechanisms that ensured the survival of communities in times of hardship and vulnerability. Conversely, the improvement of communications and the expansion of commerce within pacified Arewa paved the way for Islam.

The establishment of colonial structures of domination and the penetration of money also deeply affected kin-based production and communal life. Individuals became increasingly self-oriented instead of relying on the pooled resources of the family. Youths, especially, were given the means to produce their own income by selling not only the crops of their personal fields but their labor as well. No longer depending upon their elders for securing bridewealth or paying taxes, they gradually escaped the tutelage of the extended family, which was, in any case, less and less able to support all of its members (de Latour Dejean 1980, 123). Groundnut production and commercialization, which the French had encouraged by imposing a head tax payable in cash (Péhaut 1970, 64), particularly hastened the transformation of the extended-family farming unit and led to the privatization of land parcels. When increasingly fragmented landholdings could no longer sustain them as farmers, men would turn to migration as a means to earn the necessary cash and relieve the demand made on the food supply of their households. Moving away from the extended household has also implied neglecting one's heritage and one's ties and ritual obligations to the lineage's spirits. In the eyes of many Mawri, this is where the crux of the matter lies. I was told ad nauseam that people had forgotten the spirits and turned to Islam because, once peace was established, they just wanted to get on with their lives and take advantage of new opportunities. Because it favored the principle of private property and encouraged the accumulation of wealth (de Latour Dejean 1975, 200), the Koranic message was more compatible with market individualism. Islam thus expanded at the expense of pre-Islamic practices centered around notions of kin-based production and community.

For those who decry the neglect of gado (heritage) and the decline in solidarity, the prosperous and self-sufficient multigenerational household that was securely anchored in kin-based networks of production and exchange stands as an icon of an idealized past that is often invoked to assess the multiple costs of modernity. Such a vision of traditional domesticity belies the insecurities faced by precolonial peasants in an area periodically destabilized by drought, famine, or war. Yet there is no doubt that the economic burden and social inequities introduced first by colonial intervention and later by capitalist expansion impacted deeply communal and kin-oriented practices.

If Islam is often blamed by spirit devotees for the current evils and epidemics befalling Mawri communities, it is not the Koranic message—which in and of itself promotes piety, generosity, and moral discipline—so much as its tendency to prevent or discourage other religious practices that non-Muslims resent. The root of the problem, most of them agree, lies not in Islam itself but in the greedy nature of mankind. Because people's increasing desire for money is often perceived to be the driving force behind changing practices, those who disregard their heritage and neglect their duties toward the spirits are consistently accused of greed (see Schmoll 1991 for a discussion of similar issues). The pressing need for cash combined with a rising inability to procure it (de Latour Dejean 1980; Raynaut 1976) has led many to turn to Islam in the hope of achieving the social mobility that attends one's entry into the privileged body of the Muslim faithful. Such widespread hunger for wealth, both Muslims and non-Muslims lament, has compelled the adoption of novel values irrespective of the cost to heritage and "tradition." The following story, a popular one in bori circles, illustrates how people perceive the interrelation between the monetization of their economy, the scramble for money, and the loss of moral value:

> In a place called Matsafa, an ox would be sacrificed every year for the spirit of the area. As no one ever purchased the ox, there was no worry about how to finance the sacrificial beast. Every year, a cow and her calf appeared from the bush at the very date selected for the sacrifice to occur. People would take the calf away from its mother and slaughter it as an offering to the local spirit. Each time the cow would moo desperately for a while, before finally returning to where she came from. Nobody knew where she went, but it mattered little because she always reappeared the following year with a new calf at her side. The day after the sacrificial meat was grilled and consumed, the rain never failed. People knew it, and the following morning they would be sowing in their fields. One year, the villagers decided that the calf in itself would not provide enough meat for everyone to have a fair share. They thus killed both mother and offspring and gorged on the meat until everyone was satiated. The following year, no cow appeared to offer her progeny as sacrificial offering, and the villagers had to buy an ox for the spirit. Ever since that time, they have had to pull together their own meager resources to finance the annual sacrifice.

"This is how greed spoiled our relationship with the spirits," a bori healer commented after recounting to me his version of the tale. For spirit devotees who know the mythical cow's tragic fate, the story is especially meaningful because it expresses a fundamental loss: with the disappearance of the breeding cow, not only has a never-ending source of food, security, and pleasure vanished but the basic values on which moral life hinged have also disintegrated. The cow was not only a symbol of life, fertility, and continuity. She also embodied the ties uniting a village and its spirit. Ideally, the story implies, a spirit should provide the animal that she requires from her devotees as sacrificial offering. No individual should have to "suffer" (i.e., "have to work hard" but also "deprive himself") in order to come up with the offering requested by a spirit. When people must work hard at procuring their spirit's favorite animal, their "suffering" becomes a measure of the widening gap between humans and iskoki.

To return to the mythic cow, the animal was not sacrificed to appease an offended spirit or to fulfill its request for an offering but rather to give full rein to people's unbridled appetites. Blinded by greed, and unheeding of the material and moral implications of their action, the villagers destroyed the very thing that guaranteed the maintenance of the spirit's goodwill and protection, and, by extension, their survival—at very little cost to themselves. In a society where the specter of famine is always lurking nearby, the villagers' uncontrolled hunger for meat provides a powerful image for stressing human vulnerability to desire, and for understanding how greed—in its various expressions—can threaten individuals and society as a whole when it is allowed to reign unfettered by ethical guidelines. The continued relevance of the myth to those who are struggling to bridge the widening chasm between past experiences and modern realities testifies to the role of familiar bodily experience—hunger and satiation, consumption and depletion—for representing and manipulating the forces of history. These images are central to the 'yan bori's experience of the world and of their changing place in it, and the hunger for wealth (often referred to as neman ku'di, the search for money), in opposition to a vanishing prosperity concretized by abundant rainfall and "free" meat, figures as a crucial parameter in local perceptions of the historical shift to modernity.

The Village and the Bush:
Delineating and Anchoring Space

An examination of the indigenous principles structuring the organization of human space in Mawri society serves to underscore the importance of spatial oppositions and the significance of ritual practices, like gyaran gari, that reinforce such oppositions. Nicolas (1975; 1966) has elegantly shown how, for the Hausa-speaking inhabitants of the neighboring Maradi valley, social activities—from the founding of a village to the erection of a market—must be spatially oriented within specific cultural parameters. Hence, to establish a ritual sphere for the building of a village is to set off a social space from the "wild" and to establish a fundamental distinction between gari (town) and daji (bush). For the Hausa-speaking Mawri as well, each new settlement on Arewa soil meant a total disruption of forces. Yet in contrast to the new occupant in the Maradi region who "settle[d] with his plants, his animals, his activities, his spirits and establish[ed] them *in the place of those which had been there since time immemorial*" (Nicolas 1975, 252, emphasis added), Gubawa newcomers in Arewa did not establish their own iskoki in the place of those who had occupied the land since time immemorial. Though there might have been some overlap between local and "imported" spirits in the Gubawa pantheon, the iskoki who were associated with particular features of the immediate landscape were, my informants insisted, "native" to the area. And it is as such that they were regularly acknowledged by human communities who owed them their very existence and survival in this precarious environment.

The newly created village was a human, domesticated space within a vaster field of wild forces. Whoever entered it penetrated a ritually circumscribed area that was protected from the influences of the bush. People still say today that upon entering the city of Tibiri (four hundred miles east of Dogondoutchi, in the Maradi valley), individuals become invisible to their potential pursuers (Nicolas 1975, 386). The safety local communities provided to residents and visitors alike largely hinged on the regular performance of gyaran gari. Originally held by the 'yan 'kasa (sons of the earth) after the harvest, when the cold season sets in and the harmattan chills the air,[3] the ceremony of gyaran gari was said to bring rain and health to the community. This is how the gyaran gari was described by the French colonial administrator Plagnol (1947): "Every year, at the start of the cold season, a sacrifice is made to Maguiro [a male deity invoked in times of epidemics] on the site allocated for this purpose. Once the sacrifice is made, everyone goes back to the village. All the inhabitants stand on their doorstep. The first roosters in sight are caught and slaughtered on every path leading to the village so that the epidemics will not come in." Because it closes village paths to foreign spirits, the ceremony is also called *tarbon iska* ("meeting the spirit"). The specific purposes of the ceremony were to hold at bay the foreign spirits who were brought in by the cold wind and to purge the community from malevolent influences. If unrestricted, these spirits entered villages to frighten the children and bring diseases such as measles, meningitis, and fevers.

Today, the Azna ritual destined to protect Mawri communities at the onset of the cold season is performed by bori devotees who are not necessarily 'yan 'kasa. The bori, which has evolved partly out of the indigenous, land spirits cult, has taken on some of the ritual obligations of Gubawa priests, whose numbers are rapidly dwindling. Yet several villages of Arewa have stopped holding the gyaran gari, because, as mentioned earlier, the notion of sacrifice offends Muslim sensibilities and is antithetical to the moral views adopted by a growing majority of Muslim Mawri. Often, the abandonment of the gyaran gari rites in a community coincides with the installment of a Muslim as village chief. In the ensuing discussion of gyaran gari, I rely on my own observations of several ceremonies I attended as well as on informants' commentaries of "how things were." My description of how the towns and villages of Arewa are—or were—ritually cleansed of evil influence will clarify what is at stake for spirit devotees who, in the face of an ever encroaching Muslim community, can only deploy the specter of illness to counter the disappearance of orientational practices aimed at defining areas as particular *places,* shielded from malevolence and sickness. As will become clear, the preservation of identity, morality, and history for spirit mediums is inseparable from a context of mythic interactions out of which contemporary bori meanings and motives emerge and evolve.

The timing of the ceremony is crucial. If too much time is allowed to elapse after the harvest season, chances are that the protective barrier drawn by the ritual participants and physically imprinted onto the land through the shedding of sacrificial blood may not prove effective. A bori devotee told me in 1988 that a few years earlier and at the spirits' request, the 'yan bori of his village had collected contributions from all local households. With the money, they had bought a white he-goat that would be sacrificed to prevent "sickness, especially measles." Because they had lingered before fulfilling the spirits' recommendation, the sacrifice had come too late to avert trouble: disease had rapidly invaded the small community and many children had fallen sick.

Aside from timeliness, regularity is also key to the well-being of a community. By performing a gyaran gari every year, residents of a community effectively redefine the opposition between the village and the bush, an opposition that is seasonally dissolved by the elusive and invisible harbinger of sickness, the wind of the cold season. It is no coincidence that wind and spirit are referred to by the same Hausa term, iska. Like the wind that often carries them across the landscape, spirits lack corporeality and are not constrained by physical boundaries. They can travel great distances in a flash and go through walls. As with the slippery wind that cannot be seen but whose effects must be endured by all during the dry season, it is difficult to escape the influence of the spirits. Though invisible to the human eye, they often leave a trace of their presence for those who can read such signs. Hence one commonly hears that *aljanu duk iska na* (spirits are all wind).

Associated with the village/bush opposition is the distinction between the domesticated and the wild. Ideally, the village should contain only identified and benevolent spirits who have vowed to protect humans in exchange for periodic sacrificial offerings, and are anchored within through the erection of an altar stone in the community. In contrast, the bush is "a wild and perilous zone occupied by fearful deities, at the same time that it is a kind of mythic reality filled with powerful forces which may clash more or less violently with human enterprises" (Nicolas 1975, 117). One may fall prey to dangerous spirits or evil influences while traveling in the bush. During my fieldwork, I heard numerous accounts of villagers who had been attacked or followed by frightening or wicked creatures of varied appearance when they were crossing the bush on their way to another hamlet. There are also those who claim to have caught a terrible illness called *ciwon daji* (sickness of the bush) while traveling across the wild. Allegedly caused by spirits who "catch" people and make them *hauka* (crazy), this affliction may last anywhere from a few weeks to several years. It renders the victims feeble, incoherent, and incapable of working, and can only be cured through treatment at the hands of a bori practitioner.

The contrast between the comforting forces of the village and the perilous hazards of the bush is nicely captured in the proverb "In town, men are all the same; in the bush, you can tell the courageous from the coward."[4] The proverb implies that while there is nothing to fear in the village, the bush is a dangerous place that cowards generally avoid. Paradoxically, everyone knows that the plants and animals of the bush are endowed with special powers, which, if properly channeled, can be used to manufacture potent medicines for a wide variety of ailments. When bori healers make periodic trips to the bush to build up or replenish their supplies of medicinal plants, they often

A stone is erected for the spirit of a newly initiated medium. After the stone is planted in the ground and washed with protective medicine, an animal of the spirit's favorite color will be sacrificed on it.

follow the guidelines provided by their spirits in a dream. Spirits who communicate with their devotees in dreams tell them which plants to pick and where to find them.

Before leaving the "domesticated" world to enter the wild, however, spirit mediums must ritually perform *darmen daji* ("tying the bush") by pronouncing appropriate words that will ensure that they cross a field of favorable forces. If no such precautions are taken, healers, travelers, or hunters run the risk of losing themselves or not finding any plants or game. Woodcutters may end up being crushed by the tree they are trying to chop down (Nicolas 1975, 117). Pronouncing apparent gibberish such as "tankin tak" creates an invisible barrier that prevents any evil force from colliding with the speaker when the latter has entered the bush. As has been shown in other contexts, the use of repetitive, formalized, or non-sense language in performative utterances delineates a special field of action divorced from ordinary experience (Malinowski 1935; Stoller 1989b; Tambiah 1985). By uttering "tankin tak" or "greetings, in front tika, behind tika tak," an individual generates a system of orientation that is uniquely relative to himself. In keeping the bush at a remove from himself, the healer or hunter creates a protective interiority that insures the success of the goal that motivated his incursion into the wild.

These magical utterances are sometimes enough to "tie" the malevolent force so that it will be fixed to one spot and unable to move and harm its intended victim. As a tangible force of the tonal field that has its own direction, velocity and intensity, the spoken word becomes both expressive and instrumental in its effect upon the world. When uttering "tankin tak," the individual walking in the bush projects his voice outward. The impact of the sound is felt like a blow by the creature at whom it is directed. The creature is literally pinned down by the word, just as the sorcerer is stopped in flight by the stick or needle that a healer has planted in the ground.[5] Like knives, poisons or blows, words can harm or protect when they are used to immobilize a force or being within a circumscribed area.

Gyaran Gari: Creating Interiority

"Tying the bush," then, involves practices that not only draw a contrast between inside and outside but, to quote from a study of Haya practices in Tanzania, also generate "an internally integrated place, one that has an independent configuration" (Weiss 1996, 43). When ritually isolating a field from malevolent forces, the Mawri speak of *kafa* (anchoring) the newly apportioned space, an action that emphasizes the stability and integrity of that space in relation to its encompassing context. The notion of anchoring or fixing a space—*kafin kasuwa:* the erection of a market—or a landmark—*kafin doutchi:* erection of a spirit altar—onto the landscape is crucial to the symbolic ordering of the Mawri environment. It stabilizes and reinforces what were by definition permeable boundaries so as to prevent evil influences from penetrating the "anchored" space. In the context of gyaran gari, this anchoring of space through the modalities of inside and outside is achieved by slaughtering a hen or a rooster at each of the four cardinal points on the village periphery.

While each village follows strict and specific rules concerning the colors of the animals and the site of their sacrifice, these rules vary from one village to the next. In the village of Mamoudou, for instance, the ceremony proceeds in the following way: first, a red hen is killed to the east, then a black hen is killed to the north. At the western cardinal point, a white hen is slaughtered, and finally a black-and-white speckled hen is sacrificed at the southern periphery of the village. The four sacrificial hens are obtained locally, wherever they happen to be found. No compensation is given to their owners because the ritual is expected to benefit everyone's health. In addition, each household must provide a ladleful of millet. Once collected, the grain is pounded—but not cooked—and mixed with water to form a thick paste, *gumba,* which is then distributed among the children.

Whether the hen is thrown to the ground after its throat has been cut or whether it is actually buried alive, the action is described as *kafa kaza*—literally, to anchor the hen into the ground. The cardinal axes of the space to be delineated are often taken as reference points because they are a crucial principle of spatial classification and organization (see Nicolas 1966; 1968). Not every gyaran gari follows the same routine, however, and the location of ritual barriers to be set up strategically around the village or along sacred landmarks may thus vary considerably.[6]

As the blood seeps into the sandy ground, it marks the spot where the bush ends and the village begins. It also concretizes the largely invisible fence that protects the community's integrity from external threats. While some villages are surrounded in some places by mud walls, woven millet-stalk partitions, or fences made of brush that afford some measure of privacy to households and shield human space from the dust-laden harmattan, other communities are not physically enclosed within any protective structures. The bloodstains on selected spots of the village periphery act as visual reminders of the protection the gari receives from spirits once the latter have been placated through sacrificial offerings during gyaran gari. By also delineating through a graphic trail that which is inside the village, the gyaran gari effectively creates a field for people to live in (de Certeau 1984, 124). It is the path the participants walk that gives shape and orientation to the space they enclose within that path. In other words, the act of walking, as a form of "pedestrian enunciation" (99), authorizes the "here" of the village and temporarily separates it from its exteriority. The itinerary they follow is largely symbolic, but it is through what de

Certeau calls the "rhetoric of walking" (100)—the art of composing a path through footsteps—that the members of the gyaran gari procession create the spatiality of the village. In other words, the motions of gyaran gari constitute "pedestrian movements which form one of these real systems whose existence in fact makes up the [village]" (97). By weaving together several places through their motions, and by positioning their bodies within the encompassing world, the walkers in the procession literally structure space by constituting, in relation to their positions, each step of the way, "both a near and a far, a here and a there" (103) and thus establishing a "conjunctive and disjunctive articulation of places" (99).

If walking affirms the trajectories it "speaks," so does speech, of course. Thus footsteps that simultaneously inscribe the contours of the village and create the space within it are sometimes complemented by words, such as the terms *here* and *there,* that enunciate space by establishing links or disjunctures between locations—in this case, between the place created as the village and the bush. In the village of Argoum, a few miles south of Dogondoutchi, participants in the gyaran gari would listen to one of the procession leaders as he recited a prayer that recreated in the social imaginary the lived space of the village. No ceremony to protect the community has been held in Argoum since 1987, so the following description of the tarbon iska is based on a 'dan bori's memories of the event.

Traditionally, two hens would be slaughtered on every path leading to the village. The carcasses were then given to the children who made a fire outside the village. The meat was grilled and eaten on the spot, since none of it could be brought back to the village. When all the meat was consumed, the following words would be uttered as a fire was lit on every site where blood had been shed:

Hey, fire, it is the fire of the bush
It is not the fire of the village
It has no path [to enter] the village of Argoum
It eats the bush; it does not eat the people of Argoum
Fire does not have a path [to enter] the village of Argoum
The blaze must get worse
So that the people of Argoum will know there is fire.

Hey, fire, it is the fire of the bush

It is not the fire of the village

It has no path [to enter] the village of Argoum

It eats the bush; it does not eat the village of Argoum.[7]

Firewood was added to the fire, and once the flames were high enough, each participant would *ketare* (jump over) them. This guaranteed that "no evil would enter the village except for what God had willed," according to Malo, a 'dan bori residing in Argoum. Thus, he explained to me, if sorcerers tried to enter the village armed with evil intentions, they would disappear—provided, of course, that the gyaran gari had been correctly performed.

In Argoum, the ritual barrier sketched onto the ground through the shedding of sacrificial blood and the footprints of the participants was thus reinforced by the fence of fire lit around the village. By visually and physically enclosing the community within a wall of flames and smoke, spirit devotees actively set apart the village from the bush. For days after the ceremony was over, the bloodstained earth and the cinder would remain as tangible—and more durable—evidence of the symbolic enclosure impermanently erected through ambulatory motion and fire. Yet fire was not simply a glowing and unstable wall of flames that reinforced the division between gari (town) and daji (bush). It was also directed at the bush in which both flames and smoke would carve out their own space, thereby forcing the wild to recede further. Tongues of fire that leapt in the air were carefully monitored so that the blaze would not threaten the village. But they were encouraged to *cin daji* ("eat" the wilderness) by feeding off the dry wood and kindling brought back from the bush, just as long as they would not touch any of the thatch or wood and adobe structures in the gari.

In the majority of villages where I attended a gyaran gari or questioned spirit devotees about the ritual, once the sacrificed animals lay on the ground, they were not to be touched or taken back to one's house.[8] They now belonged to the bush and could not be consumed by any human except musicians of the bori for whom the restrictions did not apply because of their low status. As one 'dan bori put it, "The hen that is brought to the bush cannot come back. If somebody tries to eat it [in the village], he will die." By shedding the blood of sacrificial animals along cardinal axes or at strategic points along the village outskirts, 'yan bori are setting up "centers of sacred energy" (Nicolas 1966, 69). Regardless of whether the meat is consumed or left to rot on the site of the sacrifice, the point is that the carcasses can no longer move inward and violate the interiority of the community once the animal's very blood was spilled to graphically reinstate that interiority. Bringing the sacrificial carcass back to the gari would dislocate the centers of energy and weaken the village's defenses against the outside, in effect ruining the 'yan bori's chances of ensuring health and prosperity for all. In addition to the hens and roosters slaughtered "to the bush," a goat may be killed on a spirit's altar as an offering to that particular iska. This was done during several of the gyaran gari I attended, presumably to ensure that the village be protected against evil influences by specific spirits. Once the spirit to whom the offerings is made has drunk the blood of the animal, spirit devotees are free to cook and eat the meat among themselves. The sacrifice reenacts the initial pact made between humans and spirits, and guarantees congenial relations between them.

The millet given to the children in the form of gumba (uncooked millet) symbolically stands for food and wealth. In the past, it was distributed among those who stood to lose the most if the gyaran gari was not properly performed: many children would fall prey to fevers and respiratory infections during the cold season, and it was largely for their protection that the ritual was staged. Today, however, when the gyaran gari is performed at all, the millet (usually half a standard measure [rabin tiya]) that is requested from each household is often collected only to be resold. The money from the sale is then used to purchase sacrificial hens and roosters, pay the musicians and the praise singers who call the spirits with their songs, and buy food for the guests who might be attending the ceremony. Since no one offers any longer to contribute freely what is needed, things are done in such a way as to reduce the overall cost of the ritual — especially when 'yan bori must justify these expenses to Muslim households generally unwilling to subsidize "pagan" practices. "No one gives freely to the spirits anymore," lamented a spirit medium who proudly acknowledged his participation in past gyaran gari ceremonies. His complaint echoed other comments 'yan bori and 'yan 'kasa commonly make about the rise of illnesses in communities where gyaran gari is no longer or inadequately performed. The question then remains as to how 'yan bori' deal with the increased vulnerability of such communities.

Permeable Boundaries, Vulnerable Communities

In Dogondoutchi, where Muslim factions, emboldened by their growing popularity, have successfully pressured local authorities into abandoning the ways of the ancestors, there has not been a gyaran gari for at least twenty years. According to Yenge, the town's chief of bori:

> In the past, the *chef de canton* gave a goat and the hens were caught throughout town. Any hen or goat seen in the street could be grabbed for the gyaran gari. But that hasn't happened in more than twenty years. . . . Now, [village and town] chiefs are always on the side of the *malamai*. If the 'yan bori ask for an animal to be slaughtered for gyaran gari, they are told that they only ask because they want some meat. But when there is no rain, it is to me that everybody comes so that I will beg the spirits [for an end to the drought].

For many who haven't relinquished their ties to the spirits to profess allegiance to the Prophet, the abandonment of gyaran gari has resulted in many evils against which Muslim medicines are powerless. In the eyes of 'yan bori, it is because their boundaries are no longer ritually reinforced that many villages have become vulnerable to outside forces. As such, these communities no longer afford their inhabitants the protection they previously offered. "In the past, when we 'arranged' the village, sickness could not enter because we closed all the roads to foreign spirits," once lamented a 'dan bori who earned extra income as a healer in a village where Muslim followers had put a stop to most bori communal rituals. "Now, with the prayer," he had concluded mournfully, "there are many dead."

As should have become obvious by now, such disenchanted comments on the limitations of Muslim power frequently open the door to further criticisms about a state of affairs that has come to characterize modernity for those who experience the progress of Islam as a sense of loss. In a growing number of Arewa communities, village paths remain open to all creatures, whether they be visible or invisible, evil or harmless. Consequently, travelers who pass through or visit a village no longer feel that they have entered a safe place, 'yan bori argue. Because, in such contexts, the boundaries between town and bush become increasingly blurred, visitors must remain on their guard even after they have reached the house of a friend. Among bori circles especially, there is a sense that some villages are best avoided.

During my fieldwork, rumors concerning "unhealthy" or danger-ous communities were consistently fueled by reports of travelers who had heard of, or experienced firsthand, a hazardous situation. South of Dogondoutchi, a village by the name of Kame Doumey, whose inhabitants had allegedly all been killed or chased away by an evil Doguwa spirit feeding on human blood, had been rebaptized by out-siders as Kamen Kundugum (Kame where there is nothing left) and Kamen Doguwa (Kame of the Doguwa). Further south, the village of Lagodo, which counted a large number of Muslims among its popula-tion, had also acquired a reputation for fostering the deadly activities of several bloodthirsty spirits. Unlike their tamer counterparts, who mount their hosts in the ritually orchestrated context of bori cere-monies, these Doguwa spirits are destructive and deadly, and little can usually be done once they have elected to rob a human victim of her blood (Masquelier 1997a). A 'dan bori, whose brother had been at-tacked by one of these spirits, explained to me that the Doguwa who had almost killed his sibling came from Lagodo. Though he made no mention of the aggressive campaign waged by Muslim residents in their efforts to rid the village of non-Muslim practices, the spirit medium was well aware of Lagodo's new openness to outside forces— it had been several years since a gyaran gari had been performed there. "I cannot count all the mean [Doguwa] who come from Lagodo," he had concluded, to emphasize the recent proliferation of bloodthirsty spirits in his brother's village.

Because 'yan bori often associate the current vulnerability of Arewa communities to evil forces with the antibori politics of local elites, they have devised formulas to avenge themselves on the individuals whom they blame for the perceived rise of afflictions and misfortunes. Nowadays, visitors entering a village are occasionally instructed to utter certain words that will redirect potentially malevolent spirits onto the chiefs held responsible for such threatening situations;[9] by failing to adequately purge their villages from malignant influence and by declining to ritually close off the paths that open onto the outside world, some chiefs have caused their village boundaries to collapse. In so doing, they have let in a host of pernicious forces that manifest themselves on the ailing bodies of those who most concretely symbolize the community's health and vitality: children.

The perceived lack of closure that leads to the infiltration of domestic space by wild and threatening forces is one of several powerful images that spirit devotees and other bori sympathizers deploy to express loss of control over the material and moral resources of their environment. With the integration of Mawri communities within a wider order of sociopolitical and economic relations and practices, the symbolic map that anchored indigenous history and identity in the physical landscape is progressively eroding, replaced by the ostensible signs of an expanding Muslim hegemony. For those who still explain the world in terms of their connections to spirits, the disappearance of indigenous practices that centered on margins and thresholds is objectified as an invasion of communal and corporeal space. As is evidenced by the anthropological literature on the shifting margins of "moral community" in postcolonial Africa (Auslander 1993; Bastian 1992, 1998b; Gottlieb 1992; Lan 1985; Piot 1999; Shipton 1989; van Binsbergen 1981; Werbner 1989), the Mawri efforts to guard local communities against invasive "evils" are not unique. From the "opening" of wombs in Zambian witch-cleansing rituals (Auslander 1993) to the confessions extracted by the Atinga witch finders in Yoruba towns (Apter 1993), these ritual struggles waged to regain control over a world run amuck exemplify some of the ways that Africans confront the experience of modernity. In Arewa, communities are no longer guarded against moral and material evils and no longer purged from external malevolence because, spirit devotees argue, they do not pay their dues to the superhuman forces that ultimately control human productivity and prosperity.

Whether it monitors access to the body, the compound, or the village, the distinction between inside and outside is crucial because it informs much of what bori accomplishes in seeking to preserve endangered values while simultaneously defusing the impact of modernity. Bori interpretations of how religious and political reforms have affected the integrity of Mawri communities echo other discourses centering on the increasing frailty of moral and physical thresholds. Just as communities find themselves more permeable to the life-threatening diseases brought by seasonal winds, there is, for instance, a widespread perception that women have become less sexually and spatially contained within the boundaries of marriage and mother-hood. The ways in which female bodies provide the naturalizing ground for expressing the conflicts and ruptures of the modern era will be demonstrated later, but for now, it is sufficient to stress how the bori's efforts to mediate the effects of Islam, Westernization, and commoditization often take the shape of struggles against forces that threaten to invade or de-stabilize the Mawri universe. Whether they address the crumbling thresholds of corporate bodies or the open-ness of individual bodies, spirit devotees thus reassert their indispens-ability in a rapidly changing world by pointing to the scourges that threaten Mawri order when, for instance, pre-Islamic rituals that re-inforced locality and interiority are replaced by Muslim practices em-phasizing the universality of Islam and the preeminence of Allah over any other agencies or subsidiary spirits.

In the past, danger was primarily experienced as coming from the outside in the form of illness or foes against whom the village, as a tightly bound moral and physical entity, prevailed. Today the source of evil has become harder to locate. Ensuring the protection of per-sons or communities is no longer a matter of erecting walls of thorns,[10] or of engaging in combat with a visible assailant; as boundaries shift and thresholds crumble, a number of evils await unwary villagers within their own communities. This alien presence is sometimes ex-perienced as a seductive encounter with one of the fantastically em-bodied female spirits who roam highways, city streets, or village paths under various guises (Masquelier 1992). Whether they rob travelers of their riches, their reproductive capacities, or their blood, these malevolent figures chillingly objectify the contradictions of an ex-panding market economy in which the emergence of new modes of production and forms of mobility have irremediably altered the poli-tics of spatiality and the power of religious signifiers. By locating the source of modern scourges in the tampering of the moral landscape, or branding newly nuanced representations of evil on the roadscapes of Arewa, spirit devotees implicitly protest the growing ascendancy of Muslim elites over trade, politics, and religious life. Bori, then, appears to serve specific motives and interests in the context of people's search for power, identity, and prosperity. What motivates individuals to seek membership in bori, how would-be mediums become officially initiated as 'yan bori, and how bori forms of symbolic capital become means of constructing and contesting social roles and statuses are explored in the next chapter.

Chapter 3

Socializing the Spirits

A spirit is like a child. He does what he is told to do.
—Mawri proverb

When he was young, Mayaki dreamed of going to Mecca. He never wanted to be a 'dan bori. But the spirits decided otherwise. One day, some thirty years ago, Mayaki became very ill. It was the kind of sickness against which human medicines were powerless. For a long time, Mayaki refused to recognize that spirits had made him sick to let him know they had chosen him as a doki *("horse"; spirit medium). So the spirits made him even more ill. Instead of attending to his work and responsibilities, he would leave his home and wander in the bush for several days at a time. Mayaki was so mad, he did not recognize anyone. He would take off even in stormy weather and while in the bush, feed on leaves, roots, and berries. He wore rags and mostly mumbled to himself. For seven years, Mayaki suffered greatly at the hands of the spirits, and his health had deteriorated so much that he never once worked in his fields. Then a* roko *(propitiatory ritual) was organized so that he could beg the forgiveness of the spirits and request that they help him regain his health. Several months later, when he felt better, Mayaki became initiated into the bori. Now he holds a wasa for his spirits every year. Since the* gyara *(initiation), Mayaki has never given another thought to his original prospects of becoming an* alhaji *(Muslim pilgrim).*

Health and the Spirits

Lahiya (health) is the most important thing one can have, Mawri friends were fond of repeating in their efforts to make me understand what made some individuals turn to the spirits and invest so many resources in costly ceremonies that few of them could generally afford. Put differently, it is not people who choose to become mediums

but rather spirits who, through their capacity to cause and cure affliction in humans, force people to commit to a lifetime of servitude in
the bori. Thus, anyone can potentially become afflicted by spirits, and
when this happens, 'yan bori will tell you, there is no use in trying to
resist them, for in the end the mutanen daji always win. Besides, they
would insist, what is the point of living if one cannot have health?
Wouldn't Allah, the merciful, understand the plight of the afflicted
and tolerate their efforts to socialize the spirits that are tormenting
them? Even Muslims occasionally admit that the only safe and reasonable thing a person can do once she has been diagnosed as suffering
from a spirit-induced illness is to "arrange" her bori—that is, undergo
initiation. "Spirits are real, if they catch you, as long as you do not
follow their path and arrange them, they are going to bother you," explained to me Malam Mamman, a sixty-five-year-old Koranic scholar
who supplemented the income he earned as a teacher by engaging in
the sale of kola nuts. "This is why" he added, "there are so many ma-
lams who have left the Koran. They have spirits. They left their *karatu*
(studies); otherwise, the spirits were going to kill them. Or the spirits
were going to take [paralyze] a foot or a hand. Because spirits are real."

It is not the person who is looking for a spirit, Malam Mamman had
concluded, but God who sends spirits onto people. While some Muslims might find quarrel with such a bold assertion (bori being, for the
opponents of possession, nothing but the work of Satan), the old man's
views on the inevitable fate of those who fall victim to a spirit's capricious love are widely shared among Dogondoutchi's female population. But if no one, not even the most outspoken opponents of bori,
would deny the spirits' existence, still few Muslim men openly agree
with 'yan bori on the proper therapy for spirit-induced afflictions. In
private, however, some appear less secure about their supposed im-
perviousness to the spirits, and they may even be persuaded about the
superior powers of bori techniques when facing desperate situations.

Spirit mediums invariably allude to the afflictions they initially suffered when questioned about their motivations to undergo initiation, but the relationship between possession and healing is lodged
in understandings of gender, power, sexuality, marriage, music, and
marketing—among other things—rather than in "illness" itself. Healing, in the bori sense, is largely a matter of repairing the fragile boundaries of the human world by socializing the spirits suspected to have
breached the divisions between the social and the wild. In short, and

as a dimension of possession, it is about learning to reconfigure the world from the spirits' perspective. Because one must continuously negotiate the terms of one's relationship to a spirit, getting well thus becomes a lifelong exercise through which hosts learn to interpret and resolve their problems through the lens of bori and with the mediating powers of bori. To characterize spirits as agents of afflictions partly oversimplifies the complex, multifaceted, and fragile relationships these capricious creatures enjoy with their hosts as each human/spirit pair learns to coexist within a single body.

Possession may transcend the context of affliction, but *ciwo* (illness) nonetheless provides a convenient idiom for defining some of the boundaries of bori activities—even as these boundaries become routinely disputed and negotiated. From the perspective of bori mediums, there are only two kinds of diseases: those that are caused by spirits and those that are not. The latter category includes afflictions of *likita* (Western doctors), which can be remedied by getting a shot or taking pills, as well as illnesses caused by bad food, heat, *sammu* (sorcery), and the like. Spirit-induced afflictions range from mild ailments—stomachaches, headaches, pimples, rashes—to serious, debilitating, and sometimes life-threatening conditions such as that experienced by Mayaki as well as madness, paralysis, meningitis, or "lack of blood." They often take the form of prolonged and seemingly incurable diseases that can only be treated by appealing to the spirit who is eventually identified as being responsible for the patient's suffering. Many 'yan bori who described the circumstances of their involvement with the bori to me often determined that their afflictions were caused by spirits. They realized this when the likita (biomedical practitioner) could not find anything wrong with them even though they were on the brink of death. The moment of revelation invariably occurred when the needle the nurse was ready to pierce their skin with would fall to the ground or break before it could penetrate the epidermis. The actual circumstances and details surrounding the event varied from one individual to the next, but the surprising outcomes all similarly highlighted an ultimate incommensurability between the dispensary and the realm of the spirits: Western medicine could not be injected into the patient's body because the spirits who had caused the affliction would not allow it. The illness was their responsibility, and so was the cure, provided the afflicted agreed to become involved in the bori.

These scenarios exemplify the degree to which indigenous healing systems have proven resilient and adaptive in Niger and in the rest of the continent as well. Far from being destroyed by the "joint assault of colonialism and biomedicine," Vaughan notes, they tended rather to " 'indigenize' those elements of biomedical practice which seemed most effective and most impressive—the most obvious being the injection" (1991, 24). Injections are indeed a popular treatment for malaria, fevers, and a variety of other ailments. That the needle applied by the nurse was not even allowed to penetrate the skin demonstrates powerfully the inefficacy of biomedicine in the context of spirit-related afflictions. Through these narratives of biomedical failure, 'yan bori also stress that possession may involve a great deal of suffering before the host learns to adjust to the various spirits wishing to appropriate her body. As the following story illustrates, a spirit's attachment to a person may cause that unfortunate individual to almost die before anything can be done to satisfy the invading force's demands.

Mamata has married twice. Her first husband was a customs officer. The man to whom she is now married is a farmer. She sells fried cakes in the market and has eight living children. When she was two months pregnant with her first child, she was caught by spirits and suffered greatly. She would leave for the bush, and neighbors had to go find her and bring her home. When the spirits allowed it, Mamata would eat. At that time, she lived in Maradi [two hundred and forty miles east of Dogondoutchi].

She was only a young girl when the spirits caught her, and the things she would see frightened her a great deal. At night, she would be lying on her bed, when suddenly she would see huge flames in the room as if the whole house had caught on fire. At other times, it was a horse that was pursuing her. When Mamata stepped out of her room, she would sometimes be surrounded by kneeling women. When they started moving closer, she would try to run back to her room and lock herself in, but they always managed to enter the locked house. Mamata would then try to escape them by running out and seeking refuge in a neighbor's house. She would remain there, silent and shivering, until her husband came back from work.

One day, Mamata left Maradi and started walking in the bush. She did not know where she was going, but she kept on walking until a car stopped at her side.

The driver asked her where she was going. Mamata answered that she did not know where her home was. So the driver took her all the way to Dogondoutchi. Her madness lingered until she gave birth to her child. After she rested for forty days, Mamata felt better and a gyara was held for her spirits. Her father financed the ceremony. Though he was Muslim and did not want anything to do with her spirits, he was nonetheless concerned about his daughter's health. He knew Mamata had inherited her grandmother's spirits, and that she would not be well until a wasa was organized for them.

Those who, like Mamata, have gone through serious ordeals thanks to their possessing spirits consider themselves fortunate to have been chosen as hosts, because, ultimately, spirits possess the people they like. Tested by the afflicting bori, they should emerge stronger from the various trials, thereby demonstrating their fortitude and integrity to both spirit and human communities. Initial suffering is then gradually replaced by tolerance and benevolence on the part of the bori as both the novice host and the intrusive spirit learn to accommodate each other. It is thus only after having been tormented at length by spirits that some mediums become reputed healers who put to use the knowledge transmitted by their possessing bori. While Mamata, like a great majority of the female mediums I met, did not prescribe the herbs she saw in her dreams, a sizable portion of the male bori membership in Dogondoutchi claimed to earn an income selling the medicines they were shown while dreaming.

Spirit-induced afflictions may appear to follow a fairly predictable trajectory based on 'yan bori's a posteriori accounts of the health crises that preceded the initiation, but bori is above all a cultural resource that is drawn upon whenever deemed necessary or appropriate. As Boddy puts it for the zar of northern Sudan, bori is an idiom "based on consensually validated, ritually confirmed information" (1989, 137). How such information is used by individuals trying to articulate their own life experiences may vary greatly, especially given the material, moral, and social constraints people face in their families and communities. What may sometimes appear to be a spirit-induced illness to one person ends up being explained differently by another, perhaps because for the latter, an alternative curative strategy provides the means to negotiate new alliances or identities

(Brodwin 1996; Crandon-Malamud 1991). Or, as the case often arises, while they might agree as to the origin of the affliction, two individuals will argue over the kind of treatment that must be sought because one is a 'dan bori, and the other, a devout Muslim who believes that exorcism, rather than initiation, is the appropriate way to solve problems caused by the spirits' intrusive presence in the world of humans.

Yet even among bori mediums who have deeply internalized the meanings and agencies of bori, the idiom of possession is sometimes too cumbersome or conceptually removed to be useful in routine matters that can be more easily explained through references to one's physical environment. Instead of claiming that his recent insomnia, apathy, or lack of appetite may be caused by an angered spirit, an individual may thus blame his wife's poor culinary skills or decide that he is suffering from "lack of blood" brought on by excessive exposure to the sun. Conversely, how and why a banal stomachache should be attributed to the spirit Zanzana rather than to the day-old (and, therefore, sour and less digestible) millet porridge one has ingested a few hours before are not easy questions to answer. It is a problem I often grappled with in my efforts to understand the largely implicit logic of affliction management. People often revised one diagnosis if another explanation made more sense after the situation evolved or as more of the intervening factors became known. Since explaining the affliction is often a large part of the therapy (Herzfeld 1986; Levi-Strauss 1963), an as detailed as possible knowledge of the social and physical context in which the misfortune or ailment occurred is necessary to assess the efficacy of the treatment and to understand the overall significance of a healing practice.

My friend Zeinabou with whom I regularly attended bori rituals complained once of suffering from acute diarrhea. Knowing that she had been "bothered" by some of her spirits because she kept putting off her initiation ceremony and because she had not granted some of their requests for clothing,[1] I became quite concerned and offered to pay for a chicken that could be sacrificed to one of her bori. This would, I thought, appease the spirits until she could come up with the money for the initiation. It would also convince them of her earnestness, for I knew how eager she was to officialize her membership in the bori. Zeinabou laughed wholeheartedly at my suggestion, saying that all she needed to get better was some of *my* medicine. To my surprise, she then added matter-of-factly that her diarrhea was caused by the plate of unwashed lettuce she had eaten the day before. I should stop blaming the spirits for all the minor troubles I experienced or witnessed, she added with a wink of her eye.

Among other things, the incident was a convincing demonstration of how healing and, more specifically, diagnosis making, are part of a semantic—as well as a pragmatic—process involving the grounding of cultural meanings in a concrete nexus of events, relations, and practices. To Zeinabou, blaming the contaminated lettuce for her bad case of diarrhea made more sense at this particular time and place than imputing responsibility to the spirits, although the former did not necessarily preclude the latter. By locating her particular troubles within the immediate context of intimate and familiar bodily experiences such as eating and digesting, my friend was able to construct an explanation that was meaningful and commonsensical, in addition to allowing her to act upon the source of her ailment by ingesting some of my medicine for diarrhea. She had drawn upon the prosaic and the ordinary to articulate her experience of a common illness instead of resorting to an interpretation involving superhuman forces.[2] Through such articulation, Zeinabou had literally constructed her experience of disease in a way that made it acceptable and coherent. As Crapanzano has put it, "The act of articulation is more than a passive representation of the event; it is in essence the creation of an event. It separates the event from the flow of experience . . . gives the event structure . . . relates it to other similarly constructed events, and evaluates the event along both idiosyncratic and (culturally) standardized lines. Once the experience is articulated, once it is rendered an event, it is cast within the world of meaning and may provide basis for action" (1977, 10).

Whether it implicates spirits in people's destinies or excludes them, disease is thus an important and inescapable dimension of bori. Yet it must be stressed again that possession resists "analytical reduction to a single component distinction" (Boddy 1989, 136). Assessing the meanings, motivations, and implications of bori thus implies attending to the multiple and diverse ways in which possession intersects with other contexts or images—sexuality and penetration, marriage and prostitution, music and work.

Contested Diagnoses, Negotiated Identities

Whether or not Mawri people have recourse to the spirits to articulate illness within a nexus of power relations, social circumstances, and bodily experience, the literature on Mawri (and more generally Hausa) cosmology and rituals (Besmer 1983; Darrah 1980; Faulkingham 1975; Greenberg 1946, 1947; Lombard 1967; Monfouga-Nicolas 1972; Nicolas 1968, 1969b, 1975; Schmoll 1991; Tremearne 1913, 1914; and others) attests to the widespread belief in spirits as agents of illness. As pointed out earlier, it is not that some Mawri do not believe in spirits so much as that they refuse the kinds of treatment prescribed by bori healers, because, they say, bori practices are antithetical to the principles preached by the Koran. Muslims view the worship of spirits and the act of sacrificing to them as religious abominations having to do with Satan. Conducting or participating in such sinful practices defines one as an unbeliever and puts one outside the community of those who shall be saved. Among other things, bori also promotes the mingling of the sexes. Rather than fostering a woman's modesty and respectful submission to her husband, bori encourages women to abandon their households, neglect their duties as wives and mothers, and become unfaithful to their husbands when it requires them to attend ceremonies that last most of the night. Possession thus speaks to notions of bodiliness, protocol, and authority that are deemed unhealthy, immoral, and undignified by Muslims because they threaten the very concept of order upon which Islamic life and morality are based (see Brink 1997; Callaway 1987; Cooper 1997; Mernissi 1987; Wall 1988).

In families where Islam has only recently displaced indigenous spirit-related practices, the first generation of Muslims is struggling to erase the cross-generational ties that still link them to the spirits of deceased parents or grandparents. Spirits are often inherited through matrilineal or patrilineal descent. First-generation Muslims must therefore live with the startling possibility that a spirit that had possessed one of their deceased kin might choose them as his or her new host despite their strong commitment to Islam. For devout Muslims or those for whom an Islamic identity is an integral part of their public personas, being initiated in the bori or even appeasing the spirits with an offering of blood or perfume is not an option even if their health is allegedly at stake. Should the most pious among them be "caught" by a spirit, the only respectable alternative to exorcism—practiced by a Koranic healer—is to ignore the repeated "assaults" in the hope that the bori will eventually capitulate in the face of such indifference.

While the great majority of Muslims publicly decry possession by bori spirits as sinful, a few do not interfere with, and will occasionally even finance, the ceremonies organized on behalf of their women-folk. Among these, most do not object to their wives having a wasa so long as it is not held in their homes. They do not doubt the efficacy of bori. They simply want to have nothing to do with the preparations or the ceremony itself. When such a case arises, the afflicted woman awaits a favorable opportunity to return to her father's or her brother's home and hold the wasa there, provided that she receives moral and material support from sympathetic kin. If some men are tolerant of their wives' involvement in bori because, as mature women, they are past the age of seductive encounters, the new generation of husbands, on the other hand, is quick to repudiate a woman who persists in wanting to meet the spirits' demands and to seek a cure through bori.[3]

Alhaji Boubakar, a prominent and wealthy Muslim merchant, at first tolerated his wife's interest in bori as long as she was being discreet and did not attend cere-monies. When, after much hesitation, Hajiya decided to assuage her spirits and put an end to her suffering by becoming initiated into the bori, he sent her back to her father to preserve his reputation as a devout Muslim. Having accomplished the hajj to Mecca, he believed that his identity as an alhaji was incompatible with his marriage to a medium. Hajiya had been his favorite wife despite her appar-ent inability to conceive children. Before she became "attacked" by spirits, she was a young and lively woman. Yet Alhaji Boubakar felt he had no choice but to repudiate her: "I did not want to stay with someone with spirits."

When faced with the prospect of divorce, women have to decide whether they value their health more than their marriage. Many, fear-ing the reprisals of an angered spirit, opt to devote their lives to bori, even if it means giving up some measure of economic security. The few who manage to juggle marriage and membership in bori often have to resort to secrecy in their activities as mediums. Muslim hus-bands know that Mawri women are often interested in bori and that, given the slightest opportunity, they would attend possession rituals. As the story of Amadou and Hadiza illustrates, female attendance at wasani is a sore point in marital relationships: while Mawri women hide their visits to bori healers from their husbands, the latter, in turn, sometimes pretend they have not noticed their comings and goings, because doing so would amount to acknowledging their lack of authority.

As noted earlier, Muslim men, despite their notorious disdain for bori, are not entirely immune from spirit attacks. More often than not, a Muslim who suspects that he has inherited a spirit from his deceased father may hide the matter or turn to other explanations to account for his troubles, because the simple recognition that he has fallen prey to bori spirits threatens his Muslim integrity. He cannot ask help from a bori healer without losing face in front of his Muslim kin, friends, and neighbors.

Aminou, a normally gentle and generous Muslim neighbor of mine, suffered from spirit attacks that made him wander in the bush for days at a time. During those periods, he would sometimes sit on the tall rock overlooking Dogondoutchi, hurling insults at the passersby and warning everyone that their lack of morality and honesty would lead them to their doom. Residents all knew about his "madness," though few were the Muslim men willing to identify spirits as the cause of his illness. On the other hand, all the women I talked to, including his wife and the wives of his brothers, implicitly or explicitly alluded to the spirits allegedly responsible for his unfortunate condition. Kabou, his wife of fifteen years, would have gladly held a wasa for him, but she had no money of her own. Aminou, of course, had always vehemently denied "having spirits."

Thus while the Muslim community recognized that the man was sick, nothing was done to ameliorate his condition, because nothing could be done—at least, not in an overt way and within the ideological framework set by Muslim principles and conventions—even though there was an implicit consensus as to the source of his malady. Since Aminou was not getting better, his brothers eventually appropriated his land for themselves, in effect negating his social existence as a peasant in addition to condemning his children and wife to a life of acute poverty.

In contrast to a Muslim majority ostensibly eager to disown kin who claim an interest in bori, a number of educated functionaries, secure in their elite status, feel an urge to return to their "ancestors' practices," as many of them put it, when Islam no longer appears to provide satisfactory solutions to the problems and paradoxes of contemporary life. Many wasani are therefore partially or entirely financed by salaried civil servants, who, regardless of whether the ritual is held for them or for a relative, hope to secure the spirits' protection in times of increased stress and competition on the job. Though members of the functionary class enjoy a comfortable lifestyle, they also face constant social and financial pressures (for example, to support a host of relatives on their salaries) and low job security. When they need support and advice, some civil servants find that bori spirits are capable of caring and attentive solicitude in addition to providing meaningful, personalized, and pragmatic solutions to the problem at hand.

·

Possession:
Porous Bodies and Amorphous Beings

Possession in bori is metaphorically referred to as a sexual act wherein the devotee is mounted by the spirit, who penetrates her. As a doki (horse) of the spirit, the medium lends her corporeality to an immaterial being that can acquire a tangible appearance only by taking possession of a human body. Interconnected with the equestrian theme prevalent in many experiences of possession (Boddy 1989; Deren [1953] 1991; Leiris 1958; Matory 1994a) is the metaphor of marriage that informs the relationship between the medium and the spirit. This is most obvious in initiation and other healing ceremonies where novices or patients are referred to as *amare* (plural of *amarya*, brides) of the spirits regardless of their sexes.[4] To understand what these various tropes of permeability and penetration entail, it is useful to briefly discuss Mawri concepts of the self. The *kurwa* (soul or vital principle) is localized in the head[5] — though it may sometimes also be found in the blood or the liver (see Monfouga-Nicolas 1972, 194) — and manifests itself in the form of a force that is specific to each individual: the 'karfi. The fact that the 'karfi can grow through the absorption of the environment by the self or, conversely, diminish through the depletion of one's substances suggests that persons can expand or contract in ways that contradict Western notions of corporeality. In addition, the soul is not attached to the body. It may escape its bodily envelope when the individual is sleeping, for instance. When it does so, the self is particularly vulnerable to attacks by witches and other evil agencies who capture souls to consume them (see Monfouga-Nicolas 1972, 194; Schmoll 1993). During possession, the spirit takes the place of the soul. Displaced, the soul is said to remain outside of the body until it "hears" the coughing that signals the departure of the intrusive spirit.

When the body is literally emptied of its *kurwa* (vital essence), it becomes the ideal receptacle for spirits who have no embodied form or voice of their own. This means, of course, that only one spirit at a time can take possession of a human vessel. By the same token, only one bori devotee will exhibit the body postures, attitude, and personality of a specific spirit at any given time. This is why, 'yan bori explain, some spirits may not mount their devotees right away when they are invited to enter the *garka* (arena where bori ceremonies are held); they are busy riding their horses at another ceremony and must finish there before they can move on to the next wasa where their presence has been requested. Though the bori pantheon allegedly contains more than three hundred spirits, only a small number of them are very visible. Because these twenty or so mutanen daji are powerful agencies as well the central figures of the major families of spirits, their presence is often indispensable to the success of bori ceremonies.

Bori spirits can penetrate the bodies of their hosts at will, but they generally wait until they are summoned by the compelling rhythms of the calabash drums. As soon as the spirit touches the head of the 'dan bori he is about to mount, the host loses consciousness. Yet possession is not immediate. This is how Hamidou, an experienced bori violinist, describes the processes leading to trance. First, the spirit sends wind (iska) on his horse. Then, after the wind leaves, the spirit sends his dogs. Finally, once the dogs have left, he mounts the devotee. From then on, whatever the possessed devotee says or does emanates from the spirit. Having surrendered to the unyielding pressure and forceful penetration of the bori, the devotee is said to have no will of her own. Like a shell emptied of its content, she senses no pain, feels no emotion, and will remember nothing of the experience once the soul has reentered its physical matrix—though at times, her convulsive gestures and violent contortions may result in painful bodily injuries, despite attempts on the part of other mediums to prevent such occurrences. If the spirit is really mounting her horse, the physical pressure exerted is such that the host's "ribs are squeezed" (*awasu sun matsu*).

When the soul leaves its corporeal frame, the body in turn is made transparent to the spirit who fills it and animates it. Thus 'yan bori believe that one cannot obtain a visible image of a spirit mounting her human horse by photographing the possessed host. When they penetrate human bodies, spirits alter the constitution of these bodies in such a way that they no longer leave a tangible imprint on the photographer's film. Since the devotee's selfhood has been eclipsed by an ethereal presence, whatever the possessed medium says or does will be attributed solely to that spirit. During possession, 'yan bori sometimes exhibit a range of bodily postures and behaviors that would be judged ridiculous, socially unacceptable, or shameful under any other circumstances. If subject to the will of the blacksmith spirit, for instance, male and female hosts alike will make sexually explicit gestures and resort to crude language when addressing the crowd. In the manner of 'yan mata (sons of women who have inherited the smithing craft from their matrikin and who feel no shame [*kumya*] in discussing sexual matters), 'yan bori who are possessed by Makeri, the blacksmith spirit, embarrass their audience by their sexual allusions and try to pull up women's wrappers so they can peek inside.

By becoming vulnerable to intrusive forces and surrendering to their control, possessed mediums are in effect feminizing their bodies; they become in a very physical sense the "brides" of the spirits. The parallel drawn between mediumship and the female body yielding itself to male penetration is not surprising considering local conceptions of women and female productivity. In Mawri society, men are associated with activity while women constitute the more passive element of this complementary pairing. The male/female distinction that informs the apportionment of space and the division of labor also connotes an essential opposition between the active principle of penetration and the passive quality of receptivity: hence men break the earth while women sow the seeds. A well digger is *namiji* (literally, husband) to the well he has made, while young unmarried women who have lost their virginity are metaphorically referred to as *rijiya* (well). The ruler (sarki) is the ritual husband of the earth, and his fecundity, as active principle, implies abundant harvests. Openness and receptivity are also emphasized in the free woman or *karuwa* (prostitute) when she is called a *zaura,* a term that derives from *zaure,* the entrance room to the Mawri compound and the structure that mediates between the house and the outside. In the past, a man who found on his wedding night that his wife was not a virgin would make a hole through the wall of the thatched house where they had slept and come out through this opening instead of using the door. By making an opening in the wall, the disillusioned groom would metaphorically make his own opening into his wife's body through his penetrating action, thereby validating the beginning of what should henceforth become a productive relation. Just as possession is controlled by the spirits who mount their "brides" at will, so sexual intercourse should ideally be initiated by the man, who expects his wife to submit willingly but passively to his desires (see also Échard 1985, 47).

Thus we see how the receptivity of women as physiological and social beings is expressed and reproduced through various tropes, gestures, and images that often contrast female passivity with male penetrating action (see Delaney 1991 for a similar case in rural Turkey). Bori initiation rituals also constitute an explicit commentary on the receptive nature of the novice host through its focus on orifices and boundaries. The gyara actively constructs the neophyte's receptivity, opening him up so that the spirits can penetrate him. Once they have been initiated, the mediums no longer fear the encroachment of the spirits, because instead of being a threat to their bodily integrity, their openness is a source of strength. Possession transforms the devotee's body, which, rather than simply being a passive receptacle for the spirit, becomes the medium of powerful transformations. Through possession and the subsequent symbiosis that is established between the spirit and its vessel, the devotee's identity is enhanced. When possessed, 'yan bori are filled with their spirits' power. The process of taming the spirit and letting oneself be penetrated by an alien being plays upon the evocative power of procreative imagery as a model of production available to women who may not be able to fulfill their reproductive roles. Whether it manifests itself as superhuman strength, the ability to predict the future, or a variety of other extraordinary skills (Masquelier 1999a), when properly channeled, the power mediums are invested with by their spirits can benefit the community as a whole and not simply its individual recipient.

It is perhaps not surprising then that barrenness in women is often a prime mover for becoming involved in the bori (Monfouga-Nicolas

1972; Smith 1955; see also Boddy 1989 for a similar situation in zar). To be barren is to lack receptivity and to be unproductive. It means not being able to participate in the reproduction of physiological life and, by extension, not being able to engage in balanced and fertile relations of exchange with other social beings. Barrenness is as much an inability to engage in certain transformative processes as it is unwarranted blockage in a physiological and a metaphorical sense. It hints at the disruption of the stable flow of substance between the self and the environment. By treating the afflicted body as an icon of social blockage, bori rituals manage the illnesses of physical as well as social bodies. At a time when orthodox Islam is constructing women as aggressively sexual beings driven by bodily instincts whose disruptive and dangerous effects men must curb and defend themselves against, female bodies that do not produce "properly" tend ever more so to personify social contradictions in the arena of bori. Though it may be less widespread in regions like Arewa where men as well as women become initiated, infertility is nevertheless a central concern of bori, giving rise to a host of images connecting physical experiences with social realities and male fears with female distress.

The Possessed

Membership in the bori is open to men as well as women, though female mediums largely predominate. Of these women, a substantial majority are socially unstable, having married and divorced several husbands. In between unions, rather than finding shelter in a father's, brother's, or uncle's home, they often resort to prostitution, if only temporarily, to attain some degree of economic or social autonomy.[6] Yet unlike in Nigeria and other areas of Niger where all bori participants are drawn from the fringes of Hausa society, bori in Arewa appeals widely to all members of society, be they rich or poor, nobles or commoners, educated or illiterate. Elites may participate. In Dogondoutchi, several members of the aristocracy have been actively involved in bori practices. The bulk of the membership is nonetheless composed of farmers, petty traders, unemployed youth, wives, and prostitutes, who altogether belong to what is deprecatingly referred to as the *talakawa* (commoners) in contrast to the *sarauta* (aristocracy). Though it is clearly the spirits who select their horses, and not people who choose to do bori, participation in the bori is seen by most 'yan bori as a *sana'a* (craft), whether or not they derive any income from such activities. Becoming initiated entails a series of moral, social, and ritual obligations. It has serious implications for the new adept, who must regularly attend ceremonies and is expected to do his share to promote good relationships with the spirits.

Going back to the preponderance of women in the bori, there is a widely shared sense that bori is women's business, as the proverb "Bori is women's war" implies. 'Yan bori themselves explain the predominance of women by saying that bori principally addresses the number-one concern of Mawri wives, namely their reproductive capacities. Whether they are enthusiastic bori adepts or zealous Muslims, married women regularly seek the advice of bori healers when they are trying to conceive, during their pregnancies, or when their babies are sick. As elsewhere in Africa, the people here easily intermix biomedicine with other therapeutic treatments, often regardless of whether the diagnoses offered by the various consulted specialists appear contradictory or not. Having had access to a local dispensary since 1940, Dogondoutchi residents have had ample opportunities to sample and familiarize themselves with biomedicine. Yet the various and complex ways in which biomedical practices have been both articulated with and kept distinctly separate from indigenous systems of therapy attests to their uneven success in Dogondoutchi and elsewhere in the Third World (Brodwin 1996; Comaroff 1981; Comaroff and Comaroff 1997; Crandon-Malamud 1991; Janzen 1978; Last 1981; Nisula 1999; Regis 1997; Schmoll 1991; Worsley 1982). While one may conceive of the pluralistic medical landscape of Niger as a spectrum of medical practices with "Western" biomedicine at one end and the enormous variety of indigenous treatments at the other end (Islamic medicine standing somewhere in the middle), evidence nonetheless suggests that few individuals understand biomedicine as a stable and bounded domain of health care that operates in isolation from other therapies. Like mothers in Cameroon or Tanzania who creatively combine biomedical and indigenous pediatric treatments (Regis 1997; Weiss 1996), Dogondoutchi women regularly attend the "well-baby" checkups during which their infants are vaccinated against some of the well-known infantile diseases, but they also pay frequent visits to local bori healers, regardless of, and often despite, their husbands' publicly acknowledged disapproval of bori medicine. Bori also deals with the problems and adversities of married life. Whether a woman wants to find, keep, or get rid of a husband, she often resorts to the services of a *jima* (bori specialist) who will help her obtain what she desires by interceding with the spirits on her behalf.

I am sitting in Dije's compound one late afternoon. My friend is carefully sort-ing through a bowl of uncooked rice, removing one by one the bad grains and pebbles that have gotten mixed in. I have brought my tape recorder and am lis-tening to an interview I recorded the day before at a neighbor's home. I want to finish transcribing this conversation before nightfall because that evening, I have to attend a wasa held for a young woman I just met. "Liar, she is a liar!" Dije suddenly interjects, no longer absorbed in her tedious rice sifting. Though I realize she is accusing the interviewee of being a liar for telling me that she never visited a bori healer, I am nonetheless troubled by my friend's harsh words. Dije is a kind woman whose friendship and optimism I value. Besides, calling somebody a liar is a serious offense. When I press her, Dije tells me that she cannot think of a single woman who has a co-wife and who has not, at one point or another, gone to ask the spirits for protection, advice, or medicine. In fact, she continues, she does not think that a wife in a polygynous household could remain married long, no matter how attractive and prosperous she was, if she did not secretly administer strong bori medicine to her husband to ensure his love for her.

Muslim husbands, of course, would rather not advertise the appeal that bori holds for their womenfolk. In conversations where we dis-cussed the predominance of women in possession, they were quick to point out that bori attracted more female than male members be-cause women are, by nature, gullible and prone to trust any scoundrel who promises to cure their troubles or who offers remedies for an ail-ment. It is because bori capitalizes on the credulity of women that the number of healers keeps proliferating, a Muslim man once told me.

Whether or not this is true, the fact remains that many women, re-gardless of their overt religious inclinations, admit to having helped finance bori rituals and say they would attend possession ceremonies if their husbands only let them, the threat of divorce being what keeps them from disobeying their spouses. Young unmarried girls who are looking for entertainment and an excuse to step out of the compound are rarely barred from attending wasani. Like many other members of the audience, most of them have never experienced the violation of their bodily integrity by an intrusive spirit, and chances are they never will, given the increasingly limited mobility young wives are afforded in a growing number of Muslim households. Of the young female mediums I worked with in Dogondoutchi, over half came to the area to break away from a rural marriage and to start a new life far from "overbearing" kin. They engaged in *karuwanci* (prostitution) to earn a living and recruited many of their clients through bori.

While bori attracts some young women looking for romantic encounters or a clientele for their sexual services, a larger portion of the bori's female population is made up of older, mature women, who, because they are past the age of seduction and childbearing, do not constitute a threat to men. If they are married, their husbands have no need to fear for their virtue. If they are divorced or widowed, they can go as they please without having to request their husbands' permission before leaving for a possession ceremony. These mature women constitute the stable element of bori membership. Many have been possessed by their spirits for much longer than they have been married to any man. If they were at first reluctant to give in to the spirits' desires and demands — no one, after all, likes to be possessed[7] — they have long learned that contracts with superhuman protectors are open to infinite renegotiations and that salubrious intercourse can eventually be achieved between the two parties. Besides, while involvement in bori is often described in terms of suffering and vulnerability, those who are "touched" by spirits consider themselves fortunate. Even when they derive only indirect material benefits from their membership in bori and gain limited visibility as religious figures, they generally insist that being chosen by the spirits already amounts to a great honor. Fear of superhuman reprisals clearly motivates their continued involvement in bori, but it hardly characterizes the Mawri experience of possession, which many describe as intense, enriching, and empowering.

Divisions and Hierarchies in the Bori

To the extent that women are allowed to work as mediums, bori appears to be a prominent institutional arena for the promotion of gender equality (Échard 1991a). Whether male or female, all participants in bori are subject to the same social and ritual imperatives. Both men and women can derive economic benefits and social status from their roles as mediums. Both are expected to dance, follow bori social and moral rules, and, generally speaking, display their capacities as mediums in a public setting. Yet women are not expected to assume leading positions. Unlike the bori of northern Nigeria (Besmer 1977) or the Maradi valley (Monfouga-Nicolas 1972; Schmoll 1991), where leadership is partly or totally in the hands of women, female adepts in Arewa rarely have the authority to supervise an initiation ceremony (see also Échard 1991a; 1991b). I only knew of two female priestesses in charge of supervising rituals at the time that I was conducting fieldwork, and both were of Zarma ancestry. These women had moved to Dogondoutchi with their families after having already established their reputations as bori priestesses elsewhere. And though their experience in matters of healing was not questioned, they nonetheless remained "foreigners" in the eyes of local Mawri, as if their female identities precluded them from becoming totally incorporated in the local bori leadership.

Despite guaranteeing opportunities for achievement not found elsewhere in Mawri society (Échard 1991b), bori also limits female participation in high-ranking roles such as those occupied by healers. Most of the women I talked to agreed that even though their spirits revealed to them in dreams how to make medicines, women were not supposed to go to the bush and pick the leaves, barks, and roots they had been shown because only men should deal with medicinal herbs. In answer to my queries, an old woman who was married to a healer said that "a seated man is worth more than a woman who comes and goes," presumably implying that no matter how hard women tried, they could never equal men. Through these words, she was also suggesting that men embodied fixity, while women were the mobile, or unstable, element in bori—as elsewhere in society. Like many other female 'yan bori who participated in bori only to serve as vessels for the spirits, she did not dispute prevailing Mawri assumptions regard-

ing women's nature and capacities.[8] Women make good hosts for the
mutanen daji, everyone agrees, but they should leave to men the task
of administering medicines and presiding over possession ceremonies.

The principal leadership position in the bori is that of the sarkin bori
(chief of bori). The chief of bori, who may also be addressed as *mai
bori* (literally, owner of bori, i.e., the one in charge of bori), theoretically oversees the bori activities of dozens of Mawri communities
within his purview, though, in practice, outside of his own town or
village he often does little more than collect fees and attend wasani as
a guest of honor. Candidates for the office of sarkin bori are subject
to various selection mechanisms within the bori itself. Access to such
status in the bori hinges first of all on one's knowledge of medicinal
plants and cures, which itself signals the terms of one's relationship to
the spirits because the bori only reveal the location and use of certain
plants to those whom they like and who serve them well.

To become sarki, one must also be the devotee of important spirits.
Certain spirits hold important places in the hierarchy of the pantheon
while others occupy secondary positions. Only the horses of such
spirits as Babai (an important male spirit of indigenous origin), Rankasso (a female indigenous spirit who had a prominent role in precolonial wars), Kirai or Souleymane (the oldest and most powerful
Zarma spirits) can hope to compete for power and leadership. Such
rules, however, apply only to men, because women are by definition
excluded from the competition regardless of their medical knowledge and other personal qualities or circumstances. Spirit mediums
laughed at my incongruousness when I asked if women could become
leaders of the bori. In their view, it was highly unsuitable for women
to hold chiefly positions. Only men possessed the qualities required
to fulfill such important roles. Candidates must compete against each
other for the support of 'yan bori by demonstrating their powers of
leadership, by showing their proficiency at solving personal crises as
well as communal problems, and by convincing people that they enjoy
the support of their spirits.

Spirit mediums who wish to become sarkin bori do not so much
"campaign for office" as work at winning the trust, respect, and admiration of bori devotees over the years. They must also have proven
their honesty and integrity, in addition to showing a willingness to
help others. They may be judged on their ability to supervise a wasa
and to resolve emerging conflicts. The winner is ultimately appointed

by the chef de canton (traditional district chief) based on the selection achieved by popular consensus. The new sarki should ideally have won the trust of a majority of bori members, in addition to having amply demonstrated his skills at managing the affairs of the district. Once the new sarki has been chosen, his title is confirmed in a turbanning ceremony performed by the chef de canton or another prominent member of the Mawri polity.

How much power the sarkin bori wields varies from place to place. Though he rarely presides over each and every wasa held in his district, he must be informed of the 'yan bori's activities. Those who wish to hold a ceremony must first secure the consent of the chief of bori through the payment of a fee before they contact the musicians or send out invitations. The sarkin bori often acts as a redistribution point for the multiple fees, resources, and gifts that have to be split among the participating 'yan bori. In addition, as the highest authority over the bori members of several villages, the chief supervises the ceremonies held to promote the welfare of entire regions, such as the *wasa watam bakwai* (ceremony of the seventh month).

Within the bori community itself, initiated members may achieve prominence by undergoing a second initiation called *shan ice*. Shan ice means, literally, "to drink from the tree." This refers to the tree barks that are collected from the bush and put to macerate in an earthenware jar for the whole duration of the ritual. The initiates regularly drink from the medicine that is believed to strengthen them. The holding of a shan ice requires such an expenditure of money and resources that few bori members are ever able to organize one. To be able to "drink from the tree" thus demonstrates not only greatness, courage, and moral integrity but also the ability to raise the cash and the goods needed to pay the musicians and healers, to feed the various guests, and to supply the sacrificial animals as well as the material required for the erection of a ritual shelter that will momentarily house the initiate. Though they do not hold any special titles, those who have drunk from the tree are treated with special deference and receive privileged access to bori resources. In theory, they no longer sit with the mass of undistinguishable 'yan bori. They are also entitled to a larger share of the money that is distributed among 'yan bori at the end of a ceremony as payment for the work they have accomplished as hosts of the spirits. At death, *masu shan ice* (those who have drunk from the tree) further receive special considerations: among other things, a

During a wasa, the calabash players and violinists play the spirits' songs while women dance. On the right-hand-side, a singer holding a copper mouthpiece waits for the money that one of the dancers will press on her forehead as a token of appreciation for her performance.

special wasa called *kashin 'kwarya* (breaking of the calabash) is held to publicly acknowledge the death of an important member of the bori community (Masquelier 1997b).

Bori priests, whether or not they have gone through the rites of shan ice, occupy various positions of prominence under the authority of the chief of bori. They generally head a troup of loosely organized mediums and musicians who live in the same village or ward. They supervise healing rites and sacrifices to the spirits and may conduct communal ceremonies. They are generally expected to mediate disrupted relations between an afflicting spirit and his victim, provide medicines to the afflicted, and occasionally perform exorcisms when the tormenting bori cannot be tamed.[9] In contrast to the jima who supervises possession performances, healers who perform cures and administer medicines but do not generally conduct initiations are called *bokaye* (plural of *boka*). The term can refer to a Muslim healer or any other practitioner of indigenous medicine. *Boka* is the Hausa term for "doctor" while jima refers to the possession priest or priestess in the Zarma language. Though a bori priest is more likely to be called a jima, given the term's specific reference to the category of healers who do bori, people also refer to him as a boka. Bokaye do not practice medicine strictly within the purviews of bori; they diagnose a wide variety of illnesses, prescribe treatments, and provide herbal medicines to their patients.[10] They usually give private consultations in their homes but may also visit their patients' homes when the latter are too sick or feeble to walk.

All mediums informally belong to a bori troup that meets periodically to attend possession ceremonies held throughout the year, except during the rainy season when every farmer is busy working in his fields. Whether or not they are initiated members of the bori, those who plan to hold a wasa must first distribute kola nuts to members of their own community and to the 'yan bori of other villages. Distributing kola nuts—together with the information about where and when there will be a wasa—amounts to sending out invitation cards to inform people that there is going to be a party. Only those who have received a kola nut will consider attending the ceremony. I occasionally witnessed the disappointment of a 'dan bori who had not received his "invitation." When twenty-four-year-old Hadiza found out through one of her bori friends that 'Dan Juma, in a nearby village, was organizing a wasa to thank his spirits for a prosperous year, and that she had not been invited, she felt deeply disillusioned about her prospects as a visible and respected member of the bori community. Yet, as much as she wanted to go, she felt that her honor was at stake. She could not therefore debase herself by showing up uninvited. Instead, Hadiza made a mental note of the omission: when it would be her turn to invite 'yan bori to her wasa, she would remember not to send a kola nut to 'Dan Juma.

Through the circulation of kola nuts and the holding of collective performances during which 'yan bori dance, chat, eat, and "work" together,[11] intricate networks of relationships are created and maintained between and among bori communities. The staging of a ceremony often brings together mediums from many different villages or neighborhoods. Newcomers to such events must rapidly learn to recognize the major players as well as those individuals to whom they owe respect. And all are expected to acknowledge and lend moral and material support to those who, each in turn, throw a wasa for the benefit of the greater community. 'Yan bori will frequently travel fifteen or twenty miles to attend the wasa of a friend, a relative, or a colleague. Wasani are festive occasions during which mediums show off their latest attire, catch up with acquaintances, and learn the latest gossip in the same way that markets attract people who want to see and be seen, spread news, or hear about current fashions.

The most favorable days for staging a wasa are Thursdays and Sundays because, 'yan bori say, those are the favorite days of the spirits, especially the "black spirits" of Zarma ancestry who regulate wind, rain, lightning, and thunder. Other days are theoretically *masu nauyi* (heavy) to the spirits in the sense that they are less auspicious and that less can be accomplished that will be significant or have lasting consequences for the host. In practice, however, ceremonies held on Friday in Dogondoutchi inevitably attracted huge crowds of 'yan bori from nearby villages because the travelers could first visit the weekly market held on that day before devoting the rest of their time to the spirits. Because individuals who want to hold a possession ritual are in theory obligated to feed their guests, especially those who come from neighboring villages, the main cost incurred by hosts is for the food they serve to the hungry crowd of 'yan bori and musicians before or after the wasa. This aspect of the ceremony is crucial because of the importance of consumption and the flow of substance (food, money) between bodies and across boundaries to the processual reality of bori. The length of wasani varies greatly. Ceremonies may last a few hours if the spirits are quick to respond to the praise of the musicians; on other occasions, they may last two or even three days if, for instance, the host is known to have half a dozen different bori who must all in turn mount their horse. I heard about, but never witnessed, wasani lasting up to ten days because the spirits could not be cajoled into possessing the novice host. In cases where the bori are reluctant to cooperate, the jima usually agrees to postpone the ceremony until a later date so that the guests can go home and the musicians move on to their next assignment.

The Musicians of Bori

The *maroka* (musicians) who sing the bori's praise to invite them to possess their devotees' bodies are at the lowest end of the social spectrum within Mawri society. Like butchers and blacksmiths, musicians (whether they be praise singers, violinists, drummers, or gourd players) make up a "cast," a social caste by virtue of their transformative capacities.[12] Butchers shed the blood of animals, thereby attracting spirits for whom blood constitutes sustenance. Blacksmiths transform iron ore into metal; maroka, especially praise singers, can make a man or, conversely, destroy his reputation so badly that he will never be able to face his peers and will have to move to another village. In a sense, praise singers play with human sound and speech more than they play with music. They appear to be poets, forging words that have an effect in, and on, the world. In the words of Irvine (in Stoller 1989b, 111), who studied praise naming among the Wolof of Senegal, people who are named by a praise singer "are thought to be morally, socially, and even physically transformed by the words that are said." The maroka's mastery over words makes them powerful individuals not to be trifled with, even if one secretly despises them. Bori musicians are particularly feared because, as one individual put it for me, "The spirits follow them." Consequently, to offend bori musicians is tantamount to offending the spirits, something no one wants to do for fear of reprisals. This became clear to me the day I attended my first wasa outside of Dogondoutchi.

When I drove to the tiny hamlet of Kare Jido, where the ceremony was scheduled to take place, the musicians whose presence had been requested by the host had not arrived yet. They were allegedly playing for another wasa in a neighboring village half a dozen miles away. We had to be patient, they would eventually arrive, my Dogondoutchi friends and I were told. We had arrived early in the afternoon and were hoping to return to Dogondoutchi before midnight, but the sun was rapidly setting, and there was still no sign of the musicians. As I was sharing with the bori healer my deprecating thoughts on the musicians, he told me not to say another word, because musicians always "travel with the spirits."

This meant that musicians can call the "people of the bush" anytime they want, for whatever reason they deem necessary, and without having to justify themselves to those they end up inconveniencing or hurting in the process. I once witnessed such an example of their "callousness" in a small hamlet where Aminou, a bori acquaintance, was hosting a wasa.

In Tamiri, the musicians had played all evening for an initiation. It was late and everyone had gone to bed. Because they had not clearly heard what the Doguwa Rankasso, through the voice of her young devotee, had said to them during the wasa, the musicians decided to call the spirit back. They stood right outside the hut where the Doguwa's devotee was sleeping and started playing the song of Rankasso. Soon after, the young woman became possessed and the musicians were able to converse with the spirit. They thus found out that Doguwa had agreed to give them her black wrapper. Having satisfied their curiosity, they then left the scene of the possession to go to bed.

The maroka were never blamed for abusing their powers in such a blatant manner because musicians of bori do not need anyone's permission to call the spirits. They come and go as they please and appear to conduct their lives in an undisciplined and carefree manner: they respect no one and no one respects them. Thus even if they should ideally play music only when requested and only in order to mediate people's relations with the spirits, they are rarely held accountable for their deeds because in some ways they stand outside the moral community of devotees.[13]

Precisely because they feel no kumya (shame), musicians are despised by their fellow Mawri. They do not hesitate to beg for money and even make it part of their craft to solicit presents from their clients. In Nicolas's (1975, 173) words, the musician "has shed his pride in order to better serve the pride of others, in exchange for riches." The fact that musicians live off the generosity of others feminizes them. They are like prostitutes in that they break conventions and manipulate powerful forces that lead to new forms of being. Like women, they constantly request and receive gifts, and they are dependent on the resources of men. The feminine qualities of bori musicians are especially salient given their association with prostitutes. In addition to the income they earn by playing at possession ceremonies, bori musicians receive money from karuwai (prostitutes) who want to dance and to attract prospective clients through their merrymaking. The musicians' poor reputation hence partly stems from the fact that they are viewed as keeping bad company (Besmer 1983, 34). For many, their close association with women in a sex-segregated society is what makes them especially contemptible.[14]

Musicians rely on two kinds of music to induce possession: vocal and instrumental. Vocal music flatters or calls a spirit, at the same time that it entertains the audience and describes who the bori are. Each song addressed to a particular spirit consists of the *kirari* (praise epithets or praise names) of that spirit and a description of who the bori is or what she does, together with salient traits and anecdotes (see Besmer 1983, 58; Erlmann and Magagi 1989). Each of the songs sung by the vocalist is linked to a specific melody and rhythm that the 'yan bori learn to recognize before any words are said. In addition to instrumentally accompanied songs for each and every spirit of the local pantheon, musicians may include purely instrumental pieces that, because they have a faster tempo, are conducive to dancing.

When musicians play the vocal music of the spirits, the sound penetrates the devotees intensely. The music is irresistible, especially if it is played well. When 'yan bori say they cannot resist its effects, they imply that the spirits cannot remain long unaffected by the compulsive rhythms and flattering words: they get excited and soon want to take part in the wasa held in their honor. The sound of music therefore transcends the boundaries between human and superhuman realms and fuses the material with the nonmaterial. Music reverberates with power—one might say that it *is* a crucial dimension of power, because, to a certain extent, it controls what people do, what they think, and how they feel. It is felt as a tremendous and compulsive force that makes people happy or, conversely, angry—when the listener has a spirit known for his long-standing rivalry with the particular bori praised by the song. The sound of words, the melody, and their combination are like tangible waves that penetrate bodies and moves them in a metaphorical, emotional, as well as physical sense.

Bori music is neither ordinary speech nor ordinary sound. Rather, like the magical utterances that delineate a special field of action and carry the power to represent as well as to perform something (Austin 1965; Malinowski 1935), the music of the spirits is a framed and formalized kind of language. As a form of intensified sound that transcends the bounds of human experience to literally echo the voice of the spirits, bori music powerfully modifies mediums' experience of being in space and time. In neighboring Songhayland, holey music (the "cries" of the violin, the clacking of the drums) is literally spoken of as the sound of the ancestors that induces the spirits to take possession of their mediums' bodies (Stoller 1989b, 161). One might say, to borrow Rouget's (1985, 120) words, that bori music "gives time [and space] a density different from its everyday density."

A troupe of bori musicians generally consists of one or two male *masu goge* (violinists) who play the one-stringed fiddle and two to five male calabash drummers, or *'yan 'kwarya* (literally, sons of the calabash). To play, drummers dig a hole at the edge of the possession ground and later overturn and place the 'kwarya (calabash) over the hole, thereby enlarging the drum's resonating cavity considerably. They strike the calabash with a set of carved wooden sticks that are tied together with lengthy pieces of cloth and that resemble a human hand (each drumstick has five fingers). The fiddler and drummers are occasionally accompanied by one or two gourd rattle players who, unlike the other musicians, do not sit and are free to walk around the dancers. A *zabaya* (female singer) can also participate in singing the spirits' songs if the host can afford the additional expense. When she is not present, the masu goge perform the singing.

Despite their low status in Mawri society, musicians are not denied power, as the anecdotes recalled above suggest. Musicians bring the spirits into their devotees' bodies. They are the catalysts of powerful transformations. Thus, as one might expect, the quality of their music and singing is crucial to the proper unfolding of the ceremony, although, as I have already pointed out, no one would ever directly blame the masu goge and 'yan 'kwarya for their lack of dedication. If the way they play their instruments is important for achieving the desired transformations in devotees, the songs are even more critical. The singer's voice is like breath; it is a tangible force that can be physically felt and, at the same time, it has an ethereal quality that allows it to reach out across the world of humans to be heard by spirits wherever they are. The power of the words emanates not only from the quality of the vocalist's voice but also from the way they are put together. To paraphrase Laderman (1991, 298–99) in her description of the power of words in Malay shamanistic performance, "although all of [the] messages are pregnant with meaning, words are the real midwives of the séance." The spirits hear what the singers sing about them; the words are carefully chosen to induce a certain mood in the spirits that will make them want to attend the wasa, but what this mood should be depends on the particular bori considered. Some spirits must be cajoled into possessing their devotees and like to hear their qualities praised endlessly. Others only come to the possession ground when they feel insulted or when they are mad. There are established song patterns that musicians learn to reproduce with little or no variation. Deviation from the repertoire is avoided primarily "because it would result in 'meaningless' music" that spirits would presumably not be able to understand (Besmer 1983, 58). At the same time, a musician's talent is often judged on the basis of his ability to embellish a text and to improvise, thereby lending his personal mark to a standard piece. Because the songs and praise epithets they sing to the spirits provide a storehouse for people's shared knowledge about the mutanen daji, musicians are the keepers of gargajiya (tradition) and the repositories of history.

Domesticating Spirits

Spirit-induced illnesses often signal the disruption of peaceful relations between spirits and humans. Healing thus entails mending these breaches and satisfying the immediate requests of the spirits who, through the suffering that they inflict upon their victims, indicate that these individuals have not fulfilled the bargain they struck with them. When someone inherits spirits from a deceased relative, on the other hand, the afflictions are not an expression of the spirit's wrath so much as a sign that the person has been selected to follow in the footsteps of the dead medium and is expected to serve the spirits faithfully. Spirit-induced afflictions today include the effects of cultural and politico-economic disadvantage, effects whose objectification through bori signs take a variety of forms, such as the disintegration of bodily capacities and the sexualization of the road (see Masquelier 1992, 1993). While possession routinely begins as an illness, only certain ailments are attributable to the spirits. Thus, while not all headaches or stomach pains are caused by spirits, persistent pains that resist Western and Islamic treatments are often diagnosed as "illnesses of the spirits."

Each spirit of the bori pantheon causes specific illnesses and misfortunes. Gurmunya, "the lame one," cannot walk and drags herself on the ground. She makes her victims wander around cemeteries—which she inhabits—and induces women to menstruate without interruption. Adama, a white Doguwa, provokes paralysis of the limbs or of the entire body. Zanzana ("smallpox, smallpox marks") gives pimples and eye sores, and produces itching and rashes all over her

Two mediums possessed by Adama and her sister lie on the ground, embodying the paralysis these spirits cause in their victims.

victim's body. Maria the prostitute prevents women from having children and renders men impotent. Because more than one spirit provokes blindness or loss of appetite, it is sometimes difficult to identify which one is responsible for a person's affliction. As shown earlier, spirits, regardless of who they are, often cause their victims to wander aimlessly in the bush for long stretches of time before they agree to let humans tame them through an initiation ceremony. Some frighten the humans they meet, while still others provoke a general torpor that lasts for months or years before it dissipates.

Individuals who suspect the suffering they are experiencing is caused by spirits or who have been diagnosed as having spirits are encouraged to beg the bori's forgiveness by sacrificing a hen or a rooster to them. This stage is referred to as roko (begging). Those who fear they have angered the spirits or become the victims of their fickle attention generally bring a sacrificial animal to a bori healer or a devotee of the spirit suspected of causing the affliction. On the stone altar erected for this purpose, the throat of the fowl is cut with a knife while one or several 'yan bori pray aloud, imploring the mercy of the presumably disgruntled spirit on behalf of her victim. They urge the spirit to bring the patient back to health so that a wasa can be held. Roko is thus an attempt to patch up, or resume, one's relationship with the bori, a relationship that entails reciprocal offerings and dialogues through which spirit and devotee mutually redefine their roles and commitments.

While obeying the spirits' instructions and fulfilling their requests may not guarantee freedom from further punishment or protection from attacks by other spirits, the afflicted know that this may be their only chance of achieving some level of harmony in their dealings with bori. Later on, those who have partially or fully recovered may choose to undergo initiation (gyara) if they can afford the cost of the performance and if they feel the urge to make their involvement in the bori official.[15] The ritual and the preparation it entails are both costly and time consuming, which is why, in some cases, individuals never "arrange" their spirits.[16] Moreover, there is never any certainty that the medium's affliction will remain under control. Possession is a lifelong condition that requires the constant and faithful nurturing of the bonds uniting mediums to their spiritual "tormentors." However, once the relationship becomes stabilized, the human host should ideally feel supported by the spirits as they each, in turn, strive to respond to the needs and demands of their "partner."

One way of accommodating one's spirits and ensuring their continued support is to acquire a set of clothing for the possessing bori. Each spirit of the bori has a specific set of clothing and attributes. These garments allow spirits to materialize their distinct identities during possession rituals (Masquelier 1996a). Thus while Kirai, a powerful and cunning Zarma spirit, wears a red *riga* (gown), a red bonnet that looks like a *hula* (phyrgian cap), and a red *damara* (sash) and brandishes a hatchet as an ominous symbol of his control over thunder and lightning, his younger brother Moussa owns a black gown, a red bonnet, and a red sash. Zanzana, who continuously scratches "herself" when mounting her devotee, wears a *kyan nyandi* (striped black-and-white wrapper), whose striking effect may be enhanced by the addition of a *mai gorori* (a white wrapper with thin red stripes).

These garments are more than simple adornments whose loud colors and varied patterns enhance the visual pleasure of bori spectators. More than a mere piece of fabric or leather, and more than a uniform reflecting one's cultural, social, or religious status, the spirits' attire is the medium through which people create and subsequently

Folded wrappers and robes are placed next to the hatchets of the spirits of lightning in preparation for a wasa.

Four mediums of Gurmunya, the lame spirit, wear their bori attire including a hat sewn with cowrie shells and antelope horns decorated with strips of leather. They are dancing during a celebration staged for the visit of a high state official.

(above) Hamissou is a bori devotee and a leather worker. He manufactures many of the leather pieces worn by bori mediums during wasani.
(right) A bori devotee wearing the striped wrappers of Zanzana dances gracefully to the music of bori.

relate to and communicate with the "people of the bush." As they are repeatedly worn by spirits incarnated by their devotees during possession, the wrappers, robes, hats and sashes that compose the mutanen daji's paraphernalia become extensions of their ethereal owners. I have shown elsewhere that by binding an amorphous entity within the confines of a physical body, clothes provide a space in which spirits can become, in a tenuous and temporary way, substantial beings (Masquelier 1996a). Here, one simply should note the important role clothing plays in establishing a viable and enduring relationship between the spirits and their human vessels.

As a wordless message symbolizing trust, friendship, and respect, the gift of clothing that devotees purchase should convince the spirits that the gift givers are serious enough about securing the bori's protection that they will go to great expense to satisfy the spirits. Though it may be worn by the devotee outside of ritual circumstances, a spirit's wardrobe requires special care. Ideally, the various items of clothing should be washed and pressed after each bori ceremony, particularly if the possessed hosts rolled in the sand and covered themselves with dirt, as mediums of Azane—an unusually strong member of the pantheon who washes his body with dirt—are prone to do. If torn or damaged in any way, spirit clothing should ideally be mended. Devotees are also responsible for periodically replacing any worn-out items in their spirits' wardrobe. Many take pride in displaying their collection of garments in their homes, while others carefully hide the spirits' paraphernalia inside trunks or baskets when it is not in use.

Initiating a Life of Servitude

If the series of initial offerings and promises made by the afflicted can cause the symptoms to go into temporary remission, there nonetheless cannot be any healthy and productive partnership between the spirit and the host until the latter agrees to hold an initiatory ceremony: there, through drumming and singing, the spirits will, each in turn, be invited to mount their human hosts and to reveal their identities. At that time and in exchange for agreeing to comply with the spirits' demands, the novice medium receives the assurance that he will be granted health, protection, and prosperity. As previously noted, not everyone chooses to undergo the initiation, even after every other curative alternative has been exhausted. Some agree, however reluctantly, to stage a ceremony to ward off the pressure they feel from kin, friends, and the 'yan bori themselves, especially when a generous relative offers to finance the whole affair. For yet others, the gyara is the welcome culmination of lifelong attempts to achieve lahiya (health). To all, becoming initiated signifies committing one-self to a life of servitude, for the new devotee agrees to periodically attend ceremonies during which spirits might take hold of her body. Commitment to the spirits also implies making periodic offerings of the blood of their favorite animals. Kirai, a Zarma spirit who wears a red robe and hat, and who is sometimes called "the red sorcerer," likes red roosters. A speckled black-and-white hen is sacrificed for Zanzana (because the rashes she causes on her victim's skin resemble a hen's speckles) while a black one is reserved for some of the Doguwa spirits like Rankasso or Wankarma, who wear black wrappers.

As its name indicates, gyara (meaning arrangement, fixing, or re-pair) reconstitutes the integrity of the initiate's body by reaffirming its openings and boundaries, and by increasing its natural capacities to interact with and appropriate the world. For 'yan bori, the initia-tion also means the resolution of mutanen daji–initiated problems and the emergence of a truce: bori spirits cannot be exorcized from their victims, who must learn to live under the "yoke" of their spiritual partners in what will always remain an unequal relationship. Finally, *arrangement* can also be taken to mean that it is the *spirits* themselves who are "fixed": by ritually possessing their new devotee in a circum-scribed setting, they are socialized into the world of bori and their identities as members of the pantheon are officially recognized.

On the outskirts of the village of Bane Ruwa, a white cock has been slaughtered one early January morning on the stone altar of Danne, next to where the ini-tiation is to take place. Danne, a Mossi military spirit of the Baboule family, allegedly eats dogs, but nowadays he is rarely offered anything but fowls. The sac-rificial shedding of blood momentarily quenches the thirst of the spirit and insures that he will protect the participants of the wasa by deflecting malignant influences. When he cut the rooster's throat, Bilen, who is in charge of the initiation, begged the spirits to come "maza, maza" (fast, very fast). His words also insure that anyone coming to the ceremony with evil intent will be harmed by the spirits.

Those who show up with a "white stomach" (good intentions), on the other hand, will be awarded everything they ask of the mutanen daji. The jima (priest) also sets some pleasant-smelling herbs on a hot bed of coals: spirits are attracted by good smells.[17]

While the jima and his assistants are preparing a calabash of medicated henna with which the initiated will be washed, the musicians have arrived. The drummers are setting up their calabashes; the violinists are tuning their instruments. The amarya (initiate), a young man in his twenties named Amadou, is sitting under a tree, guarded by a 'dan bori and away from the crowd of devotees, who are waiting for the musicians to begin playing. Following instructions, Amadou remains silent, passive, and motionless under the white handwoven wrapper that covers his entire body. One of the two violinists and a gourd player have started playing the song of the Doguwa spirit suspected of possessing the young man. Meanwhile a woman is sweeping the grounds where the devotees will be dancing barefoot: this is to ensure that no one steps on a sharp stone or a pot shard. Someone shouts to the musicians, to whom fura *(millet porridge) has been brought for lunch: "Since you've drunk fura, now get to work and do a good job!"*

It is time for the kokobe, *the first phase of the gyara, in which the possessing spirits are invited to partially identify themselves. Still veiled, the amarya is led into the bush. The musicians, the jima, a handful of 'yan bori, and all the village children follow behind. Bilen and his assistants are looking for an anthill. They walk among the dried-up millet stalks that remain after the preceding year's harvest to locate the anthill that will best suit their purposes. The first one they find has sunk in the middle and is too flat. The second one appears suitable. The drummers settle with their calabashes and when the violinist has finished tuning his instrument, they all start playing the spirits' music.*

The *gidan toruruwa* (anthill) is the opening through which the invisible forces of the wild will emerge before being channeled through the initiate in order to be tamed as bori spirits. Also referred to as *uwa yawa* ("the mother of many"), the anthill is a particularly important symbol of fertility and abundance (see Griaule 1965): anthills always contain grain, even when people's granaries are empty, people say. Wall, who writes that *toruruwa* are a species of black ants known for their indus-

A bori healer sacrifices a white chicken at the onset of a wasa to insure the protection of the participants.

The jima (bori specialist) and three assistants prepare a calabash of medicated henna with which the amarya will be washed.

trious efforts to collect grain, also notes that these ants (or the earth forming the anthill) are used by the Hausa of northern Nigeria in the preparation of medicines "destined to increase one's business, drawing it to one's market stall or shop as effectively as the ants carry home their stores of corn" (1988, 307). Though in Arewa 'yan bori have other means at their disposal for attracting customers, the image of industriousness and wealth projected by the anthill is nevertheless exploited here to increase the initiate's chances of a prosperous start after he has been restored to the social community.[18]

By drawing a large circle around the gidan toruruwa with his foot, the jima thus constructs the anthill as the center of the ritual arena the spirits will be heading for. After having gone over the circle's circumference three times, Bilen then draws two perpendicular lines that go from one side of the circle's periphery to its opposite side and intersect at its center. He is drawing paths for the spirits to converge on the anthill where they will "materialize" by taking possession of Amadou's body. After being led around the circle three times, Amadou is made to stand in the center of the drawn circle. With both hands, he is holding a large stick planted in the opening of the anthill.

The musicians keep on playing. An assistant of the jima now washes the amarya's entire body with the medicated henna prepared earlier. The tools of some important spirits are then brought and set on the faifai (round mat) covering the calabash of henna: the ax of Kirai, the leader of the Zarma spirits; the riding crop of the Baboule, the antelope horn adorned with leather fringes belonging to Gurmunya, the lame sister of Kirai. Four chickens are also brought into the circle. Each chicken is of a different color and associated with a specific family of spirits.[19] Holding the four chickens by the legs in front of the amarya, the jima praises the "people of the bush" and exhorts those who have chosen Amadou as a medium to manifest themselves. He then brushes the chicken against the amarya's entire body starting with the head and going down until he reaches the ground. Soon the young man shivers. His whole body soon shakes and trembles as the first spirit mounts him. Suddenly, Amadou seizes the red chicken from Bilen's strong hands. It is the preferred animal of the Zarma spirits. Bilen gently takes the fowl back, but Amadou twice more snatches it violently before brandishing it in the air for all to see.

A senior bori medium (assistant to the jima) washes the amarya's body with medicated henna. A spear has been planted in the opening of the anthill to mark the spot to which the spirits will converge. (below) While the amarya, covered with a white wrapper, holds on to the spear planted in the anthill, the ritual supervisor brushes a white chicken against her body to induce possession.

One last time Bilen asks the possessed amarya to grab one of the chickens. If other spirits are possessing Amadou, this is their opportunity to make their presence known. But the amarya's hand, guided by the spirit, once again chooses the red hen, as if to show that no other mutun daji wishes to possess Amadou. Letting go of the red fowl, the "amarya" then grabs the ax of Kirai to provide further proof of his identity. The four chickens can now be sacrificed. Bilen slashes their throats and throws each of them in a different cardinal direction to satisfy all and any spirit who might have ventured there, attracted by the drums. The 'yan bori proceed back to the hango (circular stone altar). They use another path rather than retracing their steps so as to avoid anyone, human or spirit, waiting to ambush Amadou.

When they reach the altar of Danne, two 'yan bori take the amarya behind a tree to wash him once more. Meanwhile the musicians have started playing again. As the sun is slowly setting across the horizon, a group of women headed by the shugaban daka ("supervisor of the pounding," the woman who oversaw the food preparation) brings food to the 'yan bori. Ten bowls of millet are split between the devotees, who eat silently in small groups. Darkness has set in. Kerosene lamps are brought to light up the possession ground. A young woman asks her girlfriend to get up and dance with her. She does not dare stand up alone in front of everyone else. The two women dance for a while after which they are replaced by a male devotee who impresses everyone so much with his style that he is soon showered with money by friends and admirers. As the rhythm slows down again, more people get up to slowly dance in a circle. When the drummers quicken the tempo, they break from the circle to perform, each in turn, dancing back and forth in front of the musicians and furiously kicking the dusty ground with their bare feet. Many young women have come from Dogondoutchi and they dance to attract attention as much as to have fun. Some of them are looking for a partner for the night, hoping to exchange sex for money. Many people also dance to keep warm on this chilly and windy January night.

The singer chants the songs of the spirits, while the drummers' frenzied rhythms compel devotees to show off their dancing skills. When the beat slows down, the dancers return to sit on the mats that have been spread in a large circle. The music's tempo picks up once again; more 'yan bori stand up to dance to the frenetic pace *of the calabash clacks. While a couple of women move with their extended arms holding stretched wrappers over their backs in the manner of giant birds gracefully gliding over the sandy ground, a devotee sitting next to the musicians becomes possessed. Soon after, another is "attacked" by his spirit, and then a third one, and another, until, progressively, the dance ground is filled with mediums whose souls have been "ousted" by invading spiritual presences. There is Kirai and his brother Bela. Sitting on the ground with her legs folded under her is Gurmunya, the lame one who cannot walk. Three Baboule spirits, recognizable by their stiff, military style of walking, have entered the bodies of their respective hosts. Two of them salute the third one, their superior, Komandan Mugu ("Commandant Evil"), who is giving them orders in a mixture of Hausa and pidgin French. The spirit everyone is expecting has finally taken possession of the amarya, who is now pacing the possession grounds in a seemingly erratic manner. Soon he is asked to reveal his name.[20]*

The possessed amarya is made to sit on a mat that has been spread in the center of the dance ground. Bilen gives Amadou, alias the unknown spirit, medicated water and then milk to drink. As instructed, the possessed initiate does not swallow but instead spits out the liquids into the big calabash of henna that has been placed at this feet. Bilen puts one of his rings in the amarya's mouth and then asks the spirit what his name is. At first the spirit says nothing. Bilen insists, coaxing him gently but firmly. A moment later the spirit softly murmurs: "Kadaruwa" ("the crocodile of the water"). He has told his name. Kadaruwa is the son of Kirai the "red sorcerer." The amarya is urged to get up and the veil that was covering his upper body is taken off. The violinist, followed by the possessed mediums of Kirai, Bela, Gurmunya, and Kadaruwa, steps several times over a black he-goat laid on the mat and restrained by two 'yan bori who are still "themselves." Gurmunya, who cannot walk because "she has no foot," moves on her knees. She uses her arms to prop herself up and hop over the goat with her legs folded under her. After the ketare *(stepping over, crossing over) is over, the black goat is slaughtered. Rabi, Awa, Iyale, and Dije, the young women who came from Dogondoutchi, are still dancing to the beat of the calabashes. Relieved to have been "spared" by their spirits, they are enjoying themselves.*

Now that Kadaruwa has received the attention he deserved, the wasa can pro-

ceed. Amadou's second spirit, who did not manifest herself at the anthill and whose identity has yet to be revealed, must now be invited to take possession of the amarya's body. All that is suspected about this unidentified spirit is that she is a member of the Doguwa family. The musicians thus start singing the praise songs of the Doguwa spirits to invite them to the wasa. The "guests" do not respond at once to the musical enticement. The calabashes endlessly repeat their harsh yet compulsive rhythms. Then Baka Giwa, from the Doguwa family, mounts her devotee, soon followed by Mai Zaure, Rankasso, and Azane. Moments after, the amarya is also "attacked." The unknown guest is pressed to reveal her name. "I am Dossa," she says. Dossa remains a while and then departs. Amadou's body shudders. As he collapses suddenly, two 'yan bori rush to avert his fall. When he has regained consciousness, Amadou is given water. Other spirits are releasing their human vessels. The musicians play a few songs, slowly, and then stop altogether. People get up and gather the mats on which they have sat all night. Tired but satisfied that everything went well, they make their way back to the village, where each guest has been assigned a place to sleep.

The wasa is over, yet there are still things to be done. The next morning the meat of the goat that has been sacrificed will be cooked and apportioned between the 'yan bori. The head of the goat, grilled on a bed of coals and later cooked in a pot with spices, will be cut up. Very tiny portions of the ears, nose, tongue, and eyes, together with a bit of the foot will be fed to the amarya. By ingesting the parts of the goat's organs of vision, smell, taste, hearing, and locomotion, the amarya is appropriating these sensory and locomotive qualities so that he will be able to see, hear, speak, and travel better. The enhancement of these attributes will help him to remain healthy and to prosper by interacting with his environment in more efficient ways. By being metaphorically opened up, Amadou will take in and process various spiritual essences and material substances more profitably, so much better perhaps that he may one day become a wealthy healer. This is what one wishes for the amarya as he embarks on a new life as vessel for the spirits.

Once Amadou has eaten his apportioned share of the goat's head, anyone among the 'yan bori will have access to the leftovers: for some it is a way of reaping some of the benefits bestowed upon the amarya during the initiation. More than simply addressing the individual plight of a tormented host, the gyara offers all participants a chance to deal with their predicament. By holding a wasa to "socialize" his spirits, the amarya thus enables the devotees to renew their ties with the world of the spirits, to resolve nagging problems, or to ask for direction. Though the principal goal of a gyara is to identify the spirits possessing a particular individual, it is also assumed that anyone experiencing a crisis or faced with a frustrating situation may ask the spirits for help. Possession ceremonies are public events staged for the benefit of everyone, including Muslims who profess to shun bori.[21] Each wasa, regardless of its official purpose, helps renew fragile ties between the human community and the spirit world, thereby ensuring the prosperous continuity of personal lives as well as communal projects. While 'yan bori often allude to the frequent severance of these tenuous ties during crises, in practice it is difficult for a bori medium not to be reminded of how the world of spirits and the world of humans intersect on a quotidian basis. It is the contiguousness and constant interpenetration of these two domains of experience that are discussed in the next chapter.

Chapter 4

The Everyday Life of *Bori*

KNOWLEDGE, EMBODIMENT, AND QUOTIDIAN PRACTICE

Zar spirits resemble their horses.
—Ethiopian saying in Michel Leiris, 1958

CLASSICAL STUDIES OF MEDIUMSHIP have largely assumed that the essence of spirit possession resides in the rituals that mediums periodically hold to invite the spirits to take hold of their bodies and commune with the world of humans. From this perspective, the experience of possession has been confined to the ritual sphere, the domain of the sacred, and the formal enactment of highly charged symbolic performances, which appear unconnected to, and bear no implications for, the presumably more transparent and "mundane" practices of everyday life. In his ethnography of Songhay mediumship, Stoller thus focuses his analysis on the holey ceremonies during which hosts periodically abdicate their consciousness to an alien spirit (1989a). These visually stunning performances are described as the constitutive elements of possession and the quintessential "custom" of the mediums' troupe. Though we are told that Songhay mediums use their powers to deal with drought and dissent, possession is nevertheless reduced to ceremonial experience and the reproduction of an enchanted realm that remains largely insulated from "real" life. In his study of *ghimbala* spirit possession in eastern Mali, Gibbal similarly focuses his attention on the ceremonies that constitute a "sacred drama actualiz[ing] the fundamental link that unites" people and spirits (1994, 89). By resolutely eschewing analytical models that explicate trance within a rationalist framework, he is able to convey more tangibly the poetics and sensuality of spirit possession, but his description fails to concretize the relations between spirits and mediums beyond their manifest moments in the possession stage.

Just as in the case of holey and ghimbala, it is mostly through its dazzling ceremonies that bori has generated anthropological interest. Hence analyses of bori have concentrated on formal symbolic processes, ignoring, for instance, the multiple ways in which bori forms influence and are shaped by everyday practice. Besmer thus prefaces his study of bori in northern Nigeria by noting that it has been "an intriguing topic for many observers of Hausa culture. *Its ceremonies have been seen by some as colourful, dramatic, and entertaining; by some they have been described as dangerous, frightening, or merely disgusting*" (1983, xi, emphasis added). In considering these rites as a privileged arena for the condensed and intensified expression of fundamental social values, analysts of spirit possession have followed a long established anthropological tendency to privilege the sacred at the expense of the secular, and to insulate ceremonial action from quotidian practice. Save for a few noteworthy exceptions (Boddy 1989; Brown 1991; Lambek 1993), possession has thus been treated as a particular kind of ceremonial action that remains irrelevant to the stuff of daily life.

Yet it is not as if bori only comes alive in the ritualized arena of trance when spiritual forces take possession of their human vessels to provide comforting advice or offer practical solutions to worldly problems. Nor would it be accurate to assume that meaningful communication between spirits and people occurs solely during elaborately orchestrated rites that stand outside of the instrumental realm of reason — what some might call the "real" world. Ceremonies are obviously an important dimension of bori, but it can be argued that they are not its only driving force. Thus rather than focusing on the bori management of affliction as an insulated field of formal practices that affords insight into how social realities are grounded in symbolic forms, in this chapter I explore how routine forms of symbolic action are implicated in the configuration and reconfiguration of collective realities and identities. Drawing on the work of Boddy (1989), Lambek (1993), and Wafer (1991), I consider the immediacy and concreteness of possession by locating particular instances of the spirit/host relationship within events of daily life as well as ceremonial action. By tracing bori signifiers in multiple schemes of action, I hope to provide a glimpse of how the patterns of ritual and daily activities interact and interpenetrate to create the cultural significance of the world mediums live in.

In his monumental and inspiring account of Islam, sorcery, and spirit possession in Mayotte, Lambek captures much of the elusiveness of possession by grounding the intimacy shared by mediums and spirits in the embodied fabric of everyday life. Arguing that possession is not just embodied in its formal manifestations as trance, he convincingly shows how mediums are "caught in a continuous relationship with the powerful being[s] who ha[ve] chosen to inhabit [them]" (1993, 316). In her finely nuanced study of possession in northern Sudan, Boddy beautifully demonstrates that "it is the mundane environment of the zar which . . . empowers it to convey a range of meaning" while also fueling its counterhegemonic potential (1989, 8). Wafer similarly describes Brazilian Candomblé from the perspective of what he calls "ordinary knowledge" (1991, 104), to demonstrate that "like any social phenomenon, trance is embedded in an everyday world in which reason is suffused with fantasy" (106). The problem with Wafer's exploration of the implications of the "fantastic" in the "everyday world," however, is that it maintains an implicit separation between the real and the imaginary even as it insists on their intrinsic connection. My own account of the "everydayness" of bori thus seeks to transcend these analytical limitations by assuming that the distinctions that have pitted reason against magic, or sacred against secular action, obfuscate, more than they illuminate, the complex interactions between humans and spirits in the context of Mawri culture. The following text analyzes bori as a living social form embedded in the realities of contemporary rural life to concretize the latent, ongoing conversations mediums have with the spirits to whom they periodically abdicate their consciousness.

My focus on the meaningfulness of the mundane has been inspired by recent anthropological and historical efforts to demystify ritual and "put it to work in the everyday world" (Comaroff and Comaroff 1993, xvi; see also Boddy 1989; Comaroff 1985; Davis 1990; Lan 1985). Despite a recent tendency to analyze ritual as "signifying" practice, the realization that the realm of sacred structures intersects with the world of the everyday is, of course, far from novel. Over sixty years ago, Evans-Pritchard insisted that sorcery was such a *normal* and ubiquitous part of Azande life that scarcely a day went by without reference being made to it (1976). Thus, paraphrasing Olivier de Sardan (1992) one might say:

> Popular, local concepts related to sorcery, to spirits, to trance and to magic charms in modern-day Africa, do not in fact hail from "another world" which follows a logic different from that of daily life. The participation of spirits in daily life or the practical efficiency of fetishes

goes without saying. All that is banal. Ancestors, spirits, sorcerers or magic charms are all familiar concepts in regard to which "disbelief is sus- pended," and *which need no justification.* There is no question of believing or not believing: it is not a case of belief, but of fact, not of the fantastic but of the routine. (11)

Just as the significance of Zande sorcery is rooted in the immediate context of daily life, so bori configurations find their meaning in the quotidian order of Mawri practices.

Stressing the everydayness of religion and ritual by tracing their roots in daily life does not mean, however, that routine action and quotidian discourse can be dismissed as simple and transparent di- mensions of human experience. This is what is demonstrated here through a focus on the subtle but far-reaching ways in which bori values and categories affect daily representations. I am interested in the processes that shape and organize everyday "pragmatic" knowl- edge and experience. Precisely because it is a practical dimension of taken-for-granted, commonplace Mawri interaction, bori offers a privileged focus on these processes. Bori does not just have an effect on Mawri reality, it is a *constitutive* feature of that reality. In stress- ing the pragmatic nature of bori and its rootedness in daily existence, I also hope to address some recent concerns about the ethnographic tendency to exoticize religious phenomena in a given culture. The work of Stoller and Olkes (1987) and Gibbal (1994) on Songhay reli- gion, for instance, has invited controversy for its overdramatization of the "supernatural," a process that Olivier de Sardan decries as "exotic occultism" (1992, 6). While productive at some level, the debate sur- rounding the politics of representation—and whether or not studies of religion have, since Durkheim, cast ritual, magic, and the so-called occult in an exotic light—is partly misguided because it does not question the distinction between the sacred and the profane that has long dominated analyses of African ritual. Just as the latter dichotomy misconstrues the object of ethnographic analysis by introducing ir- relevant categories, so the academic insistence on "de-exoticizing" anthropological accounts equally distorts the terms through which communities everywhere make sense of, and shape, the world they inhabit. To suggest that the ethnographic or analytical focus of a work exoticizes the phenomena studied is to presume that the "mundane" is somehow transparent, immediately recognizable as such in all times and places—and perhaps even unworthy of anthropological scrutiny.[1] Mindful of Olivier de Sardan's observation that "coming to grips with the indigenous system of daily representations and . . . gaining access to autochthonous ordinary conceptions . . . are the only ways for the researcher to escape from the clichés which his or her own culture's system of commonly shared meanings continually projects onto other cultures" (1992, 20), I thus describe bori as integral to everyday life to the extent that it cannot be circumscribed as a discrete field of knowledge or as a separate form of practice. As will be shown, the strength of bori—and the source of its resilience despite censure and competition—resides precisely in its deep embeddedness in mundane practices that provide sets of culturally constituted images and techniques through which mediums and others are able to share, transform, or contest changing social realities. Paradoxically, as I hope to demonstrate, people's relations with the spirits also lead quite decisively out of the everyday. Conversations about the marvelous exploits of the mutanen daji may be routine occurrences in bori circles, but one only need listen to Muslim elites' condemnation of possession as repulsive and dangerous—or witness the 'yan bori's own "manipulative" strategies in the face of Muslim insecurities—to recognize the extent to which (Evans-Pritchard's and Olivier de Sardan's contributions notwithstanding) bori is also part of the extraordinary. To play down the inherent magicality of bori simply in order to conform to a certain Western political correctness would ultimately distort and impoverish the very reality one seeks to understand. Possession has to be viewed from a variety of refracting angles that illuminate the multidimensionality of its practices. I am focusing here on what I call the everyday life of bori, not so much in deference to the scholarly sensibilities that have arisen "in defense" of African religion as in response to what struck me again and again as the ubiquitous nature of spirit-related discourse and practices in Dogondoutchi.

By treating possession as an integral dimension of everyday existence, I show that bori practices are a pragmatic attempt to construct and act upon the world rather than an ineffective form of ritual. My focus on particular incidents, conversations, and histories that highlight how bori is intimately and intricately woven into the Mawri lived world is motivated by a specific concern: not to present bori configurations as a set of unequivocal and coherent meanings. Rather, the stress here is on the shifting, contested, and at times contradictory nature of bori representations. Bori spirits are the product of local imaginations. But they are also "persons" with complex histories, personalities, and relationships, whose own trajectories at times intersect with those of their hosts to create long-term intimacy, but also confusion, indeterminacies, and heartaches for those involved. They depart from the bodies of their hosts after the intense moment of possession, yet they do not entirely "leave" their mediums. Instead, they "become part of the context in which people act or think or experience rather than simply the means or the product of their actions" (Lambek 1993, 334).

The "Playful" Nature of Bori:
Possession as Re-creative Practice

In her account of bori in the Maradi region of Niger, Monfouga-Nicolas focused on the ways in which the therapeutic impact of mediumship practices transcends the female domain of experience (1972). She suggested that bori might be providing a meta-commentary on the conditions of social life in this increasingly Muslim culture. Though she did not explore the bori's creative use of signs, tools, and techniques to remedy disjunctures between subjective experience and social context, she rightfully described how local adepts mediated severed domains and experiences. First, by virtue of their ambivalent identities, devotees bridge the widening gap between men and women: in Maradi, members of bori are women, yet they sometimes act like men; they may suffer from reproductive disorders, yet they are able to fulfill their culturally ascribed nurturing role through their relationships with the patients and initiates they care for. Second, through healing they reaffirm the vital but fragile interdependence between humans and spirits. At yet another level, they mediate the rupture between Muslim and Azna populations—by incorporating both Muslim and Azna spirits into the bori pantheon.

Monfouga-Nicolas's analysis is insightful because it suggests that through the management of ambiguities and indeterminacies, the bori discourse extends far beyond the domain of ritual to infiltrate the fabric of everyday life. However, her interpretation of urban bori as a desacralization of the "real," traditional form denotes a problematic tendency to subscribe to the Western categories of sacred and secular

that, as already noted, do not adequately describe indigenous rendi-
tions of what the varied experiences of bori entail. Though the bori
of the city has obviously taken on new facets and expanded its message to accommodate the conditions and constraints of urban life, one
must be wary of interpretations that confine possession performance
to the realm of the secular simply because the bori has acquired a ludic,
theatrical dimension. Salamone (1975, 201) has rightfully noted that
by insisting on the serious nature of religion while treating "play"
as synonymous with "frivolous," some anthropologists fail to focus
on an important aspect of the sacred, namely its playful nature. In
his examination of the interrelation between religion and play, Huizinga (1955, 17) has characterized play as "order, tension, movement,
change, solemnity, rhythm, rapture," a definition that could well apply
to ritual as well. And in her study of Yoruba ritual, Drewal shows
that the notion of "play" is difficult to communicate because of the
capitalistic presupposition in the West that play is necessarily opposed
to work. "Performing ritual," she writes, "is at once 'hard work' and
'playing.' What play is not for the Yoruba is unserious, frivolous, and
impotent. Yoruba have a different term for what we might call frivolous play—*yeye*—usually translated into English by Yoruba speakers
simply as 'nonsense.' . . . Play—like Yoruba spectacle—is, more specifically, an engaging participatory, *transformational process* that is often,
but not always, competitive" (1992, 15; emphasis added).

Janzen has similarly pointed out that "playing" the drum in Ngoma
healing rituals is at once a therapeutic technique, a form of entertainment, and a demonstration of embodied knowledge (1992). I find
Drewal's and Janzen's respective understandings of the Yoruba and
Bantu notions of "play" are particularly useful in the context of the
present discussion of what I have termed, for lack of a better word, the
"everydayness" of bori in Mawri society. The Hausa word for "possession ceremony" is *wasa,* a term that can also be translated as "play"
or "game." Here, already, we get a sense of the essentially *re-creative*—
that is, at once diverting and transformative—nature of bori practice.
Considering ceremonial practice from such a perspective allows us to
treat ritual as something more than the mere enactment of a timeless
"tradition." Indeed, it forces us to think of ritual action as a more embracing concept that includes secular, yet meaningful, practices that
seek to *create* or *transform,* rather than simply reproduce, the world that
gives them form (Comaroff and Comaroff 1993).

Spirit-Possession in the Context of the Everyday

It is market day in Dogondoutchi and the cool morning air is already filled with the solid and rhythmic sound of wooden pestles being pounded into mortars. As I enter Issa's home, his daughter, Balki, is sweeping the dirt of the compound in a methodical fashion, raising curling waves of dust on her path. She greets me demurely and points to a group of old men sitting under a wooden canopy. Issa is among them, and as I proceed toward the small assembly, he stands up to greet me. He and his friends are talking about a spirit who attacked a young woman the night before. The victim's husband refused at first to recognize that it was a matter for the bori people. "Spirits can't be ignored like that," one of the men notes philosophically. "Besides, if you do what they ask, they help you. They provide for you," his neighbor replies, as if to add more weight to his friend's observations. Though none of them mentions it, I know what they are all thinking: that spirits can sometimes be demanding but that one learns, of necessity, to negotiate with them. In the long run, resisting them always ends up being more painful than accommodating them.

In Dogondoutchi, references to spirits crop up in every conceivable conversation and setting. Mediums like Issa are always prone to discuss matters related to the spirits, but even those who only tangentially participate in bori have an interest in the mutanen daji. I heard snippets about possession at the market, at funerals, naming ceremonies, and in countless Muslim households. Spirit matters most often surfaced during gossip sessions, embedded in larger arguments about bori's and Islam's competing claims to authority and legitimacy. Through conversations or in dreams, as disembodied forces or corporeal beings, spirits are constantly interacting with their human counterparts. They never cease to interfere in people's lives and one cannot avoid crossing their paths. A seemingly innocent gesture, like getting out of bed and going out to urinate in the middle of the night might provoke the wrath of the spirit who has been inadvertently stepped on. Stepping on a spirit is a diagnosis that bori healers commonly make when no other reason can be invoked for explaining why a bori might have been angered enough to make someone sick.

Bori devotees meet the spirits on the possession grounds, but that is not the only place they meet mutanen daji. They will more than likely encounter a few of these superhuman creatures on their weekly visits to the market. For the market to become a hot place of fertile transactions and transformations is in fact contingent upon whether there will be an intense flow of human and superhuman forces there. Hence one never knows in advance whether one's visit to the market will prove to be a fruitful enterprise or a disastrous one: evil and dangerous spirits intent upon causing havoc inevitably mingle with benevolent ones who are searching for human company. Similarly, roads are fraught with spirits who may track and assault unwary travelers when they do not simply kill them (Masquelier 1992). There is no telling when and why they will appear, but one thing is sure: even the protection that drivers and passengers might secure from a variety of ritual specialists does not prevent the frequent occurrence of accidents, as is attested by the empty shells of wrecked vehicles abandoned in road ditches.

These local representations of markets, motorized transports, and other postcolonial configurations are summoned to "counter the magic of modernity" as much as to capture the power associated with things modern (Comaroff and Comaroff 1993, xxv), but that is another story. The point to be made here is that spirits do not appear to, or communicate with, humans simply when they are summoned through music, offerings, or prayers. Nor can we say that bori possession just "happens" on ceremonial grounds. As the following story illustrates, individuals may become spontaneously possessed while they sit in their compound, performing some daily tasks.

One day, while I was interviewing an old widow about her brush with death at the "hands" of a dangerous Doguwa spirit, her niece Halima, a usually shy and reclusive young girl, suddenly started shivering and trembling. The old woman interrupted herself to watch the budurwa *(unmarried girl). Halima was now shaking her head back and forth, back and forth, as her eyes were rolling in their orbits. She was perspiring profusely and twisting her face as if she were in pain. The rest of the children in the compound were staring at her with wide eyes. "Don't come and bother Halima. Shoo! Go away!" the woman was screaming. "Who is it?" I cautiously asked.*

"It's the spirit of her grandmother," the woman replied. She could not, or would not, tell me the name of the spirit who had so unsuspectedly mounted Halima. I wondered if such an incident had happened before and what was keeping the family from "arranging" Halima's spirit. Perhaps she was too young to be undergoing an initiation—she was only sixteen. Perhaps, it was a matter of gathering the resources needed to hold the ritual, an affair that usually proves quite costly and involves the financial support of several kin. Meanwhile Halima was still in the throes of possession, her entire body now bent and twisted.

"This is not the right moment! Go away," the old widow was gently telling the spirit.

While I watched in embarrassment, not knowing whether I should leave or stay, the woman wrapped a head scarf tightly around Halima's waist to prevent her wrapper from inadvertently falling off, should the possessing spirit prove violent and disorderly. Sensing something was amiss in the compound, a neighbor had arrived to lend a helping hand. She was not a medium herself, but her husband took an active part in local bori rituals and the sight of Halima groaning and bobbing did not seem to daunt her.

"Please, she is only a child. Do not hurt her! Your time will come," the neighbor was calmly saying to the intrusive spirit. Then, as suddenly as she had come, the Doguwa left and Halima fell to the ground. She opened her eyes as the two women were attending to her. Looking both fearful and relieved, Halima drank some water from the jug her aunt was holding against her lips. She felt sore and tired. Her face still bore the marks of the struggle that had taken place within her young body only moments before.

When spirits make undesired and unexpected incursions into the bodies of uninitiated hosts, they are usually pressured to leave immediately. Sudden, unexpected possession is by no means unusual, especially among young, inexperienced hosts who have not fully internalized the constraints and possibilities associated with being the medium of a particular spirit. Mature mediums almost never relinquish control of their bodily capacities in inappropriate contexts. They are not passive objects of their spirits' attention but rather willful and engaged participants in the production of collective meanings. They have learned to negotiate the terms of their relationship with their spirits, and this is a skill they have gradually acquired over the course of their lives as hosts. "Full possession behavior is highly skillful," Levy, Mageo, and Howard note (1996, 16), adding that "it requires a mastery of role playing, and of subtle, specialized kinds of communally significant communication" (16). While junior mediums may be "caught" by their spirits almost every time they attend a wasa, older devotees rarely get possessed. In fact, the rarity of their trance episodes becomes an index of their maturity and a measure of their knowledge and confidence.

Dreams are another channel through which spirits violate the boundaries of their hosts' selfhoods. Mediums may have recurrent dreams during which the spirits provide practical advice, recipes for medicinal treatments, or moral guidance. In fact, many healers proudly claim that their knowledge of medicinal plants and their practice of dispensing medicines are based on these nightly visions in which spirits reveal the secrets of healing. While most mediums have only occasional direct "contacts" with their spirits, some devotees perceive the members of the bori pantheon as a set of familiars who never leave their mediums' side even if their presence is not perceptible to the naked eye. Such is the story of Baidou, a fearless war veteran, who claimed he owed his life to the Doguwa spirit who had protected him on countless battlefields (Masquelier 1993). Like others for whom the almost constant presence of a spiritual companion is the locus from which to make sense of one's life, one's luck, or one's prosperity, Baidou knew, of course, that spirits cannot possess more than one person at a time and that they have a human mount in every village. Yet because these ethereal forces can travel so fast, the limitations entailed in a spirit's seemingly continuous proximity to a particular medium is not an issue. Spirits are bound neither by territory nor by schedule when they intend to manifest themselves or communicate to humans. They come and go as they please. At any time and without any warning, they may decide to appear in the open and public range of the market, on the ominous roadways of Niger, as well as within the (seemingly safer) secluded space of one's compound. They sometimes show up when nobody is expecting them—or, as in the case of Halima, when their presence is not wanted—and where nothing has been set to welcome them appropriately, that is, with offerings of money, blood, or perfume. Understanding the cultural dynamics of their relations to humans thus presupposes enlarging the horizons of possession studies to include a focus on the processual reality of the quotidian. For in the theater of the everyday, people are not the only actors: spirits, too, play a role, and this role cannot be ignored if we want to understand the pragmatic significance and existential immediacy of bori.

Play and Work in Bori Performances

It is worth lingering a bit longer on what it means to hold a wasa. Simply put, having a wasa entails creating a social, spatial, and temporal setting in which spirits are invited to take hold of the bodies of their human hosts so as to borrow their voices and enter in a dialogue with the human community. That bori rituals always begin with some dancing and merrymaking suggests that the distinctions between sacred and secular do not correspond to indigenous categories of experience. During wasani, women show off their nicest wrappers, and men compete for their attention by dancing or ostentatiously rewarding other dancers with money they stick on the performers' glistening foreheads. The music, the brightly colored gowns, the men playing card games, the cigarette and candy vendors hawking their goods on overflowing trays, the giggling of the prostitutes looking for clients all contribute to give a highly cheerful character to bori ceremonies. As heightened "transactions," such deviant (from the perspective of Islam) activities as card games and prostitution are part of bori, since it is the possession performance that creates a space of license while also constituting a discourse about licentiousness. Bori involves transcending established boundaries and dealing with threatening forces, of which prostitution and other socially "deviant" practices are but an expression. For it is partly from these heightened experiences and the channeling of potent, yet potentially dangerous, forms and beings that the bori derives its power to capture the human imagination and to bring some unity to otherwise fragmented lives. In the forum of the wasa, it is in fact the excitement, heat, and gaiety generated by the music and the dancing that are supposed to attract the spirits. This is how a villager from Kome Jabo explained to me what "having fun" implied during a wasa: "If people don't dance, spirits don't come. If people dance, they come. During a *suna* [naming ceremony], people are happy, they scream, they dance, they laugh, they show joy. They don't do that at the house of some-one who has just died [*wurin mutuwa:* 'place of death']. For a wasa, it is the same thing. If people do not dance, spirits think people are not happy about their coming, and so they feel no pleasure. They refuse to come." Fun is therefore an essential ingredient for success when it comes to holding a wasa. The artificial distinction between sacred and profane, between serious and playful, ultimately distorts rather than enlightens our understanding of what bori is about in Arewa.

Though there are "fake" performances and deceptive demonstra-tions of spirit possession, these practices themselves are revealing of the ways people use bori as a mode of empowerment and as a sen-sual experience. Possession in Arewa is about the display of power (both as an expression of knowledge and as a demonstration of moral strength) and about the aesthetics of theater. If the trance of some devotees attracts suspicion and generates heated debates as to its genu-ineness, such occurrences never endanger the authenticity and efficacy of bori, because, ultimately, possession transcends the easy distinction between reality and illusion, reason and imagination. Those who are skeptical of the sincerity of a medium's performance on the posses-sion grounds do not altogether question the reality of bori and the existence of possessing spirits. Besides pointing to some of the ways in which trance may be used as a resource by differentially motivated individuals, such skepticism highlights the divergences and inconsis-tencies that are generated around the experience of possession. More important perhaps, by pointing the finger at the impostor, the skep-tics ultimately reinstate the validity and legitimacy of spirit posses-sion, for their accusations of fraud imply that there is a "real" way of being possessed. At a more practical level, people know that no one can trifle with the spirits with impunity and that "faking" may prove a dangerous game. Those who poke fun at the spirits and do not "play by the rules" end up paying for their mistakes sooner or later, as is illustrated by the following incident.

My friend Zeinabou, who had been attending a wasa in the small village of Garin Zaroumei, had spontaneously remarked to some of her friends after the ceremony was over: "Look how Abdou mounted his spirit. This is how he did it!" And grabbing a wrapper, she pretended to be attacked by a Doguwa in the same man-

ner that Abdou had been mounted by his spirit. By her own account, the young bori devotee meant no harm and just wanted to make fun of Abdou when she imitated his gestures while in trance. But her own Doguwa spirit, Rankasso, became very angry at her devotee's lack of decorum and respect toward another spirit. Soon after, and without any warning, the spirit possessed Zeinabou very violently. During her trance, Zeinabou fell on a wooden log and cut her leg very deeply. The next day, upon the bori healers' advice, Zeinabou offered apologies to Rankasso, pleading for her indulgence. She promised to behave in a more mature and dignified manner from then on. She also begged the spirit to be patient and understanding with her because she was still a young and inexperienced medium.

Zeinabou's case provides a wonderful demonstration of the latent dimension of possession: the young devotee knew it was morally wrong to poke fun at a fellow medium, because through him she was offending his spirit. Only by being inadvertently possessed by her own Doguwa, after the wasa was long over, could she create a situation in which the wrongs she had committed could be rectified. Through the Doguwa's possession (by acting as a mouthpiece for the spirit), she could acknowledge to all something she felt inwardly guilty of without having to go through the embarrassment of a public confession. Moreover, the spirit's own tolerant understanding of Zeinabou's immaturity was convincing proof that the young medium should not be excessively faulted for her disrespectful behavior.

Going back to the more general discussion of wasa, the point is that bori performances are neither trivial nor extraordinary; they cannot be understood as either strictly religious or simply ludic phenomena. Though they belong to the realm of dance, fun, and entertainment, they also speak to the danger of allowing invisible, powerful, and sometimes violent forces to reveal themselves to humans. Claiming, as Last (1991) does, that bori (of Nigeria but presumably of Niger as well, since certain ceremonies are now broadcast on Nigerien television) has been "trivialized" and exoticized through its incorporation in the media as "folklore" or "tradition" does not begin to explain the impact and power of bori in Mawri communities (see also King 1966). For one thing, such trivialization is an inherent part of the reality of bori, given the attacks it has repeatedly suffered at the hands of conservative Muslims. Furthermore, bori is no less real because it is packaged for television broadcasts. Nor are its rituals "desacralized" simply by virtue of their new status as cultural entertainment for Nigerien television audiences. The notion of desacralization necessarily implies a prior state of "sacredness" that was never there in the first place.

The issue of what to make of televised wasani is also a thorny one for the 'yan bori themselves, given their particular understandings of the ethereality of spirits. I came to appreciate the ways in which the Western insistence on capturing phenomenal reality through audiovisual technology threatened local notions of the mutanen daji's power the day I offered Ibro a photo I had taken when he was possessed by Aga, a bellicose spirit of Tuareg ethnicity. "Your photos of spirits [mounting their mediums] will be blank," several 'yan bori had assured me, after noticing that I was taking pictures of the possession performance, "because spirits are invisible." If my clear pictures of Ibro in the throes of possession served to demonstrate how flawed the mediums' reasoning was, it did nothing to solve the problem of whether or not one can, and should, create pictorial representations of the spirits. After all, the sight of one of these powerful creatures, whom God, in a fit of anger, allegedly rendered invisible, usually signals the viewer's imminent death. The very ability to represent a being who, by definition, eludes ordinary perception therefore presupposes extraordinary powers, powers that some Mawri associate exclusively with Western identity and technology (Masquelier 1992). Thus if television has altered popular perceptions of bori, it is not by invading a "secular" realm somehow divorced from the magicality of possession so much as in its capacity to erase the distinctions between corporeality and ethereality, substance and spirit, so vital to the workings of bori.

The Imagined Community of Spirits

Enduring assumptions and taken-for-granted categories of Mawri culture inform bori constructions of the world as much as bori meanings, principles, and conventions help shape Mawri lived realities. To stress how closely and deeply the spirit and human worlds intersect and how they might, in fact, be considered part of the same social reality (for a similar argument see Boddy 1989, 9), one may look at the way that spirits operate as social persons whose personalities mirror, contradict, or alter those of their hosts. The distinction to be made here between these "two worlds" is somewhat arbitrary, since in lived experience, spirits and people interact within the same social reality. Spirits constantly intervene in the lives of their human counterparts to disrupt and punish or to heal and protect. And 'yan bori continually draw upon the principles and paradoxes of the spirit world to explain discontinuities in their own experience and to (re)fashion their visions of history.

Rather than resorting to the analytical distinctions between natural and supernatural, or secular and sacred, which derive from Western epistemologies, I have found that the opposition between daji (bush/wild space) and gari (village/town/inhabited space) captures more accurately Mawri constructions of their lived-in world. Though they are commonly translated as "bush" and "town," the terms *daji* and *gari* encompass more than delineated spatial fields. As previously noted, daji connotes that realm which stands outside of human control together with all the forces that occupy it. It continually threatens to impinge upon the domesticated space of the village, and that is why the village paths that open onto the wild must be regularly sealed to prevent the unknown and destructive forces of the bush from penetrating the gari. Daji is the realm of the unknown and the mysterious, yet when appropriately controlled, it offers limitless resistance to human penetration.

All spirits originally belonged to the bush prior to the intrusion of humans, who appropriated portions of the land for themselves. As already shown, such domestication of the wild was always achieved under the guidance of spirits, whose first encounters with Mausri initiated enduring relationships between the "people of the bush" and "people of the village." Whether or not they have been domesticated through nature cults or through bori, spirits are still thought to belong to the realm of the wild and the mysterious. Their nonhuman qualities and their instability of form and being—ethereality, invisibility, and capacity to invade matter and change their appearances—significantly distinguish them from humans. And, paradoxically, they are an intimate part of people's daily lives, though not simply by virtue of their capacities to invade human bodies.

The lives of spirits parallel the lives of people (Boddy 1989, 1992; Lambek 1981; Stoller 1989a). Like humans, spirits are born into families, marry, produce children, and become grandparents. They also steal from each other, commit adultery, and have illegitimate off-spring. Some are known for their propensity to lie or cheat, others for their avarice or laziness. Like their human counterparts, they feel pleasure, pain, and anger, and they sometimes experience jealousy, irritation, or impatience. And just as humans do, they befriend one another or, conversely, dislike, fight, and compete with one another. In this sense, bori spirits are neither totally evil nor one hundred per-cent benevolent. Rather, as Brown (1991, 6) succinctly puts it in regard to Vodou spirits, "They mirror the full range of possibilities inherent in the particular slice of life over which they preside." A large part of the apprenticeship of bori involves learning the names and person-alities of these spirits as well as the way they relate to one another. This learning process is both formal and informal. Devotees under-going the ritual of gyara (initiation) are lectured about proper be-havior and initiated into some of the secrets of bori. But it is mostly by attending ceremonies and watching spirits interact through their human incarnations, by asking questions and listening to casual con-versations, that 'yan bori become socialized into the bori — that is, that they learn what Lambek calls "ethical know-how" (1993, 308). By ob-serving bodily practices and witnessing breaches of protocol, by argu-ing with their neighbors or offending their peers, initiates slowly be-come attuned to the sometimes silent signifiers and taken-for-granted conventions of bori. As will become evident, the spirits do not simply embody but also act out their natures and personalities. Hence they teach about human qualities and relations, and about moral values and social roles.

Virtual Kinship:
Crafting Identities and Families for the Spirits

The conventions and values of bori are not all silently absorbed as implicit structures of shared meaning. Prohibitions, avoidances, and affinities sometimes have their roots in the stories 'yan bori tell about the spirits and how they came to be who they are. Through these tales, anecdotes, and myths, which often take on the character of gossip, spirits are remembered before they can be literally embodied in the arena of possession. For instance, according to a well-known story, the rivalry that prevails between a Doguwa called Bagurma and the

Fulani Doguwa known as Wankarma originated when they both gave birth to their first child.

Bagurma and Wankarma were the co-wives of Mashi, the first son of Rankasso. One day, their husband said to them, "You are both pregnant. The one who gives birth to a son will receive a bag of millet, the one who has a daughter will receive a bag of bran." One night Wankarma delivered a daughter while Bagurma bore a son. Their husband had gone to the bush and would only be back the following morning.

When Bagurma went out to urinate, Wankarma entered her co-wife's room, took the baby boy and substituted it with her infant daughter. When Bagurma came back, she found a baby girl where she had left her son. She did not understand. She had seen the male genitals of the baby she had given birth to, and now she was staring at a female infant. When she saw her co-wife receive a bag of millet while she was getting a bag of bran, she became furious and started to fight with Wankarma. The two spirits have fought and confronted each other ever since.

To this day, devotees of Wankarma and Bagurma do not talk to or exhibit friendliness toward each other, regardless of circumstances. They avoid each other's paths and very rarely become possessed by their respective spirits at the same time; if they do, it is only to hit each other until someone separates them. Thus we see how bori mythology reproduces the human order of relations and practices while also reproducing gender values of inequality: co-wives are expected to fight and compete for attention and favors from their husbands. Conversely, husbands expect their wives to produce male offspring. It is because they think, act, feel, and react like "real" people that spirits such as Bagurma and Wankarma can be so intimately a part of the devotees' everyday lives instead of simply making up a pantheon of dull, abstract, and distant figures. In this instance, that Wankarma is jealous and cunning has practical and moral implications for her medium, who must learn to discern whom to avoid and whom to befriend, whom to provide favors for and whom to feel sympathy for. While a bori devotee's sense of self should ideally remain separate from that of her spirit, there is no telling to what extent the two will mesh together as the medium learns to make sense of her actions and perceptions in terms of her spirit's hold over her.

At another level, the fact that the mediums of Wankarma and Bagurma never (or rarely) simultaneously relinquish their consciousness to their spirits testifies to the primarily embodied nature of their knowledge. It is through their bodies that mediums learn to be Wankarma or Bagurma. Wankarma's hatred for Bagurma becomes part of the medium's lived experience as her body learns to remain untouched by the enrapturing effects of the music the instant Bagurma mounts her own devotee on the possession grounds. "Embodied knowledge," Lambek notes (1993, 307), "is less an object handled . . . than an activity performed." Such attention to the embodiment of knowledge and its embodied manifestations helps emphasize the continuous and quotidian dimension of possession rather than its formalized expression in marked rituals. Though a medium of Bagurma can provide a reflective statement as to why she should not sit next to a devotee of Wankarma, in most daily interactions her avoidance of that medium has sunk beyond the level of reflectiveness to become part of the naturalized system of perceptions, actions, and bodily dispositions that Bourdieu calls the habitus (1977).

Before considering this notion of embodied knowledge, which provides a fruitful perspective from which to analyze how the cultural rules and values of spirit possession become legitimated and naturalized for those who have been recruited to serve as vessels for powerful external forces, it is important to look at kinship and its realization in the spirit world. Like Mawri kinship, the spirits' kinship system is based on the dual principle of kumya (avoidance) and wasa (joking). An individual may play with his or her grandparents, tease and vex them, ask for presents and favors from them, while they, in turn, show kindness and generosity to their grandchild. On the other hand, an individual for the most part has an avoidance relationship with his or her father, mother, spouse, and first child. This means that a mother cannot pronounce her first child's name, nor can she publicly exhibit any displays of affection toward this child. Similarly, a woman may not utter her husband's name, betray feelings of intimacy in public, or speak to her spouse in a direct or confrontational manner. In possession ceremonies, kinship is enacted; or one might say that it is the ties that exist between spirits as well as their various rivalries, estrangements, and hostilities that inform the structure and unfolding of a wasa. Two spirits who dislike each other or who must preserve an avoidance relationship do not, as a rule, take possession of their human vessels simultaneously. Should this happen, the first one to manifest himself or herself usually leaves soon after the other spirit has materialized.

On the other hand, spirits who are siblings, or who like each other for some other reason, generally possess their horses in synchrony. Doguwa spirits, for instance, are the grandmothers of Zanzana ("smallpox"), a spirit who gives pimples and stomachaches, and provokes rashes and eye sores. In the possession arena (as well as in everyday life), devotees possessed by Doguwa spirits thus act kindly toward the human incarnation of Zanzana, who typically cries and whines. As one 'dan bori put it for me, "Zanzana cries all the time; when she cries, the Doguwa will forgive her. Anything she wants she can have. When she cries, they console her because she is spoiled." Another devotee assured me that Zanzana was not the granddaughter of Doguwa spirits but rather, the wife of the Doguwa's son. This is why, he said:

> Technically, Zanzana should come and prostrate herself face against the ground and cry a lot during a gyara of a Doguwa. This way, her mother-in-law, Doguwa, will come to find out what is the matter, it is a way to make sure that Doguwa will come [to possess the initiate]. If she does not come on this particular occasion, the initiate who has the Doguwa on his head will not be able to walk correctly. If Zanzana and the others do not come, Doguwa will come, but she will just peek in, she will not stay. She must be attracted by Zanzana's cries in order to come for good. Zanzana is the daughter-in-law of the Doguwa spirits, so they do not want to hear her cry.

Bori rituals are typically held for an entire family of spirits. This means that if Tsirahako, a Doguwa, is invited to possess the initiate, her kin—sisters, daughters, grandchildren, husband, and so on—are invited as well. It is only if the guest spirit is surrounded and helped by her kin (and the more the better) that proper communication can be established between people and mutanen daji. Just as spirits enjoy the company of humans, so they like to be surrounded by kin. As a team, they work better and more efficiently, and this is why every effort should be made to invite a maximum of spirits. Ideally, this means insuring that for each family involved, at least one medium of each "family member" is attending the wasa.

When Kirai, a powerful spirit of Zarma origin, is called to incarnate himself in the body of the 'dan bori for whom the wasa is held, his brothers Souleymane, Moussa, Danne, Bela, Yabilen, and Kwada will probably manifest themselves as well. If they fail to, or if only one or two show up, the wasa will not be a success. Spirits are thought to hang out with those they like and get along with; siblings, in particular, will help and support each other so that when one of them is requested at a possession ritual to do work, his or her brothers and sisters typically share the load. On such occasions, their chores may include supervising the identification of new spirits during an initiation, setting up fines for individuals who have offended spirits, revealing the future, providing advice, and warning people of incoming perils.

The kinship logic that regulates spirit interactions works very much like the human model: spirits trace their descent bilaterally, but the patrilineage dominates. Marriage is virilocal and polygynous. True siblings are expected to be supportive of each other while half-siblings exhibit the suspicion and competitiveness one finds in human families. Age is an important parameter in the definition of social identity. In fact, being host to one or several senior spirits is a necessary condition to becoming a ritual expert and a successful healer. Individuals of whom I asked if they dispensed medicine would reply that their spirits were not senior or important enough to "show them the way." There is one aspect of this social configuration that is at odds with its human counterpart. Unlike Mawri women who are offered few avenues for achieving social prominence if they have not received a Western school education, some of the most powerful and respected spirits are female. Many of them have achieved fame on the battlefields, the male realm par excellence and something that suggests one of the ways in which the status and interrelations of spirits might differ from the human configuration of social and sexual identities. Some spirits are also the aberrant inversion of their human counterpart, allowing people to catch a glimpse of what it must be like *not* to be a fertile or submissive housewife.

Old or young, powerful or humble, calm or violent, all spirits have a role to play when their presence is requested. Musicians of bori thus play the melodies and sing the songs of each and every kinsperson of the guest spirit so that as many as possible will come to the wasa. Upon hearing the music of their particular spirits, devotees feel great pleasure. The music "sinks right into their hearts," as 'yan bori say. Soon after, they lose consciousness as their bori mounts them. While the music of one's own spirit is particularly conducive to trance, the tunes of other, related spirits are also very gratifying. My friend Zeinabou, who is the devotee of Rankasso—a senior member of the Doguwa family—explained to me that whenever she heard the music of Mai Daro, she would mount her own spirit. Mai Daro is the youngest and favorite sister of Rankasso. When Rankasso hears that her little sister is being urged by the musicians to come possess her horse, she herself cannot resist the temptation of being with her sibling. "When they play Mai Daro's music," Zeinabou said, "it goes right to my heart. You won't see my eyes anymore.[2] And if I happen to be near the musicians, I will give them gifts."

Devotees of sibling spirits will typically sit together on the same mat during a wasa. They are bound by special ties since they are brothers or sisters. As members of the same family, they are thought to enjoy and seek each other's company, especially if they are full siblings (i.e., share the same father and mother). In fact, 'yan bori who are each possessed by a member of the same family of spirits are expected to hang out together. Together, they constitute a *zangon 'yan bori,* that is, a team or a group of bori mediums. But the siblingship of spirits does not correspond to that of living people. That is, two individuals may end up becoming siblings by virtue of being possessed by two spirits who are siblings even though they shared no prior kinship ties in their lives as humans. In other words, human and spirit kinship do not necessarily overlap as they do, for instance, in the case of rural zar described by Boddy (1992, 4). Conversely, a husband and wife may be possessed by spirits who are totally unrelated, thereby adding layers of complexity to the marital relationship.

If, most of the time, bori adds new dimensions to existing kin relations, in a few cases it actually leads to the severance of some existing ties. This happens when certain combinations of spirit/human relations become unacceptable because the duties, attitudes, and expectations that are associated with each set of relations conflict with each other: thus if a man and his wife are possessed by spirits who respectively are sister and brother, they will have to get a divorce because their relationship as a married couple is incompatible with the way they should behave toward each other as mediums of their respective spirits. A healer to whom I recounted that I had met a married couple who were the respective devotees of spirits who were mother and son told me that if no misfortune had yet befallen them, it would happen soon. In his opinion, the two devotees should separate or else, one of them, perhaps even both, would die at the hands of their spirits for having committed what amounted in his eyes to incest.

As selves thus become layered by the acquisition of new spirits, mediums sometimes face difficult choices: on the one hand, securing one's ties to a spirit—a safe choice if one values one's health, prosperity, and peace of mind—might entail giving up a perfectly good marriage. On the other, ignoring the proper "code" of conduct between two mediums whose spirits are siblings on the grounds that following such a code bears too high a cost might provoke the spirits' wrath and lead to disaster. The latter possibility became a reality for Tahirou, a young medium who dreamed of achieving a certain prosperity and visibility when he persisted in prolonging his affair with an older bori devotee.

Tahirou had inherited his spirits from his grandmother. Ambitious and determined, he actively attended ceremonies and could always be seen hanging around the house of the sarkin bori (chief of bori). Through the bori, he had met Mamou, a large and fair-skinned medium in her mid-forties, who, despite her lack of youth, fitted the standard Mawri description of a beautiful woman. It so happened that one of Tahirou's spirits was the mother of Mamou's own bori. Many had advised Tahirou to break off his relationship with Mamou on the grounds that having sex with the medium of his spirit's son was a grave offense that would not remain unpunished forever. The young medium paid them no heed and kept on parading with his lover at every possession ritual held in the area. Mamou was rich and she fitted in with Tahirou's plan to become a sarkin bori (chief of bori) one day. Ever since his initiation into the bori a decade earlier, he had tried to become indispensable to the old chief of bori, running errands for him, assisting him during possession ceremonies, and altogether playing to perfection the role of the devoted apprentice. Giving up Mamou, for Tahirou, would have amounted to recognizing that he had a weakness, something he was not prepared to do given his future plans to assume leadership of the bori.

When he started having health problems, it did not take the young medium long to guess that he had angered the spirits, but he was not yet ready to admit that the "incestuous" liaison he valued so much was what had proven offensive to the members of the bori pantheon. He stubbornly carried on his affair even as his health deteriorated steadily. People started noticing that while he looked tired, skinny, and older despite his youth, his lover, who was already a big woman, kept on getting plumper and more youthful in appearance. Whereas his skin had turned an ugly grayish-black color, a sign of ill health, Mamou's skin was shiny and beautiful, with a healthy reddish glow. That Tahirou looked "wasted" came as no surprise to those who knew of his relationship with a woman almost old enough to be his mother. Aside from the improper nature of such a union (men can and should be older than their wives, but women should not marry younger men), it is widely believed that when in a couple one of the partners is much older than the other, the older one of the two will drain his/her younger lover's vitality each time that they have sex. Thus the more they mingle their maṅyi *(sexual fluids) during intercourse,[3] the more the younger individual will show physical signs of being drained of his vital substance as the other partner steadily enjoys renewed vigor and youth. I left the field too soon after the onset of Tahirou's illness to find out whether or not the ambitious medium had finally listened to the spirits and stopped wasting his nutritious fluids on an older sexual partner, who, to complicate things, was also his putative "son."*

Tahirou's problematic relationship with Mamou eloquently demonstrates how locally articulated categories and hierarchies of age, gender, and power are covertly—and sometimes overtly—challenged when spirit kinship is mapped onto human kinship. In this particular story, it is difficult to assess whether the young medium's troubled health stemmed from his having sex with a woman considerably older than himself or from the incestuous nature of the relationship. What is certain is that, despite his violations of the moral code, Tahirou had internalized these sets of prohibitions in his bodily dispositions to such an extent that his body had produced its own pathological response to the transgression of the taboos.

Plural Selves, Singular Bodies:
A Model of Multiple Embodiments

Parts of the obligations of bori devotees entail behaving in accordance with the moral character and social status of their spirits. This has important implications for the way that 'yan bori lead their lives, especially when it comes to relating to other mediums. Take, for instance, a young woman who has Maria "on her head." Maria is a young, vain, and pretty prostitute who spends a great deal of time admiring herself in looking glasses and seducing the men who cross her path. Maria's medium will be able to joke with, and mock, a much older man with total impunity simply because he is the devotee of the Doguwa Rankasso, a grandmother of Maria. Whenever she meets this man, it is the relationship between their two spirits rather than their own human statuses that dictates the way they should interact with one another. Hence this man she might avoid looking at, and speaking to, in normal circumstances can now treat her as if she were his granddaughter: this means she can tease him, display affection toward him, and ask him for money or for a sweet treat—Maria, the spirit, has a sweet tooth, and so do, therefore, her devotees.

The principles of kumya (shame/avoidance) and wasa (joking/play) that structure spirit interrelationships must be strictly followed by 'yan bori. This is how a bori healer from the village of Salkam described the unfolding of such interactions:

> All those who have the spirit Harakwai cannot sit with the horses of Kirai, because Kirai is the oldest son of Harakwai [who therefore feels kumya]. The horses of Arnya cannot sit on the same mat as the devotees of Adama, and they cannot eat together. It is like a father-in-law who cannot eat with his son-in-law. They feel shame. If they get together to eat in spite of the prohibition, one of them will die. Even if they don't know each other, they cannot eat together because of their spirits. The *tuwo* [thick porridge of millet] will get stuck in their mouths; it won't go through. Or else, one of them will become ill. Also they cannot call each other by their names. They can speak to each other but from far away. . . . The grandchildren and grandparents have a joking relationship. They play together. All the things that grandchildren see in their grandparents' houses they can take if they want. The [horses of the] sons

of Kirai and the sons of Souleymane, if they see something they want on the horse of Harakwai, like a hat or a scarf, they can take it. If the horse of Harakwai has money, they can take the money. Sometimes, [the horses of] Kirai and his brothers come to chase away [the horses of] their sons because they bother their grandmother too much.

Thus mediums learn to pay attention whom—that is, to the medium of whose spirit—they speak to, sit next to, or eat with. It is as if another distinct web of relationships were superimposed on the already complex patterns of human interactions. Like the human configurations on which they are modeled, the kinship system of the spirits is not a rigid structure but rather a fluid set of relationships, subject to negotiation, interpretation, and manipulation.

Devotees must never lose sight of this overarching network of spirit relationships; for those who have recently become involved with the spirits, such a network might appear distant and abstract, while for others who have long dwelled in bori, it is a self-evident and natural part of life that is rarely scrutinized. While rules are usually significant in a prescriptive sense, their objectification as a model that lends itself to manipulations occasionally serves as a playful commentary on the proper way 'yan bori should address each other. I witnessed such a display of wit between Tsakani, a woman who had a Doguwa spirit, and Ma'azou, a 'dan bori who was the horse of Azane, the husband of Doguwa.

A bori ceremony was under way in the small village of Yankassou. A large ring of spectators had formed outside Ali'ou's compound, attracted by the drums. The sun was still high in the sky and the rhythmic beat of the music shook the still and stifling air. Sheltered under a canopy, the musicians played spirit songs in a random order while a handful of bori dancers were busy "warming the spot" so as to entice the spirits into attending the event. Tsakani and Ma'azou were both sitting on the same straw mat, watching friends and acquaintances dance to the rapid tempo of the beaten calabashes. Tsakani asked her "husband" Ma'azou alias Azane to buy her some fried cakes made of bean flour. When Ma'azou flatly refused, Tsakani declared that their marriage was over. Without missing a beat, Ma'azou retorted that he would give her the takarda (paper, i.e. divorce papers) as soon as possible.

It was all a joke, a spontaneous and lighthearted parody of the taken-for-granted responsibilities of a husband toward his wife. Men are expected to provide their spouses with sustenance so long as they remain married, and failure to comply is grounds for divorce. Yet the playful conversation between Tsakani and Ma'azou also hinted obliquely at the obscure relationship between an acceptable model of marriage and femininity, and the muddled grounds of resistance to it (conscious as well as unconscious): a wife should remain submissive and let her husband decide what food, and how much of it, he needs to buy for her. The avoidance relationship between them dictates that she should refrain from addressing him directly and asking for *more* food after he has provided her with the usual ration—all the more so since showing signs of hunger is interpreted as an expression of rudeness and deviance. Through its portrayal of the Doguwa spirit as a provocative, quarreling, and demanding wife who takes matters in her own hands and asks for divorce, Ma'azou and Tsakani's diverting skit was a sobering commentary on the problems and adversities of marriage, a theme that is all too familiar to the bori scene.

On another level, Tsakani and Ma'azou's lighthearted argument exemplifies one of the important lessons of bori, one that echoes Boddy's claims about zar as a reflexive discourse: namely, that the moral demands enjoined by a spirit provide a critique on Mawri codes of conduct, something that enables people to step outside their world and gain perspective on their lives. Through the objectification, exaggeration, critique, and perhaps resolution of the dilemmas they face, Mawri mediums, like Hofriyati women, can distance themselves from their cultural contexts and "ponder the taken-for-granted world" (Boddy 1989, 344). This is perhaps the fundamental—though never explicitly stated—value of possession: by allowing mediums to contemplate, question, or negotiate their identities through the objectification of previously unquestioned categories, bori permits a kind of transcendence of lived experience. Like zar, which Boddy describes as a "powerful medium for unchaining thought from the fetters of hegemonic cultural constructs" (1989, 356), bori provides an analytical—one could almost say, ethnographic—commentary on Mawri culture.

Fostering this awareness of alternate realities is, of course, primarily achieved in possession through the transcendence of the self in the other. It is by becoming other that mediums grow aware of, and teach about, the arbitrariness of cultural constructs. Mutanen daji not only shape people's vision of their moral world by making them ill, miserable, or by conversely bestowing rewards and support, they also inscribe themselves onto the subjectivities of their devotees in such deeply internalized ways that the mediums take on the personalities and outlooks of their spirits. Leiris describes similar processes in zar, noting, for instance, that in Ethiopia, one of his informants had become a nun under the influence of her spirit Abba Josef, a Christian zar from Jerusalem (1989, 91–93). Taking on the moral or social identity of one's zar or bori can lead to conflicts, when, as in the following case, the human host feels pulled in two opposed directions by two different spirits:

As I prompted her one day about whether she would ever marry one of the handful of lovers whose generous gifts she was always bragging about, my pretty friend Zeinabou confided that her spirits were giving her a hard time and that they were the primary reason why she had not yet chosen a husband. When I had first met Zeinabou, she was desperately in love with a young economics student who wanted to marry her but did not relish her recent involvement in bori. A year after they had broken up, she was still not married. While she had no trouble finding wealthy lovers who could indulge her taste for fashionable dresses and expensive trinkets, it was clear that few men would have wanted her for a wife. Besides having earned a reputation as an easy girl, she had directly disregarded her father's injunction not to become involved with the spirits. As a prominent Muslim and an assistant to the local chief, Zeinabou's father did not hide his contempt for the people of bori. Knowing very well she should not disobey him, Zeinabou had ignored the spirits' attentions for as long as she could. But as her ailments increased in severity, she had finally given up resisting the call of the spirits and become initiated into the bori—in a distantly located hamlet, away from home so as not to embarrass her Muslim relatives, who could therefore safely admit that they had nothing to do with the whole affair. As Zeinabou became more confident in her role as a medium, she also found it increasingly difficult to conform simultaneously to the divergent moral dictates of two of her spirits. The virtuous Doguwa Rankasso projected high standards of respectability, morality, and modesty. In stark contrast, the spirit Maria defiantly ignored the ethics promoted by Rankasso to reveal a profligate and wanton nature. Like Maria, the prostitute spirit who enjoys seducing men as well as male spirits, Zeinabou could be easily swayed into spending the night with an admirer if he promised her gifts. She liked nice clothes, spent without thinking, and enjoyed the attention of her male friends. At the same time, she desperately wanted to marry and have children but at twenty-two remained single despite her stunning looks and pleasant personality. She felt that Maria manipulated her into having so many lovers and flouting Mawri ideals of womanhood, while Rankasso, the Doguwa, made her feel shame and a longing for the more tempered pleasures of marriage and maternity. Not able to reconcile two different lifestyles and two opposed visions of sexuality, she struggled to redefine her own selfhood, mindful that what would please one of her spirits would inevitably upset the other.

Aside from hinting at the profound ways in which subjective experience can be continuously and routinely subordinated to the categories of bori, Zeinabou's confession reminds us that the morality of bori is not "universal" but contextual. How individuals experience the world, why they sink into one set of normative roles and bodily dispositions rather than another depends heavily on what spirit(s) they are possessed by—and it is spirits who choose their horses, not the other way around. According to Brown, morality in vodou is tailored not only to the situation but also to the specific person or group involved: "A moral person, in vodou, is one who lives in tune with his or her character, a character defined by the spirits said to love that person" (1991, 241). Such a description fits the practice of bori as well, for bori conditions individuals to live, and act, in tune with the spiritual personality they are embodying. From this perspective, bori is not embodiment simply because disembodied creatures are temporarily incarnated in their human receptacles during a wasa. In a more subtle—yet profound—way, and on a quotidian basis, devotees *embody* spirits as their selves are enmeshed with the social representations and cultural definitions of these spirits. During trance they partially renounce their own personalities and absent themselves to make space for the spirit, but the latent dimension of possession persists well beyond its manifest moments. Through the partial and, at times, problematic renunciation of their selfhoods, the human hosts create a new order of relationships (we might even say a new society) that interpenetrates, often mirrors, yet at times conflicts with the system it parallels.

Zeinabou's painful dilemma also demonstrates the intrinsically pragmatic nature of bori knowledge, serving as a reminder that understanding bori activities is always a matter of situating actions temporally and socially. Only by focusing on the realization of specific activities as embodied experience can one fruitfully describe spirit/host relations in their concrete realizations. Zeinabou's intimate knowledge of her spirits, of their histories and personalities, cannot be simply expressed as a structured sets of propositions and outlines, for such knowledge is more "a capacity to do things" (Weiss 1996, 165) than an objectified expression of wisdom. Despite her recent incorporation into bori, Zeinabou had deeply internalized the motivations of her spirits for whom she had become a vessel. She knew so well *how* to be Maria or Rankasso that she could no longer extricate herself from such roles. Having appropriated the personae of the spirits who had in turn appropriated her body, she could only make sense of her own actions and aspirations in the context of her status as a vessel for Maria and Rankasso. One may argue that such a strategy enabled Zeinabou to project onto the spirits a measure of the guilt she felt burdened with—it was not completely her fault if she had not married. More important perhaps, having had to surrender part of her capacity to act as a willful and self-centered individual enabled Zeinabou to bring a degree of meaningful unity to her somewhat fragmented life.

Zeinabou's disclosure further shows that if bori addresses and resolves tensions, dilemmas, and indeterminacies, it also creates further complications from which there is no escape. Once an individual has become a spirit devotee, there is no turning back. When I returned to Dogondoutchi in the summer of 1994, Zeinabou was married to a bori violinist from a nearby village. But she was childless like the prostitute spirit to whose history she had merged her own destiny. Two years later, I learned through another friend that her marriage had ended in a divorce. I expect that Zeinabou will marry and get divorced again. The only constant in her life will be her attachment to Maria, Rankasso, and the other spirits who have chosen her as their medium.

In most cases, the only way to end a relationship with a spirit is to die. Death effectively deprives the spirit of her or his human receptacle. Those who choose to sever their ties with the mutanen daji and leave the bori only end up angering the spirits and exposing themselves to painful retaliations. For those who cannot reconcile their commitment to bori with their aspirations as followers of the Prophet, life becomes an exacting series of unresolvable quandaries, as the tragic fate of Amadou demonstrates.

Amadou, a forty-year-old man from Dogondoutchi, who had known for years that he had inherited the spirits of his father, decided, after he had gone to Mecca (as a result of an invitation by one of his brothers), that he did not want anything to do with bori anymore. Eager to polish his image as an alhaji (pilgrim back from Mecca) and to regain the esteem of his Muslim acquaintances, he turned his back on the bori and stopped attending possession ceremonies. The spirits eventually retaliated by making him so sick that he could no longer work in his fields. At harvest time, his brothers had to hire day laborers to take care of his crops. After being confined to his bed for several months and upon the advice of several bori healers, Amadou finally consented to beg for the spirits' compassion and to undergo an initiation. A goat purchased on his behalf was sacrificed to Kirai, the fierce spirit of thunder, to appease him and his brothers. By shedding blood in such a manner, Amadou renewed the ancient pact established between people and spirits and demonstrated his own commitment to further serving the mutanen daji.

Some months later, when Amadou's health had shown some improvement—a sign that the spirits had agreed to help and support him—the initiation ceremony was held to officialize his involvement in the bori. Amadou's brothers strongly disapproved, of course, and so did his Muslim friends, but their objections did not alter Amadou's determination to go through with the initiation. For a few months things seemed to improve for Amadou. But behind the apparent recovery, he was deeply troubled: he felt ostracized by his Muslim peers and rejected by the community he had worked so hard to conquer. At last, unable to reconcile his Muslim aspirations with his obligations as a 'dan bori, and too weary to fight simultaneously the spirits and the members of the Islamic community, he hung himself. Suicide was the only way the troubled man could escape the grip of the spirits without suffering from debilitating illnesses for the rest of his unhappy life.

This is, of course, a case of extreme conflict between one's identity as a medium and one's social persona, but it highlights the inherent tensions existing in all individuals, whether they be Muslim or bori devotees, men or women, as they learn to balance the often contradictory demands of indigenous, Muslim, and Western lifestyles and ideologies. Most of the other cases I heard of or witnessed involved milder contradictions between one's identity as a human person and one's identity as a medium or between two spirits of divergent orientations occupying the body of a single devotee. Bori devotees whose personal pantheon includes both a Muslim spirit and an indigenous "pagan" spirit often face painful choices when it comes to satisfying both Islamic and non-Islamic requirements. Several mediums of Malam Alhaji whom I knew thus felt pressured to learn to write Koranic verses, knowing very well that their involvement in Islam would inevitably anger those of their spirits who were opposed to Islamic ways. A man once told me that he kept on feeling sickly no matter what he did to please the spirits. When he prayed (to Allah), Wankarma, his "pagan" spirit, became angry and made him suffer from stomachaches, but when he stopped attending prayer, it was Malam's turn to punish his lack of faith by sending him a sickness. In such cases, following the moral dictates of one's spirits is not enough to insure health, fulfillment, and prosperity. One must also be able to make judgments in order to evaluate beforehand the consequences of such actions in the context of their realization: will the potentially fruitful effects of obeying Malam Alhaji's injunction to pray outweigh the negative consequences of one's commitment to Islam? Besides underscoring the subversive potential of all bori activities, the dilemmas so many mediums face through their mutually antagonistic encounters with spirits express the conflicting aspirations of individuals who, like Amadou, cannot choose once and for all between bori and Islam. Boddy similarly recounts that "because one can be possessed simultaneously by different spirits, who likely come from different homelands in the spirit world, a woman's personal zar pantheon may represent the different facets of her social identity or express her internalization . . . of domestic political tensions" (1992, 8). For those who are pulled in divergent directions by their possessing spirits, learning to compromise—so as to satisfy one bori without, in the process, angering another—is the key to enjoying a fulfilling and healthy life as a medium. In this respect, a medium's situation is not unlike that of a married man who must keep each of his wives happy through the right mixture of attention and gifts while simultaneously insuring that such displays of affection do not incite jealousy or competition between the objects of his concern.

Devotees are thus enjoined to assume the moral self-image associated with their spirit(s); yet recognizing when and where it is appropriate and necessary to do so sometimes proves difficult in practice, especially for those who have only recently joined the bori.

Upon learning that Hawa, one of my young neighbors, was sick in bed, I decided to pay her a visit. A housewife and a mother of two, Hawa was currently struggling to balance the conflicting demands of marriage and mediumship as her increasing involvement in bori became more time-consuming. After thanking me for the aspirins I had brought her, she confided that the spirits were punishing her because she had inadvertently offended her spirit-husband a few weeks before:

"The spirits gave me terrible stomach pains. I thought it was because I was delaying the purchase of the clothing they had asked for. For three weeks I was in pain. I was vomiting all the time, fura was giving me nausea. I couldn't drink any. Now, I only drink kunu.[4] This happened because I refused to give a kola nut to the horse of Zahoho. At first I did not know why I had such stomachaches. Zahoho [later] mounted a woman during a wasa and came to see me, he said: 'Why did you refuse to give me some kola since I am your husband?' "

Hawa further explained to me that she had bought this big, lovely, white kola nut to offer it to the healer who was going to supervise her initiation into the bori the following month. She wanted to show him that she was grateful for his help—he had given her medicine to prevent miscarriages—and that she knew how to be generous. When the horse of Zahoho, the husband of her own spirit, Maria,[5] came over and asked her for a share of the kola nut, she had said no, because she did not want to waste her expensive kola nut on a man whom she inwardly despised. In her eagerness to please the ritual specialist who would initiate her, she had dismissed the medium's demands as unimportant and irrelevant. It had not occurred to her at the time that her unequivocal refusal would have such heavy consequences.

Hawa's painful lesson illustrates the difficulty of "finding and cultivating a voice . . . that is manifestly not one's own" (Lambek 1993, 336) and to make judicious use of it even in the most mundane circumstances. Unlike what happens during a possession ceremony where the devotee's consciousness slips away to make space for the spirit who seeks to concretely manifest himself or herself, having a spirit "on one's head" on an everyday basis entails living with multiple subjectivities that might be at odds with each other. In certain contexts where differing roles and relationships interpenetrated, Hawa's persona as female devotee soon to be initiated clashed significantly with her persona as Maria, the dutiful wife of Zahoho. Yet precisely because she was so inexperienced in the matters of bori, Hawa had failed to discern what should have been, in response to (the horse of) Zahoho's request, the most appropriate course of action. Like all mediums of Maria, she knew, of course, that the spirit was overindulging her lazy husband. What she did not know yet was how to use that knowledge as a practical resource to variously draw upon in specific situations—such as when it was Maria the spirit, and not Hawa the medium, who was being addressed. We see once more how knowing bori is inseparable from doing bori, and why the reality of possession cannot adequately be translated into an abstract set of rules divorced from practical concerns and contexts. Like Hawa or Zeinabou, young or inexperienced devotees make mistakes and experience conflicts before they learn to become confident and competent mediums who comfortably share their bodies with powerful forces on a daily basis.

Perpetually Possessed:
Embodiment, Agency, and Subjectivity Revisited

The foregoing has focused on the central role bori plays in the daily life of its members so as to trace both the *systematic* and the *fluid* ways in which spirit mediums generate, embody, and reproduce—but also subvert—the values that meaningfully shape their world. Now the question arises, in light of the previous discussion of embodiment, what it means to be a "vessel" for the spirits. Addressing this question presents an occasion also for rethinking the relationship between subjectivity and the body in order to consider some potentially fruitful avenues of inquiry regarding agency and control in the realm of possession.

When they describe the ties uniting an alien force to its human host, both anthropological observers and bori mediums assign most—if not all—of the power to the spirit. Whether mediums perceive a spirit as a deus ex machina or a petty agent of an omnipotent but distant god, they do not question the basic ascendancy these creatures of the wild have over humans. Spirits, it is widely acknowledged, choose their devotees, and resisting them is futile, as Amadou's story tragically demonstrates. More important perhaps, spirits show how powerful they are when they obliterate their mounts' consciousness in order to fully articulate a wholly "other" persona in the act of possession. What my exploration of the everyday implications of mediumship suggests, though, is that the concept of the medium as a mere "vessel" limits one's understanding of the kinds of bodies that have the *capacity* to become hosts to alien forces. In other words, the lesson to be drawn from Tsakani's, Hawa's, Amadou's, or Zeinabou's struggle to assert their *own* agency as they pursue their "careers" as mediums is that the adept's body is not just an "empty" container passively submitting to the invading spirit's will. Instead, this body must be configured and oriented toward others—including the spirit, other 'yan bori, and Mawri society as a whole—as an entity that can accommodate, and interact with, these various forces.

Part of what the discussion of the overlay of spirit relations with human relations has revealed, then, are the ways in which the recognition of a person as a potential, or realized, host in a variety of quotidian contexts works to establish new bodily dispositions for that person. Thus when Zeinabou experienced pain or sickness and interpreted her troubles as the result of one of her spirits' angry response to her foolish behavior, she was not passively submitting to a spirit who could control her health from afar. Nor could we say that Zeinabou's own sense of inadequacy and guilt is what caused her illness. Insofar as consciousness is necessarily embodied, Zeinabou's dispositions actively participated in defining or, at least, constraining the consciousness of the spirit that ostensibly "made her sick." In other words, having a spirit "on one's head" entails the imposition of "new" conventions that sink in to become eventually sedimented in the adept's body to such an extent that one can no longer isolate human agency from some "external" will identified as the spirit's. Even as one talks of spirits "taking" the bodies of their hosts, it would be more accurate to speak of their *inhabiting* these bodies. From this perspective, the host's consciousness is not really displaced in any straightforward way but always exists in the embodied forms that enables the spirit to come into being in the first place. That personhood is continually reconfigured through the vortex of interactions a person engages in—through dietary restrictions, modes of dress, marital exchange, rules of kinship—partially accounts for some of the profound dilemmas faced by adepts on a quotidian basis. Recognizing, for instance, that an active consciousness was realized in her bodily dispositions helps one understand how conflicted Zeinabou was about her identities as an unmarried medium and as a would-be wife and mother.

In my exploration of the implications of bori possession in everyday practice, I have thus far demonstrated how such experiences entail living with multiple subjectivities. In a very real way, though, it is not just the selves that are experienced as plural by bori adepts because an intrinsic dimension of these subjectivities are the bodily qualities they are grounded in. Turning, once again, to the case of Zeinabou, one might very well imagine how the ongoing fragmentation of her selfhood was concretized anew in evolving sets of bodily dispositions as she reached the successive stages of budurwa (unmarried girl), wife, and finally divorcée. Yet in her relation with Maria, the prostitute spirit, she always retained the body of the youthful, unmarried, but promiscuous girl that the spirit wanted her to be. Zeinabou, like any other adept who had successfully learned to accommodate the demands of others—be they spirits or humans—lived with multiple *bodies* as well as multiple selves.

Possession, then, is about learning how to be other. In this respect, one might see local pantheons of spirits as ethnographies in which the experience of otherness is carefully and dramatically articulated even if the awareness of such a process remains only partially conscious. Much like the possessed traveling through space and time heighten their sense of self through their engagement with the other, so anthropologists come to terms with their selfhoods through the detour of the other. Devotees who have only recently been initiated into bori sometimes appear clumsy and unskilled in contrast to their more experienced counterparts who have internalized their bodily dispositions to the extent that they can spontaneously and "naturally" think or act as their spirits would. "Learning possession" also means learning to control the spirits' access to one's body. Since, mediums will tell you, possession is about pain and hard work, most would rather avoid being "caught" (possessed) by their bori if they could. This is why old 'yan bori rarely enter into trance even though they faithfully keep attending wasani. At the same time, the fact that older mediums are much less often possessed than junior devotees suggests that the process of learning possession, as a lifelong project, entails a gradual evolution in the spirit-host relation. As the pair learns to co-exist, the original assertiveness of the possessing spirit progressively gives way to the eventual power of the medium, so that at the end of her life as a devotee, a person should have gained an important mea-sure of control over the once dominating spirit. This is not to say that the spirit has become weak or potentially less dangerous. To be sure, one should never forget that all mutanen daji can and will strike an offender for the pettiest of reasons and when they appear least likely to commit violence. Older mediums know this and avoid creating situations in which they can anger their spirits. But they also know that they no longer need to be tested, because over the course of their lives as mediums, they have proven their dedication and respect for the spirits.

The assertiveness gained by a medium, as her relationship with a possessing spirit matures, is concretized in the form of bodily attune-ments to the requirements of that spirit. That is, with time the more senior mediums are able ever more to perfectly embody the demands of their spirits. To pick an example close at hand, one may surmise that Zeinabou may, with age, become more attuned to her spirit's wishes so that instead of offending the spirit Rankasso by her girlish behavior, she will "instinctively" want or need what the spirit requires of her. Because Zeinabou will have developed the necessary know-how, there will be no need for Rankasso to remind her host through warnings and punishment that mediums must selectively follow the *ethic* appropriate to each of their spirits. Going back to the connec-tion between seniority and subjectivity, I don't think it is that senior mediums rarely become possessed but rather that their own sensibili-ties emerge in such close harmony to the spirits they incarnate that possession becomes for them less and less a matter of "displaced" and "replaced" consciousness. Since, from this perspective, acting in accordance with their spirits' requirements no longer necessarily means acting against their *own* impulses, one could almost say that senior mediums are perpetually possessed as their selves—bodies and all—become increasingly spiritlike.

The various vignettes and narratives recounted here illustrate the concrete, intimate, and far-reaching ways in which spirits are enmeshed in the quotidian lives of their mediums. By constantly intervening —sometimes subtly, sometimes dramatically—in human existence, spirits profoundly alter the mechanics of power and identity inherent in Mawri codifications of gender roles, social statuses, and moral orientations. Spirits are not confined to ceremonial events that insulate the participants from the "real" world. Because as ethereal beings they can transcend the boundaries of spirit and matter, village and bush, their realm also encompasses the worldly and quotidian processes their devotees are continuously engaged in. Their fluidity enables them to mediate between distinct worlds of being and experience. Only by focusing on the mundane environment of possession can one understand the meanings and motivations of bori as well as the degree to which it shapes daily actions and interactions. Only by tracing the strands of coherence as well as the ambiguities and indeterminacies of everyday life can one explain how bori activities constitute an effective, pragmatic, and powerful way of dealing with misfortune and coping with the pressures and contradictions of material existence. Possession pertains to the domain of illness, suffering, and healing, but it also inserts itself in interpersonal relations, family disputes, business strategies, and personal destinies. As will be seen in the following chapters, it may also play a role in travel and marketing, marriage and sexuality, politics and the historical imagination.

The focus here has been on spontaneous happenings and small slices of social interaction, so as to stress the dialogic quality of possession and show that the reality of bori can be reduced neither to ideal types nor to a set of frozen conventions followed by unreflective actors. Bori is not a collection of abstract formulas that individuals consult when they need to make sense of a reality "out there." Of course, knowledge of spirits partially derives from a body of shared conceptions and understandings about the world, but as mostly "ordinary knowledge," it also has its source in personal experiences, repeated participation in possession rituals, spontaneous battles of wit, and, most important, in quotidian involvement with *specific* spirits in *specific* circumstances. What constitutes a morally appropriate action for one medium may prove problematic or even dangerous for another, because the actions and moral commitments of devotees are tied to the identity of their spirits. Conversely, the shadowy identity of mutanen daji takes on a sharper socio-moral focus through their intervention in human affairs, because, as Lambek notes, spirits are intrinsically connected to the contexts in which they appear (1996, 243).

Analyzing possession as a force in perpetual motion thus requires paying attention to the multiplicity of motives, the open-endedness of definitions, and the provisionality of meanings that emerge through a contextual exploration of the spirits' engagement with the world of mediums, healers, *'yan biya* ("those who follow"), and would-be hosts. By focusing on knowledge in its pragmatic realization in quotidian contexts, I have tried to stress the diverse, polyphonic, and at times conflicting nature of bori experience. In the context of people's interactions with spirits, things happen *all the time.* If ritual performances of bori possession generally provide fruitful settings for anthropological analyses of symbolically packed slices of human experience, so less momentous circumstances such as a dispute, a spontaneous joke, or a wordless interaction offer, for those who can "read" them, similarly "dense" moments in which much is implied, even if little is stated. The map of spirit relations that interpenetrates the tight web of human interactions is thus routinely concretized as each medium struggles, in his or her *own* way, to mediate, subvert, or reinforce bori relations, conventions, and contradictions that are often the echoes of his or her own muted voice.

Chapter 5

Kinesthetic Appropriation and Embodied Knowledge BABOULE SPIRITS AND THE MAKING OF VALUE

Consciousness is in the first place not a matter of "I think that" but of "I can."—Maurice Merleau-Ponty, *The Phenomenology of Perception*

It was with the arrival of the French that the craziness of the Baboule started. People went to Niamey, bori musicians were invited [to play]. The 'yan bori were staying by the river [Niger]. [Once possessed,] they stepped into the water, they crossed the river. They came out on the other side like a herd of cattle since they did not know how to swim. So the French saw that the spirits were real because no one had drowned.—Guzaye, Mawri medium, May 1989

It was almost dusk in Dogondoutchi. The cool harmattan had started sweeping across the town as the syncopated and loud sound of the calabash drums resonated across the mud walls of the neighborhood. Old women shivered as they readjusted their thin cotton shawls across their bony shoulders while men wrapped in the thicker layers of their riguna *(robes) appeared not to notice how the evening air had suddenly chilled. Notified by an offering of kola nuts that their presence was requested at a wasa, bori mediums had started gathering at the house of Teshi, a 'dan bori who wanted to thank his spirits for helping him find a new job. After having praised the Zarma spirits, the musicians were now playing the music of the Baboule, the fire-eating spirits who come from the East. They had performed uninterruptedly for the last two hours, sweeping old and young mediums onto the dance ground, where they gracefully performed, kicking their feet in the sand in unison with the music beat. Shatu, a frail old griotte (praise singer), was praising the Baboule Arna with her melodious voice:*

"Arna, here is your problem
Here is what you like
Kankama [insult] your mother your father
If you whisper
You ate your mother [you had sex with your mother]
Soldiers of fire, husband of Halima
Arna, those who have the brains of a camel
Black water from the seaside
No one is superior to Dodo except Allah
Hyena, you ate a lot [insult]
Uuhhh Uuhhh
Thanks, that's what I do, I give thanks
Kure, I thank you
Soldiers of fire, husband of Halima
If you are not capable, don't take me"

A young man suddenly stood up from the crowd of onlookers. The wise mixture of flattery and insult hurled by Shatu was finally having an effect. With his hands on his hips, the medium started walking in a rigid and hurried gait toward the musicians. His eyes were bulging and he was frothing at the mouth. He was possessed by Komandan Mugu ("Major Evil"). Soon two other entranced mediums followed in his path, taking long strides, their bodies stiff and erect. One of them was Teshi. He spoke in a mixture of Hausa and pidgin French, shouting orders at the other two as he thrust his right arm in the air. Shatu kept on singing Arna's song:

"You don't pray, you don't invoke blessings on the Prophet
I said, there are no men Baboule
No one is superior to Dodo except Allah
Arna, here is your problem
Here is what you like

Today it is your turn to do the work
Because of death, men are afraid of war
But death will find you even at home
Here is the problem, here is war
One must drink [eat] fire
One must whip oneself
Today you men go in the army
Death finds you even at home
Kura I thank you
The men are called as if they were women
Soldiers of fire, husband of Halima
Allah killed and destroyed
This one "drinks" fire as if it did nothing to him
Another "drinks" fire, his body burns
One must go home and spread the news
The good spirits are only those one inherits

Meanwhile, the spectacular performance of Komandan Mugu had unleashed a series of possessions among the crowd of devotees. Salma and Danne, the Mossi spirit who eats dogs, were riding their mediums. Gwamna ("Governor") had also caught his mount. Two other women were also possessed by members of the Baboule family. The musicians kept on playing; the griotte dutifully sang the praises of every Baboule in turn. With tense and measured steps, Gwamna moved around and shouted orders that seemed to increase the confusion that already prevailed among the other soldier spirits. Soon one of them grabbed a handful of thatch from a nearby roof and someone scratched a match to light the bundle. Holding the burning thatch to his bare chest, the soldier started walking furiously around the dance ground while onlookers prudently moved out of his path. Another, General Marsey—he is from Marseilles, France, and is allegedly so mean that he does not get a riding crop but "works" with his hands, instead— was staring at the Major while holding his hand to his glistening forehead in an extended salute.[1] After performing a series of drills in front of Gwamna, who was signaling with a whistle, the soldier spirits were now ready to help people with the *problems of life. Standing in their red robes or black shirts, they listened restlessly to the requests of those who came to seek help or counsel. After providing advice in characteristically breathless and repetitive sentences punctuated by grunts and hiccups, the Baboule departed one by one, leaving their devotees thirsty, disoriented, and exhausted.*

Possession and Remembrance

So far, the significance of bori spirits has been explored in broad, general terms to capture the poetics of identity, alterity, and intention at work in possession. In the remaining chapters, the focus shifts to concentrate on specific spirits whose particular histories and identities highlight the bori's capacity to simultaneously mediate the forces of tradition and address the challenges of modernity. The Baboule spirits, their cultural significance, and the political implications of their emergence in the 1920s are the subject of this chapter. Taking these figures of the bori pantheon as historical signifiers, I focus on one particular moment of Niger's history through its re-*membrance* in contemporary ceremonies and individual memories, and examine spirit possession as an embodied practice and a politically significant discourse in the colonial context of conquest and transformation. The colonization of Arewa by the French and its subsequent integration into what would one day become the Republic of Niger introduced new relations of power and production, new levels of transactions, and new forms of authority. Unsurprisingly, even after the territory of Niger was allegedly pacified, the efforts of colonizers to rule and exploit their colonial subjects were met by resistance and defiance. More often than not, such resistance remained implicit and inchoate. The Baboule spirits, who enjoined their mediums to carry weapons, wear army uniforms, and rebel against local authorities, were a notable exception to this state of affairs.

PISimultaneously sublime and ridiculous, frightening and funny, the Baboule—known in Ghana and western Niger as Hauka—have repeatedly captured the anthropological imagination of those who sought to make sense of the spirits' intriguing parody of the French military. The haunting images of Jean Rouch's film *Les maîtres fous* reveal the convulsive violence and theatrical chaos of possession, but this evocative portrayal of Hauka mediums in the former Gold Coast (Ghana) provides only a fragmented commentary of the visual drama explored by the ethnographer's camera. Fuglestad (1975), Stoller (1984), and Olivier de Sardan (1993) have variously addressed the politics and performance of resistance in their analyses of the Hauka movement. In a prior version of this chapter (1993), I suggested that it was not enough to label the Baboule's multiethnic phenomenon of ritualized opposition as "cultural resistance" (Stoller 1984). More recently, Kramer (1993) has argued that spirit possession, such as in the case of the Hauka, provides means through which to articulate a sense of self, and of the stranger within oneself, by focusing on and imitating the alien and the foreign. This fruitful argument is further developed by Stoller (1995), who builds on Taussig's (1993) concept of mimesis to comment on the significance of Hauka aesthetics in the configurations of power in colonial and postcolonial Niger.

In a recent reassessment of the scholarship on the Baboule, Olivier de Sardan (1993) criticizes former analyses that have cast the movement as political action and argues that the mediums who aped the French colonials in the 1920s were not resisting a foreign power. Arguably, the followers of the Baboule movement were only partially able to localize and identify the source of their distress and subjugation, but their actions cannot be dismissed, in the manner of Olivier de Sardan, as mere religious manifestations of limited historical consequences. The spirit mediums who imitated the oppressing Other through their theatrical antics were playing a very serious wasa (game) in their attempt to grasp the mystifying manifestations of colonial power.

More significant perhaps, through what Taussig (1993, 247) calls "'mimetic excess' spending itself in a riot of dialectical energy," Baboule mediums subverted and transformed the system put in place by their oppressors. To comment on the Baboule's stunning disruption of the neat and tidy categories of French conceptual hegemony, I will focus primarily on the ways that mediums appropriated this alien world and its sources of power with and through their bodies. It will be seen that primarily through the internalization of what they took to be embodied forms of foreign selfhood and authority, Baboule mediums were able to gain understanding and mastery over the alien universe of French colonial rules. First, however, it will be helpful to describe briefly the birth of the movement in southern Niger.

The Emergence of the Baboule Movement

During the dry season of 1925, barely three years after the military territory of Niger had officially become the Colony of Niger, a series of
"religious" manifestations came to the attention of the French administration. Not knowing the exact nature of these displays, yet suspicious of any gathering that could evolve into a Muslim conspiracy—
Muslims were still distrusted by the colonial government—French
officials became worried. In the village of Toudou Anza, in northern
Arewa, a priestess by the name of Chibo was "attacked" by a female
spirit from the brand-new Baboule family (Fuglestad 1983, 128–29).
Chibo and her followers, who were also possessed by the new Baboule
spirits, started manifesting overt hostility toward the sarkin Arewa,
the local chef de canton. The French administration intervened to re-
establish order among the local population and impose by virtue of
the indigénat—according to this legal code, penalties could be imposed
upon subjects without any judicial procedure—disciplinary sentences
on some one hundred demonstrators (Fuglestad 1975, 203).

Such measures did not stop the Chibo sect—as it was now called.
In May 1926, more incidents occurred in the predominantly Mawri
southern and eastern corners of the subdivision of Dogondoutchi and
in the Filingue region (also known as Kurfey, northwest of Arewa),
where villagers responded enthusiastically to Chibo's call for protest
against the colonial administration. During the day Chibo's followers
trained for guerrilla war with wooden rifles, while at night they
held rituals during which the Baboule spirits possessed their mediums
and hunted for witches. The French once again intervened to penal-
ize Chibo's followers. Meanwhile Chibo, who had been fomenting
trouble all along, returned to her native village of Chikal, in Kurfey,
where her father was chief. By February 1927, all the villages of Kurfey had been, in the words of Niamey's commandant, "contaminated"
(Fuglestad 1983, 129).

All members of la secte de Chibo claimed to be possessed by spirits,
who, by virtue of their names (Kabral Gardi, Komandan Mugu,
General Marsey, etc.) and behavioral traits (spoke pidgin French or
English, wore army uniforms, carried guns, etc.), bore uncanny resemblance to the colonial powers. Because their human vessels were
able to swallow cinders and walk into fires unharmed, the spirits—

as well as the manifestations they initiated—became known as the Baboule (meaning "fire-eating spirits" in Zarma; see Rouch 1989, 74). In the west of the colony, they acquired the name of Hauka because their frenzied histrionics recalled the frantic and aimless deportment of the mentally ill (*Hauka* is the Hausa term for "madness" or "folly"). Though it first appeared as just a bizarre and exotic "cult," it soon became clear that the Baboule movement was more than a series of "religious" manifestations in which a group of predominantly young mediums were possessed by particularly violent and strong spirits of foreign origin. Those who joined Chibo's movement refused to pay taxes, participate in forced labor, and submit to the authority of local chiefs (Fuglestad 1983, 129). As the movement grew throughout south-central Niger, more and more young followers founded villages, named governors, and arrested local guards. Chibo and her father, Ganji, had created a sect that "copies our administration and wants to supplant our authority," wrote Scheurer (n.d. in Stoller 1995) in his *Rapport de tournée.*

The French did not wait long to respond to the Baboule offensive. In 1927, eager to repress the movement and put an end to the general agitation, they sent a young and inexperienced administrator who found himself facing widespread and stubborn passive resistance on the part of the villagers (Fuglestad 1983). The French envoy had been ordered to tour the Kurfey canton and take a census of the indigenous population. Censuses constituted an effective means of reasserting the colonial presence and sounding out the general mood of villagers. In addition to furnishing the perfect justification for punitive action—the so-called disciplinary measures—they also provided more recent figures of the human and cattle population for taxation purposes (taxes were established per capita). Lacking any precise instructions as to how to deal with the general upheaval he was confronting, yet determined to make a display of authority, the young administrator took a series of brash measures that, he thought, would punish the culprits and restore peace and order in Kurfey villages (Fuglestad 1983, 129). But he behaved in such a clumsy and inconsiderate manner that his superiors later had to disavow his actions and repeal the penalties he had inflicted. Not only that, but he had to pay compensation to some of Chibo's disciples, an unheard-of action in the annals of colonial administration (129).

The embarrassment that the French envoy caused the colonial ad-

ministration seemed to consolidate the position of the Baboule movement and contribute to its expansion, according to Fuglestad (1983,
129; 1975, 204). So did two other significant happenings: the death
of the old sarkin Filingue (Kurfey), Gado Namalaya, in March 1927
and the attack on the post of Tessaoua on June 5 of the same year.
Gado's death left a political vacuum that was hard to fill, given the
lack of consensus among the local population. The French finally decided to support the candidacy of one of Gado's sons, Chekou Seyni,
although he was far less popular than his father, even among his own
family. Chibo and her followers, who favored another candidate, Mai-
nassara, refused to recognize Chekou Seyni as chef de canton. Soon
after the French toured the Kurfey region to restore order and put
an end to the agitation one more time, the post of Tessaoua, east of
Dogondoutchi, was allegedly attacked by a small band of Madhists
(Muslim reformers) from northern Nigeria, with the tacit approval of
the local chiefs (Fuglestad 1983, 126). Though the incident, which cost
the lives of three men, was a rather isolated event, it was exploited
by Chibo and her adherents with considerable success. According to
Fuglestad (126), the fact that none of the culprits, except for the chief
of Tessaoua, were ever apprehended by the French justice was interpreted locally as a sign that the 'karfi (strength) and sa'a (luck) of the
French was eroding.

   In fact, soon after the Madhist attack at Tessaoua, the French and
the indigenous chiefs in Kurfey found themselves confronted by a
widespread movement of protest that had grown out of the turmoil
sparked by Chibo's movement. More than a simple manifestation of
dissidence against local authorities, the amplified movement was now
an open rebellion against the sociopolitical system imposed by the
French. The Baboule or Hauka movement, as it became known, established an entirely new social order, or, to borrow Turner's (1969, 69)
term, a *communitas*. Refusing to submit to the authority of local and
colonial administrations, Baboule mediums departed en masse for the
bush, where they created their own villages and their own economies
(Fuglestad 1975, 205). Guard duty was organized and any representative of local chiefs or the colonial administration who ventured into
Hauka communities was arrested and beaten (205). The most influential members were awarded titles such as "gouverneur" or "commandant," titles that also referred to the spirits of these mediums. They

carried wooden guns and imitated ("aped" according to colonial reports) the French army.

In neighboring Arewa, the Baboule movement was not so much related to the loss of "force" of the indigenous chieftaincy (in the person of Chekou Seyni, the current chef de canton) and the colonial administration as to the long-standing enmity between the Azna of the village of Lougou and the sarkin Arewa of neighboring Matankari. (It will be recalled that some of the first Baboule appeared in Azna villages.) In 1934 Leroy (1934), the chief of the subdivision of Dogondoutchi, noted:

> The enmity between the people of Lougou (indigenous Azna) and those of Dogondoutchi-Matankari (conquering Mawri who came from Bornou) existed before our arrival in the country. Indadaou, a candidate evicted from the post of village chief of Lougou, and more belligerent than the others, refused to follow the advice of the *chef de subdivision* and made demonstrations of a military nature. He was arrested and condemned by the tribunal to two years in prison for disobeying the chief of his village and the chef de canton, inciting villagers to disobedience and disorder, and threatening to beat the village chief and the representative of the chef de canton. What is true for the village of Lougou is true for every other Azna village. In 1934, one can notice everywhere a continuous hostility [between the Azna and Arewa populations].

Leroy does not say whether Indadaou belonged to the Baboule movement, but one may surmise that he probably did, given his rebellious attitude and the "demonstrations of a military nature" he indulged in. Whether or not he belonged to the movement, his behavior was characteristic of the kind of resistance that both local and colonial authorities encountered at the hands of the Baboule. The French had modified the indigenous Arewa polity by bolstering the power of the sarkin Arewa (who became the chef de canton) and ignoring the influence that the Sarauniya of Lougou and the Baura of Bagaji (Azna religious leaders) wielded over the Azna population. By favoring the Arewa chief over the Baura and the Sarauniya, the French administration destroyed the fragile and continually renegotiated balance between the sarki's political power and the Azna priests' ritual authority (see Fuglestad 1975, 211). How exactly such a disruption contributed to the rise of the Baboule movement in Arewa will become clearer below. Before discussing how the Hauka movement constituted an effort to deal with the colonial experience, however, it will be helpful to examine more closely who these Baboule figures were.

Soldiers from the Red Sea

The Baboule had allegedly been brought back from the Malia (Red Sea) by a Hausa peasant, a veteran of World War I, who had gone on the pilgrimage to Mecca. "They followed him with their strength," writes Rouch (1989, 80). The chief of the Baboule was Istambula, an "inhabitant of Istanbul" and a Muslim. When they arrived in Hausa country, the Baboule remained in the bush for a while, lurking around villages where people saw them for the first time (either in Arewa or in Filingue) (80). Muslim or "pagan," male or female, disciplined or insubordinate, the Baboule were mean and brutal but also courageous and not easily intimidated. Most of them were soldiers, and this is perhaps why, in contrast to what can be said of other bori spirits, they possessed primarily sturdy young men (Échard 1992). People said they could destroy or protect villages. They were known to turn bullets into water. They allegedly had the ability to read the past, predict the future, and identify witches (Stoller 1995, 12). This is how Kane, an old spirit medium and an active participant in bori affairs, remembers his experience in the Baboule movement: "There were many of us. We used to walk around together. This is when people heard gunshots in the night. The Baboule did this to scare [the people]. People were terrified. They [the Baboule] were dressed like soldiers. They were walking around with clubs."

As will be argued below, the Baboule's uncanny resemblance to the European military had more to do with the embodiment of foreign practice than with the wearing of military attire. From the testimonies I was able to gather from a few surviving devotees, it appears that few in Dogondoutchi managed to procure the appropriate outfits that would have identified them as army personnel while also helping to distinguish the commandant from the simple soldier. None wore pith helmets, and, more often than not, the wooden guns described by colonial administrators were replaced by clubs, pestles, or riding crops made from automobile fan belts. The robes and red sashes of the mediums bore little or no similarity to the uniforms sported by the French: it was in their parody of military salutes and gaits, in the orders they shouted in pidgin French or English that the Baboule successfully tapped the power of their colonial masters. Flouting colonial conventions by fleeing villages and refusing to pay taxes, yet paradoxically appropriating signs of the dominant order, the young men and women possessed by these foreign spirits managed to deflect the impact of the colonizers' institutions while simultaneously redirecting the flow of power in the world.

The rebellion initiated in 1925 by the priestess Chibo was ultimately followed by a severe repression that led to the imprisonment of several hundred Baboule mediums. Chibo and other leaders were deported to the colonies of Upper Volta and Ivory Coast (Fuglestad 1983, 130). By the late 1920s, the movement had been dismantled, save for a few strongholds in Kurfey—in Chibo's village of Chikal, for instance. Yet the brutal intervention of French colonials did not ultimately prevent the integration of the Baboule spirits in the Songhay (Rouch 1989; Stoller 1984) and Mawri pantheons. Échard (1992) situates the synthesis of Baboule and bori practices around 1940, when the spirits known as "eaters of fire" were recruited in the fight against witches. Today the spirits' influence can be felt as far as Maradi, where the Baboule occasionally make an appearance at possession ceremonies (Monfouga-Nicolas 1972; Schmoll 1991). In Arewa, they are now regular participants in wasani aimed at propitiating the babba'ku (black—or Zarma—spirits), of which they are the alleged children. Possessing mostly young men—though women, too, can become hosts to these bold spirits—the Baboule are just as violent and dauntless as when they first appeared to challenge the might of their colonial masters. And no Baboule performance is complete until at least one of them has "drunk" fire, as if, to borrow from the words of the griotte, "it did nothing to him."

Resistance, Power, and Efficacy

In his analysis of the Hauka/Baboule, Fuglestad (1983; 1975) argues that the movement sparked by Chibo and her adepts constituted a defense mechanism invented by a stable society threatened by the imposition of abusive and exploitative laws. He concludes that since the Baboule movement was crushed by the French a few years after its inception, it failed in its attempt to revolutionize the social order it was ostensibly opposing. Suggesting that the Baboule movement evolved in response to the "crisis" provoked by the colonial experience, Fuglestad (1975, 216) adds that the "modern" Baboule manifestation in possession rituals, in contrast to its earlier forms, has an integrative role and aims at mediating disruptions in a rapidly changing society. Such conclusions concerning the status of the movement, its role on the political scene, and its impact on the Nigerien people raises the issues of what is meant by resistance and what criteria we must use to assess the success or, conversely, the failure of a protest movement.

Consider briefly the problem of resistance as a ritualized mode of action. Recent studies (Comaroff, 1985; Lan 1985; Ong 1987; Ranger 1977; and others) have stressed the need to transcend the binary oppositions between matter and mind, secular and sacred or magic, and religion and politics. By focusing on ritual as a signifying practice whose meaningful dimension is not dissociable from its pragmatic impact, social scientists have turned their attention to the creative and expressive practices of minorities and subcultures (Abu-Lughod 1986; Hebdige 1979; Marks 1987; Ong 1987) that until now were confined to the ahistorical margins of history (Wolf 1982). By expanding the horizons of history and politics, they have shown that rituals do not necessarily perpetuate or reassert unchanging cosmologies and social orders but that they are often implicated in the reformation and transformation of the world in which they take place. Hence the cultural value, political impact, and historical implications of so-called resistance movements, be they nationalistic revolutions or humble forms of everyday protest, reside not in some narrowly conceived utilitarian scheme but in the imaginative, creative, and persuasive ways in which they appropriate the world in the face of a shifting landscape of opportunity.

From this perspective, the Hauka movement is not, as Fuglestad (1983, 131) maintains, a failure in the strict utilitarian sense, because even if many of Chibo's followers ended up in prison, their actions and the memories of these actions would have significant implications for the colony as a whole. Though their protest did not give rise to an articulate consciousness about colonial domination, the Baboule were nevertheless effective in forcing the French to reconsider the nature of their relation to their colonized subjects. Following the Baboule protest, the French reorganized the region of Filingue into a new subdivision and appointed a French administrator, thereby stripping the chef de canton of what had previously been his nearly unlimited authority over the local population (Fuglestad 1975, 207). Fuglestad (1983, 132) also notes that the strongholds of the Hauka movement became bastions of the first political party in Niger, the PPN (Parti Progressiste Nigerien), which was instrumental in the emergence of the authoritarian one-party rule of President Diori Hamani at independence.

If one agrees with Ileto (1979 in Comaroff 1985, 262) that "no uprising fails" and takes ritual as an inherently, and inescapably, historical activity, it follows that labeling the Baboule movement "resistance" is not enough to account for its importance and impact in Mawri communities. It is necessary to assess the movement's significance by locating it within its local cultural context instead of interpreting it mainly and primarily as a people's opposition to the external powers that oppress them. Though the arena of resistance provides a privileged perspective for examining the relation between structure, history, consciousness, and practice, one must recognize, along with Marcus (1986), that people's actions and creations are more than a *reaction* to forces impinging on their reality. For instance, Lan's (1985) study of Zimbabwe's revolution falls short of providing a holistic picture of Shona society and history because it focuses too narrowly on rebellion as a monolithic and unambiguous discourse. Intent upon challenging the conventional view that "bullets are more effective than spirits in the struggle against . . . colonizers" (Lewis 1989, 105), Lan locates the revolutionary agenda within the contextual logic of Shona culture to demonstrate the power of collective representations in unifying divergent paradigms and interests and providing the legitimacy guerrillas needed to overthrow the Rhodesian government. But his concern with resistance and political conflict leads him to overlook certain important dimensions of Shona cosmology and history. Hence, by assuming a single symbolic system that applies uniformly to guerrillas, mediums, and peasants, he simplifies the complex reality of Shona people and reduces what might be a plurality of voices to a homogeneous construction of the Shona world.

In tracing the manifold strategies by which subordinate groups insert the terms of their protest into the "public transcript" (Scott 1990), the challenge is to avoid reducing social consciousness to resistance by assuming that colonized subjects are by definition insurgents who reject en bloc the hegemonies they are opposing. This is where the crux of the matter lies. The colonial encounter and the subsequent collision of global markets, marginal economies, modern states, and regional cultures have engendered numerous, locally specific responses whose significance can be assessed neither by general political models of imperialism nor by a narrow focus on the symbolism of resistance. Colonization and the struggle against it are processes of " 'challenge and riposte' often much too complex to be captured in simple equations of domination and resistance" (Comaroff and Comaroff 1991, 5). This presents several implications for the way to examine the Baboule movement as a product of the colonial encounter and its aftermath. First, in analyzing Mawri experience and consciousness of the colonial encounter, one must not unduly systematize the collision of two worlds, as if Mawri society and French colonial culture were both closed systems of unambiguous and uncontested signs and practices. On both sides, cultural meanings and historical values were constantly questioned and transformed. Before one can speak of Baboule practices as a syncretism through which existing signifiers are realigned and disengaged from their former contexts to produce novel significations, one must recognize that the signs and images drawn from local and global cultures by Baboule mediums were themselves bricolages in which the old and the new, and the alien and the familiar, were the object of ongoing, and sometimes differing, interpretations. This means, for instance, that though the colonized subjects anthropologists and historians are studying may have presented a seemingly consensual opposition to an external power, they also experienced differences, dissension, and cleavages within the immediate communities in which they lived.

Second, one cannot reduce the significance of a resistance movement to its narrowly conceived political impact on the local and national scene. The Baboule movement did not overthrow the colonial government, but this does not mean it was ineffective in stirring the imagination of both the dominating and the dominated, or in altering the balance of power. Its efforts to reform the world cannot be accounted for in raw economic or political terms. Nor can these efforts be assessed as a merely overt confrontation of palpable force. For individuals struggling to redefine their field of action in the face of colonial intrusions, the Baboule's seemingly defiant response to French domination was an attempt to gain a practical understanding of, and a symbolic handle over, a rapidly changing universe. In this sense, it was a successful project: though the imaginatively constituted world of the Baboule was never fully realized, it nonetheless endures in the em- bodied memories of Baboule mediums who learn to recreate through their possessed frames the experience of Baboule being-in-the-world, even if, to some extent, the younger generation of spirit devotees is more concerned with contemporary realities than with past history.

Third, to define a protest as political does not imply that its actors have a distinct awareness of the coercive structures they are resist- ing. For the most part, the Baboule movement was neither guided by an explicit agenda nor motivated by an articulate consciousness of domination. Often inchoate, yet effective, Mawri villagers' response to French rule was inspired by a *recognition* out of which "there typi- cally arise forms of experimental practice that are at once techniques of empowerment and the signs of collective representation," as Coma- roff and Comaroff (1991, 31) put it in another context. As the following will demonstrate, the novel forms that Baboule adepts crafted to ap- prehend the cryptic nature of shifting realities were as expressive of the colonized's consciousness as they were constitutive of it.

This leads to the fourth point, namely the complex and multidimen- sional nature of the interplay between center and periphery, coloniz- ing and colonized. Just as people who embrace a new faith or system do not assimilate alien sets of values and practices without reshaping them in meaningful and practical ways, so resisters do not protest against colonial hegemonies or the modern state without simulta- neously acting in complicity with these very powers. Recent studies of colonial societies (Comaroff 1985; Comaroff and Comaroff 1991; Scott 1990; Taussig 1984) have shown that ritualized resistance against a hegemonic order is made up of complex processes through which the oppressed simultaneously attempt to reject and to incorporate dimen- sions of these dominant orders. The Baboule protest shares similari- ties with these so-called utopian movements in which contestation is intermixed with appropriation, and condemnation with identifi- cation. If one follows this line of reasoning, one sees that the Baboule appropriated icons of power they associated with military force and reforged them to serve their own interests and to articulate their local world with broader horizons. While it is very tempting to see the Baboule movement, its aftermath, and its contemporary reenactment on the bori scene as a heroic performance of African might, one must cautiously avoid reading these events in an overtly celebratory light simply because they are couched as a glorious epic. In his provocative analysis on the production of history, Trouillot offers a useful perspective for assessing events that cannot be accepted as they occur and for writing what he calls a "history of the impossible" (1995, 73). Mindful that historical production often involves a process of "silencing the past" and that the re-membering of Baboule history in bori possession is not simply about correcting an oppressive past, I offer the following discussion of the Baboule spirits as an example of the Mawri's imaginative and pragmatic response to rapid structural transformations.

The Baboule: Spirits of Fire, Soldiers of Strength

The focus in this section is on some of the physical characteristics of the Baboule spirits, in order to understand some of the ways in which the movement constituted more than a narrowly conceived display of ritual power. The Baboule distinguished themselves by their tremendous strength. Today when they attend a bori ceremony, they possess their hosts very violently and sometimes even beat each other up with their riding crops and clubs. Kolonel (or Kabral: corporal) Gardi, a tough and imposing officer, can break iron with his hands (Rouch 1989, 81). When taking hold of their devotees, some of his colleagues are able to knock down thick mud walls with their bare fists (Stoller 1989a). Salissou, a middle-aged Baboule medium and Dogondoutchi resident who faithfully attended all the ceremonies held in honor of the soldier spirits, once assured me that when mounted by his bori, he could dig a large pit with his bare hands and feet in the hardest, most barren soil. In Salissou's opinion, even "an old woman [could] quickly dig a hole to bury three big men if she was possessed by her Baboule spirit. And the strongest man [would] not be able to overpower her as long as the spirit was on her."

This uncommon strength exhibited by the Baboule mediums plays a central role in the construction of the mythology that emerged around the movement. No matter how brutal were the disciplinary measures taken by the French, the Baboule adepts were always able to escape unscathed from the most perilous situations. Their alleged victories over the French are still celebrated today in the numerous tales that bori adepts tell each other. When several 'yan bori told me the story of Chibo's imprisonment, their rendition contrasted significantly with the "official" version circulated by historians and anthropologists. According to Rouch's informant, Alhaji Moham-madou (Rouch 1989, 80–81), the events took place as follows: the chief of Filingue sent a message to Niamey to inform the comman-dant de cercle, Commandant Croccichia, that Chibo was provok-ing disorder and dissent among the Hauka throughout the region. Croccichia then ordered that the mediums fomenting the trouble be brought to Niamey. Sixty young men and women were arrested and brought to Croccichia, who locked them up without food for three days and three nights. When they were allowed out of their cells, they danced until they were possessed by the Hauka. Chibo was mounted by Gwamna Malia (Governor "Red Sea"). The commandant had his guards bring him Chibo, and when she stood in front of him, he slapped her. Then he asked her: "Where is the Hauka?" He slapped her again until she finally admitted that there was no Hauka. All the other mediums were treated in the same manner until they all rec-ognized that "there are no Hauka." Then Croccichia sent them back to Filingue, from which Chibo was later spirited away by the local population.

Though the narrator concludes that the Hauka later came back to Filingue and eventually spread throughout the country, the story he tells is one of defeat and humiliation for Chibo and her followers. In the version recounted to me some sixty years later, the evil com-mandant (he was immortalized in the Baboule pantheon as Koman-dan Mugu,[2] the "Commandant Evil") never had a chance to display his power by beating the troublemakers and forcing them to publicly embrace his reality. Soon after they were imprisoned, the Hauka me-diums were possessed by their spirits. In a matter of minutes, they knocked down the walls of their prison and escaped before anyone realized what was happening.[3] This triumphant conclusion of the incident was a powerful demonstration of the force of these spirits, who, not unlike the Doguwa of the precolonial era who protected their devotees from arrows and swords and helped them to escape captivity or slavery, stopped at nothing to save their devotees from starvation and ill treatments at the hands of their colonial oppressors.

But more important perhaps, this version of events is a way of re-affirming the existence of the Hauka/Baboule to the French, who until then did not believe (Croccichia in the "official" version is testimony to the general skepticism of the French), that these powerful spirits existed. For those who witnessed the rise and spread of the Baboule movement, the imprisoned mediums had scored a victory, not simply because they had escaped, but because they had proven that they had indeed been invested with superhuman powers through possession. For how else would the French explain, to themselves or to others, that a handful of prisoners had been able to knock down a thick cement wall armed only with their bare hands?

The Baboule mediums' lasting bond with their spirits also manifested itself as an invulnerability to fire. That is why these mighty creatures were called the Baboule ("spirits of fire") (Fuglestad 1983). When possessed, their hosts would swallow cinders and walk into fires without feeling pain. To this day, a Baboule medium who has consistently nurtured his relationship with his spirit can allegedly walk into a thatched hut that has caught on fire and retrieve its contents without feeling the effect of the flames. During wasani (possession ceremonies), Baboule horses regularly take off their shirts or robes before they grab handfuls of thatch from the roof of the nearest hut. After someone lights the thatch for them with a match or a lighter, they walk around holding the burning bundle right up against their chests with no sign of pain. If the Baboule are invulnerable to fire, the rest of the world is not, as the singer Shatu reminds us in her song for Arna; that is why after they have walked around the possession ground a few times while brandishing their torches, the remainder of the burning grass is often taken away from them lest they inadvertently set fire to a house or harm someone else.

The surprising strength and immunity of the Baboule have long been known to Mawri villagers who witnessed firsthand the exploits of the spirits' first human vessels in the 1920s. As rumors of those alleged exploits spread, soon everyone in the Dogondoutchi region knew what these Baboule mediums were capable of. An old 'dan bori recalled for me that one day—when exactly during the colonial period was not clear—he, along with all those in the village who had Baboule spirits, was summoned by the commandant.[4] The commandant had apparently heard about their special capacities and wanted to test their alleged claims to invincibility. He locked all the young Baboule mediums in a house and had his soldiers set it on fire. All the mothers and fathers witnessing the event started crying and lamenting the deaths of their children, while the rest of the village stared in disbelief at the burning hut. But just as the hut was about to collapse, everyone, including the commandant, saw the youths they had already presumed dead burst out of the blazing structure. None of them had been harmed by the fire. Nor had their clothing been damaged by the flames. By allowing the French to lock them up in a burning house and by willingly submitting to colonial authority, the Baboule successfully passed the test. Moreover, they proved to all who were present that they were stronger than the commandant and his entire army.

Kane, the sarkin bori of Garin Darimey once told me a similar tale demonstrating the powers of the Baboule:

> One day, in Matankari I was summoned to the *sous-préfecture* [of Dogondoutchi] with all the other horses of Baboule. We were all dressed in red, we, the Baboule horses. They made us undress. They burned all the spirits' clothes. They took the robe of Danne [Kane's spirit] in order to burn it. I refused to throw it into the fire and told the guards to do it themselves if they wanted to burn it. I said I didn't want to touch it. They grabbed it, but just as they were going to throw it into the fire, there was lightning. . . . The spirits had sent lightning on the desk of the sous-préfet. The sous-préfet heard the noise and came to see what was happening. Just as he was about to question the guards, a second lightning bolt hit his own house. So he went to get the chef de canton [the sarkin Arewa], who told him that if he burned the clothing of Danne, he [the sous-préfet] would die. There were many horses of Baboule in the sous-préfecture. Together with the musicians, their number reached forty. The next day the sous-préfet let us free and gave us 2,500 francs. The spirits also gave him a fine of two he-goats, a red and a black. He gave them [the goats], but then he got very scared and left for Dòsso. He said he didn't want to stay in Dogondoutchi anymore. Then the bori people asked the spirits to let him work in peace.

This time the Baboule allegedly triumphed over colonial force by demonstrating how spirits controlled lightning and could use it to punish anyone, even the supreme authority of the Dogondoutchi subdivision. It is the only instance I learned of in which the Baboule spirits were described as having mastery over heavenly fire. Prior to the coming of the Zarma spirits at independence, lightning was held to be caused by human *mayu* (sorcerers) who flew in the rain and struck people's houses out of malice. After the Zarma minority gained control of the government and started to overtly favor their own ethnic members, the Zarma or black spirits made their appearance in Arewa to address local populations' marginalization from the Zarma-controlled centers of polity and economy. These spirits are the only ones who fine people who, like the sous-préfet, have been struck by lightning or have had their possessions—a house, a tree, cattle—destroyed by lightning. Perhaps my old friend was creatively rewriting history, embellishing it as he went along with details that made it more meaningful and persuasive.

Whether or not the Baboule actually used lightning to frighten a French administrator, what is significant is that, according to the storyteller, the spirits did gain the consideration of the sous-préfet. In retaliation for the burning of their clothes, the Baboule struck the commanding officer's office and home with heavenly fire. They showed that if the sous-préfet could intimidate local villagers with fire and bullets, they in turn could really frighten him through their mastery over unworldly powers. It is worth mentioning also that by burning the clothing of the spirits, the sous-préfet was (intentionally or not) committing an especially sacrilegious and subversive act. The clothing of one's spirit is the extension and materialized expression of that spirit (Masquelier 1996a). It is so imbued with its owner's essence that people use it to communicate or to reassert their bonds with superhuman powers. Wearing the wrapper of one's spirit is a demonstration of one's veneration for the bori, but, conversely, destroying or getting rid of the clothing amounts to a powerful rejection of its owner. The perpetrator of such a foolish (by bori standards) act never goes unpunished, however, as is attested by the scores of stories that circulate about the retributions incurred by negligent mediums (Masquelier 1996a).

All the stories recalled here focus on the special bodily qualities of the Baboule mediums—their strength, their ability to withstand the effect of fire, and their endurance. This suggests that the Mawri's experience and appropriation of colonial wealth and value were grounded in bodily movement and techniques rather than in verbal representations. The Baboule's collective attempt to grasp the force of an alien hegemony was an embodied rather than objectified knowledge of the colonial experience. This notion of embodiment and bodily praxis will be discussed again because it is central to the way Mawri colonial subjects apprehended their changing world.

Embodied Wealth and Wealthy Bodies:
The Making of Value

In addition to exhibiting an uncanny strength, the Baboule mediums who resisted the colonial administration also allegedly demonstrated an ability to magically produce money. The sarkin bori of Garin Za-roumei recalled that among the Baboule mediums he hung out with in his youth, "there was a horse of Baboule who could vomit gold. And he could make money in coins. [After he publicly made use of his wealth-generating powers,] the chef de canton took all the money and gold." Not only could Baboule devotees magically vomit money, but if they simply raised their open hands, they would receive whatever they needed. Today many have lost these superhuman powers because they are not as faithful to their spirits as their predecessors used to be, I was often told. However, a few Baboule mediums are still able today to produce money magically. Money magic is the specialty of one Baboule, 'dan Mama, who can also transform sand into medicine to be used for a variety of ailments.

'Dan Mama is a regular client of Maria, the prostitute spirit who supports her husband Zahoho with what she earns through her trade. He magically produces the money he gives to Maria in exchange for sexual services. During one ceremony I attended in the compound of a neighbor, a horse mounted by his Baboule spirit picked the leaves of a nearby acacia tree, rubbed them in between his palms, and soon proudly exhibited a crumpled 1,000 CFA franc note for all to see. When I asked why the bill was old and not brand-new, given its recent creation, Yaro, a 'dan bori and regular participant at possession ceremonies, told me that the crinkled appearance of the note was further proof that the medium had not stolen the money from a bank, as other spirits are prone to do when they want to help out their devotees. The crumpled bill did not come from the bank—where smooth and shiny new notes are produced—but had been made from the very leaves the possessed devotee had picked. Like the tree leaves out of which it had been manufactured, the 1,000 CFA franc bill had been weathered by the elements.

Some of the 'yan bori I discussed such matters with thought that all Baboule spirits can make magic before their adepts are initiated into the bori. Before the spirits are "arranged" (that is, before their mediums are initiated), they are wild and untamed, and that is why they help their devotees achieve extraordinary things. Once they are arranged, the spirits become docile and reasonable, because their relationships to particular mediums have become an institutionalized part of bori—which, above all, regulates the behavior of spirits and mediums toward each other. Hence Baboule who have revealed their identities during the initiation no longer steal money to help their devotees survive without having to work. However, before the terrain of action for spirits has been officially circumscribed in bori terms during the initiation, they have much leeway. "Baboule will do whatever they can to help their new hosts," volunteered Yaro, in his efforts to clarify for me the still puzzling connections between Baboule, banks, and shiny new notes. "For this reason," he added, "they [the Baboule] bring banknotes that are brand-new. Some of them take them directly from the bank. That is why sometimes banks go bankrupt and have to go to court. It is actually the spirits who have taken the money that is found missing. Sometimes they return it to the bank. Sometimes people say there's been a thief who committed a crime, but it is the fault of the [Baboule] spirits."

Thus we see how the Baboule spirits who steal from the bank and redistribute the precious cash to impoverished individuals serve to situate rural people in the wider landscape of social and monetary transactions and to mediate between local communities and more global economies. Few Dogondoutchi residents have a precise understanding of banking, and even fewer have a bank account in which they regularly deposit their earnings or from which they withdraw cash. There are no banks in Dogondoutchi. The closest bank is in Dosso, the capital of the *département,* some 150 miles away. While some people are familiar with the process through which civil servants convert their monthly checks into cash, a great majority never deals with anything but hard currency. Through their reports of the Baboule spirits' coming and going between banking institutions and rural communities, 'yan bori are, in effect, crafting novel techniques for symbolically mastering the production and transaction of wealth. Being possessed by spirits who allegedly shower them with money, they are able to gain conceptual control over the elusive centers of wealth that banks are for those who are not prosperous. It is in this respect that the Baboule are like the French colonials whose demonstrations of authority they originally mimicked in an effort to both resist their power and tap into its very source. By allowing their devotees to participate in the production and circulation of value through money magic, Baboule spirits are endowing these individuals with the capacity to ground the largely unknown and uncontrollable process of moneymaking in the more familiar nexus of bori practices. Unlike their predecessors, who, in the colonial era, refused to pay taxes and defied the French authorities, the Baboule of today exhibit more restraint. There are no prison walls to knock down and no commandant to poke fun at. Yet at a time when the Mawri are faced with an escalating gap between increasing monetary needs and decreasing resources, the Baboule's creative potentialities are just as relevant as they were some eighty years ago.

But to return for a moment to the mediums who took part in the movement against colonial forces, one sees that by manifesting the ability to regurgitate gold and produce wealth at will, the Baboule at once promoted and subverted the colonial forms of economy and authority established by the French. Through their attention to the processes involved in the production of money, a medium that was now sorely needed to pay taxes and acquire essential commodities, the Baboule celebrated the centrality of the coin in their newly emerged social order. Vomiting gold and producing money out of tree leaves constituted the Baboule's way of capturing the power of the successful and channeling it beyond the reach of those who sought to destroy their world. Significantly, in the universe of the Baboule, the production and transaction of money did not obey the rigid laws of capitalist logic; instead, they were a measure of the "force"—in terms of both sa'a (luck) and 'karfi (strength)—that was bestowed upon hosts by the spirits in the form of arziki (good fortune, wealth) as a sign of the spirits' goodwill toward their devotees.

Because the production and use of wealth by Baboule mediums was independent of any notion of labor, agricultural production, exchange, or property, it implicitly subverted the forms of economy and polity imposed by the colonial administration. By producing money without having to work or sell the product of their labor, the Baboule defied the French administration, which imposed harsh taxation and forced labor on its colonial subjects. They represent the only instance of a concerted effort among Hausa populations to oppose colonial hegemony and an exploitative tax system. As Schmoll (1991, 280) notes, allusions to taxation are conspicuously absent from bori discourse. Yet we know that the tax burden imposed on the Nigerien population was quite heavy. In fact, tax payments had been steadily increasing before the Baboule resistance broke out, but the colonial government offered little in the way of services or economic opportunities to its taxpayers in exchange for their monetary contributions. Confident that the colony had a bright economic future, the French administration kept imposing heavier taxes to promote the extra-subsistence sector of agricultural production. The rate of the poll tax doubled between 1914 and 1915, and it trebled during the period between 1906 and 1916 (Fuglestad 1983, 83). Furthermore, after 1910, Nigeriens were no longer able to pay their taxes in cowries or in kind. By 1916 onward, the colonial administration insisted that taxes be paid exclusively in francs (Collion 1982, 264).

To make matters worse, the censuses upon which the tax rolls were based were often inflated and did not reflect the huge population drops caused by the massive exodus southward during periods of drought. This meant that those who stayed behind were stuck paying more than their share of taxes, since taxes were levied per capita (Fuglestad 1983, 83–84). It is not surprising then that the Baboule's rejection of the political and economic system put into place by the French should include a refusal to pay taxes. What is particularly significant here is that the Baboule resisted subordination not only by rejecting the French taxation system but also by forging an alternative economy that transcended colonial monetary networks and provided a meaningful alternative to the French extraction of indigenous wealth. In channeling their mimetic ability toward the production of money, the Baboule demonstrated that it was not the medium itself they hated and despised but rather the social system that controlled and authorized the production and circulation of this currency.

Other Bodily Techniques of Empowerment

As noted above, the ostentatious and defiant display of bodily capacities involved in the production of a kind of wealth that was not tied to Western notions of labor, market, and discipline cannot be understood simply as a way of sabotaging colonial hegemony. This subversive bricolage was also a way to concretely articulate new relations of power and production on the most immediate repertoire of signs and symbols, the body. To make sense of the Baboule movement and of the certain kinds of power and agency it entailed, one must focus on the body and the way "embodiment is the existential condition for the possibility" (Csordas 1994, 12) of an alternative world that Baboule mediums still remember and reproduce every time they are possessed. But before proceeding, a few clarifications are needed concerning the way I understand the body and bodiliness in this discussion of Baboule practices.

The body has conventionally been analyzed as a medium for the expression and communication of social categories, relations, and patterns (Douglas 1970). From this perspective, the body is reduced to a thing, an inert ground onto which are projected unchanging social realities. Such a view has long been been criticized by Merleau-Ponty and Dewey (1929), who have shown that the notion of the body as a mere instrument of the mind or of society cannot be reconciled with our experience of the "lived body." Consciousness, Merleau-Ponty tells us (1962, 138–39), is "being-toward-the-thing through the intermediary of the body." In other words, the body is the knowing instrument of our being-in-the-world rather than the unknowing medium for the objectification of the world surrounding it. To quote Merleau-Ponty (1962, 139), "Motility, then, is not, as it were, a handmaid of consciousness, transporting the body to that point in space of which we have formed a representation beforehand. In order that we may be able to move our body toward an object, the object must first exist for it, our body must first exist for it, our body must not belong to the realm of the 'in-itself.'"

The primacy of bodily techniques over verbal expression to effect understanding of, and literally grasp, the world has been emphasized by Jackson (1983, 338), whose analysis of Kuranko body praxis and cognition in initiation rites shows how "bodily movement can do more than words can say." Mindful of Lambek's (1993) insistence that we pay attention to the persistent dialectic of embodiment and objectification at work in social experience, I follow Jackson's fruitful perspective to consider Baboule practices and techniques for producing wealth. The Baboule were able to recognize the alien world of relations introduced by the French because they mimetically appropriated it with, and through, their bodies. To argue along with Jackson that bodily awareness precedes verbal skills and moral representations does not imply that all mental forms can be reduced to bodily praxis.

Rather, we must recognize that "within the unitary field of body-mind-habitus it is possible to intervene and effect changes from any one of these points. By approaching cognition in this manner we are able to enter the domain of words and symbols through the back door, so to speak" (Jackson 1983, 336).

Mawri mediums who were trying to make sense of the superhuman force of the French had no prior model for understanding the processes at work in the production of coins, for instance. The Mawri who used cowries prior to the introduction of francs knew they came from the sea. Metal coins, on the other hand, were introduced ready-made in Mawri society. To the colonial subject, they were not embedded in a historically meaningful network of production, circulation, and transaction. In other words, villagers had no knowledge of the coins' origin. Nor did they know by which techniques they were produced and what process was required to accumulate riches. They could only grasp intuitively that which they knew so little about, and this recognition process entailed engendering through the body a sense of mastery, a sense that they knew because they felt it with their bodies.

By vomiting money or producing it through magic, Baboule mediums provided a model that explained not only how coins were made but also what the superhuman powers of the French consisted of. By showing that they could make money thanks to their privileged status as mediums for the spirits, the Baboule demonstrated that the French's arziki could only emanate from supernatural powers. Using their corporeality to "realiz[e] and manifes[t] the 'outer world' " (Devisch 1985, 401), Baboule adepts capitalized on the transformative and creative capacities of their bodies to elucidate the elusive processes at work in the making of money. Moneymaking became a "naturalized" process just like eating and defecating, but it remained an extraordinary capacity with which only Baboule mediums were endowed. By experiencing the world through their bodies (Devisch 1985, 401), Baboule mediums utilized their corporeality as both an object of representation and a medium for constituting the world not in an intellectual but rather in an experiential way. One could say, paraphrasing Kramer (1993, 253), that when faced with the task of reducing the diversity of a foreign culture's visible manifestation to its essential nature, the Baboule chose suggestive, intuitively grasped images that captured the seeming irrationality of monetary production so characteristic of modernity.

The power of these images was such that the mediums' own imagination was in turn seized by the "money machines" they had created (253). Alleged reports or testimonies of mediums vomiting money were more powerful than any claims to an intellectual understanding of what went on in the production of cash and gold because, to quote Merleau-Ponty once more, the mediums' bodies were "permanently stationed before things in order to perceive them and, conversely, appearances [were] always enveloped for [them] in a certain bodily attitude. In so far, therefore, as [they knew] the relation of appearances to the kinesthetic situation, this [was] not in virtue of any law, or in terms of any formula, but to the extent that [they had] bod[ies], and that through [these] bod[ies], [they were] at grips with the world" (1962, 303). By focusing on this kinesthetic model of moneymaking, I do not mean that the Baboule spirits' devotees had a distinctive way of experiencing and constituting the world through special modes of body use. Mawri understanding is often embedded in praxis—that is, enveloped in bodily attitudes—rather than enunciated through words, concepts, or formulas. Spirit possession, in general, is a mode of understanding and acting upon the world that is based on bodily practice rather than verbal performance. The meanings communicated through such embodied performances are rarely fully articulated, but they are hardly less eloquent for being more corporeal than textual. As is perhaps best illustrated by the brilliant jump-cut made in the film Les maîtres fous (in which the cascading plumes of the governor's hat become the focus of Rouch's camera immediately after a close-up on the broken egg running on the statue of that same governor during a possession ceremony), the evocative power of entirely wordless messages can be such that they require no explanation.

For the young men and women who became possessed by Baboule spirits, getting a grasp of the colonial situation involved imitating the bodily movements and attitudes of the men who had conquered the central Sudan through military force and who would subsequently administer the newly founded colony of Niger. In this preliterate, pre-Islamic society where educating oneself and learning were mostly based on direct observation and imitation (see Jackson 1983, 337; Mauss 1936), coming to an understanding of the colonials' power and learning to be strong like them was thus a matter of using one's body the way the French did. Imitating the gait of army men, learning to march in a fast, stiff, and upright manner and to salute one's superiors became bodily techniques for grasping the sense of the French's activities and learning to inhabit their alien world. In other words, learning the process through which to become wealthy and powerful like the French did not involve mastering formulas and articulating words—though shouting orders in French during possession was part of the practical tasks Baboule mediums learned in their efforts to create their own source of authority. Rather, it meant acquiring an embodied knowledge, a sort of bodily awareness—of their colonial masters' production of power and riches—which was beyond words and verbal understanding.

Most of the Baboule spirits were soldiers, and this is why their mediums were supposed to wear khaki uniforms and carry wooden guns or riding crops. They learned to respond to the drill of their commanding officers and to salute them. Yet other Baboule were administrators, sitting behind desks: like the French models they imitated, their power resided in the words they inscribed on paper. Literacy for the colonized subject manifested itself as an ability to see and know things that could not be apprehended by usual means. Mastering this skill in order to get at the truth was a way to harness the somewhat mysterious power of their colonial oppressors, thereby capturing their means of producing wealth and value. Comaroff (1985, 203) has shown how illiterate South Africans have appropriated the word in their ritual healing of the afflicted body to regain control over a rapidly changing world. I suggest that this is what was happening in the Baboule movement—but with one main difference. Here, making sense of the mysteries of literacy and drawing upon the power of the word were not intellectual tasks. Put differently, they were not accomplished by gaining mastery over foreign signs on the conceptual and linguistic terrain. Nor was it a process that involved the fetishization of the written word, as is sometimes the case among bori devotees of Muslim spirits who pressure their hosts to learn the Arabic script. Rather, this appropriation of bureaucratic authority involved sitting at a desk and positioning one's body as if it was resting in a chair in front of a table, even though there never were any tables or chairs.[5]

Here again one sees the importance of kinesthetic learning. It was the pattern of body use that created the furniture and engendered the images associated with certain bodily postures. By creating the desk and the chair through their bodily interactions with these imagined objects, Baboule hosts made present to their audiences and to themselves what had been noticeably absent. In so doing, they created and asserted their own bureaucratic authority. It is not hard to imagine how intimidating an interview with a French colonial sitting at his desk must have been for people who had no furniture, except for the mats they slept on and the short stools women sat on to cook. Today many people have acquired beds, and women stock brightly colored enamel pots in large cupboards. Chairs, on the other hand, are still associated with high status and the educated elite, and while families generally own one or two, they are mostly reserved for important guests and patrons. During possession ceremonies, for instance, only bori chiefs and high dignitaries may be seated in chairs. Everyone else, even the healer supervising the ceremony, sits on mats spread in a circle around the ceremonial grounds where 'yan bori dance before some are possessed by their spirits. In their efforts to appropriate the power of their colonial masters, Baboule mediums thus fashioned a corporeal awareness of the media they perceived as suffused with this very potency. For people whose understanding of the world was based neither on a distinction between process and product, nor on that between mind and matter, the tables and chairs they created did not simply represent authority and literacy; they were these things inasmuch as they seemed to bring on special might to those who used them to sit or to write on.

The same processes of corporeal articulation seem to have been at work in the creation of a Baboule spirit who goes by the name of Mai Mota. Mai Mota—which means "owner of a vehicle" and refers here to a lorry driver—drives a truck. He holds his hands in front of him, palms open to simulate the bright lights of the truck he is supposedly driving.[6] By forging the persona of Mai Mota, the mediums are redirecting to themselves neither the moneymaking capacities of the French nor their power of literacy. They are dealing with a different but related form of superhuman potency that hinges on novel notions of mobility and speed tied to the technological wonders of *motoci* (cars). Perhaps we should not be surprised to find that in their quest for power, Baboule mediums have used their corporeality to become trucklike in order to symbolically travel at high speed. As I have noted elsewhere (Masquelier 1992), automobiles are one of the most concrete and widely recognized expressions of wealth in contemporary Niger. For the young male mediums who, like so many other youths in Dogondoutchi and elsewhere, aspire to making a living by driving a bush taxi or a lorry, motor vehicles are not only emblematic of socioeconomic success, at a time when being "modern" often hinges on velocity and mobility. Through their association with physical rapidity and movement, cars, or, in this case, trucks, embody the very qualities that, together with brute strength, make the Baboule so frighteningly effective in the eyes of their devotees.

Renewing Ties, Making History

In their pragmatic attempts to capitalize on the colonizing culture's production of wealth, power, and value, the Baboule mediums mimetically appropriated the technologies (weaponry, money, the alphabet) they associated with French 'karfi. Unifying diverse signifiers on the Baboule personae or imbuing familiar signs with new signification was their way to reassert a sense of identity and viability that had been shattered by the French conquest. I am thinking here particularly of the blow to Mawri polity dealt by an administration that took for granted the distinction between profane authority and sacred power and that bolstered the sarkin Arewa at the expense of the sarauniya—priestess of the Azna—whose role as a mediator between the spirits and the people was particularly crucial. To insure the success of colonial policies, the French legitimized the *sarakuna* (chiefs) as mediators between the colonial powers and their colonized subjects while ignoring the tight interconnection between the temporal and the spiritual that inhered in Mawri society and polity. Stripped of their military and economic independence, and retaining only a few judicial responsibilities, Mawri chiefs became mere puppets in the hands of the French administration (see Crowder 1968; Collion 1982). Invested with what the French saw as legitimate authority and familiar with customary law, they became responsible for carrying out such unpopular measures as the enforcement of cash-crop cultivation, the collection of taxes, and the recruitment of workers and soldiers. Thus where local rulers, whose worldly powers hinged on nurturing their relations to the spirits, formerly constituted the epicenter of their social, political, and religious world, they now frequently became the most hated members of their communities.

In the eyes of his subjects, the sarki's authority and legitimacy were traditionally rooted in the alliance established years ago between the sarauniya and the baura's mythical ancestors and the spirits. With the advent of colonization, chiefs who had customarily been chosen from the ruling lineages by a divinatory process involving the spirits, and which together with the ritual of enthronement officially sanctioned their sacred authority, were now elected by French administrators, often according to criteria of convenience and expediency that threatened the fragile balance of power between the three poles of Mawri polity: the Sarauniya, the Baura, and the Mawri chieftaincy. By establishing their own networks of power relations and drawing an unbridgeable distinction between religion and politics, the French did more than remove the ruler's control over political processes. They, in effect, loosened the bonds between human and spiritual agencies that the local population saw as essential to its survival and reproduction.

People's good fortune and well-being hinged on maintaining a balanced and nurturing relationship with the spirits either through the intermediary of the Baura or Sarauniya acting on behalf of the entire society, via the priests of specific lineages, or by personally propitiating a particular spirit. The spirits preside over people's destinies, and nothing productive can be accomplished prior to having secured their consent or support. Conversely, spirits need people to provide them with regular sustenance. As previously shown, this symbiotic relationship between people and spirits was closely tied to and reinforced by the wars that people fought in precolonial times. By providing booty in the form of grains, cattle, and slaves, war—even as it promoted instability, insecurity and famine—was a means of subsistence for poor peasants and a way for power-hungry chiefs to acquire riches and recognition.

Since no military victory could be achieved without the help and protection of the spirits, the relative ease with which the French conquered the territory of Niger must have convinced the villagers of Arewa that these foreign invaders possessed an uncommon strength.[7] In Mawri communities, the infamous Voulet-Chanoine expedition is especially remembered for the atrocities it committed in Northern Arewa. The French column led by Voulet and Chanoine was welcomed by the sarkin Arewa, who saw in these new conquerors eventual allies against his own enemies, but the archers of the sarauniya put up a vigorous resistance in Lougou. Their opposition was crushed by the superior force of French troops. Many of Lougou's inhabitants were subsequently massacred and the village, like many others in the area, burned to the ground. In the eyes of local villagers, this appalling victory and the subsequent colonial domination of local populations were a powerful demonstration that the power of the French was superior even to their own, despite the support they enjoyed from their Doguwa spirits. It should be recalled that in the social imaginary, Doguwa had led warriors and chiefs to victory throughout the precolonial era. How could the villagers of Lougou and elsewhere explain to themselves that they had been overcome by these foreigners? Did they come to the conclusion that such extraordinary force and superiority could only have originated in an alliance with very powerful spirits? The precise answers to these questions will never be known. What is more certain, however, is that the Baboule movement constituted an attempt to capture the might of the successful so as to regain some control over an increasingly fragmented and contradictory world.

By becoming invulnerable to fire and vomiting money at will, Baboule mediums proved to those who believed their stories that they were equal, if not superior, to the French. If they were not able to erase from the collective memory the humiliating defeats suffered at the hands of ruthless French conquerors, they could at least mediate the devastating impact of colonial rule by constructing and circulating positive scenarios of their encounters with "evil" French commandants. Through their compelling performances, Baboule mediums promoted an awareness of the forces of history and the structures of domination. In their efforts to recreate their sense of self in a Eurocentric world while probing the mysteries of Western productions of value, they selectively highlighted certain events while obliterating others to produce a version of the "facts" that actively contested conventional history.

Not unlike the 1791–1804 epic of liberation that promotes among Haitian elites a positive image of blackness quite useful in a white-dominated world (Trouillot 1995), the Baboule mediums' account of the colonial encounter offers a version of history that can only be assessed by attending to the means and process through which the colonized "heroes" recorded their alleged exploits for posterity. When historical narratives "convey plots that are unthinkable in the world within which these narratives take place," at the same time that they celebrate a people's resistance to an oppressive power, analyzing them without undue romanticism is a challenging task (1995, 73). I have focused here on the processes of embodiment that structured the Baboule mediums' experience of the colonial Other to illuminate how these Mawri peasants demonstrated their control over foreign notions of value, power, and agency, and how, more than half a century later, they remember their youthful exploits.

Today, most of the younger mediums feel little connection with the glorious past of the older bori generation. They know the Baboule stories, of course, at least enough to be able to function in the social world of bori relations, and their own possession performances regularly concretize and sustain the memory of these events for the wider community. Yet the fearful figures who brandish a handful of burning thatch or hurl orders at their platoons on the possession grounds speak more to Mawri concerns with present-day realities than to their understanding of an ever more distant past. Through them, one understands that while bori is a powerful vehicle for embodying and remembering history, it is not restricted to preserving an idealized past bearing no connection with the material reality of everyday life. Bori is, above all, a way of living in and adjusting to the world of today. For contemporary 'yan bori, the contested authority is no longer a colonial administration but the ever expanding community of Muslims who have taken control over local markets and trade. And while devotees no longer vomit gold at will to fill the chests of the Baboule rebels, they are nonetheless trying to regain access to the resources that now flow almost exclusively into Muslim coffers.

Chapter 6

Taking Hold of the *Kasuwa*

THE RITUAL ECONOMY OF BORI IN THE MARKET

The official picture of what does and does not constitute ideological orthodoxy is the officially constructed picture, molding and remolding the "past" to provide an effective backdrop for the revealed truth of the present. In this process the invention of tradition is just as important as the invention of antitradition. —Ioan M. Lewis, *Religion in Context.*

On Fridays, the peasant becomes trader. —Jean-Michel Guillon, *Étude économique d'un milieu urbain sous-développé*

DURING MY FIELDWORK, I routinely heard people make striking comments about the kasuwa (market). One statement in particular puzzled me. I had been told once that "those who go to the market are not afraid." I often spent several hours walking among the stalls of the weekly market but could never quite see what made the kasuwa such a threatening place. When I asked a couple of friends what dangers one should fear from the market, they shrugged their shoulders and answered that they were not afraid of anything but Allah. Others told me that since so many strangers came to the market, you could never know about the people with whom you spoke. What they meant was that the old woman who had just sold you a liter of peanut oil might actually be a witch or a spirit in disguise, and not an old woman at all. In the absence of further clarifications, I assumed that there were no other reasons for remaining on guard when entering the marketplace.

But I also knew that men (especially those who professed to be devout Muslims) would often strictly prohibit their young wives from going to the kasuwa, preferring to entrust the task of purchasing the weekly household necessities to their unmarried daughters or their mothers. Some men would even do the marketing themselves rather than allow any women of the household to venture into the marketplace. It seemed that a husband's fear of having another man cast an eye on, or even seduce, his wife could hardly justify the deep-seated yet unspoken fear I felt pervading Mawri attitudes regarding the market. If seduction was the primary reason for women to avoid the kasuwa, any public place where young married women were not supposed to be seen should have been perceived as equally dangerous. Yet that was usually not the case. Moreover, in my experience, men would express reservations about going to the market almost as often as the women. As the months went by, I became more involved in bori activities and put aside my investigation of the mysteries that the market held. In June 1989, however, an incident occurred in the area that shed some light on the dangers of marketing.

On the first Friday of that month, the weekly market of Dogondoutchi, traditionally held on the west side of town, was transferred south, to the outskirts of the town. The newly appointed mayor, eager to make some innovative changes, had decided that the closer proximity of the market to the highway would improve the economic prospects of the area.[1] Holding the market at a place along the highway linking all the major cities of southern Niger would undoubtedly increase the flow of prospective merchants and customers and facilitate access to, and transportation of, locally unavailable or perishable goods.

Such a major transformation in the spatial organization of the town did not meet with everybody's approval, however. Added to the inconvenience of having to walk an extra half-mile to reach the market, proximity to the highway implied a whole array of new dangers. People were especially concerned with the rise in theft and robbery that they perceived as the inevitable outcome of having to venture by the *kwalta* (tarmac). The weeks preceding the event nevertheless witnessed the feverish activity of carpenters busy setting up stalls in the newly apportioned market space. I myself was eagerly awaiting what I thought would be an important celebration that a great many people would attend. But as I was sharing my excitement with my neighbor, Halima, on the eve of the opening day, she warned me not to go to the market the next day, because, she said, evil things happened the first time a kasuwa was held at a new site. When I attempted to press the issue further, Halima just responded that she really did not know much about it and that I should ask my bori friends.

The next day, still resolved to attend the kasuwa in spite of (or maybe because of) Halima's intriguing warning, I made my way to my friend Mamou's house to see if her eldest daughter, Rabi, would come with me. Even though Mamou was one of my most valuable bori friends, I had not consciously gone to her on my way to the market to ask about why I should follow Halima's suggestion and not visit the new ka-suwa. Upon learning of my intentions, Mamou became very alarmed. I should not go to the new marketplace under any circumstances, she warned me. When I asked her why she and Halima were both trying to prevent me from accomplishing such a routine task, she seemed to be at a loss for an answer. After I insisted that attending such an important event was crucial to my overall research project, Mamou could only repeat that it would be very dangerous for me to go there that day. She then added that she could not tell me anything more at this point, but that if I promised not to go, she could perhaps explain later what had been so threatening about the kasuwa on that particu-lar day. In spite of my intense curiosity, I agreed to forgo the day's main attraction and limit my activities to visits and interviews.

It was not until the next day that I learned what had motivated Mamou's and Halima's mysterious warnings. That morning, right after sunrise, Halima told me she had just been informed that the day before three people from the nearby village of Kieche had died in an auto crash soon after leaving the Dogondoutchi marketplace. Their deaths were not accidental, I was told. The Kieche villagers had been the victims of a bloodthirsty spirit whom I came to know as the Doguwa of the market. Although most spirits belonging to the Doguwa family bear proper names, I was never able to find out what this Doguwa was called. Either out of fear or ignorance, nobody could tell me whether or not she had a name.[2]

In Arewa each market has its Doguwa. And each time a market is transferred to a new site, the spirit of that market must be propiti-ated by an offering of blood so that commerce will thrive. People say that a new market requires the shedding of blood. Theoretically, the sarkin Arewa should provide the sacrificial ox for the *kafin ka-suwa* (establishment of the market). I have often been told that in the past, Doguwa spirits would not associate with mere commoners, but only with chiefs. Only chiefs were rich enough to be able to sat-isfy the voracious appetites of these fearful iskoki. Legend has it that human blood was the Doguwa's favorite sustenance. Local chiefs thus kept slaves whom they would regularly sacrifice to appease the spirit.

Nowadays, the ritual killing of an ox would fulfill the Doguwa's request for blood and insure the prosperity of the market. A thriving market was, in fact, a sign that the spirit was satisfied and had agreed to protect the kasuwa and its people.

There was a concomitant assumption that on the first market day, the Doguwa would kill a young man and a young woman, or a budurwa (unmarried girl) and a *samari* (unmarried boy), regardless of whether or not an ox was sacrificed. Why the spirit needed victims of this sort, no one could tell me. It seemed that the Doguwa had been ignored for so long that no one could trace the logic behind such requirements. If the spirit did not kill two such persons, the market would not "take" (become a place of prosperity). Individuals who belonged to these social categories hence ran the risk of becoming the spirit's next victims if they ventured to enter the new marketplace on the first day of its sitting. This meant that I could have been the Doguwa's prey had I not been warned about the potential danger.

My friends' fears were heightened by the fact that no offerings had been made to the spirit. In contrast to the 'yan bori who were often scorned by the local administration, the *malamai* (Muslim clerics) had powerful connections with town officials. Eager to demonstrate their loyalty to the representatives of Islam and to promote their own agenda, the mayor and the *mai gari* (customary chief of town) had thus agreed to pay the malamai for their services and forgo the traditional sacrifice of an ox. Thus, on the eve of the market day, the imam of Dogondoutchi led his assembly of followers to prayer and called on Allah to make the new market prosperous. After this ritual was accomplished, the 'yan bori swarmed the marketplace to hold a ritual of their own. They called on the spirits whose support they saw as essential for the success of the town's enterprise, but they had no ox to offer the Doguwa. Every one of them was bitter and angry that local officials had ignored their claims to a part of the money that had been turned over to the malamai. Besides seeing their prospects of getting free meat ruined, bori leaders felt insulted by the fact that their role and responsibilities in promoting the market's prosperity had been so grossly overlooked. In their eyes, it was a dramatic sign that times had changed irretrievably.

Were the spirits angry as well for not having been offered a sacrificial ox? Nobody could say. But the fact that all the mutanen daji declined to possess their devotees during the possession ceremony that day was taken by some as an inauspicious sign of the evils that were yet to come. It did not take long for these premonitions to be realized. The sun was still high up in the sky when, the following day, the three unfortunate passengers of a Peugeot 404 had a fatal accident on their way back from the market. Among them were a young man and a young woman.

The following Friday the tragedy was, if not forgotten, at least no longer the main topic of gossip in local households. If, the week before, the newly established market had had a limited attendance due to people's fears of the Doguwa's requirements, in its second week it presented, in the opinion of onlookers, all the signs of becoming a prosperous institution. Muslim leaders had been vehemently denying that the deaths of the three travelers had been caused by anything else than the will of Allah. The 'yan bori, on the other hand, were eager to erase from their memory the painful humiliation they had just suffered on the eve of the first market day. For although they had held a possession ritual and paid the musicians to play the spirits' music, no money had been available to perform the required sacrifice. As if Muslim subversive tactics and their open disapproval of bori practices were not enough, no spirits had deigned to mount their devotees that evening. At the same time, 'yan bori were reluctant to acknowledge that their defeat implied the abandonment of yet another non-Muslim communal ritual. To them and to all those who, in spite of their adherence to Islam, believed in the power of the iskoki, the fatal car crash was an unmistakable confirmation of the Doguwa's potency and of her fierce temper. It therefore provided bori devotees and sympathizers with an effective weapon with which to challenge the supremacy of Muslim authority. For in the eyes of many, the imam's prayers, no matter how convincing, had clearly been of no avail against the Doguwa's anger.

A number of studies (Arnould 1982, 1984; Cohen 1969a; Grégoire 1992; Hill 1969; Piault 1971; Works 1976) have discussed the importance of trade and markets in Hausa society. Yet except for Schmoll's (1991) insightful description of the kasuwa's spiritual dimension, those who have explained the institution of kasuwa in relation to pre-Islamic religious practices have done so only in passing (Nicolas 1966, 1975; Smith 1962), usually reducing the market to a field of socioeconomic forces. Overplaying the narrowly conceived economic dimension of this cultural enterprise at the expense of the immaterial and the richly symbolic has obscured what the market has come to signify for Mawri like the 'yan bori who routinely feel alienated from the centers of institutional wealth and power. In particular, such an approach ignores how the 'yan bori tap into their stock of traditional concepts and historical imagery to accommodate the new demands of the market economy and to mediate their understanding of wider social forces they cannot clearly pinpoint, much less control.[3] Besides alerting me to the crucial role played by the spirits in the seemingly mundane sphere of commerce, the market incident convinced me that a very real battle was being waged in the kasuwa between 'yan bori and Muslims. The fight involved no overt confrontation of palpable power but found expression in an "argument of images" (Fernandez 1982) and practices whose impact on the collective imagination remained long after the Doguwa's victims were buried. Taking this argument as a point of departure, this chapter explores how the 'yan bori's ongoing efforts to retain control of the town's moral and material prosperity is motivated by an urgency to preserve the rapidly disappearing symbolic chart that anchored indigenous history and identity in the immediate landscape.

Contemporary Mawri Markets

Writing almost forty years ago about Hausa markets in northern Nigeria, Smith (1962, 305) noted:

> Even today, when population or other changes lead the authorities to establish a new village and village-chief, one of his first tasks is to promote the development of a regular market at his headquarters. If this fails and another settlement in his area has a viable market, the chief will go to live there. Likewise, when the capital of an old village area declines and the market dies, the chief will select a new headquarters where the market is likely to flourish. I can recall no Hausa community having an officially recognized chief which lacked a market at its center, even if it meets but once a week.

Such a description could well apply to Arewa markets, which constitute a fundamental institution of Mawri economy and polity. The majority of Mawri rely on wet-season cultivation of millet, guinea corn, ground nuts, and beans, and domestic pastoralism—raising goats, sheep, and chickens—for the bulk of their subsistence. Yet trading is an important, and probably the most common, occupation of Mawri men during the dry season. Though their operation does not match that of their urban counterpart in the Nigerien capital or in northern Nigeria, rural Mawri are nevertheless "market venturers" (Wall 1988, 37). Just about everybody engages in trade, however limited the scale and the variety of goods sold. The incessant exchange of coins, banknotes, and kola nuts in greeting procedures exemplifies the deeply rooted transactionalism of Mawri society (1988).

Although children hawk cooked food throughout the village from dawn until dusk and petty traders set up tables covered with cigarettes, soap, candy, kerosene, and kola nuts in busy streets, the bulk of the transactions takes place at the market. Unlike informal gatherings of petty traders who generally lack official recognition and control,[4] the kasuwa meets on an officially designated and ritually apportioned space on certain days of the week. City markets are centrally located, while in rural communities, markets are erected on the edge of the village next to the road to permit access by car or truck and to allow for expansion if necessary. Urban markets usually meet on a daily basis; in contrast, rural markets assemble once a week. It is in fact the frequency—as well as size—of its market that determines whether a settlement will be classified as urban or rural, Smith argued (1965, 128). In rural areas, days of the week are identified by the name of the town where a market is held that day. Around Dogondoutchi, the most important day of the week is Friday, because it is the day of this town's market which many villagers from northern Arewa attend. In such contexts, it is not unusual to meet women who have walked a dozen miles simply to procure a little salt, some cassava, or a few morsels of meat (Guillon 1967, 118). That day, the town as a whole is busy, not simply the marketplace. Many visitors take advantage of market day to participate in the communal prayer at the central mosque. As noted earlier, those who take an active part in bori will attend a scheduled ceremony after they have paid a visit to the market. Others may just wander through the crowded streets to greet friends and visit their kin.

The layout of a Mawri market is simple yet orderly: rows of open-sided sheds covered with thatch provide shelter for the merchants who assemble themselves by commodities. Hence the grain sellers are grouped together. The potters sit in one place, the mat makers in another. Butchers remain together, and so do bokaye (healers), enamelware traders, and women who sell cooked food. While young boys and girls walk around hawking processed food, homemade candies, or kola nuts, Fulani women settle on the edge of the market to sell their milk and butter. The kasuwa is a vital institution because it is where commodities may be exchanged and valuable cash obtained, but its significance for local populations goes far beyond its economic role. That markets are lively and alive is not simply attributable to their being privileged arenas for material transactions. In fact, Piault goes so far as to say that the striking thing about Mawri markets "is not the movement of goods but of persons; it is the exchanges between the people, rather than the buying and selling of goods which character- izes the market-place" (1971, 300, my translation). Furthermore, the exchange of goods, the transformation of value, and the circulation of people in and out and within the market depend primarily on the support of the spirits who patronize it. Without the backing of super- human powers, the kasuwa literally withers and dies. Markets have a life of their own. When they thrive, they are the prime example and indicator of the movement, vitality, and flow that characterize health in the body and society (Schmoll 1991, 148).

This does not mean that markets only bring good things. Indeed, the widespread reaction of doubt and uncertainty that followed the announcement of a new site for the weekly kasuwa in Dogondoutchi is a good measure of the extent to which markets are perceived as mixed blessings. On the one hand, the influx of visitors, goods, and in- formation generally enhances local exchange and may even stimulate the diversification of formal and informal economies. In addition, the emergence of a merchant class may give rise, as is the case in neighbor- ing Maradi and to a lesser extent in Dogondoutchi as well, to a large network of patron-client relationships (Grégoire 1992).[5] On the other hand, external competition may pit small artisans and local producers against the modern sector. In Arewa and other regions of Niger, the sales of imported, mass-produced goods has forced some professions out of the market: the arrival of plastic shoes in massive quantities thus disrupted the shoemakers, whose control over their access to leather had previously forestalled any competition (137). Ironically, the best clients of these shoemakers today are 'yan bori who must pur- chase traditional leather sandals for their spirits. Weavers and calabash carvers were similarly hurt when cheaper, foreign cloth and enamel- ware flooded the local markets (137). While some Mawri might have mixed feelings about market forces they cannot control but on which they depend—for instance, when the price of certain goods essential to their own production fluctuates over the course of the year—there is nonetheless a widespread sense that marketing is the surest way to arziki (good fortune, wealth).

According to the philosophy surrounding arziki, life is nothing but a game of chance; some individuals, being more fortunate, have more chance of winning than others (Nicolas 1964). Given the widespread assumption that spirits intervene in people's lives to increase or decrease their arziki, securing the protection of iskoki will ensure an individual's chances of staying, or becoming, healthy and prosperous. Although agricultural production is the main source of income for Dogondoutchi residents, its unreliability—due to frequent droughts and devastation by crickets—has turned trade into the only avenue to arziki for those who do not practice a craft or work as civil servants. According to my Mawri friends, engaging in trade is, if not the best, at least one way to enhance one's economic position and prestige. The fact that most, if not all, of the rich and prosperous alhazai are merchants testifies to the opportunities associated with commerce in people's minds. Without demeaning the importance of faith, one might say that the title alhaji symbolizes economic success more than it does religious piety: the pilgrimage to Mecca is very often the first major expense of any successful merchant. At the same time, because life is a lottery and because success in any human enterprise, whether it be a commercial transaction, marriage plans, or the taking of an exam, is still often credited to the favorable intervention of a spirit, it is only after having promised allegiance to a bori that a person can achieve wealth and prosperity through trade.

While spirit devotees and bori sympathizers unanimously recognize that the establishment and maintenance of a successful market entails fostering a relationship with the spirits, many in Muslim circles would rather forget previously secured alliances with iskoki and rely simply on God's will to make markets prosper. Because Muslims have been largely successful in taking control of the terms of trade, the bori membership (made up mostly of small artisans, healers, and petty traders) has been progressively estranged from the central loci of power and wealth. Yet the 'yan bori are hardly powerless. Their power resides less in the manipulation of concrete quantums of force than in the creation and transformation of images of wealth and potency.

Effective yet elusive, this form of power is not easily located and circumscribed in time or space. As the incident recalled here suggests, one must recognize, along with Foucault (1977), that power can be creative and productive if one wants to account for the social and historical relevance of bori.

The power of bori thus consists of the creative energy focused through ritual and the imagined community of spirits. Drawing on the notions that the instrumental value of bori symbols cannot be abstracted from their meaningful dimension and that ritual is always a conversation about the dynamic world that contains it, the following discussion focuses on the relevance of bori representations that, like those of the Doguwa, reassert the centrality of a minority that has often been silenced by Islam. Though largely alienated from the tangible structures of wealth and authority, bori devotees have successfully managed to channel their own forms of potency through the ritual manipulation of empowering signs and techniques. In attempting to reassert their independence from the hegemony of Islam, 'yan bori are in effect reworking the bases of a moral economy that rejects the rules and principles laid down by Muslim clerics and merchants. Their protest against Muslim structures of economic, religious, and political control remains largely implicit, but the bori images they use are nevertheless a powerful vehicle of collective consciousness. Because they are rooted in indigenous cosmologies that Muslim practices have not managed to erode, these images become an instrument of coercion in the hands of a marginalized faction seeking to transform alienating structures of control.

The Emergence of a Market Economy

Twentieth-century Arewa experienced major socioeconomic and political transformations following the imposition of peace, the abolition of slavery, the colonial imposition of taxation and cash cropping, and the emergence of Islam. With its emphasis on the solidarity uniting the believers and its association with commerce, Islam has had a transformative impact on the religious life of local communities, even as it appeared to sweep away the indigenous rituals in its path. In the process of reconfiguring themselves in the midst of rapid social, economic, and political upheavals, both Islam and bori have been involved in a mutual "struggle for possession of the sign" (Hebdidge 1979, 17). While Islam thus taps into the sacred instrumentalities of bori signs to adapt itself to the local cultural milieu, bori has recontextualized Islamic temporalities, images, and values, thus acquiring a cosmopolitan dimension it previous lacked. Despite bori's active participation in the creation of a moral order, there is a widespread sense in bori circles as well as among certain nominally Muslim individuals that the Islamic expansion witnessed by Arewa has been unidimensionally destructive and detrimental.

Simply put, the progress of Islam is perceived by many as a direct outcome of the suppression of war and a symptom of the society's malaise. De Latour Dejean's (1982, 264) informant touched on a crucial point when he declared that "Islam has spread because of peace. War necessitated recourse to the spirits." The advent of peace is thus experienced as one of the many evils brought about by colonialism through the disintegration of the socio-religious structures that guaranteed survival in times of hardship. The improvement of communications and the expansion of commerce within, and outside of, pacified Arewa conversely facilitated the expansion of Islam: those Mawri who perceived the potentials of trade converted to the Muslim faith to legitimize their activity and earn the trust and consideration of the French, who, after World War II, generally favored Islam. For those who remained faithful to the "old" ways, colonial peace only implied that to retain or regain control over the ritual centers of power and access to material resources, they would have to wage a new kind of war: they were now confronted with moral and material forces they could not clearly identify, much less fight with conventional weapons. In this sense, peace was evil.

With the penetration of money and the introduction of such new notions as private property, individuality, and free enterprise, members of society became increasingly self-oriented, instead of relying on the pooled resources of the extended family unit. According to Sutter, "collective ties, based on reciprocal responsibilities centered on the extended family production and consumption unit, have become progressively replaced by social relationships mediated through money. The family as an economic unit has become less important in supplying the needs of the individual, who has become more isolated and responsible for his own subsistence" (1979, 1). Sutter further notes that "it [was] the need for money that push[ed] young men, and even family heads, into working as salaried laborers and into selling land" (1979, 1). Groundnut production and commercialization, which the French had encouraged by imposing a head tax payable in cash (Pehaut 1970, 64; Baier 1980), particularly hastened the breakdown of the extended-family farming unit and led to the privatization of landholdings. When increasingly fragmented landholdings could no longer sustain them as farmers, men turned to migration as a means of earning the necessary cash and relieving the demand made on the food supply of their households (de Latour Dejean 1980; Guillas 1983).

Islam contributed to the increasing individualization and monetar-ization of the economy by favoring the notions of private property and social differentiation, and by encouraging the accumulation of wealth (de Latour Dejean 1975, 200). The Koranic message thus ex-panded at the expense of pre-Islamic religion because it was more compatible with market individualism. But this is only part of the picture. It should be recalled that Islam was used by indigenous elites eager to demarcate themselves from French colonials, and to promote a sense of national unity among Nigerien masses at independence. De-spite its egalitarian message and its emphasis on the concept of a com-munity of faithful, Islam has never succeeded in abolishing all ethnic, cultural, and social differences. Partly because of its prominent role in the politics of the first two governments of independent Niger, it has become tied to national hegemonies and class domination.

The spirits were thus neglected. They allegedly ceased to intervene in human existence, except to cause diseases, poverty, and degradation in retribution for people's forgetfulness. Incurable afflictions and re-peated misfortunes are often taken to be the spirits' way of reminding people of their heritage, whether they be Muslims or 'yan bori. While people see their struggles as originating in French domination and in the profound changes that have come in its wake, they nevertheless impute a great part of the responsibility for such a state of affairs to their own lack of fidelity and honesty. "It is our own fault," they say, "if things have become so bad." This widespread sense that it is ulti-mately people themselves who "ruined everything" is shared mostly by 'yan bori, who can thus put the blame on those who have strayed from the path of the ancestors, that is, the Muslims. Yet one finds some followers of the Prophet who also believe that the troubles they are experiencing stem from their disregard of traditions and the values of their forefathers. They may have ostentatiously adopted the Muslim way of life, but they remain interiorly convinced that the spirits are responsible for some of the misfortunes and injustices that befall Muslim converts. As already shown, some see no contradictions in attending both communal prayers at the local mosque and possession ceremonies, but others, who cannot reconcile these two divergent orientations, hide their ties to the bori in order to stress their Muslim identity.

In a sense, it is as if the bori priests see their role as having shifted from a focus on prospective propitiation to one of retrospective amelioration. Punishment is dispensed by the spirits who, by denying an individual wealth and good fortune, are thought to strip him of all he possesses in the form of money, land, offspring, and social prestige. A formerly prosperous individual lacking arziki will not only lose all the traces of his fortune but will also have to abandon all hope of enhancing his economic standing, social status, and the enjoyment derived from being rich and wealthy (Nicolas 1964, 105). On the other hand, a person, who is endowed with arziki, thanks to having nurtured his relationship with spirits (for pious Muslims, only God dispenses arziki to those who deserve it, and listening to the teachings of the Koran is the only way to achieve prosperity), must risk everything in the game of chance.[6] Besides card games and the lottery, the best way for an individual to try his luck and test the power of his arziki is to go to the market.

The market is now a fundamental institution of Mawri society, but it was not so in precolonial times. On the eve of colonization, Mawri society had a limited orientation toward trade. A local administrator reported the following in 1913 (Belle 1913):

Non-existent before our occupation, commerce in this sector only started to develop at the end of 1908 with the transport of telegraphic materials. Though the transport of such materials required a considerable effort from them at the beginning, indigenes have now realized what profits can be gained from such activities. The transport service has been an economic and political benefit for the region. It has stirred a people which was previously unwilling to move away from the corner of earth to where it confined itself. It has given villagers the desire for acquiring possessions, and the idea of engaging in trade. By convincing Mawri and Azna that they could work, it has rendered them bold enough to speculate.

With the imposition of peace and the introduction of money through the levying of taxes, the indigenous war economy was progressively replaced by a market economy. When taxes were first introduced in 1914, they were paid in centimes and cowries.[7] Cowries were suppressed in 1920 and replaced in 1921 by silver coins (République du Niger n.d.). This region, in which twenty years before no foreign merchant would have ventured for fear of being attacked, robbed, or captured as a slave, began to welcome Nigerien merchants and foreign traders (Belle 1913). Many tradesmen who left for Madaoua, Niamey, or Gaya exchanged parts, or all, of their salaries in these towns to acquire goods that could be sold on Arewa markets. Others, who traveled to Nigeria, would stock up on cloth, wrappers, and turbans that they would then resell at an inflated price in Dogondoutchi (1913). Belle noted that as early as the 1910s "the traffic of Dioulas is heavy; they bring back from Nigeria, sometimes from Dahomey: wrappers, *boubous* (Muslim robes), turbans, British or German knick-knacks, showy cloth manufactured in Europe, needles, thread, pearls, copper or glass bracelets, etc. Kola nuts, which used to be in scarce supply and solely for chiefs, are now plentiful, markets have been created and are flourishing. . . . A commercial movement has been created, it can only grow" (1913). By that time, six weekly markets had been created in the villages of Matankari, Dogondoutchi, Doumega, Tibiri, Lokoko, and Lougou; they gave signs of continued growth, affluence, and prosperity (1913).

By 1941 the number of markets in the subdivision of Dogondoutchi had risen to nine (République du Niger 1941), providing further evidence of the growing role of money in the local economy. The main commodities traded in the markets of Fadama and Nassarawa were millet, wrappers, cattle, sheep and poultry, and goods imported from Nigeria. In the markets of Dogondoutchi, Matankari, Bagaji, and Sukukutane, villagers could sell or purchase millet, cattle, skins, and salt. At the lesser markets of Ligido, Kilia, and Bougou, the main goods were millet and wrappers (1913). Aside from animals and millet, one could acquire locally grown cotton, tobacco, cloth, peanut oil, butter, eggs, milk, and locally dyed wrappers. The money obtained from the sale of cash crops also enabled villagers to purchase the Western goods that eventually replaced locally produced items. Kola nuts, white cloth, matches, colored cloth, sugar, and *chechia* (Sudanese hats) figured most prominently among the imported goods available at local markets (République du Niger 1941). As people were forced to sell their labor or a portion of their harvest or herds to take care of tax requirements, more coins began to be used in transactions and barter gradually died out (de Latour Dejean 1980, 110).

In a geographic area already subject to periodic natural disasters, the new colonial economy deepened the peasant's vulnerability to climactic changes and price fluctuations, and increased dependence on cash-crop revenues. Encouraged to buy manufactured goods of generally poor quality at high prices in return for the sale of unprocessed products grown or collected locally, villagers were continually indebted. Having spent large sums of money in marriage negotiations, they then had to feed their wives and children and provide them with nutritious food, clothes, medicines, and comfortable housing, all of which—save the millet and guinea corn harvested from the land—had to be purchased with cash. In their attempts to surmount the contradictions of the capitalist economy and meet the never-ending monetary needs of their families, they would inevitably fall back on the market to find the necessary cash (de Latour Dejean 1980, 124–25). This was the beginning of a vicious circle from which the peasants could never disentangle themselves.

Take, for instance, the case of a villager who derived his subsistence from field cultivation. Sowing more peanuts (at the expense of his millet field acreage [8]) to get cash meant that the man would be faced with a shortage of millet—the food staple—before the next harvest. If he hired himself out as a laborer to buy extra millet with his wages, he would wind up having little or no time to tend his own field (de Latour Dejean 1980). To make ends meet, he would often be forced to sell parts of his livestock, an option that resolved short-term demands for cash, but since animals were the currency for bride-price, also prompted greater long-term needs for money. The last recourse available to a peasant faced with the fearful prospects of ruin and famine was the sale of his land or labor and, possibly, emigration. These were commonly chosen alternatives as more and more households found it increasingly difficult to sustain themselves solely from their agricultural revenues.

Faced with increasing monetary obligations and decreasing, or unstable, revenues, peasants were obliged to resort to the market, even if the market absorbed not simply surpluses but also what was indispensable to the cyclical reproduction of labor and resources. The market thus became a trap, to paraphrase de Latour Dejean (1980, 124). Added to the fact that in this new economy money had become the indispensable instrument of exchange without which one could not survive, let alone prosper, was the problem of the limited amount of currency available in the colony. This only made the need for money more acute. On one occasion, it also deeply upset the entire economic structure erected by the French: according to a colonial report of 1913, the rarity of bronze coins in the Territory induced some villagers to desert the market and revert to barter (110). No further information is available on the incident, so it is difficult to say whether this return to barter was the only possible course of action. Besides raising the question of African resistance to new economic policies, the incident shows how the market was perceived by villagers. For them the market was indeed a trap, and money was the embodiment of what they could not have and the source of their many problems. Solving their immediate difficulties implied abandoning the market as the main locus of trade and exchanging goods and services without using cash as an intermediary.

For those who were unable to benefit from the move toward a capitalist economy, money was such a symbol of the alienation from traditional values and of the uncertainties of the future that it was feared as much as it was coveted. I was told that up to a few years ago, those who would hire themselves out as day laborers often insisted upon being paid in grain rather than in cash. In these people's minds, millet would go a long way, whereas money literally burned holes in their pockets. The comments of de Latour Dejean's informant expresses these fears very vividly: "We prefer millet to money. Money gets spent right away; millet is kept in our gullet" (140). As people became increasingly controlled by the market economy and helpless in the face of adversity, there was the sense that money only made the poor poorer and the rich richer. Such a feeling still prevails in Arewa today as money has invaded virtually every area of Mawri life. It was not only nostalgia for the "good old days" that impelled an eighty-year-old man to observe that "before the Whites, we had no money and everybody was rich. Now, we have money but everybody is poor."

Yet while these various constructions of an idealized past highlight the very real difficulties peasants are facing in these times of neman ku'di (the search for money), paradoxically they also conceal the fact that some Mawri make substantial profits and that for them, at least,

the system "works." I have spoken of the expansion of monetary relations and the diminution of bori power largely in terms of the vic-
timization of certain Mawri so as to address the subjective perspective
of 'yan bori who decry the waning of pre-Islamic tradition and, by
extension, morality. For many spirit mediums, money—a necessary
evil—aptly exemplifies the corruption of moral values and relations
(Masquelier 1999a). At the same time, even the most disillusioned are
busily engaged in moneymaking activities. My old neighbor, who
nostalgically reminisced about a past devoid of money and poverty,
participated like everyone else in the daily reproduction of the very
system he was denouncing: he was known in the neighborhood for
manufacturing protective amulets, which he sold for a modest sum
to subsidize his kola nut addiction. As significant and sincere as these
discourses on disempowerment may be, it is therefore useful to remind ourselves that the experience of money and markets has been
diverse and uneven across Mawri society. From this perspective, the
conspicuous wealth of Muslim elites becomes both a measure of their
ambition in the lifelong search for arziki and a convenient target of
recrimination for those who perceive the success of Islam as a fundamental loss.

Flux and Forces of the Market

Earning money, by any means and at any cost, has nevertheless become a major concern of the Mawri, whether they be rich or poor,
peasants or civil servants, of humble or aristocratic descent. If in 1913
a handful of villagers decided to eliminate the market and its chief
instrument, money, in an attempt to regain control over the means of
production, there is no sign today that their momentary withdrawal
from the channels of monetary transactions had any historical impact.
The kasuwa is now a thriving and popular institution in Arewa.

   Villagers and merchants from nearby or faraway communities attend
the market not simply to sell or buy goods but to meet friends and
relatives and to renew acquaintances. In fact, the need to make a purchase is irrelevant to whether or not someone will go to the market.
One goes to the market to see and to be seen. Men parade in their
most elegant gowns and women show off their newest outfits. The
market is the place to hear news and gossip and to discuss marriage

plans. It is the place where new fashions and trends are started. It is the "public" sphere par excellence. This is why no secluded women may ever attend the market.[9] For the same reason, even husbands who do not keep their wives in *kubli* (seclusion) are sometimes reluctant to let them enter the kasuwa. In the past, chiefs would inform their subjects of their general orders or important decisions in the market (Smith 1962, 309). Village and neighborhood chiefs in charge of tax collection often visit the market for the sole purpose of collecting the money from family heads or to remind them of their monetary obligations.

The establishment and growth of a market is not simply a matter of allocating a space, laying out stalls, and inviting everyone to come. Attendance at the market may fluctuate dramatically; when everyone might expect a market to be flooded by traders, customers, and onlookers, it could nonetheless fail to attract anyone. Market performance is so unpredictable that people say that "a river, a chief and a market are too capricious to prognosticate about them" (see Abraham 1962, 532). So capricious are markets, in fact, that no matter how experienced, cunning, and calculating traders might be, there is no telling what the future of a market will be. For a market's success essentially depends upon the arziki of the community founding it. According to the 'yan bori, this arziki is contingent upon the power and goodwill of the spirits (Nicolas 1975, 390). For this very reason, choosing the site of a new market should never be conducted haphazardly. A divinatory rite should be held in order to determine the most auspicious location for a market. For should the site chosen for a new market be on the customary path of a spirit or too close to the stone or tree in which an iska dwells, the kasuwa will never become a successful enterprise (Nicolas 1975, 391). If the spirits like the place for the new market, they will make it thrive, but in the manner of a river—sometimes full and flowing, sometimes dry and empty.[10]

What the proverb further suggests is that markets, as already noted, have a vitality of their own. Rather than being merely a "thing," in a reified sense, or a space of interaction and transaction, markets are animated with life and are personified. In the same manner that bodies are animated by the flow of substances within their boundaries, and in and out of their orifices, markets are endowed with life—that is, subject to the flux of people, the exchange of goods, and the circulation of news and values (see Schmoll 1991, 145).

But perhaps more important, the vitality and, by extension, the health of a market derive from the spirits who protect and animate it by their presence. Spirits are thought to enjoy attending people's markets. Although they have their own markets, where they can sell and buy goods, they never miss an opportunity to mingle among a crowd of humans for the sole pleasure of contemplating piles of colorful enamel bowls or of smelling the fragrant aroma of ripe mangoes and guavas. Spirits are attracted by fragrant smells and beauty,[11] and they are said to be curious, envious, and sometimes greedy, just like humans. They are also attracted by the blood that butchers spill in the slaughter area and that they drink. As Mary Smith's informant Baba recounts: "The market is the people's, but it belongs to the spirits also. If you give them alms, you please their hearts, then they settle down and cause men to come with their loads, they draw people and draw people—lots of people" (1955, 220). It is thus the sum of all these relations, material and spiritual, that gives *rai* (life) to a market. Baba's depiction of the kasuwa was recorded almost fifty years ago, yet it could well pertain to a contemporary market, judging from Schmoll's (1991, 144–48) account of the "life and death" of the Djirataoua market. This market, created in 1924, originally thrived and soon became a major center of exchange and transaction in the Maradi area. One of Schmoll's informants said that "when the market was alive people came from everywhere, and each (person) benefited from the other" (145). Another villager told Schmoll that he had seen an individual (from her account we must presume that he was the butcher who was entrusted with the responsibility of protecting the market) bury medicines in the local kasuwa so that the spirits "would bring lots of people to the market, for the market IS the gathering of [people]" (146). According to a third individual to whom Schmoll spoke, the prosperity of the market was due to the chief's mother, who visited every "strong" market in the area, took their spirits, and brought them back to the Djirataoua kasuwa (146). The market prospered for many years and then it died, principally because as it slowly lost its strength and arziki, the spirits withdrew their power and support from the village. People became afraid to come to Djirataoua, the spirits ceased to attend the kasuwa and infuse it with vitality, and the previously steady flow of goods turned into a mere trickle until it stopped altogether, leaving the market empty, silent, and lifeless.

Though I never heard of individuals stealing spirits from other markets to start a new kasuwa in Arewa, I found a concern for the liveliness of the market that resonated with the comments of Djirataoua residents. In the eyes of local 'yan bori, propitiating spirits before the first market day is essential to the prosperity of the establishment. In the past, bori ceremonies, whose purpose was to invite one or several iskoki to settle at the marketplace, were held with the tacit, if not complete, approval of town officials. If Muslim authorities interfered and prevented the propitiation of benevolent spirits, disastrous consequences would generally follow. According Baba (Smith 1955):

> There was also no market at Old Giwa [Nigeria]. The market refused to take. The bori adepts danced for fourteen days, and it looked as if the market might settle, but since there was no water, it did not take. . . . They [the spirits] said that they were to be given a black bull and black goats and black cloth, but Fagaci [the District Head, a Muslim] would not give them their things. After that they were here, they went on living here, but the market wouldn't go. They didn't go anywhere else, they were here, they just put a stop to the market. (188–89)

Thus not every market takes, but if and when it does, it becomes (like a bori possession ground) a hot place of fertile transactions and transformations. Since the market is so full of spirits (it is where they are said to often reside when they are not in the bush or participating in a bori ritual), it is also a potentially dangerous place. There are evil as well as benevolent spirits who stroll in the kasuwa in search of human company. These iskoki may take on the appearance of a harmless animal, such as a donkey, a horse, or a goat, to trick humans. They can also make themselves look like somebody a person is familiar with, such as one's sister or one's neighbor, in order to communicate with this person. More often than not, they look like pretty Fulani women, pacing the market alone or walking in pairs. One should be especially suspicious of these creatures, I was told, because their beauty is equaled only by their cruelty and fierceness. The only way to find out whether or not they are real women is to take a look at their feet: these female spirits have a camel's, a donkey's, or a horse's hooves in place of feet.

While an encounter with a spirit can be beneficial and fruitful, meeting a spirit can also have tragic consequences if the iska turns out to have evil intentions. Many dreadful incidents, which resulted in a person's death or illness and involved an evil spirit, were said to have originated in the marketplace where the victim had gone to buy a calabash or some tomatoes. This is why one should not go to the market without protection. It is thought that those who have one or several spirits never enter a marketplace without them. Thanks to her spirits, a woman will know what dangers await her, and she will see through strangers to find out what the intentions of their spirits are. Moreover, just as one does not walk into the arena of a bori ceremony without having washed with, or ingested, powerful medicines, one never enters a market without being protected by medicines, for the openness of the kasuwa, like a lack of bodily closure or the permeability of villages, implies, and leads to, vulnerability. Some medicines act as a protection against evil spirits, blows, metallic weapons, and the like, while the aim of others is to insure that the people who have used them will be liked by everybody, and therefore will be offered a profitable exchange for every transaction they undertake.

Besides the evil spirits who visit the marketplace, one must also fear the presence of mean old women who practice medicine only to hurt and gain power over individuals. Men in particular should be especially careful not to leave any hair and nail clippings on the ground of the kasuwa if they have resorted to the services of a barber. After everyone has gone home, these old hags are thought to roam the marketplace in search of forgotten hair and nail clippings with which they will prepare potent and harmful medicines. When the medicine takes effect, the man to whom the shaved hair belonged may, for instance, become impotent.

The dangers of markets do not reside solely in the fact that one may cross the path of a dangerous spirit or become the victim of an evil healer; markets are inherently dangerous by virtue of their unboundedness. Usually located on the periphery of a town or a village, they are not, like houses, enclosed within walls.[12] Because there are no boundaries to limit access, and no restrictions as to the identity of visitors, anybody is free to walk in and out of the kasuwa. Although the pre-Islamic installation of a market aims at ritually circumscribing a space that will be protected from external evil forces and will be where benevolent agencies converge (Nicolas 1966), there is no telling who enters the kasuwa and under what disguise. Markets must be "open" and free, but this very condition promotes potential instability. So, "to eat the market" (that is, to engage in profitable transactions, whether one is selling or buying), one must be "open" to intrusion and risk. But one must not be so open that one gets consumed, or literally "eaten" by the market.

Part of the attraction that a market holds for Mawri seems to reside in these very dangers. Just as in the past, battles, wealth, and fame could only be achieved by taking risks and courting death, so in the market one must be willing to expose oneself to certain threats in order to conduct trade and hope to attain prosperity (by enhancing or altering one's person). Visiting the market is seen as a risky yet potentially rewarding venture if one knows when and how to seize opportunities. In this respect, the market is not unlike the bush, described earlier as a wild and dangerous place. Like the healer looking for medicinal plants, like the hunter tracking guinea hens, the market venturer must be both brave and alert to potential perils as he prepares to enter the kasuwa. One way to enhance one's chances of becoming prosperous, of course, is to obtain supernatural powers. This is achieved by spending one or several nights within the deserted marketplace in order to meet the spirits and become infused with their potency (Nicolas 1975, 345–46). Since, as the proverb goes, *kasuwa bai gidan kowa ba* (a market isn't anybody's home), people who are found wandering in the market at odd hours are generally suspected of "messing with the spirits." Marketplaces, like cemeteries, threshing grounds, and garbage dumps, are avoided outside of neatly circumscribed times and activities, for they are situated on the community's spatial and ritual boundaries (Douglas 1966). The dangers of these places also stem from the fact that they are arenas for the dissolution of material categories and boundaries; it is the margins of persons, goods, and elements that fade and disintegrate on spots such as graveyards, threshing grounds, and rubbish piles.

In spite or perhaps because of its inherent dangers, the market is thought of as the place where "things happen."[13] It is where wealth, in the form of goods, animals, people, spirits, and information, converges in a seemingly inexhaustible flux. For Mawri, the concept of the market is synonymous with abundance and opportunity.[14] If in precolonial times war was the sole avenue to riches and social advancement, now the market has taken on that role for many unschooled Mawri. There is a saying that speaks to that view: "Anything one sees in the chief's house can be found in the market" (Whitting 1940, 112). Some individuals seem to set up a trade business with almost no capital and end up rich a few years later. Ironically enough, most of them have turned their backs on the spirits to embrace Islam and its social values. Yet they (like everyone else) conceive of the market as a place where one competes in order to get the best deal. First, people compete against the buyers or sellers with whom they transact. For trade is achieved through barter: no transaction worthy of the name is successfully made without long negotiations consisting of offers and counteroffers. The prospective buyer usually initiates the process by inquiring as to the price of an item. He will be quoted a price that is much above what he would consider a reasonable bargain and will counter by offering an invariably low price, only to hear the reply "*Albarka!*" (literally, "blessing"; in this context, "no, thanks"). The seller and his client will keep on haggling until they reach a price with which both parties are comfortable. They strike a deal, and if the buyer is especially happy with his purchase, he may give the seller a small sum of money—small, that is, in relation to the price of his acquisition—to express his satisfaction. The seller may reciprocate by offering a small gift—an orange if he sells fruits, a plastic bowl if his client has bought a set of enamelware—as a token of his gratitude and appreciation. Thus trading involves maximizing one's position and competing for profit. The goal is to fight for better prices without alienating those against whom one is fighting.

Second, people compete against the market itself in a more metaphorical sense. Those who come back home after striking good deals will say that they have "eaten" the market (they have figuratively bested their opponent, the kasuwa), just as they would an enemy. In contrast, those who have "lost" money in transactions will feel that the market has "eaten" them (they have been consumed by a superior force). In this sense, too, markets can be traps for those who are not quick enough to seize opportunities and shrewd enough to strike good deals. Yet, as in battles, only in trying their luck can individuals find out if they are blessed with arziki—whether bestowed by God or by the spirits. And if one is not successful this time, there is always the hope one will have better luck on the next market day.

The Market as a Muslim Institution

Trade in Doutchi is mainly in the hands of Muslims. In fact, as several studies have pointed out (Lovejoy 1971; Works 1976), for the rest of Hausaland the development of trade went hand in hand with the spread of Islam.[15] Trade provided the means for the spread of Islam because adherence to the Muslim faith worked to maintain ties between dispersed trade settlements as well as to enable merchants to feel part of an "imagined community" and to experience a "consciousness of connectedness" (Anderson 1985, 57). Those who converted to Islam knew they were instantly becoming part of the great brotherhood of the faithful that was united against pagans and infidels. Even far away from home, traders were able to establish contacts and conduct transactions with strangers simply on the basis of their common faith. Lovejoy (1971, 543) notes, for instance, that because Islam provided a status system (based on education and religious piety), it furnished a religious rationalization for the hospitality that landlords extended to passing strangers out of economic motives. And Cohen (1969a) has stressed the role of Islam in consolidating communities of Hausa migrants who, in Yoruba towns, face economic and political rivalry from their host society.

Conversely, Islam paved the way for commerce by providing a religious rationalization for economic motivations and success, just as the Protestant ethic provided the hardworking and successful European capitalists with an ethical justification. Like the Protestant ethic, Islamization represented a marked shift away from what it constructed as a parochial past: it facilitated the region's opening to the vaster world by locking local history into the framework of a universal time scale and linking it to world geography (see Anderson 1985). It enabled the new converts to communicate at a distance, to record the passage of the years, and to learn about the history of past centuries or faraway lands (Goody 1971, 460). It also subjected them to moral judgment by an external, monotheistic standard of values (Hiskett 1984, 81). This had important implications for the way newly converted Muslims dealt with the increasing monetarization of their economy in colonial and postcolonial Arewa. Besides the fact that French colonial policies eventually reflected an overriding preference for Islam, Muslims seemed to be more advantageously adapting to the newly emerged cultural order, and also seemed better equipped than 'yan bori to deal with a nascent capitalism.

Today the social veneer provided by Islam is a crucial element in successful trading (see Grégoire 1992). Only those who openly profess allegiance to the Prophet will see doors open up before them; only those who enjoy visibility and conspicuously parade at the mosque for the Friday prayer will be able to establish the network of relationships

needed to practice commerce on a large scale. It is through ostentatious displays of piety and sobriety that one may claim membership
in the universal and egalitarian brotherhood that, in theory at least,
recognizes no tribal, racial, or geographical cleavages. As Hausa merchants striving to maintain social and commercial ties far away from
their home bases realized long before the nineteenth-century Islamic
jihads, becoming a Muslim can be purely a matter of wearing Islamic
garb, taking a Muslim name, and professing some knowledge of Arabic. By conforming to Islamic custom, adopting Islamic values, and
following an Islamic schedule, one can soon earn the prestige and recognition needed to enter the world of trade.

It is not surprising then that all the successful traders in Doutchi are
Muslims. More often than not, these *attajirai* (wealthy merchants) have
accomplished the pilgrimage to Mecca and are very respected and
powerful members of their community.[16] For their fellow Muslims,
their achievements — highlighted by the trip to Mecca — are a measure
of their commercial abilities and a sign of God's will. In the eyes of
the 'yan bori, however, their material success stems from their faithful allegiance to their lineage's spirits. Just as rich and powerful Muslim leaders allegedly owe their arziki to a spirit whom they secretly
propitiate, so wealthy merchants are thought to regularly sacrifice to
their spirits in the privacy of their home to ensure their continued
prosperity. The annual commemoration of Abraham's sacrifice is also
interpreted by some of the 'yan bori as another disguised attempt on
the part of the Muslim community to propitiate the spirits. Although
I never witnessed or heard Muslims admit to such practices, for the
'yan bori they exemplify the proverbial bad faith of the Muslims. It is
common knowledge within the bori community that the Prophet's
followers lie about their dealings with the spirits and hide behind the
deceptive facade of Islamic conventions.

Despite popular perceptions that commerce is the sole road to riches
for those who have no political connections and little education, not
everyone who trades ends up rich and respectable. In fact, wealthy
merchants remain a minority among the multitude of petty traders
who resell the goods they have bought from a wholesaler for a nearly
insignificant profit. The increasing commoditization of their economy has forced many farmers to fall back on trade as a secondary occupation during the dry season in an attempt to supplement their meager agricultural revenues. Studies (Arnould in Horowitz et al. 1983)

conducted in the eastern part of Hausaland have shown, for instance, that three-fourths of the traders interviewed in markets were cultivators or herders seeking to earn cash through market transactions. Like their counterparts in Dogondoutchi, they held limited inventories and usually bought and resold goods in the same market in a single day (Horowitz et al. 1983). Whether they were selling cigarettes, kerosene, kola nuts, candies, or laundry soap, their profit margins were usually narrow. Because farming is no longer an adequate means of livelihood, many Mawri go to the market to sell as much as to purchase, in the hope that their (often speculative) transactions will bring the much needed cash. It is as if "more and more part-time traders [were] competing for a decreasing share of the limited 'surplus' in the country" (1983).

Bori in the Market and Market in the Bori

The apparent bad faith of the Muslims, who openly condemn the rituals that the 'yan bori suspect them of secretly resorting to, only exacerbates the mounting tension between the Islamic and the 'yan bori communities. For if Muslims are thought to have a monopoly over the market, the 'yan bori would like to retain unlimited control over the realm of spirits. With the growing disappearance of once-popular pre-Islamic rituals in the Dogondoutchi area, the 'yan bori see the extent of their authority and the sphere of their power diminishing progressively. In their attempt to retain what they still have and to regain control over what was once theirs, they blame the Muslims for all the evils of this world. Hence the source of profit to which they have had little access, the market, became identified by the 'yan bori as the source of misfortunes after the Muslims denied them the ritual powers that they once held over the institution. Because the new market was a triumphant symbol of Islamic hegemony rather than an emblem of unity and cooperation between opposed factions, the tragedy associated with its opening provided bori devotees with the perfect occasion to brandish the fearful images of a not-so-distant past and shake up people's admiration for Muslim ways. By conjuring up the powerful vision of the Doguwa, which spoke to all Mawri and resonated with the forgotten images and symbols of the precolonial past in all its glorious and legendary dimensions, the 'yan bori

were also attempting to rework the historical roots of their predicament and locate the cause of their misfortunes (of which the death
of three innocent villagers was only a facet) in the practices of those
who sought to overpower them.

Reclaiming the marketplace as a "place of, and for, the spirits" was
also a way to redefine the kasuwa location as part of the moral landscape in which were encoded so many beliefs and practices relating
to bori. I have already noted how the rocks, trees, and caves inhab-
ited by spirits have long been perceived as the tangible objectifications of the interconnections between the world of humans and the
world of the iskoki. By periodically redefining this moral topography through offerings at the various sites, villagers also symbolically
re-anchored their identity and history. Like the caves, anthills, and
mounts that had been imaginatively appropriated by early settlers to
domesticate and historicize the local landscape (see Ranger 1987 for
a similar case among the Shona), the market has become part of this
mystical geography. For the 'yan bori, denying the Doguwa of the
market her ritual offering essentially amounted to relinquishing one's
identity and consciousness of the past, because it meant letting Muslims erase yet another sacred site in the landscape and redraw a new
moral topography that would only bear the imprint of Islam. This
reconfiguration of the local landscape started with the advent of colonialism as French engineers redesigned the topography of Arewa to
build roads and connect towns and administrative headquarters. As
shown elsewhere (Masquelier 1992, 1993), the new network of roads
unfurling on the land partially eclipsed a prior order of meaning and
exchange based on people's symbiotic relations with spirits.

Cast out from what they see as the main avenue to economic prosperity, the 'yan bori have attempted to change the real world and
recreate their own inherent source of wealth through the ritual manipulation of signs, objects, and relations capable of channeling riches
and potency. A recent practice of bori adepts involves building houses
for spirits who are allegedly Zarma. Spirits are more likely to remain
with their devotees and to help them become (or remain) healthy
and prosperous if they can be physically anchored to the land. In the
past, this anchoring was done by erecting one or two stones in a place
chosen by the spirit himself. These altars sometimes took the shape
of a hango (circle of stones), with one opening to the west through
which 'yan bori entered the "house" of the spirit. They were modeled

after the old funerary sites that the Gubawa used to erect in their communities. Just as they did it in their own homes, 'yan bori would cover the area enclosed by the stones with fine sand to provide comfort for the spirit.

Some spirits had their homes in the village, inside or just outside the compound where their devotees lived, while others, who were considered wild and dangerous, had their altars in the bush, away from the human community. Ritually apportioning a site that the spirit could call home for as long as she wished, and usually long after the stone's first keeper had died, insured her fixity both in space and time. Anybody could go to the house of this spirit to request her intervention in times of need or desperation. The spirit's devotee periodically held a possession ceremony at the stone site and made offerings of blood to the bori by slaughtering animals on the altar. The stone was both a timeless reminder of the spirit's presence and a marker of the finitude of human lives: seven days after a 'dan bori died, the stone would be dug up and replanted in the ground upside down to warn the spirit that one cycle had been brought to an end and that another was about to begin if she chose a new adept among the descendants of the deceased.

The last decade or so has seen the emergence of a new kind of house for spirits whose appearance in Arewa coincides with the end of the colonial period. This is how Zumbaye described the changing architectural practices of bori adepts: "Before, there were no houses for the spirits. Only stones. People in the past considered the stone as a place of reunion for the spirits [and people]. Now it is the Zarma spirits who have started this new practice of constructing spirit houses. . . . And now many people [Muslims] have abandoned the hango because no one needs them anymore." The new houses constructed for the Zarma spirits look just like, and are the same size as, the thatch-roofed huts in which many people themselves are living, except that they are the object of an elaborate and costly ritual during which the bori is invited to take possession of his new home. From then on, anybody in need of that spirit's assistance is free to come to the hut and ask for the spirit's support, usually promising payment in the form of a piece of cloth or an animal after the request is granted. One of the most significant aspects of the ritual marking of the hut as the bori's home involves filling a minuscule earthenware cooking pot with a long series of ingredients before burying it on the right-hand side of the hut entrance. Over the pot is erected the sacrificial stone on which animals are ritually slaughtered to propitiate or thank the spirit.

What bori specialists use to fill the little cooking pot varies from one village to the next, but it usually includes tufts of cotton, which stand for clothing and which are supposed to elicit gifts of cloth from those who come to the house of the spirit in search for help. There is also grain, which represents the food the spirit's medium will receive from those who are thankful to his bori. A handful of sand from an anthill, referred to as uwa yawa ("the mother of many"), is often included. As seen previously, the anthill, where a crucial part of initiation into the bori takes place, is a major symbol of fertility and abundance for the Mawri. The visions of growth and fertility associated with water are also contained in the pot by including a handful of sand from a riverbed, usually that of the Niger, which flows in the extreme southwestern part of the country.

Each time an ingredient is placed in the cooking pot, the bori specialist supervising the ritual whispers the words that will define the purpose of this performance while imbuing the object with the necessary potency. By assembling together these potent elements and by describing how each symbolizes a type of arziki or stands for a spatial landmark of ritual importance, the bori priest is weaving together familiar images to create a powerful instrument of wealth. Juxtaposed with these symbols of prosperity is the image of the market that evokes notions of plenty and draws forth visions of unlimited commodities: among the ingredients that are always included are seven handfuls of sand collected from seven different marketplaces.[17] During one ceremony I attended, while he poured the sand of various markets into the cooking pot, the priest supervising the ritual whispered the following:

the soil of the market will be poured (a market will be set up)
anyone who comes with his things
when the market is over
he goes home
the thing that we want
anyone who comes to the house of spirits
whether man or woman
the one who comes with good intentions
whether it be night or day

may he receive that which he wants
this is what one wants for a market
the soil of the market
the soil that they will put in the cooking pot
the soil of the market
the one who comes to look for prosperity
may he receive it in a flash
that which he came to look for at the house of spirits
may he receive in a flash

Formulas for infusing power into the substances buried in the earthenware vary from one practitioner to the next, but no matter how varied, all these prayers have the same aim. I would suggest that by concentrating these images of abundance, wealth, and growth into a cooking pot that is then buried to the right of the doorway, the priest is actually bringing the market into the bori devotee's house or perhaps making that house into an icon of a market. Through this condensation of symbolic wealth, he is recreating and redefining a source of prosperity for the 'dan bori. For the burial of the pot is thought to ensure that the 'dan bori who owns the house will never be wanting. Following the ritual, there should be a never-ending stream of "customers" who, in return for the spirit's protection or forgiveness, will amply reward the devotee with money, clothes, animals, or the bori's favorite perfume.

The simple presence of the bori in the house attracts all those who need to communicate their problems or concerns to the spirit. Even when the owner of the house is not present, these individuals can sacrifice a fowl and tell the spirit what they need or fear. Upon receiving satisfaction, they will go back and recompense the spirit's devotee with whatever they feel is appropriate to the service rendered. Presents actually belong to the spirit, but devotees are able to make use of them for their own enjoyment and benefit. Some 'yan bori claim to receive so many presents in such manner that they do not need to buy everyday necessities for themselves and their families. Whether or not this claim can be made by most bori devotees who own houses for their spirits, it nonetheless objectifies the 'yan bori's efforts to circumvent the "official" market and to create a network of transactions that does not bear the stamp of Islam—though, of course, those who ask a favor from a spirit and who later reward the bori's devotee with a piece of cloth or a pair of sandals may well be Muslim.

By manipulating the signs of wealth and diverting the flow of market goods to their houses, the 'yan bori are drawing on the signs and symbols of Islamic superiority to justify new claims to authority. They are also laying the bases for their own moral economy, an economy that remains anchored in a mystical landscape of hills, rocks, and caves, and objectified through the myths and ceremonies mapping out moral and material relations of power. But more than simply an attempt to recreate their own networks of exchange and power, these new houses of spirits must be seen as an objectification of the interconnection of human and spirit worlds. As more practices and institutions (such as the marketplace) progressively fall in the hands of the fast-growing Muslim community and hence are uprooted from local spirit moorings, 'yan bori feel an urgent need to reassert their connection with the realm of mutanen daji by physically inscribing this connection on the landscape for all to see. While planting stones as spirits' altars is a practical and efficient way to redesign a moral topography, erecting a costly house to store the material possessions of a bori is a far more vivid and powerful testimony to the strength and lasting nature of the alliance established between people and spirits. The fact that in the last forty years mosques have sprouted like mushrooms to accommodate the ever-expanding crowds of Muslim believers may have influenced 'yan bori in building these costly dwellings. Perhaps the houses of spirits emerged as a direct response to the Muslim erection of monuments that celebrated the almightiness of Allah. Inspired by the Muslims' success in "taking hold of the land" to create holy sites (Ranger 1987), the 'yan bori borrowed freely from a Muslim tradition whose monuments and symbols spelled prestige and authority. This is suggested by the fact that a man I knew actually built a mosque for his spirit, a spirit who was a Muslim preacher and who taught his devotee how to write verses of the Koran. After witnessing how Muslims were remapping towns and villages by destroying spirits' altars,[18] erecting mosques, and forbidding the indigenous rituals that closed off village entrances to evil forces, 'yan bori needed to objectify their control over local networks of moral, spiritual, and material relations by physically imprinting on the landscape the visible signs of the wealth they wanted for themselves.

Thus one sees how a marginalized minority's response to Mus-

A house built for a spirit. Note the spear of Rankasso propped against the wall, next to the stone where offerings of blood are made.

Mosque built by a bori medium who claimed that his spirit, a Muslim scholar, requested such a structure.

In the house he built for his spirit Kirai, a bori healer has assembled a variety of enamel bowls and calabashes in which he stores the medicines he provides to his patients. Note the cowrie shells hanging from the central post.

lim hegemony is not overt protest but rather a complex and enduring process (concretized through the redrawing of maps threatened by obliteration) of rejecting yet appropriating the dominant order whose signs, practices, and values sometimes provide the terms for indigenous expressions of contestation. Hence while Muslim attitudes toward spirits are openly condemned by bori members, Muslim architecture—mosques, for instance—provides models for spirit devotees eager to rechannel the might of pious followers of the Prophet. Though Muslim policies are criticized by the bori minority for causing much evil and suffering, one of the most triumphant symbols of Muslim domination, the market, is symbolically brought to spirits' houses so as to divert the flow of its goods and riches to 'yan bori.

Although satisfying the spirit's desire for a home is taken to be the major reason prompting the construction of a hut for the bori, visions of the wealth that that spirit's house will bring to its human owner —in the form of general prosperity, of which the presents brought by satisfied customers are just one expression—is a powerful incentive that usually justifies the actual cost incurred through the entire ceremony. No matter how few and small these gains really are for some, they remain convinced that their hard-earned income is boosted thanks to the gratefulness of an occasional visitor who has come to the spirit's house and seen his request fulfilled. All of the 'yan bori who owned a house for one of their spirits told me that if it were not for this extra revenue, they would never be able to afford to buy new clothing for their families every year. In their eyes, the ritual aimed at capturing the essence of wealth by burying a "little bit" of the marketplace under their spirit's altar was an efficient and meaningful way to regain control over local contexts of wealth and power without capitulating to the Muslim world view and its concomitant work ethic.

The erection of a home for a spirit does not benefit only the owner: if the latter stands to profit from it more directly, thanks to the goods and notoriety he will receive for having mediated his fellow villagers' interactions with the spirit residing in the house, those who ask for the help of superhuman powers also reap benefits. Should they need to communicate with the bori, they know where to go. Now that so many have forgotten who their lineage spirits were and where the altars of these spirits lay, the houses of bori spirits are convenient sites for addressing the invisible "people of the bush."

When French colonizers imposed peace and a cash economy in what is today the Republic of Niger, villagers of Arewa who had at first shunned the market and ignored its laws, progressively came to the hard realization that the kasuwa had become one of the only paths to power and wealth for those either unable to land a job in the administration or unwilling to emigrate. Along with the increasing monetization of Mawri society, the last few decades witnessed the rise of Islam, which paved the way for capitalism by promoting a moral economy based on individual success, private property, and the accumulation of wealth. Converting to Islam meant adopting a world view that provided better ideological tools for coping with the complexities introduced by the emergence of a market economy. It also meant straying from the paths of one's forefathers and relinquishing the traditional view that individuals' well-being depended essentially upon the nature of their relations with spirits.

Confronted with the rapid disappearance of pre-Islamic beliefs and

practices, and constantly provoked by the members of the ever growing and powerful Muslim community, the 'yan bori can only blame
the followers of the Prophet for the far-reaching disruptions that have
come in the wake of colonialism and capitalism. Feeling increasingly
pushed aside and dominated by Muslims in the spheres of politics,
economy, and ritual, they are desperately trying to reassert their control over the area that they see as a crucial locus of power and a
source of infinite wealth: the market. When Muslim officials denied
the 'yan bori the religious responsibilities they traditionally held over
the marketplace, the latter's response, though seemingly inarticulate,
proved a potent weapon with which to question the legitimacy and
supremacy of Islamic values. Drawing on a notion of authority rooted
in ritual practice and legitimated by the weight of history and tradition, the 'yan bori conjured up a fearful figure of the past, a figure
that spoke to all Mawri regardless of their religious affiliation. That
the shadow of the Doguwa hung over the town of Dogondoutchi
several weeks after the tragedy connected with the opening of the
market testifies to the viability of such mystical figures in the collective consciousness and speaks to the effectiveness of bori images and
conventions in dominating the community's moral imagination.

For the most part, Muslims, especially the men, refused to comment
on the accident, producing only such laconic statements as "It was
Allah's will." Yet their reluctance to speak about such issues did not
conceal the ambivalence many of them felt toward the powers of the
spirits. Pious Muslims may openly declare that, in general, the bori's
procedures are backward and irrational, yet many of them remain interiorly convinced that these practices are sometimes instrumental in
restoring health and prosperity. The bori's mixed response of identification with, and rejection of, Muslim values and ethics, its largely inchoate protest of the structures of domination, and its creative efforts
to understand a world threatened by forces beyond local control all
point to the elusive and subtle forms that power, history, and agency
can take in the context of ritual practice.

Chapter 7

The Mirrors of Maria

SWEETNESS, SEXUALITY, AND

DANGEROUS CONSUMPTION

Maria, she is beautiful, she looks so young, but I tell you,
she can be mean! You should never underestimate her.
—Iyale, Mawri medium, April 1989

"*The beautiful Maria, come here, stop crying, Maria*
With her scarf, Maria, the white kola, Maria
The perfume, Maria"

Shatou sings melodiously to coax the vain spirit into possessing the young amarya
who is being initiated into bori on this chilly December night. But Maria stub-
bornly refuses to make an appearance despite the griotte's insistent praise. It is
very late and the 'yan bori will need their rest soon. If appeals to Maria's vanity
do not persuade her to come, a change of strategy is in order. Shatou's high-pitched
voice quivers and then stops altogether. The musicians pause. Moments later, the
sharp claps of the calabashes cut once more into the moonless night, and Shatou
resumes her singing. She has decided to address Zahoho, Maria's husband:
"*Black dog, he with the black anus,*
He only drinks millet porridge with milk
Lazy one, husband of Mangu [Maria]
He who does not work, good-for-nothing, husband of Mangu [Maria]"

Shatou has not completed the song when the amarya starts shivering and roll-
ing her shoulders. The musicians quicken the tempo. The amarya suddenly gets
up, propelled by some invisible force, and marches toward the musicians. With
her hands on her hips, she stands for a second in front of the calabash players,

panting and quivering. She angrily reaches for a handful of change, previously thrown there by cheerful dancers, and without a word starts walking around the possession ground. Other possessed mediums follow in her path.

When Maria cannot be quickly cajoled into taking hold of her devotee's body, bori singers may strategically opt to insult her husband for whom she has much affection. The spirit occasionally remains deaf to flattery, but when she hears Zahoho being called a "good-for-nothing," she can no longer pretend she does not care. Opting to anger Maria is not without risk, however. While the spirit is known for her unrestrained generosity, devotees and musicians have also learned at their expense how quickly she will take away her gifts—even a few coins—in retaliation for an offense. As a complex, endearing, yet also frightening character of the bori scene who condenses in her persona some of the most central paradoxes of contemporary Mawri life, Maria is a "pastiche" of cultural elements "constructed from the disordered fragments of social life . . . that are left out of education, established ritual, and socialization—fragments that intrude upon experience in a particular way because of this neglect" (Levy, Mageo, and Howard 1996, n 6).

  This chapter examines the relationship between possession, female sexuality, and power by focusing on Maria and her passion for sweet things. The multifaceted image of sweetness, which lends itself to numerous metaphorical evocations of how life tastes or feels (Masquelier 1993), concretely ties together the contexts of prostitution, alimentation, and obstetrics. It is also a particularly illuminating component of the temptations of consumer culture and the dangers of uncontrolled consumption that the sugar-loving Maria embodies for a number of Mawri. The centrality of gustatory metaphors, the sensory qualities of food, and the symbolic implications of eating, feeding, and consumption in Africa and elsewhere have been explored at length in several studies (Counihan 1988; Fabian 1990; Hugh-Jones 1979; Meigs 1984; Ohnuki-Tierney 1993; Popenoe 1993; Stoller and Olkes 1986; Weiss 1996). Whether they focus on the thickness of sauces (Stoller and Olkes 1986) or on a moral gastronomy of value (Weiss 1996), these ethnographies of culinary and feeding practices point to a dimension of human experience that, despite Levi-Strauss's concern with the semiotics of raw and cooked food, has long remained unexplored.

Drawing on recent perspectives on sensory experiences (Howes 1991; Stoller 1989b), my discussion of things sweet nevertheless attempts to go beyond a "taste" of Mawri life to explore how deeply the value and power of sugar are grounded in the concrete qualities and cultural meanings of Mawri practice. The concept of sweetness is central to the Mawri's conception of sexuality, gestation, and parturition. Its implications are also manifold for devotees of Maria the prostitute, who, besides indulging in the luxuries of sugar and other sweet commodities, causes infertility in her victims. Thus woven together by the unifying principle of sweetness, the imagery of consumption and reproduction provides a subtle and meaningful discourse through which bori devotees address the challenges and contradictions of contemporary life. Through a focus on the interrelated contexts of alimentation, obstetrics, and possession, I thus show how sweetness, as a synonym for luxury and eroticism, has become a meaningful, if not tasteful, currency for dealing with disturbing social realities.

Sweet Symbols and the Meaning of Sugar in Arewa

Zaki (sweetness), whether literal or metaphorical, is a very desirable quality among the Mawri, but its presence beyond certain culturally demarcated boundaries can be detrimental and even potentially lethal. Zaki has several literal meanings: (1) sweetness, (2) pleasant flavor, (3) pleasantness, (4) eagerness (Abraham 1962, 963). Zaki is also a condition in pregnancy that blocks the expulsion of amniotic fluid. Although seemingly unrelated, the domains of alimentation, reproduction, and the erotic are inextricably intertwined by virtue of the connotations and effects attributed to zaki. Sugar is the embodiment of sweetness and is also a luxury that few people are able to afford on a regular basis:[1] a kilo of sugar costs half of a worker's daily earnings. Even so, refined sugar is an essential component of the Mawri consumer culture, which did not take hold until the beginning of the twentieth century and the French colonization of Niger. Before this time, Arewa was closed off to external trade and plagued with permanent internecine wars (de Latour Dejean 1980). When trade was launched in 1908, the goods traded consisted mostly of cloth, wrappers, turbans, and trinkets brought from Nigeria and Dahomey by merchants eager to take advantage of the apparent prosperity of local populations (Belle 1913). By 1941, sugar figured prominently among imported goods, but its price already made it a luxurious commodity: while a liter of milk cost a paltry .50 francs and a kilo of goat meat 3.00 francs, a kilo of sugar could not be had for under 12.00 francs (République du Niger 1941). Today sugar remains expensive, and even unaffordable, for many Mawri. Sugar cane is grown locally in southern Arewa, but as there are no refineries in Niger, refined sugar is essentially imported.

Unlike the Carribean case described by Mintz (1985) where the plantation system was specifically developed on the periphery to serve as the supplier of raw sugar for a core metropolitan society—a process that had a huge impact on the emergence of the so-called world system—Niger's limited production of sugar cane plays no role in international trade. For years, the peasants of Fadama, in southern Arewa, proudly cultivated their reputation as great producers of sugar cane. Local families, which counted at least one sugar cane grower among their members, allegedly never had to worry about hunger, for even the smallest parcel of land could ensure the subsistence of a whole household for a year if planted with sugar cane (Kotoudi 1988b). Successive years of drought have shrunk the already limited availability of land for sugar cane, however. And since the project of building a local sugar refinery never materialized, whatever hope peasants had had to enrich themselves through cane production disappeared. More and more villagers now plant cassava where cane once grew and go to Nigeria to procure the cane bundles that they resell on local Arewa markets. It is also in Nigeria that local smugglers obtain the refined sugar that has become such a familiar, yet costly, addition to the local diet. Thanks to the continued devaluation of the naira, goods like sugar or cloth that could be easily purchased on the other side of the border were very affordable, at least until the devaluation of the franc CFA in 1994. When it is not smuggled from northern Nigeria, refined sugar is imported—at a much higher cost—from France, Niger's most important trading partner and its largest creditor (Charlick 1991, 135).

Like the enamel bowls—made in Eastern Europe—in which food is served and like the jewelry—made in China—with which women adorn their wrists, the sugar that so many men consume in their morning cups of instant Nescafé exemplifies rural Nigeriens' involvement in national and transnational circuits of wealth, production, and information. Whether sugar is smuggled or legally imported, its local consumption also highlights Niger's lack of self-sufficiency and its dependence on powerful neighbors or former colonial masters. That Maria's fondness for sweet things should express itself as an addiction to white sugar, rather than locally produced sugar cane, should not therefore surprise us, aside from the fact that white is the pretty spirit's favorite color. As an icon of modern and unrestrained consumerism, the sweet-toothed Maria beautifully condenses through her own dependencies on the world market the multiple connections operating between rural peripheries such as Dogondoutchi and cosmopolitan centers of knowledge, production, and consumption.

Sugar is used to enhance the taste of fura, the traditional midday meal of cooked millet flour to which water, and sometimes a little milk, is added. So wonderful is the flavor of sweet fura that any self-respecting host in Arewa will borrow money to buy sugar rather than serve unsweetened fura to his guests.[2] Even when I tried to discourage my friends from putting sugar in my bowl of fura because I knew they could not afford it, they would stare at me in disbelief and disregard my efforts to spare them the expense. Operating under the commonly held assumption that wealthy people drink only sweetened fura (because they can afford it), they saw it as their responsibility to make sure that I would not go one day without my ration of sugar. "Besides," one woman pointed out to me one day, "you Europeans have fragile stomachs, so the sugar will make the fura more digestible for you." Sugar is not considered *abinci* (food) that one consumes to nourish the body;[3] it is rather a gratifying ingestion and a pleasurable addition to the actual nutrients consumed during the three daily meals. This indulgence often takes the form of sugar cane, which sells for a few francs at local markets. Children and women also buy a variety of sweets made from honey or sugar, which is sold door to door by young boys and girls. Thus, in contrast to the British case where, through its transformation from a luxury ingredient into a commonplace "food," sugar became a paradigmatic commodity in the evolution of capitalism (Mintz 1985), *sukari* (sugar) for the Mawri remains an expensive treat.[4]

Sweetness as a synonym for pleasure is linked to sexuality in a literal as well as metaphorical fashion. *Zaki* connotes love and sexual desirability. *Ya zakina* (literally, "he is doing my sweetness"), for instance, can be translated as "he loves me" (Abraham 1962, 963). Since the quality and quantity of food that a person consumes are believed to affect her moral constitution, foods with a high sugar content are consumed to make sexual intercourse sweeter (Darrah 1980, 132). Darrah also cites the practice of applying sweet substances to the genitals to increase pleasure in sex (132). In the same vein, many love philters and other remedies intended to increase sexual attractiveness are concocted with honey or sugar (264). If zaki can be metaphorically and literally equated with sexual desire through its effects upon an individual's emotions, it remains that, as in all things, moderation is advised: too much sweetness causes impotence. A high consumption of sugar may also lead to a relapse of *ciwon sanyi* (literally, sickness of the cold), a form of gonorrhea (267). Sugar, then, is simultaneously synonymous with pleasure and decay: a little sugar, I was often told, helps fragile constitutions, but too much sugar "rots" the constitution.

The "Sweetness" of Pregnancy

Another commonly held assumption among Mawri women is that if they eat sweet things such as sugar or sugar cane during their pregnancies, they will have a long and painful delivery. Sugar in the diet of a pregnant woman will cause zaki (sweetness), a potentially dangerous condition in which an excess of sugar builds up in the uterus and acts as a plug on the cervix, thus preventing the expulsion of the amniotic fluid and the fetus at birth, and endangering the lives of mother and child. Those who cannot resist the many temptations of sugar or who suspect they are afflicted with zaki will drink fura to which has been added *toka* (ashes made from the upper part of the millet stalk once the grains have been removed). This concoction is believed to clean the *ciki* (insides) of the pregnant woman and prevent zaki from accumulating. Should any sugar build up despite such treatment, the delivery will be long and painful, because the zaki has to be expelled before the fetus can go down the birth canal. In a similar vein, a woman known to indulge heavily in mangoes will be encouraged to soak the bark of the mango tree in water and drink the liquid (Darrah 1980, 270), lest she be afflicted with "sweetness."

Once the baby is born, the dietary restriction is lifted and it is even beneficial for the new mother to consume foods with a sugar content. A special gruel of millet to which is added sugar is made by the woman's co-wife or by a neighbor. This gruel, which is often drunk hot, gives the new mother strength and makes her hot. Several plants are steeped in the cooking water with which the gruel is made, to add sweetness to its taste.[5] Sugar is a hot substance — sweetness then is also heat — and its ingestion helps the new mother to literally fight the coldness. Drained of the heat she has spent on the fetus developing in her womb, she must replenish her vital substances. Aside from sugar, she will be given extra rations of meat and spicy sauce, meat and spices being hot foods. Since insufficient food contributes to prolonged bleeding, it is crucial that she eat a lot so that she will not lose much blood (Piault 1963, 77).

The Transformative Powers of Heat

In several contexts, sweetness and its associated referent, heat, are prominent markers of potential or realized fertility when their use is carefully monitored. Heat is necessary to the making of an embryo, a process that the Mawri metaphorically equate to the now extinct practice of smelting iron ore. Just as the blacksmith depends on the transformative capacity of fire to produce metal out of stones, so the woman needs heat to produce a child (see also Échard 1985; Échard and Bonte 1978).[6]

Once the child has been "fired," every precaution must be taken to ensure that the new mother regains an adequate measure of heat. Having spent her own heat on the firing of the child during pregnancy, and having being opened through the passage of the child at birth, she remains thereafter very vulnerable to outside influences such as cold. Women are strongly advised not to go out at night following the delivery for fear that dangerous amounts of cold may enter their bodies through their enlarged genitals (Darrah 1980, 315–16). For similar reasons, they are told not to sit on the floor. Cold is the most frequently asserted cause of illness (see Last 1979, 142–43), and the application of heat is curative inside and out, but especially so for the postpartum condition. Heat is thought to affect the quality of a woman's blood, rendering it too thin or conversely too thick (see

Masquelier 1994; Wall 1988), and therefore a constant application or ingestion of heat will stop the bleeding after childbirth. An extreme form of this logic was related to Mary Smith (1955) by Baba, an old Hausa woman:

> A new mother . . . lies on the bed and turns from side to side so that the heat of the fire under the bed shall get into her body. After seven days it is warmed thoroughly, the blood of childbirth has stopped flowing, her womb has gone back again into place . . . the washing with hot water and the warmth from the fire under the bed and hot spiced food make this happen properly. She is washed morning and evening with hot water, the water is splashed all over her body, and it is poured into her inside so that it shall heal. If this is not done, the mother's inside will putrefy. . . . (126)

Later on, Baba says that when she took care of a young woman named 'Yardada, the latter "washed for five months and she became strong and healthy, she ate hot drinks; everything must be hot so that the chill will not seize her. . . . You give her delicious food with plenty of meat and spices, and you heat the bed. . . . I washed 'Yardada, I boiled the water, and took her behind her hut and dipped leaves in the water and splashed her all over so that the water should enter her skin and make her feel good" (250).

Rattray (1913, 186) and Tremearne (1913, 92) also noted that an important task of the husband before the actual delivery consisted of gathering firewood to heat the water with which his wife would bathe. Postpartum women in Karo or elsewhere are no longer confined to heated beds, but washing with hot water remains a prerequisite to regaining one's health after childbirth. In a 1973 article on obstetrics among the Hausa women of Zaria, Nigeria, Trevitt (1973, 226) recorded that for forty days postpartum, about twenty to twenty-five liters of water are boiled morning and evening, and she measured the heated water at 180 degrees Fahrenheit just before use. Contemporary Mawri mothers also wash with very hot water, splashing it over themselves with a twig so that the heat penetrates the skin. Although Mawri mothers do not heat up the beds of parturients, they would nevertheless implicitly agree with the overall logic governing the postnatal practices described by Mary Smith's informant.

The coldness symptomatic of the postpartum condition implies not only that the mother would be unable at this point to conceive another child but also that her capacity for sexual desire should be low. Because zaki, the desire-inducing substance, has been literally and symbolically eliminated from the woman's body prior to the birth of her child, she should feel no desire other than that of nurturing her newborn. Thus we see at work here a corpus of practices aimed at bringing sharply into focus Mawri women's fertility by dramatically curbing their sexuality.[7] It is as if the two could not coexist. In effect, blood (from menstruation) in its association with female sexuality should alternate, not overlap, with the prime symbol of maternity, milk (Échard 1985, 55). In most cases, everything is done to limit the flow of blood while augmenting the flow of milk (Échard 1985, 55). While the new mother must consume foods high in sugar and therefore hot, she must ignore whatever sexual desire might have been rekindled by the sweet diet and concentrate on the more immediate task of feeding her baby. Women should ideally remain celibate from the seventh month of pregnancy until the delivery and forty days thereafter. They are told to avoid intercourse as long as they nurse, but such advice is never followed in practice. According to Darrah (1980, 272), this avoidance is rooted in fears that should they become pregnant, their milk would spoil, resulting in their infants' probable death.[8]

Sexuality Versus Maternity

The practices described so far demonstrate a mutual concern for the enhancement of fertility and for curbing sexual impulses antithetical to Mawri conceptions of healthy maternity. These views are held strictly by women; the male segment of the population ignores the presence of any incompatibility between a woman's marital duties and her role as childbearer, as Darrah points out (1980, 284). While the dilemma women face is by no means unique to Mawri society, there are no rituals to speak of that deal with this central concern, in contrast to those that exist in other parts of the continent. In the Muslim community of northern Sudan described by Boddy (1989), an entire body of practices, ranging from the most mundane to the most ritualized, aims at emphasizing and redefining women's fertility in ways that leave no doubts as to the primary and central role of wives. Implicit beliefs about women's procreative powers are constantly reinforced by objects and processes that are associated with women and that evoke the qualities connoting female fertility. Sudanese ideology about womanhood finds its most salient affirmation in pharaonic circumcision, a practice that brings into focus the fecundity of women through a negation of their sexuality (Boddy 1989, 55).

Unlike the Sudanese woman whose status and position in the household depend solely on her ability to conceive children, the Mawri woman is confronted with the conflicting tasks of satisfying her husband's desires and nurturing her progeny. Without openly challenging Muslim and male views on this issue, some women choose to insure the viability of their infant by adding to their food *kanwa* (natron), which, in this context, is used to suppress sexual desire while simultaneously enhancing milk production. It provides temporary relief from the double burden placed on the woman as both wife and mother, but it offers no solution to the dilemma. In the context of possession, however, a rich collection of practices that speak to the issue of female identity has emerged in recent years. In particular, the prostitute spirits collectively known as Maria[9] weave a finely textured discourse on sexuality and reproduction by playing with the symbols that unify the experiences of consumption and prostitution. Addressing concerns vital to contemporary Mawri women in their embattled relation to marriage and maternity, these frivolous spirits also speak to the age-old issues of life, death, and sterility in the context of Islamization and sweeping social changes. More than a simple form of resistance in the face of Muslim and male hegemony, the Maria spirits, as they are known in Arewa, offer a poignant commentary on women's ambivalence about their marital and motherly roles and on the destructive excesses of consumerism.

Among the things that these spirits are particularly fond of is sugar or, more precisely, sweetness, which they use and misuse to intensify pleasure. The representations of these spirits as consumers and abusers of sweet commodities tells us a great deal about the way people apprehend their experience of commoditization. As is attested by the anthropological literature on commoditization in postcolonial Africa (Bastian 1998a; Burke 1996; Comaroff and Comaroff 1990; Durham 1995; Gottlieb 1992; Hutchinson 1996; Jewsiewicki 1996; Lan 1985; Piot 1999; Schmoll 1993; Weiss 1996), the Mawri are not alone in attempting to regain conceptual control over their rapidly changing universe through the imaginative interpretation, use, and transformation of commodities of all sorts. From plastic teeth (Weiss 1996) to "cattle without legs" (Comaroff and Comaroff 1990), the adoption—or rejection—of consumer goods in moral and social economies vividly testifies to the imaginative ways in which many Africans challenge the indiscriminate logic of a monetary economy at the same time that they hope to reap the benefits of "modernity." Bori representations of female forms that personify reproductive as well as destructive processes exemplify how bodies and body substances have become commodities in Mawri communities. Maria spirits, in particular, speak to the damaging impact of female sexuality when, no longer connected with fertility, it becomes just another good that can be sold and purchased.

Possession, Prostitution, and Marriage

In Arewa, popular perceptions of women as the embodiment of purity, modesty, and productivity seem to increasingly give way to disturbing images of female identities profoundly at odds with indigenous and Islamic notions of femininity and fertility. These emerging conceptions of women as sexual and moral threats are most effectively expressed in the forum of bori. As previously noted, despite the popularity of bori among women, membership in the bori is itself often tantamount to becoming a karuwa (prostitute) in the eyes of many men, Muslims and spirit followers alike. There are at least three reasons for assuming that bori circles are dens of vice. First, as the epitome of lasciviousness, unrestrained behavior, and excessive gratification, bori ceremonies stand in direct opposition to Muslim ideals of modesty and control. Second, bori ceremonies are held to be conducive to romantic encounters. Third, it is common knowledge that many of the young women who attend wasani are karuwai (prostitutes) looking for male customers. That bori is so profoundly associated with sex stems, of course, from the potent tropes of sexuality at work in possession. Possession, we have seen, plays with the image of physical penetration. Aside from explaining why Mawri husbands might object to their wives' involvement in bori, such relations between humans and superhuman forces show that sex is an integral dimension of bori.

Bori values clash with Islamic and indigenous notions of femininity and motherhood in many ways, not the least of them being that bori affords its devotees a degree of power and independence that, in the eyes of men, no woman should have, especially if she is married. As studies (Coles and Mack 1991; Cooper 1997; Hill 1969; Pittin 1983; Schildkrout 1983) of wives, mothers, and karuwai in postcolonial Hausaland have amply demonstrated, Hausa women are struggling daily to balance the often competing demands of indigenous, Islamic, and Western ideologies as their society itself strives to articulate local values with more global concerns. The Islamic tide that has swept over Arewa in recent years has only served to reinforce women's financial and social dependency upon male relatives. Because bori offers women possibilities of social and economic achievements not available to them otherwise (and not all of them involve prostitution), it threatens the very foundation of Mawri marriage, the supremacy of male authority.

Bori devotees commonly assert that the most important thing to have is health, but few are the women who do not recognize the inherent conflict that exists between bori and marriage. This conflict is often expressed in the saying "*Bori daban, arme daban*" (Bori is one thing — marriage is another), which communicates the fundamental incompatibility between devotion to the spirits and devotion to one's husband. Aside from being a potential object of seduction, a woman who does bori is more likely than other women to neglect her wifely duties and gain a certain degree of emancipation. Moreover, should she be endowed with special curative powers, she might be able to earn enough not to have to rely on a husband for food, clothing, and shelter. This suggests, as noted earlier, that the whole modus operandi of bori challenges the norms of established social orthodoxy in addition to presenting an image of female power that can rarely be reconciled with men's views of the passive, submissive, yet productive wife.

The Poetics of Food in Bori and Marriage: Being Married and Being Fed

Some female devotees actually claim to make a living with the money and gifts they receive from customers anxious to express their gratitude at having regained their health. This is where the crux of the

matter lies. One spirit devotee who had been married twice summa-
rized the situation very aptly: "I don't like marriage. I like only bori.
The reason why a woman marries is so that her husband may feed her.
Now that the bori is feeding me, I don't need a husband anymore."
Although it did not tell me anything I did not already know, the old
woman's statement summoned a host of images that addressed the
heart of Mawri women's world. Most significant, the old bori adept
had chosen to set marriage in opposition to bori in order to make
sense of her own history. Though she is not unique in downplaying
the values of marriage, her case is significant because, unlike many
women who keep trying to reconcile married life and mediumship,
she had resolutely made up her mind that the benefits of bori far out-
weighed those of having a husband.

Of particular interest is the theme of sustenance evoked here, a
theme that shapes Mawri people's reality in a variety of contexts. For
this woman as for many others who, like her perhaps, fought their
way through several marriages before committing to bori, eating and
feeding are essential parameters in defining one's social status. One
of the primary obligations of a husband is to feed his wife, even if
it means borrowing money from her in times of hardship. Though
the millet or sorghum used as the main staples are usually produced
through farming, the other ingredients (spices, sugar, meat, vege-
tables) must be purchased. In recent years, macaroni and rice have
gained popularity as the rich man's staple and some wives insist upon
having *maka* (macaroni) every so often. Husbands must therefore
struggle to maintain a constant and readily available flow of cash if
they are to keep their wives happily fed. A wife's tasks, on the other
hand, include cooking for her husband. In fact, so long as her husband
fulfills his obligations to provide her with raw foodstuff, cooking is
the primary duty of a wife, says Saunders in regard to the Hausa (1978,
247). In a society where the sexual division of labor pervades virtually every dimension of life, the few times a husband will address his
wife or come into contact with her may only be when he gives her
the daily or weekly ration of food with which she will have to cook,
when she presents him with a meal, or when they engage in sex.

Because relationships are defined to a certain extent through food—
its preparation and consumption—showing signs of hunger is not
simply very shameful but has implications of social deviancy (Darrah 1980, 3). A man who is hungry is clearly a social outcast who has

no means of support or no wife to cook for him, or else he has so alienated himself from his kin that they won't even invite him to the family meal. As already pointed out, the quality and kinds of food consumed tell a great deal about an individual's moral and social constitution. Sugar added to the fura on a daily basis, for instance, is an indicator of relative prosperity. Whether it is obtained fresh from a Fulani woman or in powdered form, milk also reflects wealth when it is mixed in with the daily fura. In several ways, food plays a complex role in defining or cementing personal relationships. To go back to the old devotee's comment, what seems crucial is the way she defines marriage: marriage is not about the union of two households or lineages, nor about pregnancy and child rearing, nor even about competition and jealousy between co-wives—it is about *being fed*. Aside from the notions of power and control being hinted at, the imagery of feeding evoked by the old woman in the context of marriage is doubly meaningful: at the literal level, it is through food that husband and wife relate to one another; at the metaphorical level, she is discussing sexual intercourse. *Ci* literally means "to eat," but it also signifies "to have intercourse." The themes of alimentation and reproduction that were brought together by the unifying principle of sweetness are here again meaningfully associated through the multifaceted imagery related to ci.

Eating and Feeding:
The Pleasures and Costs of Bori

If one turns now to the realm of spirit possession, which the old devotee contrasted with marriage, it becomes evident that food and sustenance constitute an important dimension of bori in several ways. One is often inevitably being reminded of it when organizing a ceremony for the spirits, because the cost of feeding all the participants by far exceeds any other expenditure. Those who hold a ritual to become initiated, or simply to thank the spirits, take great pains to ensure that all the guests are satiated, for the surest way to insult a host is to tell him that there was not enough food for everybody.

Upon her return from the bush where she had been initiated, my young friend Zeinabou spent days going around town, telling bori members who had not at-

tended the event how much food she had served at every meal. Since I had been present during the entire three-day ceremony, closely following her every move, I could back up her claims. I was nevertheless dismayed that such an intense and important event of her existence would elicit only comments about the quantity and quality of the food served, and would go down in history as a culinary feast. All her acquaintances heard that she not only served milk with the fura but that she put so much sugar in it that, in addition to "sweetening" her guests' experience of the event, it caused everyone zahi (in this case, zahi means discomfort, burning sensations in the stomach, diarrhea). Tirelessly, she repeated the fact that she was serving not millet (which is the poor man's staple) but rice, and not once (for dinner, as is usually the case) but twice a day. To all who wanted to hear it, she kept describing in minute detail the numerous ingredients that had gone into the preparation of each sauce. She insisted that those who complained that they had to buy kola nuts were liars intent upon damaging her reputation, because she had bought three and a half calabahes of kola to be distributed among the guests. While I was expecting people to rave about how well the initiation had gone, everybody only wanted to hear about Zeinabou's friend, who had helped with food preparation and had stolen most of the meat to feed to her lover, who happened to be one of the bori musicians.

Each detail about the cost or the preparation of the meal served, and each reference to incidents relating to the distribution or the consumption of food, confirmed my suspicion that feeding and sustenance were indeed crucial parameters in evaluating the success or failure of a bori ceremony. It was ironic perhaps that for a young unmarried woman who never cooked and who considered herself ambitious, educated, and talented, the only way to acquire a reputation as a respected medium was to cook for the bori community. "I want them to remember my wasa for a long time," Zeinabou had said to me several times.

So significant is the amount of food preparation carried out for a possession ceremony that when they want to criticize 'yan bori, Muslims jokingly observe that it is to go drink fura that bori people get together and call the spirits. A mockery commonly heard in Muslim circles is that instead of praising the spirits during a wasa, the musi-

Food is a crucial dimension of bori. Here millet and corn paste
await guests.

cians sing the following verses: "Harakwai is fura and milk; the black
spirits are tuwo and meat." Without delving too much into the symbolic significance of this parody of a bori song,[10] I must note that
it implies that spirits are food. Spirits constitute a meal, and that is
why 'yan bori call them when they organize a wasa. Bori ceremonies,
which are preceded and/or followed by a meal that sustains the participants, are thus implicitly contrasted to the Muslim prayer sessions,
which do not involve any food or water intake. If water is used prior
to the *salla* (Muslim prayer), it only serves as a purifying device. Muslims see themselves as morally superior to the followers of the spirits
because they can perform a "ritual" without showing hunger or letting
their hunger control them. Of course, the comparison is hardly fair,
given that bori ceremonies can go on for two or three days while salla
only takes a few minutes. Moreover, while bori meals are about sustenance and nourishment, they are also about sharing and conviviality,
as previously noted.

While Muslims have refined to an art the practice of controlling and
curbing one's appetite by fasting during *azumi* (month of fast), the
'yan bori know how draining the role of a medium can be when she
is possessed by particularly violent spirits. After the spirits are gone

and the 'yan bori are resting, those whose bodies have been the arena of powerful processes need to replenish their strength. This is no time to deny them food, even if it would demonstrate to the Muslims that spirit mediums do not attend possession ceremonies in order to be fed. The above-quoted mocking statement demonstrates that for the Mawri the language of food can become a weapon as used by their adversaries. When Muslims want to deny the spirituality of bori rituals, they accuse the mediums of holding ceremonies solely to satisfy their need for food.

During arguments with 'yan bori about the legitimacy of Muslims' criticisms, Muslims are quick to point out that no one ever saw a spirit mounting his devotee in times of famine. 'Yan bori are quick to retort that when the hunger came, the Muslims did not pray either, because—like everyone else—they were too weak to do anything. The 'yan bori further contend that the Muslims were so controlled by their own hunger that they ate the meat of goats that had died of famine or disease, instead of restricting themselves to the consumption of ritually slaughtered animals. Although it is an insult to hint that mediums attend wasani because they want to be fed, it is nevertheless true— as the 'yan bori themselves emphasize—that "feeding" is an icon of what bori achieves by *providing* for its devotees.[11]

While hosting a wasa constitutes a blatant demonstration of one's wealth, it also offers irrefutable proof that one can make a living through bori. Although the costs of the actual bori ceremony usually far outweigh the income earned by selling medicines, advice, or services, 'yan bori insist that whatever they possess or have received they owe to the spirits. Many 'yan bori who are not ritual specialists maintain that the spirits provide for them, not only by ensuring that they will have a plentiful harvest but also by revealing the location and use of a number of medicinal plants through dreams. Whether or not a substantial income can be earned by selling cures for infertility, stomachaches, or rheumatism, every bori adept remains convinced that bori can be, and is, a profitable occupation. Thus, for my old friend who had chosen not to remarry after her second divorce so that she would not have to ask anyone permission to attend a wasa, bori was a way of living and a means of livelihood. If she had chosen to ground her discourse in the mundane reality of food, it was not simply to point out that participating in a bori ritual meant that she would be fed by the host, just as performing her duties as a wife implied that she would be nourished by her husband. Doing bori was a practical as well as meaningful alternative to marriage because on the one hand, bori provided an easily graspable idiom to articulate the problems of everyday life, while on the other, it was a means of livelihood that "took care" of food, sociality, "mating," and all else. In this respect, bori was a complete substitute for marriage.

Maria Spirits: The Commoditization of Sexuality

The Maria spirits most saliently express the concerns, fears, and aspirations of contemporary Mawri women. These wanton beings who possess only women—and mostly young women with a history of marital instability—simultaneously condense the notions of looseness usually associated with prostitution and present an alternative to the traditional Mawri marriage. Donning sparkling white dresses and brandishing mirrors in which they endlessly admire their own reflections, the Maria spirits turn their ceremonies into cosmetology sessions. In addition to the customary offering of money, which is presented as a welcome gift at the beginning of a wasa, these spirits are given an assortment of candies, dates, and sugar cubes, because they are known to have a sweet tooth. Such an indulgence for sweet food speaks directly to the kinds of deregulated sexuality that these flirtatious spirits embody for the Mawri. As icons of dangerous powers and rampant consumerism, the Maria spirits provide rural Mawri with a moral critique of what they perceive as an increasingly "immoral" economy governed by the uncontrolled and uncontrollable flow of commodities of all kinds. These new images of femininity are but one among several cases in which Mawri popular discourse on the changing nature of evil centers around the female body. Yet these particular representations are significant because while they are anchored in the categories, relations, and values of everyday life, they articulate the conflicting signs of an evolving cultural dynamic. Rather than being labeled as "subculture" (Callaway 1984), and in view of its impact on the moral imagination of so many individuals, Muslims and non-Muslims alike, this bori discourse must be interpreted as the Mawri's attempt to address the challenges of their current socioeconomic situation in the language of their own experience.

Maria spirits are the epitome of impulse, lasciviousness, and profli-

A young medium posessed by Maria is offered a bowl filled with candy, money, and perfume as she straightens her head scarf to express vanity.

gacy. Known to be wanton teasers, whose favorite game is to seduce both married and unmarried men, they are the antithesis of the ideal Mawri wife, who must show modesty, obedience, and respect to her husband or to any man. They engage in sexual activities that are consuming and destructive rather than fruitful, and they render their victims and devotees infertile. Here again one can trace the implicit logic at work in the way 'yan bori speak of what Maria does: while "proper" unions between men and women involve marriage in order to produce children, "improper" unions, such as those related to prostitution, do not involve marriage and are therefore barren. As the perfect personification of the financially independent, self-assured prostitute who has escaped her family's tutelage to enjoy without restraint the luxuries of consumer culture, the Maria spirits embody the predicament and aspirations of many young Mawri women who must reconcile the apparent freedom and pleasures of a Western lifestyle with Muslim as well as indigenous ideologies.[12] For if prostitution and commoditization endanger Muslim values, they are also perceived by many 'yan bori to be a threat to the longer-standing Mawri gado (heritage) (see also Schmoll 1991). Not surprisingly, a large number of Maria devotees—such as Zeinabou—are themselves prostitutes who recruit most of their clients through the medium of bori. Unable to sustain previous marital relationships (often because of their involvement in bori), they have provisionally opted to improve their personal circumstances by engaging in karuwanci (prostitution), despite their increasingly stigmatized positions in communities where conservative Muslim norms of respectability have gained wide currency.[13] In times of increasing divorce rates and disintegrating family ties, when a substantial number of women sell their bodies to feed themselves or to be able to pay for the nonessential commodities an impoverished husband cannot provide, the Maria spirits afford a glimpse of the seemingly unrestrained and lavish life one can lead by engaging in prostitution. These spirits are not pure inventions (Ranger and Hobsbawm 1984); rather, they symbolize yet another strand in the tangled web of mythical interrelations through which the Mawri articulate present-day inconsistencies with past realities.

Controlling Bodies, Affirming Fertility:
Old and Novel Burial Practices

Old people, who recall the origin of these spirits, say that before the Muslims started to change everything, women who had died in pregnancy were buried separately from the other dead, in an area outside the village that was set aside for this specific purpose; the burial was conducted according to very precise rules. These women's belongings (their clothes, cooking pots, or mats) had to be buried with them. Otherwise, they would forever haunt their families to claim their possessions. I was told that if only a sewing needle was forgotten or given away to a neighbor or a relative, the dead woman would come back for it, needlessly scaring the entire village and frightening little children in the process. Like her modern personification as Maria, she would not part with anything that was hers. Only the women possessed by Gurmunya, a spirit of alleged Zarma origin who is lame,[14] were entrusted with the dangerous task of washing the corpse and bringing the deceased and her belongings to the cemetery. And only the devotees of Gurmunya and her numerous brothers, such as Kirai and Suleymane, could carry the body and bury it without fear for their lives. A he-goat was sacrificed and the meat presented to the soul of the dead woman, to assuage it and convince it not to go back to the village in search of food. Some gumba (raw millet paste) mixed with sugar would then be spread thinly on the tomb. The gumba represents the pounded millet that the deceased woman left in her mortar before she died. It was believed that if she was brought all the food she needed, she would not be tempted to go back to the village to harm people. While she was being buried, all the pregnant women of the village would be safely kept inside their compound, for it was known that Maria disliked children and babies and would render sterile any woman whom she "caught." [15]

These ritual procedures must be examined in light of what has been said earlier about Mawri views of female sexuality and gestation. Dead pregnant women are dangerous to the Mawri community because they have died before they could fulfill their procreative role. In a society where female sexuality is valued only insofar as it bears fruit, such women are a threat to both the living and the unborn. As symbols of unrealized fertility, their bodies cannot be allowed to rest untouched, because the survival of the entire community is at stake. Bringing food to the tomb was a way to metaphorically bring the interrupted pregnancy to its successful completion and satisfy its unrequited purpose. What was brought to the deceased was the unprocessed millet that she was in the process of pounding before she died. The mortar symbolized the womb,[16] and the food stood for the unborn baby (see Darrah 1980, 38, 171). Just as she failed to process the millet from its raw state (gumba) to its cooked state (kunu), the pregnant woman failed to "cook" her fetus to term. While gumba, as unprocessed food, was identified with the uncooked baby, and cooking metaphorically stood for gestation, the sugar added to the raw millet paste symbolized excessive sexuality and failed reproduction—by leading to a buildup of zaki (sweetness) in the uterus, a condition that might have caused the death of the mother and/or child. No matter what caused the woman to die, I suggest that the fact that she could not carry her child to term is, if not the outcome, at least an apt expression, of uncontrolled sexuality, stimulated by the consumption of sugar. Rather than tempering her excessive desires by ingesting natron, this woman perhaps even indulged in the pleasures of sweet food and sex. Because it wasted her nutritious fluids on her sexual partner,[17] this indulgence caused the unborn child to die.

An additional connotation of dangerous sexuality is supplied by the raw gumba that is presented to the deceased. Gumba also means the mucuslike discharge from the genitals that signals a case of gonorrhea (Darrah 1980, 266–67). Because of its association with improper sexuality and its role as a prime factor in infertility, gonorrhea suggests the dangers of female sexuality unbounded by the constraints of marriage. The implication is that although the deceased demonstrated her fecundity by becoming pregnant, her failure to deliver the finished product identifies her to a certain extent with the countless other women who were infertile, and even died, because of ciwon sanyi. In other words, her reproductive failure also indicates an excessive, unproductive sexuality.

Finally, the offering of gumba can be interpreted as reproduction gone awry in another sense. It is from the raw gumba that kunu, the hot and sweet porridge drunk by new mothers in need of replenishment, is made, but the goat meat stands for food prepared through the application of heat and consumed in a cooked rather than in a raw state. Because it is considered a hot food, whose hotness is further enhanced by the addition of spices, it is one of the preferred aliments given to the parturient, so that she will replenish her own heat and heal quickly. Goat meat is also considered a woman's food that "real men" who want to assert their masculinity avoid at all cost. In this case the offering of meat symbolizes the fulfillment of fertility. Thus, condensed in these two foods—one raw and cool, the other cooked and hot—is the dead woman's history, rewritten so as to correct what went wrong. The presentation of the goat meat establishes that the woman gave birth to a live child and that her successful maternity is to be rewarded with rich and savory food. As an affirmation of her fertility, it also turns the woman into an adult. Although marriage is the essential rite of passage that defines social adulthood (Smith 1959), the critical feature and most valued endowment of female identity is parenthood. Children are valued not simply because they are a potential source of wealth (and security in old age), but because they *are* wealth.

In addition to contributing to one's prosperity, children bring "sweetness" to one's life in the form of pleasure and fulfillment. They are all the more treasured since the infant mortality rate remains high in Niger,[18] despite the government's efforts to ameliorate pre- and postnatal care in urban as well as rural areas. If children help make one's life sweet (that is, pleasurable and flavorful), one might say then that by denying a woman the experience of motherhood, the spirit Maria is also denying her the zaki (sweetness) that she, herself, craves, though in a different—because edible—form. In considering once more burial procedures, it is apparent that after she had received simultaneously food that would sustain her during her supposed re- covery period and symbols of the fulfillment of motherhood, the dead woman would have no reason to go back to the world of the living so as to finish her interrupted task. Having metaphorically fulfilled her culturally ascribed reproductive role, she could rest in peace, feeling no need to wander as an unrequited consumer.

Today these ritual procedures have been abandoned, and everyone is buried in the same cemetery. Many older 'yan bori deplore the changes, however. According to a bori member who, as a young woman, had witnessed the special burial ceremonies, "now, with the prayer everything is mixed up.[19] They don't bury women who have died in pregnancy separately anymore." Because these women are no longer properly buried, they come back as Maria to possess other women and cause trouble."[20] Incarnated in Maria, the dead pregnant woman who has not received the proper treatment transforms her- self into an icon of unproductive sexuality. At death her reproduc- tive potential—which had been demonstrated (through pregnancy) but not full realized (through maternity)—translates itself into nega- tive capacities that signify, or lead to, infertility, miscarriage, and in- fant mortality. By engaging in sexual activities that are not only im- moral and fruitless but also destructive for her partners, Maria spirits symbolize female sexuality in its most dangerous state, when it has been detached from reproduction. No longer contained by the rules of marriage and maternal life, female sexuality becomes a threat to society, because instead of being the foundation for reproduction, it becomes its antithesis. Herself barren of children, Maria renders her devotees sterile or at least infertile, and she visits dreadful illnesses upon her lovers. As such, she epitomizes rampant desire that, because it cannot be fulfilled, destroys its very object.

Sweet Maria, Bitter Encounters, and Fruitless Unions

Maria dislikes dirt and wears only sparkling white dresses. If her outfit is somewhat spotted or dusty, she may refuse to wear it, an ominous gesture that may have dire consequences for her devotee. She will not be associated with the spirits who make their horse roll on the ground or wash themselves with sand because they are filthy and repugnant. Her diet also expresses the fancy she has for whiteness: she loves sugar cubes and chews only kola nuts that are white. When possessed by Maria, bori adepts spend their time admiring their reflections in a mirror and brushing flecks of dust off their dresses. They will not sit on the usual mat tossed on the ground that other spirits satisfy themselves with. At one wasa to which I was invited, the attendants laid a mattress of millet stalk on which they added several successive pillows, a blanket, and a white wrapper before pouring several bottles of perfume over the last layer. Only then did they invite the group of young women mounted by the Maria to seat themselves.

Another dimension of the barrenness Maria embodies is expressed by her inherent dislike of children. She especially hates babies, because they are the living embodiments of the transformative capacities she negates and destroys. While she expresses disgust at any kind of dirt, she has a special abhorrence for the *daudar haifuwa* (dirt of childbirth). Because she is a symbol and a bestower of barrenness, her presence is not welcome at feasts that celebrate healthy maternities. Women especially fear the destructive powers of Maria during the naming ceremony held a week after a child is born. One Maria devotee told me that although she was allowed to go to naming ceremonies because people trusted her, she could never do so if she wore Maria's outfit. Donning the spirit's sparkling dress also meant that she could not hold a baby in her arms or even go near one, for fear of endangering the child's life.

Neni, a forty-year-old woman who had given birth to four children before falling prey to Maria's destructive schemes, had given me a fairly good idea of the spirit's capacity to wreck human lives. She had been married four times, and the first three times, the spirit had broken up the marriage. She had suffered from worms, had become blind, and, on one occasion, had gotten so sick that people thought she was

Maria devotees possessed by their spirits are offered an assortment of candy, perfume, and sugar cubes during a wasa. They wear spotless white outfits and sit on layers of mattresses and blankets topped by a white wrapper.

dead and wanted to bury her. As if that weren't enough, she had had to quit her job as a governess for a French family in Niamey, for although she loved taking care of children, Maria would not hear of it and punished her by making her very ill. She was making good money in Niamey, but she nevertheless came back to Dogondoutchi because she wanted to regain her health more than anything else.

Testimonies such as this one add another dimension to the already multifaceted personality of the dangerous Maria and speak to some of women's deepest concerns; Maria does not simply attack men and women's reproductive powers—she also denies women their nurturing role by using whatever means possible to ensure that her victims will not care for their own or anyone else's children, regardless of their own inclinations. Like the spirit of which they are the human replicas, Maria's devotees must be barren and devoid of any motherly instincts in order to be able to concentrate on, and satisfy, their consuming passions. As one bori member put it: "Once a woman has been attacked by Maria, she doesn't like her children anymore. Sometimes, she will even refuse to hold her baby and the grandmother has to force her to feed it."[21]

The many tales that vividly recount the way Maria leaves her victims impotent, diseased, or dead have earned her a reputation as a dangerous spirit never to be trifled with. She is especially feared by faithless husbands, whom she lures away from home and later kills without mercy.[22] Before dying, the victims are said to see a very beautiful woman with long, flowing hair and hooves in place of feet.[23] One of my friends, a schoolteacher, described her as follows: "Her feet are those of a donkey,[24] but she is very well dressed. At first, nobody notices her hooves. Men don't look at her feet—they see her face and Maria is very beautiful. She is dressed very elegantly." Always emerging suddenly from nowhere, Maria strikes men by her beauty. She often vanishes into the night as suddenly as she has appeared. While some men have portrayed her as a sophisticated lady, others insist on her youthful and radiant appearance in the dark of the night: "She was a teenage girl, with very long hair held by a barrette. She had very fair skin and eyes as white as milk." One of her devotees told me that the spirit came to visit her at night in her sleep. She would see a pretty woman dressed in pure white sitting by her side. Once again, Maria is portrayed as the epitome of seduction and of the evil of commodities. That she was described as wearing a barrette is significant: Mawri girls and women wear braids and tie them with thread. The barrette (part of the creature's seductive apparel) came from the market, thus emphasizing Maria's status as both an alluring commodity and a consumer of commodities.

There is a deep-seated fear among contemporary communities that prostitution, as unregulated female sexuality, threatens to drain essential fluids from men's bodies and leave them as empty shells.[25] I was told the story of one of my neighbors who nearly died after he had been seduced into having sexual intercourse with a beautiful and mysterious woman. Upon his return home, his testicles had become extraordinarily swollen, reaching the size of a small gourd, and they bled profusely. After he had admitted his sexual encounter, a bori healer identified the unknown woman as one of the Maria spirits reputed to lurk in the vicinity. Had it not been for the healer's powerful medicine, the man would have bled to death, in my neighbor's opinion. No exegesis was offered as to why the man's testicles bled and swelled after he had sex with the spirit. Nevertheless, I suggest that the man's condition was caused by the unusual nature of the exchange of bodily fluids that might have occurred during the encounter. His testicles swelled because he was prevented from "properly donating" his semen toward reproductive ends.

This story typifies what a man's encounter with a Maria spirit entails, and it vividly addresses the dangers of female sexuality when it is separated from productivity.[26] Such dangers are most palpably brought to life through the idiom of sweetness. It may be remembered that a hint of sugar is not nourishing—rather, it enhances experience—while too much sugar ruins one's health and constitution. In contrast to food that gives the body strength and vitality, excessive sweetness is counterproductive. The same relationship is at work between productive sexuality (that is, fertility) and seduction; in other words, when no longer fettered by moral principles, seduction becomes an end in itself rather than a means of using one's reproductive capacities; it becomes destructive, just as immoderate consumption of sugar (which is itself the source and symbol of impotence and infertility) is deleterious to one's health.

The Consumed Consumer:
Maria's Model of Sumptuary Excess

A symbol of profligacy, Maria condenses the double image of the childish and immature budurwa (unmarried girl) and the cunning and dangerous seductress. On the one hand, she is often referred to as "the little one" or "the granddaughter," to emphasize her low status as opposed to some of the older, more important figures of the bori pantheon. On the other hand, she is a vicious temptress who does not hesitate to kill once she has gotten what she wants. Her uncontrolled lust for men is only matched by her insatiable appetite for sweet things and her desire for cosmetics. Like prostitutes who spend all the money they earn on expensive clothes and jewelry, Maria is a profligate who never tires of accumulating luxury items. She had appeared regularly in dreams to a woman who had been her host for nearly twenty-five years, asking her for cosmetics. This faithful devotee, like others, spent a great deal of her earnings buying perfume, sugar, and kola for the pretentious spirit. Neni, the soft-spoken ex-governess who did not even own a bed and who often relied on her neighbors' generosity for food, spent lavishly when it came time to update her spirit's wardrobe. She had a trunk full of heavy white brocade dresses, bright scarves, and sheer veils embroidered with gold threads, and she also owned two heavy silver bracelets and a pair of silver earrings, which were her most prized possessions.[27]

In an effort to behave and become like the spirit in a moral as well as a material sense, the devotees of Maria thus equip their personae with the material trappings of women who make a living at seducing others. The responsibility of devotees as mediums includes living and acting in accordance with the moral constitution of the spirit they are personifying. Maria devotees, then, should be, and often are, lavish spenders who worry more about updating their—and their spirits'— wardrobes than about having enough to eat. As objectifications of the rather deceitful and destructive attractiveness of Maria, they must concentrate on appearance rather than substance, on sugar rather than food, and on prostitution rather than motherhood. Bani, a young woman whose life had been forever changed the day that she crossed Maria's path (see note 20), kept having visions of white dresses and perfume bottles wherever she went. The fateful day when Maria followed her home, she had been accused by a teenage girl of stealing her perfume bottle. She knew now that the theft had been perpetrated by Maria, who was driven by her passion for perfume and makeup items.

Like perfume, mirrors are an integral part of Maria's self-centered persona. By gazing at her reflection in the mirror, the spirit reassures herself that she remains beautiful and alluring. But more than a simple icon of vanity, the mirror symbolizes the kind of selfish antisociety that Maria has created through her refusal to participate in balanced, reciprocated, and productive exchange. Looking glasses have long been associated with the contained and egocentric self that is no longer tangled up in a mesh of forces and relationships (Babcock 1975). Mirrors were also the bait used by explorers and missionaries to attract indigenous populations (Comaroff and Comaroff 1991).[28] Motivated by her selfish love of goods and her thirst for sweet pleasures, Maria uses the mirror to turn her subject self into an object. That self is partially divorced from the surrounding context insofar as she only takes in and consumes without ever giving out anything besides deceitful temptations and unfulfilled dreams.

From this it follows that Maria exemplifies a special type of attractiveness that has little to do with indigenous conceptions of beauty related to one's ability to interact productively with one's environment. For the Mawri, a healthy, and therefore, beautiful body is unblocked and porous not only in that it is capable of absorbing elements from the outside but in that it is able to let out what it cannot use and to interact with the forces, persons, and bodies that surround it (see Schmoll 1991, 170–74). In contrast to this picture of health, Maria exemplifies the woman who is willing to treat her body as a malleable medium that can be refashioned at will through the use of tools and the consumption of artifices. By literally coating herself inside out with sugar and cosmetics, she manufactures the kind of appearance behind which she hides her rapacious nature when she is looking for prey. In that sense, too, she is a symbol of impermeability and ill health. The coating of sweetness in which she has wrapped herself to disguise or, rather, transform her appearance acts as a barrier that prevents the balanced and constructive flow of substances in and out of her self. Hence not only does she personify blockage through the infertility, miscarriages, and infant deaths she causes, but she is, herself, a blocked being.

Maria is a prostitute who loathes maternity and domesticity. Perhaps this is why she has no home, in contrast to other spirits whose high status in the bori pantheon is expressed through the ownership of houses, be they trees, a couple of stones, or a thatched hut. In other words, she lacks the very possession that is at once the locus of domesticity and the embodiment of "proper" man-wife relations. People would invariably tell me that Maria was "too small" to own a house. By "small," they meant that she was unimportant. Her lack of status refers to the fact that she is a young spirit—she is young of age and she is a recent incorporation into the bori pantheon. To ritually mark their devotion to Maria, her devotees keep an enameled bowl filled with all the sweet things that Maria loves so much: candies, caramel, sugar cubes, dates, and peanuts. Since there is no telling when the spirit will pay a visit to her devotee and grab a few candies, the bowl must always be filled with tempting items. Maria's perfume bottles and eyeliners are usually kept in the same bowl, mixed in with the sweets.

To appease her carnal appetites, Maria must prove irresistible to the men whom she intends to seduce. She artfully enhances her already uncommon beauty with cosmetics. Hence the perfumes, eyeliners, and lipsticks she avidly collects are the signs of her self-indulgence and consuming habits at the same time that they become weapons of seduction in her hunt for consumable bodies. Cosmetics render Maria more desirable and enhance her sexuality by separating it further from productivity—after all, the spirit wants to experience her sexuality outside the constraints of a "normal" marriage. Cosmetics are, in effect, the counterpart of sugar and sweets. While the consumption of sweet treats induces or sharpens a woman's desire for sex, perfume and other beauty tools work to make this woman intensely desirable to others. While sugar in the diet of a mother-to-be presents threats to the health of her child and is thus seen as antithetical to maternity, heavy makeup implies loose morals and is usually taken by men as an invitation to seduction. And just as sugar is a pleasant and luxurious addition to one's diet rather than a necessary item, perfume is a superfluous commodity once the body has been washed with soap and water. Also, they are both market goods par excellence: neither is a locally produced commodity. As already pointed out, sugar is imported from Nigeria and France. Several brands of perfume also come from Nigeria, like the cheap Binta Sudan that is regularly poured on the bori spirits' altars. The more prized varieties are all imported from France or Nigeria.

Both perfume and sugar are intrinsic parts of Maria's image because of their connotations of sweetness and images of sumptuous excess. These two luxuries in effect define Maria as an inherently and excessively sexual being whose only goal is to consume and be consumed. Maria herself is the embodiment of sweetness, a sweetness that not only enhances bodily experience but also ultimately destroys it because its excess cannot be controlled. This multifaceted model of un-controlled consumption is further complicated by the fact that Maria uses and abuses perfume not simply to smell good but also to drink. When they are offered bottles of perfume, the women possessed by Maria drink their content with delight. Perfume is Maria's favorite drink, but it is also a food to her: if she swallows the content of a bottle, her hunger is satisfied until the next day. In contrast to people who make sparing use of these two luxuries and who consider them enhancers of experience, Maria regards sugar and perfume as basic commodities that must be consumed plain because they in themselves constitute the experience of pleasure. Thus while sweetness acts like the "spice" in the healthy and productive exchange of food and fluids between married men and women, it is the basic substance on which Maria and her husband feed. In this form of extreme consumption, perfume does not enhance the experience of Maria's body for her lovers, because she partakes of this experience herself (by physically ingesting it) without having to share it with anybody else. It should be noted again that such a gesture resonates with the narcissistic gaze in the mirror. By not sharing, Maria once again proves to be the epitome of individualism and vanity.

The Use and Abuse of Sweetness in Marriage

Maria is a prostitute who sells her body to any male spirit who can afford her. As previously mentioned, she is also married to Zahoho, a "lazy bum" who does little but wait for his wife to come home.[29] Maria's relationship to Zahoho is the perfect inversion of a proper Mawri marriage. While Zahoho stays home and sleeps, doing nothing important, Maria takes on the role of the male figure by going into the "public" world and making a living "selling her sex," eating everybody just as a man in business would. With the proceeds she earns from her trade, she provides for her incompetent and lazy husband. This could mean, of course, that Maria is not so self-centered after all. However, it is the couple that Maria and Zahoho form together that is significant, I argue. Their association projects the image of a selfish, unproductive (they have no children) marriage. As a karuwa (prostitute), Maria is thought to have several lovers (who, interestingly enough, are referred to as her husband's) with whom she has had long-lasting relationships,[30] but she is always on the lookout for new "affairs," should any handsome spirit come her way. Maria also seduces human males. The terrible fate suffered by her mortal partners eloquently testifies to the perceived evils stemming from marriages such as Maria and Zahoho's, where the wife is given so much space to assert herself that she inevitably ends up trespassing the culturally demarcated boundaries that define women's position within the marital household. Moreover, Maria's multiple "unions" and the fact that her lovers are called "husbands" symbolize the female appropriation of polygyny as defined by Islam: it is not Maria's legitimate husband

who contracts several marriages but rather Maria herself. In this inverted marriage, not only does Zahoho not provide for his wife but
he lives off other men via the earnings of his wife.

The praise song performed to invite Zahoho to possess one of his
devotees at a wasa sheds light on this shadowy figure and is also very
revealing of the particular kind of threat Maria presents to men:

> You [Zahoho] do not cut, you do not prick
> You do nothing but sleep.
> His wife only takes sugar to put it in his mouth
> So that he may suck on it.[31]

Zahoho is cast as a gentle, unassertive husband whose lack of authority
and masculinity is contrasted with the fierceness and manliness of
Tuareg nobles. Unlike the Tuareg spirits who reputedly pierce their
victims with a spear and never spare offenders, Zahoho "does not cut
and does not prick." Tuareg spirits' habit of spearing their prey symbolizes aggressiveness and virility, whereas Zahoho is known as a spirit
who is too lazy to even harm anyone. As a fundamentally unproductive figure, he lives only to open his mouth and receive what others
give him. Zahoho's refusal to penetrate further suggests that Maria
is his wife in name only. Perhaps that is what is meant when Maria's
lovers are called her husbands: it is they who have sex with the beautiful prostitute while her impotent husband sleeps alone in his bed.

Unable to satisfy his wife sexually, Zahoho is also unable to provide
her with food. In this totally transformed marriage, it is Maria who
feeds her husband, and in the song the symbols chosen to illustrate this
kind of union are particularly suggestive of what the inversion signifies. The song cited at the opening of this chapter describes the way
Zahoho is spoiled: he only drinks fura with milk. In the second song,
above, Zahoho lazily indulges in the pleasurable consumption of the
sugar provided by Maria. As pointed out earlier, an excess of sugar in
the diet causes impotence, so it would seem that it is Maria herself
who induces her husband's lack of virility. Maria further feminizes
Zahoho by her gesture of depositing the food in her husband's open
mouth. Not only are Zahoho's passivity and impotence contrasted to
the masculine images of piercing and cutting, but they are under-
scored by his becoming the object of his wife's action (*she* "takes sugar
to put it in *his* mouth").

As if having no spear were not enough, it appears that Zahoho has no teeth: he sucks like a toothless baby. Not able to bite, he lets his wife metaphorically penetrate him with sugar, a luxurious treat and a symbol of sexual desire. Consumed by sugar and plagued by impotence, Zahoho can only open his mouth and become a receptacle for sweetness. At another level, the image of sucking is revealing of the kind of inverted relationship Zahoho and Maria are having. The sugar Zahoho sucks on presumably melts in his mouth, thus facilitating ingestion. For Mawri, the ingestion of somewhat liquid or juicy foods—whether fura, mangoes, or popsicles—is likened to drinking, in contrast to the ingestion of more solid food, which is thought of as being eaten. The verbs *ci* (to eat) and *sha* (to drink) also have a sexual connotation that is related to the consumption image. While both verbs mean to have intercourse, *ci* describes the male perspective (*shi ci ta:* he slept with her), whereas *sha* is used when a woman is the subject of the action (*ta sha maza:* she slept with men) (Gouffé 1966, 90). In the song above, the image of Zahoho drinking the sugar that his wife pushes into his mouth robs the impotent spirit of the last bit of virility he ever had by identifying him once more with the female figure in the couple he forms with Maria.

"Life is a mango," people in Dogondoutchi routinely remark to capture the sweetness of life but also, paradoxically, its slipperiness. Beyond the proverbial and real pleasures of life, there is a recognition that life can be as fraught with uncertainty as the enjoyment of a mango—as, for example, when it slips from one's hand to land into the sand. Like the luscious grafted fruits whose sweet fragrance is an irresistible temptation to so many who cannot afford them, the pretty but artificial Maria epitomizes the sweetness of commodities and their slipperiness—slippery because they can be simultaneously dangerous and unattainable. This chapter thus has traced the implications of sweetness and the multiple forms it takes in several contexts in order to illuminate the fascinating figure of Maria, the prostitute spirit of the bori pantheon.

Mindful of White's recommendation that when writing about prostitution one stop "isolating women in the categories of deviancy and subculture" (1990, 11), I have attempted to privilege women's experience and the central role that constructions of femininity and female power play in the bori's articulation of social and historical contradictions. Other ethnographies of female possession practices

equally embedded in their own peculiar nexuses of capitalist dependence, religious competition, and gender hierarchies (Boddy 1989;
Brown 1991; Ong 1987) have convincingly shown what a focus on
women's perspective and practice may reveal about local appropria-
tions of alien commodities and popular representations of the West.
Such studies also demonstrate how attention to the seemingly peripheral discourses of spirit possession can illuminate the multiple ways in
which people make sense of the historically changing configurations
of power and production in which they are enmeshed as they become
variously drawn into the global landscape of capitalist labor, city life,
and consumer culture.

Summarizing this chapter's discussion of the world of Mawri prostitution and one of its iconic figures, it becomes clear that Maria—half
child, half woman, immature yet cunning—combines the role of the
nurturing wife with that of the seductive karuwa, thereby presenting
followers and victims alike with a complex identity. By condensing
the images of the virginal budurwa, the sexually mature wife, and the
independent prostitute, she embodies different temporal moments of
a woman's life and speaks to the ambivalence of marriage and maternity. As a multifaceted personality bridging past and present realities, she addresses the predicament of Mawri women who aspire to
be proper wives and mothers but who are lured away by the many
temptations of consumer culture. Though Maria presents some very
real dangers to men, women, and children, the message she delivers is
a valuable one because she expresses very vividly and eloquently the
plight of many Mawri who feel consumed by economic forces they
do not understand.

To those who are struggling to make sense of the disturbing socioeconomic changes that have come in the wake of colonialism and
capitalism, the Maria complex provides a subtle discourse based on
the threat of uncontrolled consumption. The idiom of consumption
meaningfully ties together the experiences of possession, reproduction, and prostitution, and concretely expresses the dangers associated
with Maria and similar figures. Maria's excessive and dangerous consumption of consumable commodities—whether they be goods, services, or people—takes the form of an uncontrollable indulgence for
anything sweet. As the embodiment of sweetness in its luxurious and
excessive forms, the figure of Maria is a particularly tragic expression of Mawri consciousness. In Africa, Rowlands notes, "to be de-

veloped is measured in terms of the manner by which the products of Western technologies are consumed rather than the capacity to pro-duce them" (1996, 190). From this perspective, the perfume-drinking, sugar-loving Maria is a very apt icon of modernity in all its simulta-neously seductive and perverse dimensions.

Chapter 8

Lightning, Death, and the Politics of Truth

THE SPIRITS OF RAIN

I am Muslim and I only fear God. I am not afraid of lightning
because I have not offended the spirits. — Hidi, Dogondoutchi resident,
November 1988

The main occupation of [fetishists in Mawri country] appears to be
the search for and punishment of religious offenses whose definition
they control and whose monetary reparations by the guilty party
constitute their main source of income — Gilbert Viellard,
Coutumier du cercle de Dosso

THOUGH THE SIGNS and values of bori, as well as its codes, colors,
and schedules, often serve to differentiate the illiterate and impoverished peasants from the core of educated civil servants and merchants belonging to the orthodox Muslim order, the distinction between bori and Islam is not clear-cut. I have already shown how bori
evolved, and continues to evolve, out of the articulation of indigenous and external cultural forms, at the same time that Muslim culture
emerged to express the influence of local ideologies. Muslims, who
preach allegiance to Allah, nevertheless admit the existence of spirits
and the fact that they can make their presence known to people by
intervening in their lives. Conversely, bori prayers are replete with
references to Allah, who, as the supreme being, commands and delegates tasks to the spirits. By addressing their supplications to the bori,
the 'yan bori are, in effect, entrusting them with a message to God.
Bori devotees call the malamai (Muslim clerics) to celebrate their children's naming ceremonies or to "tie" a marriage. The array of Muslim
figures incorporated into the constantly evolving bori pantheon,[1] the
ways bori mediums use Muslim prayer schedules as temporal markers,
and the growing number of bori healers who wear Muslim attire and
plan to accomplish the hajj also attest to the extensive and complex

interaction between Islam and bori. The overlap between Muslim and non-Muslim identities in Niger has been noted by several scholars who have stressed the integrative and synthetic nature of local religious practices. Bernus has written that Islam and indigenous religious practices are "part of a relatively coherent whole" (1969, 190). Speaking of Songhay society, Rouch notes that Islam appears "less as the dominant religion than as an essential element of a religious complex . . . to which it has deeply incorporated itself" (1989, 17).

Despite the interconnectedness of bori and Muslim visions of the world, Muslims and 'yan bori often stand divided along a host of issues relating primarily to the role that spirits should be allowed to play in human projects. Moreover, partly because a follower of the Prophet can no longer be distinguished from an "animist" based on attire, now that every man owns at least one Muslim robe (Nicolas 1975, 32), Muslims anxious to eschew the stigma attached to bori identity will often denigrate possession practices to redefine their own worthiness as members of the umma. Bori is thus the foil against which those who need to reassert their social identity can look good in contrast to the provincial and unrefined 'yan bori; conversely, Islam is the foil against which 'yan bori reaffirm the creative powers of possession when disease, drought, or financial insecurity threaten local communities.

Malamai who have secured wealth and respectability through their membership in the community of believers point out that bori and Islam are two divergent routes that cannot be followed simultaneously, although there is always time to switch paths and profess allegiance to the Koran. Aspiring to greater prestige and better economic conditions, and eager to escape the imputation of rusticism often connected with bori, many Mawri call themselves Muslim although they possess only a minimal knowledge of what conversion to Islam entails. Their limited understanding of the Koran and their flawed knowledge of Arabic in no way reflects their degree of piety and sincerity. Nonetheless, the fact that few in Dogondoutchi can translate many of the Koranic prayers they have so assiduously learned by heart has largely contributed to the localized and syncretic character of Islam. As a result, if some Mawri appear to be very devout Muslims, others are less so. As argued earlier, it is precisely in these sometimes tenuous distinctions that the subtleties of power and domination lie.

French colonials and, soon after, Muslim merchants capitalized on

All three bori leaders, who are erecting a stone altar for a spirit in someone's compound, wear Muslim attire. Note the mosque design, a characteristic Muslim motif, embroidered on the collar of the grand boubou
worn by the man in front.

the local flow of goods, values, and substances—the former, by encouraging the emergence of markets; the latter, by taking hold of
these central nexuses of social and economic transactions. As previously seen, the 'yan bori, who feel largely estranged from the mechanisms controlling access to power and prosperity, have continually and
tirelessly sought to redirect the wealth that flows into other hands,
and these efforts to craft an alternative economy have hinged on creatively appropriating the dominant power's techniques for producing
and reproducing value. This chapter discusses the 'yan bori's attempts
to gain control over yet another kind of economy, that having to do
with the politics of burial and the control of bodies. Of late, burials
have become the sites of various ideological contestations in communities struggling to establish competing moral identities (Masquelier
1997b), but the present discussion is limited to disputes rooted in 'yan
bori's and Muslims' conflicting management of lightning. Through an
examination of the images, practices, and arguments relating to these
divergent conceptualizations of lightning, I return to issues raised

earlier about the unconventional forms that power and resistance take in the context of bori. Focusing on the interrelated themes of fire, rain, and smithing, lying and oath taking, and burial and justice, I show that while in other contexts bori remains a forum for negotiating the complexities and contradictions of living with Islam, in situations that involve death or destruction by lightning, it becomes a means of resisting Islam.

As elsewhere in West Africa (Herskovits 1938; Matory 1994a), lightning provides the tropes and techniques through which people re-word the local terms of justice. In Arewa, lightning is often specifically used by 'yan bori to intimidate Muslims. Yet bori practices and the logic that guides them cannot be reduced to a simple reaction to Islamic influence. As Rasmussen notes in the context of her research on neighboring Kel Ewey Tuareg, possession "emerges not solely as a response to conditions, but as a factor in creating or re-articulating contradictions" (1995, 7). While bori provides some Mawri with an idiom of resistance, it also exists in its own right. Central to my argument, once again, is the notion that bori articulates various levels of experience by mediating distant and elusive forces through the management of corporeal signs and immediate contexts. Bori theories of lightning are part of a coherent vision of the world that, as I have shown elsewhere, centers around notions of flow and balance at the personal, social, and cosmological levels (Masquelier 1994). The focus in this chapter is on the frightening images of supernatural retaliation and morality so adroitly manipulated by 'yan bori to demonstrate once more the vitality and relevance of bori practices for Arewa residents for whom the world is replete with potent possibilities, both tempting and threatening, despite the alarming ascendancy of Islam and its concomitant system of values.

Rain, Lightning, and Death

Until a few decades ago, a host of *mayu* (sorcerers) who struck people, cattle, and trees alike with deadly bolts of fire would appear in Arewa every rainy season. Traveling with and in the rain, they flew over the houses in which people sought shelter from the storm. Armed with a rake, a club, or a pestle, the sorcerers would hit the roof of a house with their weapons. This would set the house on fire and cause the death of the villagers trapped inside (for a slightly different version, see Échard 1978 on sorcery in Ader). During this time of year, insomnia was attributed to a sorcerer lurking around people's homes. And when people felt their bodies become very hot, they knew a sorcerer was probably hiding in the clouds above their house. Thus before lightning ever struck a house, the dangerous heat emanating from sorcerers radiated over the house and could be felt by the occupants. The heat these sorcerers radiated was produced by their antisocial behavior and selfish motives as well as by the potent medicines they had ingested so as to be able to fly.

To protect themselves from "the evil in the rain," villagers in Arewa held a particular ritual prior to the beginning of the rainy season. Known as *tuwon damana* (tuwo of the rainy season),[2] the ceremony simultaneously addressed the well-being of each participant and redefined the fragile interconnectedness and boundedness of the wider social order. After millet had been collected from every household in the village, it would be cooked with special medicines and later redistributed; each person was to eat a portion of it. If the various steps of this operation were carefully followed, no one would fall sick, and sorcerers would not be able to enter the village to bring disorder and death.

Today old people reminisce about the times when a jealous neighbor could hire a sorcerer to kill them, but communities have stopped holding the tuwon damana rituals that close off village paths to deadly sorcerers. Just as with other indigenous rituals described in earlier chapters whose discontinuation is ascribed to increasing Muslim pressure to turn away from "pagan" practices, the abandonment of the tuwon damana practice is attributed to the wave of Islamization that swept over Arewa since after independence. Muslims, who believe lightning and thunder are sent by Allah, now outnumber those who fear the sorcerers, who are primarily followers of the bori. Because they often hold most of the high-ranking positions in the sociopolitical hierarchy, the followers of Allah have successfully put a stop to several indigenous rituals that they considered sacrilegious and antithetical to Islamic doctrine. As described earlier, Muslims in many Arewa communities now forbid gyaran gari ceremonies that close village paths to external evil forces, on one occasion even refusing to allow the propitiation of the market spirit in Dogondoutchi. They have also put an end to burial practices whose object was to protect

This tree was struck by lightning in 1994. A wasa was held soon after to beg the spirits' forgiveness.

local communities from the attack of wandering souls coming back to claim their possessions. The disappearance of tuwon damana is just one more setback in a series of defeats and humiliations that the 'yan bori have suffered at the hands of the Muslims.

In Mawri communities at present, other kinds of sorcery- or witchcraft-related deeds appear to proliferate at a disquieting rate (Masquelier 1993, 1997a), but memories of sorcery-caused lightning progressively fade away as local discourses about lightning are reframed so as to incorporate current socioeconomic and political realities. Though Muslims theoretically invoke the power of God to account for thunderbolts, Mawri who have not severed their ties to the spirits and turned to Islam now believe that lightning is caused by a family of spirits that has only recently appeared on the bori scene of Arewa. Striking their victims with deadly thunderbolts, these spirits only direct their fire against those who have gravely offended them. Individuals who die, lose cattle or sheep, or see their trees burn because of lightning are not victims but offenders, according to 'yan bori. As such, they or their families must ask for the spirits' indulgence and pay a monetary compensation to bori devotees.[3]

Offenders who must incur the cost of a possession ceremony and pay the high fines set by the spirits are often Muslims who do not belong to bori and would rather not be associated with any spirit devotee. Although some remain unshakable and staunchly deny having committed any crime, most people, regardless of the degree of their devotion to Allah, are not able to ignore what many believe to be warnings sent by angered spirits. Pressured to settle their debts with the spirits, they often give in and finance the costly ceremony that will enable 'yan bori to determine the cause of the spirits' wrath (that is, if the guilty party has not yet confessed). Blamed by their peers for their lack of faith and trust in God, Muslims who "fall prey" to the 'yan bori's scheme are also ostracized by the Islamic community for adopting bori notions and speaking the "language" of bori, which has evolved to counter dominant Muslim discourses.

My concern here is not whether more Muslims actually die or suffer damage from lightning than do non-Muslims, nor have I made any attempt to determine the accuracy of spirit followers' testimonies, having myself witnessed very few of the incidents recounted in this chapter. It is worth reiterating that the negative portrayal of Muslims emerging from my discussion exemplifies bori constructions of Islamic identity. Bori narratives that depict local Muslims as wealthy and greedy individuals removed from nexuses of exchange contrast strikingly with Islam's own promotion of almsgiving and good citizenship. Because the intent here is to discuss bori statements of defiance in the face of a dominant order as meaningful and instrumental modes of self-assertion and empowerment, I have tried to reproduce as faithfully as possible the climate of suspicion, fear, and competition that surrounds the experience of lightning in Mawri society.

Constantly discredited by the members of the ever growing Islamic community and estranged from the centers of economic and political power, spirit followers have attempted to create a meaningful and viable order of practices to negotiate their place in the local economy and act upon the forces that threaten to overpower them. When these forces of material and political domination cannot be clearly pinpointed, the tangible wealth and success of the Muslims become a more accessible target for bitter and impoverished Mawri.[4] In an attempt to contest the logic of the Muslim culture in which they live, 'yan bori also draw on the raw power of lightning, which, they say, is thrown only to punish those who manage to escape human justice. Allegedly feared even by pious Muslims, the spirits of lightning present a significant challenge to the hegemony of Islam in Mawri communities. These personalized moral forces also provide 'yan bori with a coherent discourse for making sense of and acting upon a world whose structures they often no longer control.

Deadly Stones and Consuming Fires: The Spirits in the Rain

The appearance of the spirits of lightning in Arewa coincided with the coming to power of Zarma elites at the head of independent Niger. Like many of the spirits who have become familiar bori figures, they are not native to the area. They are Zarma, and like the Zarma people, they come from the West. In the Zarma-Songhay region of Niger, where they first appeared, they constitute a family of noble spirits, the Tooru, who govern the winds, the clouds, lightning, and rain, in addition to controlling the Niger river. Originally integrated into the nature cult through which members of a lineage derived prosperity and protection, the Tooru progressively became public figures in the *holey* possession practices that emerged as Islam gained prominence in Songhay country (Rouch 1989; Stoller 1989a). In Arewa the Tooru are known as the Zarma. They are also referred to as babba'ku (black ones), presumably because some of them wear black robes and hats. "The ones from above" is another name for them: the black spirits live in the sky, from which they control the clouds that bring the rain.

When exactly these fearful spirits started possessing Mawri villagers is not certain. A prominent member of bori described their coming to Arewa:

Before the Whites, everybody was Arne, and some evil man would eat *tuwon maita* [food of sorcery], and then, when there would be a storm, he (the man having become the sorcerer) would kill people in their house (with lightning). . . . And then, the Zarma came; the sons of Harakwai. Since then, sorcerers don't go out in the rain to kill people during storms. The Zarma prevented them. It is they, themselves, who now throw lightning on people who have offended them. . . . Now there are no more sorcerers or sorcery-related problems.

In the neighboring region of Ader, "those of the West"—as Zarma spirits are often called—started throwing lightning in the late 1960s (Échard 1992). By 1969, chiefs of bori had determined that the series of lightning-related incidents that had occurred over the last three years were caused not by human sorcerers but by spirit sorcerers who had come from the West to destroy the country (1992). Their brutal possession of bori devotees symptomatized the unethical politics of the pro-Zarma regime and the economic abuses of the PPN-RDA politicians who after independence "looked more like a privileged caste than the authentic representatives of the Nigerien masses" (Fuglestad 1983, 178). Eager to promote their own corporate interests, Zarma/ Songhay political leaders had cut short the nascent political awakening of the Hausa and monopolized power for themselves. In a country where until Gen. Ali Seybou came to power in 1987, there was no freedom of expression, spirit possession provided Hausa populations with a convenient medium for interpreting their political and economic marginalization.

In Arewa the babba'ku's (black ones') potency and cruelty also stands for the neo-imperialist character of the Zarma-controlled government that ruled the new Republic of Niger, though I never heard that the famine of the seventies—exacerbated by the regime's abuses and mismanagement—was also attributed to the Zarma spirits, as Échard (1992) found in Ader. There are very few Zarma living in Dogondoutchi. Apart from the two female healers I met who were held in high esteem by bori leaders, none of the Zarma-speaking individuals who were devotees of the spirits had achieved any prominence within the bori. The young men and women actively took part in possession ceremonies (one young man even underwent the shan ice ritual that was financed by a Zarma functionary who had come all the way from Niamey), but older Zarma devotees rarely showed up for a wasa. They felt that the people of Dogondoutchi were taking too many liberties when it came to inviting the black spirits over. "They don't know how to dress them and how to deal with them," I was told by a Zarma healer, "but since people don't like it when I tell them what they do wrong, I have stopped going to ceremonies."

Feared for their cruelty and ruthlessness, the Zarma are also among the most highly regarded spirits of the local pantheon. It should be recalled that they control not only lightning but also rain. As such, they share the spectrum of benevolent and retaliatory activities that Herskovits describes in his discussion of Xeviso, a Dahomean spirit of thunder. Xeviso, also known as Agbolesu, is "the possessor of the sky. He is the judge who renders supreme justice, for he understands what the world needs. He sends heat and he sends the rain. He kills men and destroys houses, trees, and fields, but he also makes humans fertile and nourishes their fields" (1938, 151). In the event of a drought or insufficient rain, bori adepts now sacrifice to the Zarma spirits, because they have the power to bring the rain. "What proves it," argued a bori chief, "is that if the black spirits kill someone, we are going to see clouds in the sky, and it will soon start raining." Frequently solicited by individuals seeking advice, help, or protection, the Zarma spirits are guests of honor during the most important annual bori ritual in Dogondoutchi.

Held on the Thursday of the seventh month of every year,[5] the *watam bakwai* (seventh month) ceremony involves a test to determine if, where, and in what quantity the rain will fall in the current year.[6] Financed by the local authorities, and drawing a crowd of spectators from bori as well as Muslim and Christian circles, the event not only focuses on communal well-being and global reproductive capacities but also addresses individual concerns and situations. After the bori chief has determined the fate of the community for the year to come, the Zarma spirits are given fresh milk. Instead of swallowing it, they spit it out on the onlookers assembled around them. To be sprayed with milk theoretically insures protection against the threat of lightning during the next rainy season.[7] People also ask for the spirits' help in solving a problem, seeking a job, or averting misfortune.

The Zarma spirits, whose merciless justice Muslims and 'yan bori alike fear greatly, are all part of the same family. At their head is Harakwai, their father, who is said to judge whether or not someone has done wrong and who sends his sons to deliver the punishment, should the accused party be found guilty. His oldest son, Kirai, does not throw lightning, but he is nevertheless a fearful creature. The praise song performed to invite him to possess one of his devotees during a ritual clearly states his relentless ferocity:

Anyone who touches (offends) Dongo[8]
Dongo will hit him
In the hollow of the ear
and not in the neck
Dongo will kill
Dongo the mad one
Everyone who swears
Dongo will hit him.

His younger brothers are the ones who actually throw lightning: Moussa, nicknamed *sarkin gaugawa* ("the king of haste") because "he is the fastest of them all," is the first one to throw lightning. The potency and harshness of Souleymane, the second son of Harakwai, is well known to bori musicians, who sing that "the fire is more compassionate than him, because the fire spares some things." His brother, Bela, comes to the scene to burn everything, and that is why he is often called "the destroyer." Bela controls fire. When he has set a house or a granary on fire, water will not be of any use to extinguish the flames. "Bela's fire is like petrol," one devotee once explained. It keeps burning until there is nothing more to burn. Thus if lightning occurs without there being any fire, one can be assured that Bela has not accompanied his brothers to punish an offender. Bela's brother, Hausa-kwai, who makes decisions as to what or who will be hit or burned (e.g., a tree, cattle, etc.), is also called Dodo because he has four eyes and can see behind him. His fierceness and cunning have earned him the name *ba'kin maye* (black sorcerer). Yandu, another son of Harakwai, is the blacksmith who is said to kill by hitting until he reaches the brain (he cracks open the skulls of his victims).

The *kankara* (thunderstones) that these fearful spirits are said to throw at the targets they choose to hit are actually neolithic axes that can be recovered by bori specialists on the site where lightning occurred. The widespread equation of polished stone ax blades with thunder projectiles throughout the world takes on a special signification in Arewa, where 'yan bori claim that these projectiles have been forged by the blacksmith Yandu.[9] Though a few people think that all the stones are the same, most agree that the size and the shape of these thunderstones vary with the size of the target to be hit. The stone used for animals is a sort of ball that hits its victim with a deadly blow. As indicated above, if Bela participates in the punitive action, the ball is covered with fire. When people are the intended target, the spirits' weapons look like needles.[10] If the spirits choose a tree as the object of their punishment, they use a stone as big as a hatchet's blade. After they are done, Kirai, Souleymane, and the others leave a sign of their presence so as to warn or remind people of their intentions. When they destroy a granary, for instance, the spirits leave three handfuls of grain aside, untouched. If they hit a goat or other animal, they put a dead lizard on the animal's back. For example, when a villager once found his bull, one ram, and two ewes lying in his field, killed by lightning, a dead lizard, the unmistakable signature of the Zarma spirits, was lying on top of one of the corpses.

When the spirits decide to kill someone because he has offended them in some way, the person must be at home. The babba'ku punish only those who are guilty and spare innocent lives. If the guilty party happens to be visiting, or staying in, someone else's house, the spirits will not touch him, because they do not want to burn down an innocent person's home. If, on the other hand, the offender is home but has borrowed something that belongs to a friend or a relative, the spirits will destroy everything but the object owned by the innocent party. In a village I used to visit regularly, I was told that a year before a house had burned down completely except for a calabash full of millet that did not belong to the house's owner.

Once it has been established that the Zarma spirits are responsible for the destruction of a granary or the killing or wounding of a person, milk and medicines are brought to the site where lightning struck. The milk and medicines are poured on the ground. Once the milk has seeped into the earth,[11] the bori specialist in charge of the operation digs until he finds the stone thrown by the avenging spirits. The milk enables the 'yan bori to find the stone that, once thrown from above, disappears into the ground "as far as water." Because the stones are very hot ("it is the heat that kills," a 'dan bori told me), only an expert in the matter may attempt to dig up the dangerous projectile.[12] Stones that are retrieved by bori practitioners become prized possessions that are proudly exhibited to colleagues and apprentices, for they are the tangible proof of the practitioner's expertise and of his ties to the spirits' world. The stones can also be purchased, I was told, by bori specialists eager to demonstrate their savoir faire and build their reputation. The city of Bilma, near the Chadian frontier, and Burkina Faso are the main sources for obtaining stones.

That these stones may be purchased is revealing of the extent to which—as Schmoll (1991) has demonstrated in the case of soul eating —magic and ritual have been commoditized. According to Schmoll, the seeds or stones (referred to as kankara, just like lightning stones) that live and reproduce in a soul eater's stomach and that could in the past only be inherited, can now be purchased with money. Hence if previous soul eaters, who had not sought to possess destructive powers and who were born that way, represented, in Schmoll's words (1991, 23), "a sort of natural evil that could, nonetheless, be socially controlled," modern soul eaters speak to the immoral and corrupt practices that have emerged with the rise of European colonialism and a market economy. Like other commodities that take on a life of their own and ultimately destroy their makers and owners (see Masquelier 1992), the stones of *maita* (soul eating) enslave and control their buyers in such a way that they can never satiate their hunger once it has been unleashed.

Lying and Perjury:
The Logic of Bori Oaths

Though bori discourse about lightning and avenging spirits apparently contradicts the logic of Muslim culture,[13] its moral implications are such that few individuals, whether Muslims or spirit followers, are willing to deny the spirits' power when pressured. Besides suggesting that the division between 'yan bori and followers of the Prophet may be more social than religious, the widespread respect for, and fear of, the thunder spirits' threatening power has given rise to a novel way of administering justice. The context in which this new practice has evolved requires some attention. The distinction between truth and a lie is not statically defined for the Mawri, and what is true at one point may later become false, depending on the situation, the actors involved, and the intentions of and what is at stake for the speaker. People are known to lie to protect their own interests or because they are afraid of the repercussions their statements may have.[14] One way to make sure a person is not lying is to ask her to swear. Spirits, too, are often suspected of lying and cheating when put on the spot. When asked for their names during an initiation ceremony, they conceal their real identities and give false names as a matter of course.

To prevent such an occurrence, spirits are requested to swear: some are made to swear on Mecca and Medina—a practice that once again exemplifies how bori contests the authority of Islam while simultaneously attempting to appropriate central signifiers of Muslim power and legitimacy; others will swear on the praying mantis and other beings whose ambiguities or oddities set them apart from other animals.[15] Swearing is crucial to establishing the moral tension needed to sort out the true from the false.

When two parties are in disagreement and need to find out who is telling the truth and who is lying, they have several alternatives at their disposal. The first and simplest method of handling a dispute is to air it openly in front of kin, friends, and neighbors (Cooper 1997, 22). Friends and family members are often pulled into marital conflicts and pressured into taking sides until the dispute is resolved to the satisfaction of at least one of the parties. If such attempts fail to yield the desired outcome, the involved parties may choose to bring their grievance to the court of the sarki. The sarki's court tends to be used, among other occasions, by alleged victims of witchcraft who want to confront publicly the *maye* (witch) they suspect of harming them. This is also where Fulani herders and Mawri farmers bring their disagreements over crop and grazing land. Another institutional forum for settling disputes is the tribunal established by the French during colonial rule. In contrast to Nigeria where a comprehensive Muslim judicial system was maintained by the British, in Niger colonial administrators instituted the Napoleonic code at the expense of the shari'a. As a result, Nigeriens rarely adopt shari'a means of dispute resolution, and the office of Al'kali (Muslim judge) is used primarily to iron out the details of Maliki Islamic law that govern family law (Cooper 1997, 28). Moreover, the prohibitive costs of travel often discourage villagers from having recourse to Islamic institutions of justice when the Al'kali court is not within walking distance of their homes (Miles 1994, 261). The bori court presents yet another alternative way of seeking justice, one that has proved popular in Dogondoutchi. In front of an assembly of high-ranking members of bori, the individual whose actions and words caused suspicion will be expected to swear solemnly on the axes of the Zarma spirits that he did not commit the deed he is accused of having committed. The axes, which are the sacred property of the spirits, symbolize thunder and the babba'ku's control over natural elements (see also Rouch 1989,

170). The ax's blade represents the stone that is thrown to harm or kill offenders, while the sound of the little bell attached to the handle stands for the noise of thunder. If the accused individual is innocent, he will not hesitate to publicly claim his innocence.

A guilty person, on the other hand, is more likely to forgo the swearing and admit his culpability rather than run the risk of being struck by lightning the following rainy season. Committing perjury will inevitably lead to death, for the Zarma spirits do not show any leniency for those who have used their names in vain. Individuals who are killed by lightning are sometimes accused retrospectively of having sworn falsely on Kirai or Souleymane. The spirits may wait several years to avenge themselves, but sometimes reprisals are immediate, as in the following case that was recounted to me by a 'dan bori eager to impress me with the powers of the Zarma spirits. In the village of Doula, a young girl, who had been given some money by her fiancé, found that the money was gone after she came back from running an errand for her mother. She accused a friend who had been in the compound at the time of having stolen the money. The friend swore that she had not taken the money, which the girl had left on a mat. They went to the house of the Zarma spirits where the axes are kept to settle the matter. The friend swore again that she was innocent. Before the sun set on the horizon, she was dead. For the bori, this alleged tragedy was a triumphant affirmation of the spirits' extraordinary might, a might that staunch Muslims regularly challenge—explicitly or implicitly—by hindering the progress of bori practices, questioning the legitimacy and morality of bori possession, or simply denying that these Zarma spirits have a connection to lightning. Each of the incidents recalled in this chapter forms a particular kind of mythical construction that bori devotees use to redefine their notions of power and agency, and bodiliness and personhood. What Muslims thought of these representations of bori authority is open to speculation. For the most part, the Muslim individuals I talked to were reluctant to agree that there might be some truth to these testimonies, when they did not simply dismiss the matter entirely. I think that, usually, they did not know how these stories were narrated and used in bori circles. 'Yan bori never tire of recounting accidents that involve lightning for those who wish to hear about them. Through these carefully crafted narratives, they reaffirm the centrality of bori within the local nexus of power relations. And by appropriating lightning

During a wasa held for the spirits of rain and lightning, two possessed mediums dispense advice to members of the audience. The medium possessed by Souleymane (right) shakes a thunder ax, symbol of the spirit's might.

as an instrument of bori revenge, they also provide an imaginative response to the political and social coercion of Islam.

The setting of these courts provides yet another instantiation of how bori taps the system to draw on its unique forms of power. The management of disputes is usually the responsibility of orthodox authority, together with other administrative and executive tasks that one likes to locate in the "secular" realm of government. Here the bori steps outside of the boundaries to which it usually confines itself to rework the terms of justice, power, and punishment and interfere in local "politics." By dispensing their own brand of justice under the spirits' supervision, bori devotees are in effect rewording local and national notions of authority without ever confronting the orthodox judicial system. This is where their strength lies: for they need no jail to imprison the guilty and no police to enforce their laws. Everyone knows that there is no escape from the spirits for those who have lied under bori oath. Invisible yet omnipresent, the Zarma spirits always catch up with offenders and liars sooner or later. Clearly, the implications of these alternative courts are far reaching, considering that many among those who considered themselves devout Muslims agreed that they risked more by swearing falsely on Kirai's hatchet than by lying after having taken an oath on the Koran.[16] Allah in his almightiness can be merciful to the sinners—as long as their sins do not outweigh their good deeds—but people know from experience that the spirits show no compassion to their offenders. And even if, as will be seen below, some malamai have come up with their own theories about lightning in an effort to confront what they see as the 'yan bori's devious schemes, their explanations appear shaky when confronted by the raw reality of lightning.

Yet bori discourse about superhuman powers is more than a simple answer to Muslim hegemony. As Échard (1978) has suggested, it is grounded in deep historical, social, and cosmological realities that are best expressed through the medium of possession. As previously noted, in Ader, the Zarma spirits are held partially responsible for the deadly droughts and famines that occurred throughout the 1960s and 1970s. They are thought to have come to Ader with the sole intent of devastating the country and killing its inhabitants. Though no such commentary was available to me in Arewa, the data so far point to the profound historical and mythical basis of the Zarma spirits. These masters of rain and lightning have clear connections to the marginal group of iron smelters and smiths who, interestingly enough, stopped smelting iron ore to recycle the metal of auto parts at the time that the Zarma complex (the axes that the spirits of lightning carry should come to mind) emerged in Arewa. Like human blacksmiths who control the transformative capacities of fire to produce metal tools (Échard 1965; Herbert 1993), the spirit Yandu embodies control over heat in his skillful forging of thunderstones. The degree of heat sent by the spirits depends on the circumstances and the deed committed. If the offense is small, the life of the guilty party may not be taken. A person who has slightly offended the spirits, for instance, will feel extremely hot all the time. A more serious offense may result in the production of enough heat to kill the offender. Spirits feel emotions and are capable of displaying spontaneity, anger, revenge, or passion, but they do not strike without reason, or so 'yan bori would like to think.

The red robes and hats worn by certain Zarma spirits adds another layer of significance to the images of heat associated with the spirits of rain, thunder, and lightning. Red, in its connotation as blood or fire, has the potential to signify power and force but also ambiguity (Ryan 1976). *Ja* (red) may also connote severity and endurance. In certain contexts, it may mean "superior" (Wall 1988, 310). The Zarma spirits could well be described as red and fierce, hot and angry. One need only listen to their praise names (Kirai, "the mad one"; Souleymane, "less compassionate than fire") to get a sense of their hot and impetuous temper. In the neighboring region of Ader, they may take on the appearance of a large snake spitting fire and are so ferocious and impulsive that "they do not know their own family" (Échard 1978, 125). Despite Mawri assertions that the Zarma spirits only throw lightning to administer justice, the portrait that emerges out of this collection of testimonies nonetheless bears definite similarities to the sorcerers these fearful creatures allegedly replaced. Like sorcerers, they kill in the rain and work with fire. Like sorcerers, their display of anger takes the form of a destructive and wrongful heat. Through their control of fire and water, the heavens and the seasons, the mighty spirits of the West thus not only address contemporary political, religious, and economic problems but also mediate between distinct levels of experience and between the present and the past.

Muslim and Bori Interpretations of Lightning

For devout Muslims who reject bori interpretations, lightning strikes everywhere in the world rather than in particular places at particular times. It is sent by God and should not scare people into thinking they have been punished by some spirits, as the 'yan bori claim. This does not mean that pious Muslims deny the existence of spirits, but simply that they do not see a reason to deal with these supernatural entities when they can pray directly to God and follow the guidelines laid out by the Prophet. Some followers of the Koran see lightning as the work of Satan and warn against falling prey to his devious schemes and becoming a victim of the 'yan bori's cupidity.[17] A malam told me:

"For the 'yan bori, it is the spirits who cause lightning. But the Muslims, they see that the person who has committed a bad action was tempted by Satan. Satan set up a trap for that person and then [Satan] will tell the

A possessed bori devotee dressed in the costume of Kirai's brother, Souleymane, helps hold a goat that is about to be sacrificed.

'yan bori: 'I have set up a trap for this man and soon lightning will strike something he owns.' And the man [who has already received warnings that revenge is imminent] has promised a goat to the spirits if things got better. Satan will say to God: 'We will see if he is a good Muslim or not, and whether he follows the Koran.' As soon as lightning has struck his field or his cow, the 'yan bori will come to his house saying: 'We had warned you that lightning would strike because you did something wrong.' If he is not a good Muslim, he will believe what they say. They will convince him that he must hold a wasa because he had promised to give a goat if things got better. And things got better, but he hadn't brought the goat he had promised to give. The bad Muslim will be convinced that he needs to beg the spirits' forgiveness and make amends. The good Muslim will refuse to do what the 'yan bori ask and he will say that [lightning] has nothing to do with spirits, that lightning is sent by God."

Such an elaborate exegesis is of course hardly representative of what the majority of illiterate Muslims living in Arewa would say. It is more revealing of the ways Muslim scholars go about interpreting lightning-related tragedies to reaffirm the almightiness of Allah and convince people that they have nothing to fear from the 'yan bori. This man, however, dismisses the spirits altogether as a ploy created by Satan to test the faith of Muslims. According to him, God sends lightning to distinguish the "good" Muslims (who never doubt him) from the "bad" ones (who are tempted by Satan into believing that lightning is caused by spirits). Though many Muslims want to believe that spirits are not endowed with the power to control natural elements such as rain and lightning, Muslim rhetoric is often of no avail against the bori images of supernatural justice, which loom large in the moral imagination of Mawri communities. The ruling discourse peremptorily proclaims the divine supremacy of Allah, but the defiant interpretations of 'yan bori address notions of potency and authority that are still more in harmony with indigenous constructs of persons, supernatural forces, and the natural world, as pointed out earlier.

The attitude of Muslim women, especially, testifies to the resiliency of bori in Mawri consciousness. Though they might have accomplished the hajj to Mecca and piously follow the words of the Koran, rare are the Muslim women who would refuse to hold a wasa for the spirits should their granaries be destroyed by lightning. Bori is part of their cultural heritage, as it is for Muslim men who take supernatural signs seriously. Rather than representing a threat to the legitimacy of Muslim leaders and a transgression of the Prophet's words, bori is a genuine body of knowledge to which anyone may turn in times of crisis, just as Mawri ancestors did. From the viewpoint of bori, some crises (such as those caused by disease, lightning, poverty, etc.) are precipitated by the spirits themselves. When this is the case, the only sensible thing to do is to find out what the spirits require in exchange for a truce, because ignoring the warning or punishment sent by the spirits would only aggravate one's already critical situation. Since a person does not go to the spirits of her own free will but because the spirits intervened in her life, a Muslim who holds a wasam bori commits no sin, according to bori devotees: it is not sinful to listen to the dictates of those who are in power when it is the only way to remain alive and healthy.

Those who adhered, implicitly or explicitly, to such a view would often say that health is the most important thing an individual possesses and that no sacrifice is too big when one's well-being and prosperity are at stake. The following testimony, given to me by a bori healer of Dogondoutchi, vividly illustrates the point, besides attesting that spirits always have the last word:

I have been doing bori for thirty years. I have inherited my spirits from my mother. My maternal grandfather is the sarkin bori of Dosso. On my father's side, however, everybody is Muslim. After he went to Mecca, my father's brother said he would not greet me anymore because he did not approve of my doing bori. He went so far as choosing someone else to take his cows to pasture after I had tended his cows for years. I was very angry and said to my grandfather, the sarkin bori: 'If really I have spirits, Alhaji must be shown that spirits exist. Then we will see if he still refuses to greet me.' That day, Alhaji's daughter had taken the cows to pasture. Upon her return to the village, she heard some thunder and decided to take shelter under a tree. There was a lightning bolt and all the cows were struck except for the one that had already been sold to a neighboring woman. She (the cow) was the only survivor. The smoke from the lightning threw the girl on the ground; she was not dead but she was very frightened. When Alhaji heard what happened, he rushed to assist his daughter, but when he tried to hold her in his arms, his hands got twisted. He could not hold her. I went into hiding because I was afraid of Alhaji's reaction and thought it was best not to be seen for a while until things calmed down. But Alhaji came and offered apologies. He said: 'The cows that the spirits have killed are nothing. Above all, I am concerned about my daughter's well-being. I want to hold a wasa to make excuses to the spirits.' He even agreed to have the ceremony at his house, for he wanted most of all to apologize and see his daughter in good health again. A wasa was held at his house, and my spirit came. Alhaji, who had sworn he would never greet me again, took my hand and said: 'I am glad! I am glad! I am glad!' He did not want the spirits to hit his cattle or his children again. The spirit said to him: 'If you humiliate Mamane again, we will do it again.' He was fined seven he-goats. So Alhaji said: 'When my cattle come back from the bush, I will dedicate an ox to the spirits. And Mamane, if you want to hold a wasa, I will give you the money. Just come to me every time you want to have a wasa. Starting today, I will follow God and I will follow the spirits.' Six months passed and his daughter was still sick. She could not get up. So Alhaji gave me 30,000 francs CFA to organize a wasa. Alhaji's wife gave me a goat and his son gave me three goats. The wasa was held and within a week, the daughter healed. Alhaji's cattle came back and he gave an ox to the spirits. Since then, he has given two more oxen,[18] because he has seen the power of the spirits.

Here a wealthy and powerful Muslim almost loses his daughter to the spirits before he finally realizes what dedication to bori means. This is where the narrative is effective in construing the power of bori, because what the storyteller is saying in effect is that money—in the form of fines—is not all that the Zarma spirits want from those who have offended them. They expect people to show them respect and commitment. As long as Alhaji held wasani and gave money only out of fear of retaliation, his daughter would not get well. When he finally understood that the spirits were really stronger than he was, he stopped resisting them and gave in to their demands by willingly becoming a strong supporter of bori.

This triumphant testimony to the might of the Zarma spirits aptly captures the subtle yet highly efficient ways in which bori signs and practices are used to undermine the coherence and legitimacy of the sociocultural scheme they contest. Of course, the contestation of Muslim principles coexists with acceptance and assimilation. Various Islamic traits and customs have been incorporated into the bori lexicon. Besides the reference to Mecca and Medina mentioned above, and the noticeably Muslim garb worn by Zarma spirits, there are many signs of Islamic influence throughout the codified body of bori practices. Often these "foreign" signs and categories are absorbed, only to be aggressively redeployed against the dominant order (Comaroff 1985). Though the power of bori remains rooted in ritual practice, its social and moral ramifications extend well beyond the level of implicit statements to become an overtly coercive exercise used against visible Muslim dominance.

In the countless narratives of spirit-induced lightning that I heard in Arewa, wealthy and respectable alhazai or malamai are favorite targets precisely because they most explicitly embody the signs and values of Muslim hegemony.[19] In the bori version of these incidents, the forces of bori always win over the intrusive structures of Islam. Hence honorable Muslim figures not only end up partially embracing the seemingly unorthodox values of the marginalized 'yan bori, but they are also pressured into paying large sums of money to individuals they despise for their non-Muslim affiliations. Again, it should be pointed

out that there is no telling whether malamai are *really* the prime object of spiritual retaliation, as these testimonies cited seem to suggest.
Yet the fact that they are *said* to be often singled out for punishment
by the Zarma spirits confirms once more the extraordinary might of
the spirits. For everyone knows that only those individuals who have
the ability to tap into supernatural sources of power and knowledge
can become malamai. That Kirai, Souleymane, and their brothers dare
harm such persons—despite all the protection they have secured—
further attests to their remarkable puissance.

A crucial moment in many of these narratives is the instant of revelation, when the Muslim individual involved comes to the realization
that his faith in Allah cannot save him from the forces that threaten to
encompass him, and that he must make public amends to the spirits.
And though the fines imposed by the court of spirits are often described in explicit detail, it may be years before the 'yan bori see any of
the money that is rightfully theirs. In the end, few 'yan bori know and
concern themselves as to whether or not the entire sum has been paid
to the appropriate party. What matters more is that Muslims should
be led back onto the path from which they have strayed, the path of
the spirits, as is pointed out in the following account by a 'dan bori:

> Once lightning struck the tree of a malam. The malam came out of his
> house and saw that his tree was on fire. It was scarlet red. So he went
> back inside the house because he was very frightened. People say that
> his wives had quarreled and invoked the names of the spirits wrong-
> fully. That is why lightning had hit his tree. The spirits said [during the
> possession ceremony]: "We spared you because one of your sons was in
> the house. Otherwise we would have burned down your house, too."
> The malam's son has spirits, so he was protected by them. When the
> malam left for the bush, his son and his wives hurriedly asked the bori
> healer to hold the wasa and beg for the spirits' forgiveness on their be-
> half. Milk was fetched. When the malam came back, he was told that
> the 'yan bori were there, on the spot where lightning had struck, to
> speak to the spirits. And he said: "It's okay."

Aside from reducing arrogant Muslims to helpless and frightened
creatures and forcing them to redistribute their wealth to the less
fortunate, these practices aim at recreating a sense of justice and
morality for a minority estranged from the centers of power and control. Through their incarnation as Zarma spirits, 'yan bori brandish

the hatchet, the awe-inspiring symbol of lightning, just as Muslim clerks wield the pen, symbol of worldly powers. In a defiant gesture of opposition to the judicial principles originally established by the colonial administration, the members of bori set up their own courts and dispense their own justice, attempting thereby to relocate the centers of social and material authority and morality. Defying further Muslim orthodoxy, they also aggressively reassert control over the terms of burial in an alleged effort to remedy the destructive effects of the babba'ku's fire.

Indigenous Burials, Muslim Practices, and the Bori Alternative

Human beings have a *jiki* (body) and a kurwa (soul). Though it has the same shape as the body and is considered its double, the kurwa is fluid and invisible (Leroux 1948, 162). It is the essence of life at the same time that it has a life of its own. At death, the soul escapes from the body, making a feeble noise. After the burial of the corpse, the soul may remain among the living, a situation that is very undesirable, since a wandering soul may scare, harm, and even kill the people it manifests itself to. Prior to the Islamization of Arewa, both the body and the soul of the deceased were the object of special care aimed at ensuring that no soul would come back to haunt the friends, neighbors, and relatives of a person who had recently died. As soon as the body of the deceased had crossed the threshold of the house, a daughter of the deceased's brother would walk behind it holding a calabash filled with water. She would sprinkle the water over the ground and say: "You belong to the dead—leave the living in peace" (République du Niger n.d.[a]). Those who had died an unusual or violent death were especially threatening to their loved ones if their souls had not been properly appeased with offerings of food. As previously noted, women who had died in pregnancy were the object of special procedures destined to ensure that they remained among the dead.

The successful integration of Islamic practices (from naming ceremonies to weddings to funerals) into the Mawri lifestyle over the last forty or fifty years has not always gone hand in hand with the adoption of novel conceptions of personhood, agency, and the cosmos. Though a majority of the population performs the five daily prayers and faithfully carries out the fast, people still see themselves as enmeshed in intricate webs of forces that must be kept at bay by whatever means available. Islam possesses comparable notions if one considers, for an instant, the role of the jinn, or Muslim spirits, in shaping people's lives. Like the bori spirits, the jinn form an invisible society that parallels human society. Yet rather than promoting the coupling of humans and spirits to institute a fruitful relation of reciprocal exchange between them, Islamic practices strive to exorcise the intruding spirit whose presence contradicts Muslim notions of bodily health, closure, and self-control.

In the past, protection against external, and potentially malignant, influences was successfully accomplished by the 'yan 'kasa, who insured global prosperity and individual success by acting as mediators between humans and spirits. Even Muslims occasionally agree with 'yan bori that the abandonment of indigenous ritual practices is the reason for the various calamities and troubles people now experience. Now that people, regardless of the circumstances of their death, are all buried in the same cemetery (except for Christians who have their own graveyard), things happen: for example, the souls of women who have died in pregnancy come back as ruthless and dangerous female spirits. Local rumors have it that one of the victims claimed by the 1974 coup that overthrew President Diori's regime is now a ghost who torments her kin. Finding no peace, the soul of this woman has gone back to her native Arewa village to wander aimlessly. Neighbors and friends now avoid crossing the threshold of her brother's compound for fear of encountering the ghost. A story like this reveals how ideas develop to make sense of new realities and incorporate new scales of action. In the present case the deceased is not dangerous to her native community because she has died before she could fulfill her procreative role and give birth to a child; rather, as a prominent figure of the political scene who passed away before her "term" was over, she symbolizes another type of failure, another sense of aborted potential. Her unfulfilled promises are treated as a "miscarriage" of a special kind. Since one may presume no ritual precautions were taken at burial to correct what when astray, it is fitting then that the tormented soul of the dead woman would haunt her kin. Like the souls of childless women, it cannot rest until it fulfills the role that it was assigned.

Because of popular assumptions surrounding thunder and lightning, how a person who has been struck by lightning must be buried remains a topic of great contention between 'yan bori and fervent Muslims. Muslims insist that nothing special must be done, since the deceased died because it was God's will, whereas the 'yan bori energetically protest that the spirits' instructions must be carefully followed when one buries a victim of lightning. From the body of a person or an animal hit by a thunderbolt—as well as from the burning cinders of a house or the remnants of a tree—there emanates a dangerously polluting heat that must be neutralized before proceeding to the burial. The heat contained in the lightning stone that hit the victim is wrongful and destructive. It not only kills its intended target but threatens to harm those who come in contact with the remains of the victim. Only the devotees of Malo, Jatau, and Dounaba, the slaves of the Zarma spirits, may touch the corpses of the victims. Anyone else who touches the bodies, or the possessions of the deceased, takes a great risk of being struck by lightning herself. A sum of money must be paid to the devotees of the slave spirits by the relatives of the deceased to enable them to accomplish their work. Milk and medicines are used to cool off the bodies so that they can be removed without harmful consequences. After a wasa has been held for the spirits on the site where lightning fell, the place is no longer threatening and may be used for its intended purpose. During this ceremony, the Zarma spirits and their slaves are invited to possess their devotees and indicate where the victims are to be buried. Mounted on their adepts, the slave spirits then proceed to dig a hole and inter the corpses, while their masters, Kirai and his brothers, oversee the operation. Ignoring such a modus operandi may only worsen the situation and increase the fines that the relatives must pay to the spirits' devotees.

The story of the young girl who had defiantly sworn on the Zarma spirits that she had not stolen her girlfriend's money is instructive:

For her family, who adhered to strict Muslim principles, her untimely death by lightning had nothing to do with spirits. As soon as she was found, she was washed, laid in a shroud, and buried in a hastily dug grave in accordance with Muslim precepts. According to the 'yan bori who narrated the incident, she had not even been buried an hour when, in the same village, Kirai suddenly and unexpectedly possessed one of the local bori devotees. Speaking in anger, he asked his horse's companions just who had given the victim's family the authorization to bury the girl without the spirits' consent. Soon after the spirit spoke, the 'yan bori allegedly disinterred the body and covered it with a mat. Still mounted on his devotee, the spirit Kirai took the mat off and then proceeded to show the exact site where she was to be buried. His orders were promptly followed, and nothing more happened to her surviving kin.

Though this vignette eloquently underscores the spirits' powers of persuasion (for presumably the girl's kin were convinced that they should let bori devotees repair their "mistake"), Muslims are usually reluctant to let 'yan bori bury a victim of lightning who professed to follow the Koran, even if they secretly agree with bori interpretations of what caused the person's death. Despite the fact that bori devotees rarely succeed in actually taking over the malamai's ritual role when the person struck by lightning was Muslim, bori narratives of such happenings usually end on a victorious note. Nothing, not even the malamai's authority and tenacity, can get the better of 'yan bori, who know that no culprit escapes the spirits unscathed, as is attested by the following story, which was said to have occurred over a decade ago in a village of Arewa:

A boy was struck by lightning. The malamai wanted to bury him, but so did the 'yan bori. The 'yan bori said the members of Kirai's family had struck him for a specific reason and that a wasa must be held to find out what had to be done to appease the spirits. Eventually, and largely because the boy's father and uncle were Muslim, the malamai prevailed. The young victim was thus buried in an Islamic manner. But this didn't prevent the 'yan bori from holding a ceremony on the site where the little boy had been killed, outside the village. The boy's uncle came back from Niamey and interrupted the ritual. He was a malam and he didn't want bori people to get involved in what he considered his family's business. The wasa was therefore suspended and no one heard what the spirits had to say about the boy's death or about the fine to be paid by his family. Then a son of the malam became very sick, and later on a second one also started to have problems. The malam himself allegedly became ill and could not find a cure for his affliction.

This testimony exemplifies the struggle for power between 'yan bori and Muslims, which earlier was shown to have centered on the terms of trade and the flow of goods and now zeroes in on the control of the bodies. Through the voices of the threatening Zarma spirits, bori devotees fight to regain dominion over the terms of burial. That they do so should not be surprising, since it was often by warning people that non-Muslims no longer deserved a "ritual" burial and would simply be dumped into a hole, without the saying of any prayer, that malamai successfully converted so many Mawri in the 1970s.

What many of these stories also suggest is that no matter what opponents of bori say or do to discredit spirit mediums or to contest the legitimacy of their attempts to intervene in personal as well as communal crises, the spirits' justice always prevails in the eyes of 'yan bori. Significantly, the majority of those who overtly, and sometimes arrogantly, deny the existence of this brand of justice rarely hesitate to secretly seek the help of bori healers when avenging spirits strike home. Besides suggesting limits to the hegemony of Islam in Mawri communities, the fact that so many believe that spirits always have the last word makes bori an appropriate symbol of the triumph of the impoverished and the powerless.

This chapter examined the rich and finely textured discourse on lightning created by a religious minority and attempted to situate the discourse within a historical field of social and material relations. It also depicted an emerging body of signs and practices that was designed to deal with the threat of supernatural justice and that has proven its value as an instrument for confronting the visible features of socioeconomic and political domination. Yet, seeing the 'yan bori's translation of lightning as "retaliation" aimed simply at gaining access to Muslim wealth would be misleading. After all, from the bori perspective, dealing with the trauma inflicted by lightning involves a concerted effort to heal and to cool. By conjuring some of the most ominous figures of the bori pantheon and controlling their revengeful instincts, bori practices related to the occurrence of lightning have a strong impact on the community at large, not simply because they adroitly manipulate images of supernatural retaliation but also because they provide a conceptual framework that remains embedded within the implicit logic of Mawri life. Bori signs and practices meaningfully relate the frightful reality of lightning to other levels of experience by building on indigenous conceptions of health, heat, and reproduction. They continually implicate the person within the vaster cosmic reality and insist on their symbiotic relationship, all in contradistinction to Islam, which strives for more bounded, independent selfhood. By construing the effect of lightning as punishment for offenses that must be forgiven before the symbiosis between people and spirits can resume its course, bori practitioners propose an alternative explanation to Muslim models of personhood and agency, as well as a way to address, and even redress, the destructive impact of heavenly fire. In so doing, they also provide people with coherent and concrete schemes with which to face some of the problems of contemporary life in post-independence Niger.

Conclusion

Continuities and Discontinuities in Bori

THE PORTRAIT I HAVE PAINTED of possession in Dogondoutchi probably differs starkly from the vision of bori shared by those who patiently and generously introduced me to the world of the mutanen daji. Whereas spirit mediums took pains to emphasize continuities, often stressing that "the bori does not change; it is people who change," I have emphasized the transformative capacities of bori. Rather than lending support to my friends' views that bori is just the same "old"—and therefore *good*—thing, I often chose to focus on the diverse ways in which some individuals adapt to a shifting social landscape through the manipulation of bori media. Discussing bori as a movement in constant flux has also meant addressing the heteroglossic qualities of the spirits by pointing to the ways their voices "join[ed], contradict[ed], or transform[ed] larger conversations" (Lambek 1996, 244). My aim has been to situate spirit possession within a historical nexus of cultural experiences and social transformations by exploring bori idioms, relations, and practices within the local contexts that led to their engendering or modification. Such attention to the ways in which bori constitutes a determinant force in Mawri society, I want to gently remind my Dogondoutchi friends, only partially reflects my original agenda. However much this book developed out of an intellectual formation whose parameters I have tried to outline throughout, its fundamental inspiration lies in a few lively debates, some wordless but hauntingly vivid encounters, and all the puzzling yet significant gestures that I was privileged to witness during my research. One need only observe the pantheon of spirits over time to be further convinced that contrary to local claims that bori "does not change," possession practices hardly constitute a static, unchanging institution that is endlessly reproducing the mores of Mawri culture. Bori possession has been constantly changing to accommodate new spirits that are chronicling the unfolding and complex engagement between Mawri society and the outside world. All the spirits—whether male or female, high ranking or subordinate, young or old, mean or benevolent—are significant for what they tell us about people's experience of both quotidian reality and drastic transformations; the cast of characters include female warriors, French soldiers, noble Tuareg, seductive prostitutes, Zarma black-smiths, doctors and lorry drivers, Muslim clerks and bank thieves. All have something to say, all offer a commentary, however subtle and fragmentary, on the Mawri's perception of their evolving reality. Though they might conventionally be seen as the "quiet" actors of history (Braudel 1980, 38), bori devotees nonetheless emphasize their centrality as chroniclers of the past and the present in the multiple ways they remember, interpret, and periodically reenact their story in the forum of spirit possession. In recollecting significant events, ma-nipulating images, and modifying traditions, they also concretize the often diffuse yet deeply felt forces affecting their social order.

Paradoxically perhaps, this book also attempts to delineate the his-torical and cultural circumstances out of which emerged the shared sense that it is *people,* rather than the bori, who change. By stressing the immutable nature of bori, 'yan bori imply that the severance of what used to be tight connections between humans and spirits is im-putable not to the mutanen daji but to people *themselves.* It is people, my bori friends repeatedly pointed out, who have shown a decreas-ing lack of commitment to the spirits, when they did not altogether turn their backs on the mutanen daji to pursue their fortunes along other paths. Thus when spirit devotees insist that bori remains con-stant, a comforting rock of tradition in a sea of disruptive changes, their intent is not so much to look for an anchoring point in a decep-tively unchanging "institution" as it is to find solace in the resiliency of bori.

Like other indigenous traditions of spirit possession elsewhere (Lewis 1991; Matory 1994b), bori has outlived the theoretical per-spectives that predicted its demise. Despite the malamai's stubborn attempts to discourage possession and to erase the tangible signs of the spirits' presence on the local landscape, bori has left its trace even in the most Islamized communities of Arewa. Dogondoutchi, where prayer grounds now outnumber Coca-Cola outlets, is thus reputed to be one of the last strongholds of bori in Niger. Such a claim to fame has encouraged spirit mediums in need of additional income to ex-port this cultural "capital" to Niamey during the dry season; there, instead of searching for poorly paid and largely unskilled labor, they pursue ambitious careers as "traditional" healers *from Arewa,* providing specialized services that reap generous financial rewards. Not everyone, of course, wants to capitalize on Dogondoutchi's reputation as a haven for spirits and a center of "animist" practice. A friend told me that her brother and his acquaintances, all staunch Muslims, avoided Dogondoutchi altogether, because, they said, there were simply too many "stones" (altars) for the spirits scattered around town. Many of these altars have now been abandoned: when the last mediums of the spirits to whom they were dedicated died, their Muslim descendants were only too happy to forget that the mutanen daji relied on people for their subsistence. Yet perhaps because no one dares to further provoke the anger of these spirits by symbolically uprooting them from the local landscape, a lone *doutchi* (rock) or *hango* (circle of stones) remains here and there, as durable relics of a time when people publicly acknowledged their ties to the bori by shedding blood on what used to be well-kept altars.

Aside from such remains, the rocky peak that overlooks Dogondoutchi is by far the most powerful reminder of a tangible, if invisible, presence hovering over the industrious Mawri town. Like other clayey crests and mesas that have been sculpted by erosion in what is now a fossilized valley, the dogon doutchi raises its tortured shape against the sky like a giant tower. Although the spirit Ungurnu, who established residence in the huge monolith long before any humans settled in the area, no longer warns the inhabitants of any upcoming enemy attacks, a black ox is still slaughtered for her once a year. The sacrificial animal is dragged up the mountain with a rope around its neck. There are no set paths along the precipitous flanks of the dogon doutchi, and the climb is steep and difficult. Once the small party of Ungurnu "devotees" has reached a small flat area, halfway up the stony peak, the 'dan 'kasa who "owns" the sacrificial knife cuts the throat of the animal so that the spirit may drink its blood.

By climbing the dogon doutchi and sacrificing an ox to Ungurnu, the 'yan 'kasa, many of whom are members of the bori, reconquer Dogondoutchi as a place of and for the spirits. They vividly remind those (Muslims and spirit devotees alike) who witness their annual ascension from the streets below that the dogon doutchi is still part of the mythical landscape in which the first settlers of Arewa originally rooted their history and identity. As objectifications of the nexus between human existence and spirit agency, "natural" landmarks such as the dogon doutchi remain the valued and resilient signifiers of an indigenous moral order at the same time that they dramatize bori rivalries with Islam. In insisting that bori is unchanging or, as one healer once put it, "above all, about gargajiya (tradition)," my Mawri friends are pointing to the complex and meaningful resonances between past and present bori practices, resonances that are concretized anew each time a few spirit mediums ascend the dogon doutchi to shed sacrificial blood on its flanks.

In attending to bori as both a locus of gargajiya and a dynamic source of agency and creativity, I have traced some of the cosmological configurations that the local landscape has taken from its precolonial form to its more recent patterns as Mawri men and women learn to deal with the multiple contradictions of an expanding market economy. The local map of moral and mythical relations that had been routinely concretized through Mawri villagers' active propitiation of the spirits who peopled their surroundings was profoundly altered as local communities were progressively engulfed in a globalizing order of social practices and historical transformations. This is not to say that Arewa remained unchanging until the arrival of the French in 1899. Like countless other societies long reified as islands of "tradition" with histories but no history (Comaroff and Comaroff 1992), the Mawri did not wait until the advent of colonization to have a past (see de Latour 1982, 1984; Piault 1970, 1975). If I initiated my argument about the historical role of bori with the colonial encounter, it is largely because the creation, transformation, or disappearance of certain practices — for example, those related to healing, spirit possession, and the articulation of conflicting experience — become more noticeable in times of rapid structural change.

The focus on local "historicities" (Sahlins 1985, 53) has aided the attempt to demonstrate the meaningful relevance of bori practices in an overwhelmingly Muslim world; this has entailed examining how such relevance lies beyond the confines of individual crises and may be located in the carefully negotiated ways in which bori addresses the predicament of communities variously confronted with the disruptive effects of colonization, Islam, or commoditization. As has been documented for possession elsewhere in Africa (Boddy 1989; Lewis 1986; Nisula 1999), the perception of a Muslim threat serves to structure bori defiance of religious "orthodoxy"; yet the multiple ways in which Islam and bori have influenced and, even, constituted each other paradoxically challenges the very notion of mutually exclusive religious identities. In a sense, the history of Arewa is a history of struggles to redefine the contours of the moral community. Born in the encounter between two seemingly distinct visions of the world and the place of divinity in it, these struggles have given rise to complex processes out of which bori images and practices have emerged and been continually re-/defined, re-/de-coded, or re-/de-valued.

Embodiment, Balance, and Interiority

To trace the politics of appropriation, resistance, and competition that have shaped bori's interactions with Islam as well as colonial and postcolonial forces, this study has focused on the multidimensional relationship between social experience and embodied forms and shown how various transformations in Mawri society have been given tangible objectification in bodily signs, structures, and processes. By manipulating and reevaluating these embodied forms, the 'yan bori have meaningfully identified and attempted to gain control over the forces that threatened to destabilize their local universe. Whether they remapped villages, houses, or bodies, those who sought to rework the terms of their marginalization and to rechannel various forms and flows of power saw themselves as working to preserve their world from the threat of external evil. As the discussion of prostitution demonstrates, of late this evil has become increasingly harder to identify and to guard oneself against, as boundaries blur, thresholds vanish, and enclosed spaces become permeable to outside influence. Destructive and threatening things — enemy invasion, congestion, fevers brought during the cold season, lightning, wandering souls — have often been perceived as originating outside of one's community. Whether it is outside one's body or outside one's compound, village, or town, the distinction between inside and outside informs much of what bori accomplishes in order to preserve endangered values while defusing the impact of modern technologies. The outside, epitomized by the bush, is where special, at times potentially productive, but often dangerous powers reside. With the progressive abandonment of bodily techniques and symbolic practices (e.g., gyaran gari, "special" burials, propitiation of market spirits, and the like) that focused on the mediation between village and wilderness and the inscription of margins and thresholds onto individual and corporate bodies, spaces that were previously protected against harmful external influences have become vulnerable to a variety of pernicious forces and malevolent beings from the outside.

In examining how bori reasserts its indispensability by translating the effects of social, economic, and political transformations into multileveled invasions of corporeal and communal space, I moved back and forth across various thresholds and onto various paths and analyzed the images that some Mawri deploy to express their loss of control over moral and material resources. As Arewa was encompassed within colonial Niger, indigenous mythico-ritual topographies were progressively eclipsed by an emerging order of power and production. As longer and broader roads unfurled across the landscape to bring the mixed blessings of "development" to rural communities, villages that gained easier access to the cities also became more open to a host of dangerous forces displaced by the erosion of a prior network of socio-moral relations. This much emerged out of my discussion of the tragedy that followed the erection of a new marketplace: by deploying the images of the market Doguwa preying upon innocent villagers, 'yan bori implicitly were protesting the growing control of Muslims over the terms of commerce as much as they were trying to regain conceptual mastery over a world overcome by forces beyond local control. As for the notion of breached borders and boundaries, bori effectively heals personal and communal bodies by restoring balance to otherwise unbalanced processes of growth, production, and exchange. One dimension of this attempt to restore health and prosperity to corporeal as well as social bodies has involved reclaiming some of the authority vested in colonial, national, or Muslim institutions. Motivated by an urgency to redraw some of the features of a mythic precolonial landscape, the 'yan bori have forged various value-generating techniques by borrowing mostly from colonial and Islamic repertoires of signifiers—for instance, building mosques for their spirits, wearing French army uniforms, or positioning their bodies as if they were sitting at desks.

The various signs, tropes, and techniques that bori uses to reconstruct bodies and redefine boundaries are not confined to an elusive realm of sacred structures and symbolic processes. Rather, they are part of a continuum of meaningful yet instrumental practices through which people ceaselessly interpret, articulate, and objectify personal circumstances and cultural experiences. Bori, I have shown, does not lie outside of the mundane and the ordinary, because the logic of its

Two assistants dress a devotee possessed by Kirai during a wasa held for the spirits of rain and lightning.

practices is embedded in the processual reality of the everyday. Nowhere is it more evident than in the domain of clothing and presentation of self. Bori clothing mediates separate realms by objectifying the presence of intangible beings and giving contours to elusive bodies during possession rituals. By soaking up and inscribing in their folds, seams, and texture the identity of their wearer, these garments recreate the physicality of the spirits and concretize their presence even long after they have left their fleshy hosts. As such, the outfits are routinely used to evoke or communicate with the spirits, thereby forging spiritual connections between distinct worlds of experience.

If clothing objectifies tenuous relations by giving shape to amorphous entities and providing the connecting threads between matter and spirit, the physical bodies covered, hidden, or revealed in such a manner are themselves the most versatile instruments available to bori devotees. The human frame offers a concrete, immediate, and easily manipulable ground for indexing wider forces that are not easily circumscribed and for grasping events that elude comprehension. In their attempt to mediate processes of historical and social transformation through the refashioning of quotidian signifiers, the followers of the spirits focus on the body's capacity to objectify and articulate social structures and processes. Female forms, in particular, provide a fertile medium for imagining and coping with various experiences of growth, decay, reproduction, destruction, and transformation. In chapter 7, I explored bori discourses on female bodies and bodily capacities to throw light on the creative processes at work in the mediation of rapidly evolving relations of power and production. Through this focus on embodied forms and bodily practices one can see that far from disappearing in the face of a growing Islamic ascendancy, as some academics and colonial administrators predicted, bori has emerged as a tangible force of Mawri history and society.

Bori as an Emergent yet Resilient Force

The resiliency and rootedness of bori are largely based in practices that enable people to selectively appropriate and reconfigure some elements of tradition while simultaneously mediating the effects of modernity. Spirit possession in Arewa exists in its own right and not ultimately as a response to deteriorating social conditions or the dehumanizing effects of commoditization or migrant labor. It raises questions about power and agency, offers practical solutions to nagging problems, and provides ethical standards to deal with moral issues or address the problem of evil at the same time that it brings a critical distance with which to assess changes, disturbances, injustices, pain, or conflicts. Whether it is dealing with infertility, drought, or business failures, bori's resolutely pragmatic outlook on the adversities of modern life is what makes it such an indispensable resource for so many rural Mawri, whether or not they choose to publicize their reliance on the mutanen daji. At another level, bori's strength and credibility hinge on the paradoxical and constantly renegotiated terms of its relations with Islam—relations that hover between antagonism and cooperation, disapproval and recognition. Explicitly controversial, public, and political, bori has evolved in response to colonial, postcolonial, and Islamic challenges, but in such a way as to become irremediably imbricated in prevailing ideologies—today those of Islam and the state. Much of my discussion has thus focused on the critical, sometimes subversive, yet always changing commentaries through which bori negotiates its coexistence with Islam, at times "domesticating" and internalizing Islamic elements but occasionally reasserting the superiority and indispensability of its own practices in the face of Muslim hegemony.

Yet if bori owes its survival and constant regeneration in part to the long-standing rivalry it has engaged in with Islam, what is one to make of the fact that at the time I write this, some Muslims seem to be more concerned with intra-Muslim competition than with the threat of "animism"? Put differently, one may wonder if, ironically, the recent intensification of the conflict in which mainstream Muslims are opposed to the growing faction of Izala reformers over a variety of moral, spiritual, economic, and political issues will not eventually weaken the creative and combative impetus of bori devotees who no longer feel the need to routinely redefine themselves in association with or in opposition to Islamic orthodoxy. My hunch is that because bori has no necessary cause or outcome and must be seen instead as a constitutive feature of local reality, it will probably always work to interpret, mediate, or contest some of the social forces affecting the Mawri world. Bori reasserts its centrality through its capacity to renew itself as a multifaceted phenomenon that caters to a variety of needs and expectations, even if this means, at times, containing contradictions and nurturing paradoxes. In this respect, it appears to differ widely from its northern Nigerian counterpart, which, despite its thriving influence in some quarters, was officially banned by Hausa emirs and has been described as a "sub-rosa court of last resort" (Callaway 1987, 84).

By stressing both the local specificity of bori and the characteristics it shares with other forms of possession in Africa and beyond, I have tried to portray both the translocal dimensions of possession and the distinct ways in which Mawri farmers define, interpret, and negotiate their encounters with spirits. Creative, fluid, and ever changing, the practices that authorize and regulate people's conversations with the mutanen daji challenge conventional understandings of history, power, and efficacy. To account for what they are, what they do, and where they belong, one must strive to retain as much authenticity as possible in one's interpretations. This implies both avoiding the pitfalls of simply seeing possession as "standing for something else" and refraining from adopting a phenomenological model that would forbid any interpretive stance. It cannot be pointed out too often that the messages and motivations of possession are numerous and complex. And while possession aims to recreate order out of chaos and confusion, it also cultivates and contemplates ambiguity. Puzzlement and mystification are an intimate part of public performances even if people manifestly attend them to find an answer to their problems. One's readings, therefore, can never be definitive; they must remain, of necessity, partial and open-ended even as they aim to clarify the language of possession. This is perhaps what I have tried to do in this book. Whether or not I have succeeded, only the spirits can judge. To them and to their hosts, who struggle daily to preserve endangered traditions while capitalizing on new possibilities, I simply say, "*Maganin zaman duniya ha'kuri*" (With patience, you can do anything).

Notes

Introduction

1 Such a list has been provided by Échard (1991a) in her study of the bori in the neighboring Hausa communities of Ader.

1. *Bori,* Power, and Identity in Dogondoutchi

1 For an insightful discussion of gender politics in contemporary Hausa households and communities, see Cooper's analysis of the lives and struggles of married women in Maradi, Niger (1997).

2 Bori healers, especially famous ones, are sometimes called *mayu* (witches), because through their partnership with the spirits they have the potential to inflict misfortunes and even to kill people. This is why Mawri mothers do not let their young children get close to prominent healers. A jima could, unknown to anyone, cast a spell on a nearby child or capture the child's soul.

3 One story claims that no inhabitants of Lougou ever set foot in Matankari after the Azna were defeated by the sarki's troops. And it is common knowledge that if an Azna from Lougou is given a handful of dirt from Matankari in the palm of his hand, the Azna will flee (Piault 1970, 123). Besides alluding to the ritual and moral signification of certain sites and landmarks, these tales of clashes and confrontations point to the permanent oscillation between alliance and war that characterized relations between Gubawa and Arewa.

4 If, in the nineteenth century, slavery had become a major dimension of the socioeconomic structures in the rest of Hausaland (during his stay in Kano, Barth [1857, 510] estimated that there were as many slaves in the city as there were free men), it never played anything but a secondary role in the Mawri economy. According to Piault (1975), there was never any systematic exploitation of slave labor in Arewa. The embryonic character of the Mawri state and the persistence of a lineage mode of production promoted the progressive integration of most war prisoners into their masters' lineages. Noble prisoners could be exchanged for a ransom from their families. Commoners made up the bulk of the slaves who were exported to Songhay country to serve as a means of exchange, but most became members of their masters' lineages. The slave trade in this region appears to have been

very limited, which is probably why colonial administrators often reported the relative absence of market relations in Arewa.

5 Many administrators deplored the inefficacy of the French administration and commented on the lack of an explicit and clearly elaborated policy (Deschamps 1963; Gouilly 1952; Le Chatelier 1899).

6 Prior to the nineteenth-century Fulani conquest, the Hausa states east and south of Arewa had remained a loose confederation of partners or rivals. After Usman 'dan Fodio launched his jihad against the Hausa kingdoms, most of these polities were incorporated into what became known as the Sokoto caliphate. Because it resisted the Fulani invasion, Arewa was largely spared from Muslim influence until the arrival of the French at the turn of the century.

7 PPN stands for Parti Progressiste Nigérien.

8 In his inaugural speech to the Assemblée Nationale, Prime Minister Hama Amadou stressed that the people of Niger "are experiencing untold suffering, beginning with poverty, continuing with sickness, and very often followed by famine. The national coffers are absolutely empty, the country's financial situation is disastrous. Niger needs to recover its dignity and its credibility, both within the country and abroad" (Mayer 2000).

9 The Movement for Suppressing Innovations and Restoring the Sunna, or Izala movement, was created in Jos, Nigeria, in 1978 (see Kane 1994; Masquelier 1996b, 1999b; Umar 1993).

10 Which household I lived in was dictated more by necessity than by choice. Upon my arrival in Dogondoutchi, I rented a house that eventually turned out to be no longer "available" when the actual owner accidentally learned that his brother had rented it to me without telling him before fleeing to Nigeria with the rent money. Across the street lived a Muslim family in whose compound I had spent many afternoons observing and participating in domestic activities. When Salamatou, the second wife, learned about my problematic housing situation, she spoke to her husband, who agreed to rent me his own quarters in the family compound. The compound was centrally located. Having my own courtyard enabled me to transcribe taped interviews in relative privacy. And hanging out with two Muslim wives who had no qualms about sharing their knowledge of bori afforded me an invaluable perspective on the not-so-"public" affinities between possession and Islam.

11 To preserve the anonymity of these individuals, all have been given pseudonyms. Except for Dogondoutchi, Lougou, and Matankari, the name of Mawri communities have also been changed.

2. Lost Rituals

1 For a similar scenario in zar, see Leiris (1958, 12–13). According to Leiris, in the Ethiopian version Eve had thirty children, but because she was afraid of God, she hid the fifteen most beautiful ones. To punish her, God declared that the hidden children would remain forever invisible.

2 Hausaphone Nigeriens are not unique in their division of the lived-in world between the domesticated and the wild. For a particularly rich account of Beng classification of the "village" and the "bush" in Côte d'Ivoire, see Gottlieb (1992).

3 The harmattan blows from the northeast during the dry season, which lasts from November through May.

4 *Cikin gari maza suke dai; cikin daji akwai bambanci.*

5 Bori healers commonly allude to the alleged sorcerers they catch during the night when everyone else is sleeping. They plant a blade, a stick, or a needle straight into the ground and in so doing, immobilize their preys. The latter, if the procedure is done right, can barely blink an eye. After requesting a ransom in cash from prisoners who usually agree to anything so as not to be found out by the rest of the village, the healers pull their "weapons" from the ground, thereby liberating the sorcerers in the process (see Masquelier 1999a).

6 In the village of Tanciya, a formerly independent hamlet that has now been incorporated as part of Dogondoutchi, more than fifteen hens and roosters of varying colors are slaughtered every year to prevent sickness from afflicting the children. After the bori devotees attending the ceremony have been possessed by one of their spirits, they walk along the village periphery, led by the sarkin bori (chief of bori) supervising the gyaran gari. It is the spirits, who, by common accord, indicate where an animal is to be slaughtered.

7 The original prayer in Hausa goes:

> *Ha, wuta, wuta daji ta*
> *Ba ta gari ba*
> *Ba ta da hanyar cikin garin Argoum*
> *Sai dai ta ci; Daji ba ta cin mutum*
> *Wuta ba ta da hanyar cikin garin Argoum*
> *Za ta yi ha maza ha mata*
> *Shi garin Argoum shina zama furi*
> *Ha, wuta, wuta daji ta*
> *Ba ta gari ba*
> *Ba ta da hanyar cikin garin Argoum*
> *Sai dai ta ci; daji ba ta cin garin Argoum.*

8 Frobenius (1913, 568) witnessed the same practice during his travel through Hausaland. During an initiation ritual destined to cure a man from his epilepsy, he wrote:

> The general custom is to sacrifice a black buck-goat to the Babba'ku, cook it and eat it. But no morsel of it may be taken to the village or town. It is an unwritten law that these sinister immolations and all traces of them must be confined to the bush. Not a single pot, not a single piece of crockery used in the arrangement of the ritual is allowed to go back into a human abode.

9 The following words, a bori healer assured me, would efficiently redirect evil forces away from me and onto the guilty party: "Greetings, this is the village we come in, we get out, headaches and stomachaches, headaches are for village chiefs, stomachaches are for village chiefs."

10 In Ourgam, southeast of Dogondoutchi, the spirit Kirsa would allegedly build a thick and thorny fence around the village to protect its inhabitants from potential invaders.

3. Socializing the Spirits

1 I show below why spirits request their own clothing from their devotees soon after (but also often before) they become initiated. It is an obligation that 'yan bori must fulfill if they do not wish to incur the spirits' wrath (see Masquelier 1996a).

2 I do not mean to imply here that spirits are not part of what Mawri people would consider as ordinary experience, for they are indeed inextricably embedded in the fabric of everyday life. In the case at hand, Zeinabou is nonetheless making a distinction between what she experiences as a direct result of her own actions in the world and what she experiences as a result of an external agency's involvement in her life.

3 Muslim men often invoke bori as the reason why they divorced a former wife. It would be a mistake to assume that husbands divorce their wives primarily on account of bori. Incompatibility, infertility, bad character, and adultery are also often cited as factors in divorce. Nonetheless, within the context of bori itself, a high percentage of the divorced women told me that their husbands had repudiated them *because* they were plagued by spirits and wished to heal themselves by undergoing an initiation.

4 For an insightful discussion of the marriage and sexual imagery suffusing Oyo Yoruba possession, see Matory (1994a, 198–204).

5 Kurwa was often associated—and interchangeable—in my informants' experience with *inuwa,* which is literally one's shadow or shade. The concept

of a soul or vital principle was occasionally translated by French-speaking residents as *image* (same word in English).

6 The relationship between bori and prostitution has been given some attention in the literature (Barkow 1971), yet little or no information exists on specific numbers, income levels, and economic opportunities of prostitutes (Frishman 1991). For more on the politics of identity and karuwanci (prostitution), see Pittin (1983) and Cooper (1997).

7 Possession is hard work, everyone will tell you. After they have been possessed by one or several spirits, devotees are usually exhausted and sore, especially if the possession has been violent. Though it is the duty of 'yan bori to attend ceremonies during which they might be mounted by their spirits, they fear the power of the spirits over them. Despite the fact that, paradoxically, many of them, especially among the younger generation, crave the visibility and attention one receives when possessed in the middle of a crowded audience, they are usually relieved when another medium is chosen to be a mount.

8 To justify their assertions, people often say that women are *not* like men. Even if the spirits teach them curing techniques and herbal preparations, they cannot, and should not, use such knowledge to heal other people, though they may prepare medicines for their personal use.

9 It should be recalled that certain Doguwa spirits possess their victims only to kill them. They feed on their victims until they have drunk the last drop of their blood. Wild and capricious, they cannot be placated, but they may, in some cases, be persuaded to leave their victims before it is too late (Masquelier 1997a).

10 Herbal medicines are sold as powders that are wrapped in rags. Such medicine can be (1) ingested as is, (2) drunk after it has been mixed with water, (3) inhaled after it has been set over a bed of hot coals, (4) or mixed with the water one washes oneself with. All types of treatments are of comparable efficacy, given the permeability of the human body to material forces and substances. The skin is thought to be a porous medium through which heat and cold, winds, and medicines can penetrate, affecting the body in various ways.

11 Possession, when initiated and controlled within the boundaries of a ritualized performance, is considered *aiki* (serious and intense work).

12 Though most musicians inherit their craft patrilineally, I met some individuals who, in their words, "had simply started to play music with some friends one day." These musicians who may not have been brought up in a household of bori musicians often credit the spirits for inspiring them or for forcing them to play even against their will. According to one violinist who had traveled throughout Niger and northern Nigeria to perform his trade, "Before, I tried to stop playing at bori performances. But the spirits

made me go on. They said they would force me to play, that if [I did not play], they would make me ill."

13 In some rare instances, bori musicians are also spirit mediums. When this happens, the maroki (sing. of maroka) learns to postpone possession until it is appropriate, that is, when he attends a ceremony where he has not been requested to play music.

14 The maroka's lack of shame and their female dimension make them ambivalent individuals who can transact bodily powers across conventional margins. Not being able to aspire to the rank, situation, and prestige that other men seek, they are also not bound by the same restrictions. As noted earlier, they can, for instance, bring back to the village the carcasses of the roosters and hens that have been slaughtered in the bush during gyaran gari. They may touch the hatchets of the terrible Zarma spirits when no one else is allowed to—after the latter have thrown them to the ground in a moment of anger. Unless the maroka pick them up, the hatchets might lie on the ground until another wasa is organized for the spirits of thunder and lightning. Because they are "nobodies," bori musicians are the only ones who can ask the fearful Gillaji spirits—Tuareg nobles and warriors—to identify themselves. Tuareg spirits are very proud and the slightest mishap might offend them. Being such lowly individuals, musicians risk nothing at the hands of the Gillaji. As mediators between the realm of mortals and the world of spirits, musicians are also an indispensable component of spirit possession. Spirits can always replace devotees, but they cannot replace those who make things happen by singing their praise.

15 Although affliction by a bori spirit frequently results in the patient's initiation, there are some spirits who do not require initiation. Known as Dodo, these powerful creatures endow their human hosts with the capacity to heal a wide variety of ailments, but like the wind to which they are often compared, they don't generally remain long with their mediums. As I show elsewhere, these spirits are very critical of the perceived excesses of bori devotees who charge high prices for their services and seem more interested in making money than healing the sick (Masquelier 1999c). In their efforts to resist the tide of modernity, Dodo devotees shun certain mass-produced goods, refuse to charge their clients a set fee, and follow strict moral prescriptions.

16 I knew several old women, many of them widowed or divorced, who, though they had attended countless wasani over the years, had never had their spirits "arranged," because of lack of funds and support. Those who have not yet undergone a gyara cannot fully participate in a wasa, because their spirits have not been socialized and tuned to the set of cultural meanings and conventions that shape bori performances. Their spirits are said

to have no *baki* (mouth): therefore, they cannot speak. Though these "un-tamed" spirits may possess their horses, their speech will be unintelligible and of no value to the community of mediums and bori sympathizers. Usually, such spirits are discouraged from possessing their horses, because, as wild and mute participants, they only create havoc and confusion.

17 Spirits love the sweet smell of perfume, but they are driven away by foul odors. Healers trying to exorcize an evil spirit thus use a mixture of plants (in pounded form) that emit a pungent or acrid smoke when heated on a bed of warm coals. It is hoped that the bad smell, combined with other powerful techniques, will drive away the wild spirit.

18 It is worthwhile to note that *torou* is the name of the first spirits to be incorporated in *holey* possession in neighboring Songhay society (see Rouch 1989). These spirits are now also part of bori. Torou also designates the physical abode of a spirit in Songhay—a stone, a mountain, a tree, and the like—while *ruwa* is the Hausa term for water. The image of water is obviously relevant because the Torou or Zarma spirits govern the rivers and are masters of the heavens, and, by extension, of the rain.

19 The black chicken is the favorite animal of the Doguwa while the red-brown one is usually associated with the Zarma spirits. The white chicken may be favored by Zaki-Sarki, a Muslim spirit and member of the Zarma family or by Maria spirits, who favor white over any other color. The black-and-white speckled chicken is associated with Zanzana, because black-and-white spots represent the ugly skin disease with which this spirit is afflicted and/or afflicts her victims: smallpox.

20 In order for the spirits to speak, they must be given "mouths." Thus people say of a spirit that "*an yi mishi baki*" (he was "given" a mouth).

21 To Muslims who pressure them into abandoning their "sinful" ways, bori devotees respond that they are working for the benefit of the entire community. Muslims should be thankful, they often argue, that others pull together their meager resources to protect the whole village from evils against whose effect Muslims prayers and medicine are powerless.

4. The Everyday Life of *Bori*

1 I am grateful to Brad Weiss for this particular insight.

2 When devotees are about to be possessed by their spirits, their eyes often protrude and roll backward in their orbits. As a result, the iris is hidden and only the white of the eye is visible.

3 It is the successful mixing of these sexual fluids that is believed to produce a fetus.

4 A kind of gruel made from millet flour to which sugar is added and that is traditionally consumed by new mothers, who must reinvigorate themselves after their pregnancy.

5 Ironically enough, if, in a different context, this medium might have had no real reason for demanding that his "wife" share with him a kola nut, in this particular case it was totally appropriate and even, perhaps, expected that Zahoho's medium ask his wife for sustenance. As will be seen in chapter 7, Zahoho is a "lazy bum" who does nothing besides waiting for his wife to come home and feed him.

5. Kinesthetic Appropriation and Embodied Knowledge

1 This spirit is cruel and vicious because his wife, Fadimata, left him for another man, I was told. When he comes to a wasa, he immediately starts fighting with the other Baboule.

2 People say that Komandan Mugu *hi tonka yaji* (is "meaner" than hot pepper).

3 In a footnote to the "official" version Rouch relates (1989, 92n), he also recounts a similar tale that I summarize here. Commandant Croccichia had the young Hauka mediums whipped and hosed with water, and then he incarcerated them in the prison of Niamey. During the night a new Hauka, the "Commandant Mugu," also called the "mean commandant" or Korsasi (i.e., the Corsican), provoked the possession of all the mediums by their spirits. They broke the walls of their prison and escaped. They went to Kumasi and Accra, where many young Nigeriens had already emigrated.

4 *Commandant* is a title Mawri often used in a generic manner to refer to any high-ranked officer in charge of an administrative subdivision.

5 According to Stoller (1989a, 139), in the *holey* form of spirit possession prevalent in Songhay, many Hauka vomit ink when they possess their mediums' bodies. Stoller does not comment on the possible significance of such a gesture, but it may be just another "technique" for embodying, and therefore capturing, the powers of literacy. By vomiting the very substance with which colonial clerks—as well as Muslim scholars—inscribe words on a palpable medium, Hauka devotees engendered literacy as an embodied form out of which emerged the might associated with the mastery of the word.

6 Interestingly, in *Les maîtres fous,* one can observe a Hauka medium portraying a locomotive, driving back and forth with his arms imitating the wheels' mechanical movements (Rouch 1956).

7 For the ideas presented in this section, I am indebted to Fuglestad (1975), whose argument centers around the notion of force and luck.

6. Taking Hold of the *Kasuwa*

1 The market transfer was the first of a series of administrative measures designed to improve the town's commercial prospects and sanitary condition. In September 1988, the town acquired six donkeys to pull carts designed for the pickup of local garbage. During that month merchants and petty traders who had not or would not pay their business taxes (which would be used from then on to cover the salaries of the mayor and his four newly appointed assistants) were promptly ordered to dismantle the canopies that shielded their merchandise from the sun. Funds were to be allocated for the destruction of errant dogs, the improvement of veterinary services, and the furnishing of local classrooms.

2 It would only be fitting for this bloodthirsty spirit to retain some measure of anonymity, since the evil Doguwa who prey on people and suck their blood remain forever nameless. They are considered too mean and vicious to be named, that is, to be properly socialized so as to interact with humans in a benevolent and fruitful manner (Masquelier 1997a).

3 Mawri people are not alone in thinking of markets as dangerous and problematic places. For an account of the dangers of markets in an Igbo-speaking community of southeast Nigeria, see Bastian 1998b.

4 *Tabliers* (from the French *table*), who display their merchandise on tables under shade trees or before the entrance to a compound, are not subject to any official control. In an effort to regulate the practices of these small-scale traders and to sanitize the streets of the town, in the summer of 1988 the newly appointed mayor of Dogondoutchi established a new tax to be paid by all the tabliers who set up their tables in a shed made of wood and thatch. Those who did not conduct their business under a man-made shelter would not pay taxes. Within a few weeks all the sheds had been torn down by their owners, who felt that they would rather be subjected to the effects of the glaring sun than submit to what they perceived as the whimsical fancies of city officials.

5 Material wealth, as Grégoire notes, is "closely linked with social status, measured as a 'richness in men,' or *arzikin mutane*. The ways in which material wealth is accumulated, employed and distributed have much to do with whether a particular merchant is also 'rich in men' " (1992, 2).

6 The widespread practice of gambling (in the form of card games), which attracts a crowd of players and onlookers during bori ceremonies, testifies to such a belief.

7 Aside from serving as currency, *farin ku'di* ("white money," or cowries) were, and still are, put to a variety of uses. As *idanu* ("eyes") through which one

can read into the future, they are used in divination (Nicolas 1986, 126). They are sewn onto the costumes worn by certain bori adepts. They are also associated with fertility and female sexuality because of their resemblance to female genitals. In the past, cowries would be used for jewelry, figured in wedding songs, and would be received by women as tokens of affection from a suitor (Cooper 1997, 92).

8 In the southeastern part of the country (Hausaland), farmers responded so enthusiastically to colonial propaganda destined to promote the cultivation of groundnut—the French saw the crop's potential for exportation— that production soared from about nine thousand tons in 1945 to nearly two hundred thousand tons in 1957 (Charlick 1991, 39). Because raising cash crops for the market inevitably meant decreasing the amount of acreage used for millet or sorghum cultivation, the French became alarmed about the possibility of chronic famine and potential political unrest ensuing from a shortage of food crops (39). Storage of surplus grain production and the implementation of modern farming techniques were seen as remedies to the threat of food shortage. Mention is made in colonial reports of the legendary "lack of foresight" of villagers who sell all their millet in Nigeria to obtain cash and who find themselves obliged later to buy it back at a higher price or who struggle to survive on wild roots and berries (see, for instance, République du Niger 1947).

9 I once gave a ride to a friend of mine who lived in seclusion—as an enclosed space, my car was an acceptable substitute for the compound, her husband had decided. As we drove through the permanent town market, referred to as *tasha* in Hausa or *autogare* (car park) in French, because this is where bush taxis load passengers, her eyes opened wide. She looked with amazement at the stalls, the people, and the various goods displayed and later told me she "no longer knew" the market (that is, she had forgotten what it looked like). She only vaguely remembered what it was like when she was a young unmarried girl. After marrying her current husband at fifteen, she had never returned to the tasha until that day.

10 This is aptly conveyed in the following proverb: "*Kasuwa kogi ce*" (The market is a river).

11 This is why one should never take one's spirit to a *gidan kallo* ("house of seeing," or museum) for fear that he will want to remain there, forever gazing at beautiful objects and rich artifacts.

12 A notable exception is the new *Grand Marché* (big market) of Niamey, which was constructed on the site where the previous one burned down approximately twenty years ago.

13 None of my male neighbors in Doutchi ever missed the Friday market unless they were sick or out of town. Failing to attend the market would have been akin to a dyed-in-the-wool gambler missing a day at the races. Beside

being *ran salla* (prayer day) for the Muslims, Friday was clearly the most important day of the week for Mawri living in or within traveling distance of Dogondoutchi.

14 In this respect it is interesting to note that one of the markets of Niamey, Niger's capital, has been named Wadata. As a noun, *wadata* can be translated as "wealth." As a verb, it also means "became rich" or "had sufficiency" (Abraham 1962, 914).

15 See also Meillassoux (1971) for the role of the Saharan trade in spreading Islam.

16 In fact, because the term *alhaji* has become synonymous with wealth rather than piety, it is often used as a respectful way of addressing wealthy merchants, regardless of whether they have accomplished the pilgrimage.

17 As the union of three (associated with maleness and male elements, cycles, and activities) and four (its female counterpart), the number seven is extremely important in Mawri culture in general—among Muslims as well as non-Muslims. It is the product of the joining of the male and female principles, principles that provide the foundation for Mawri conceptions of the universe and its reproduction. As such, it is intimately associated with concepts of growth and generation. That seven markets, no more or less, are needed for the successful completion of the hut heightens the significance of the ritual as an attempt not only to create wealth but also to ensure its subsequent reproduction.

18 In 1988 and 1989 there were rumors that in northern Nigeria, malamai went around systematically destroying spirit houses in an attempt to discourage people from practicing bori.

7. The Mirrors of Maria

1 This is even more true since the recent devaluation by half of the franc CFA. As of January 1994 the price of imported goods had more or less doubled for Nigeriens.

2 If sweetened fura is associated with high standards of living (and often reserved for guests), poverty, in Mawri eyes, often implies not simply unsweetened fura but sour fura. When fura is left to stand overnight, it ferments and takes on a very bitter taste. Leftover fura is considered very unsavory, and women usually give it to beggars when they ask for food.

3 The same goes for mangoes, which are seen as a sweet and luxurious addition to one's diet but which by no means constitute what the Mawri call *abinci*. During the mango season, I would often eat two of these fruits at midday and call it "lunch," to the dismay of my neighbors and friends, who thought I was starving myself. Even though I explained that I was quite

full and satisfied, they once retorted, "No one eats *mangoes* for lunch. One must drink fura or eat macaroni or rice with meat in order to feel full."

4 Mintz's *Sweetness and Power* (1985) is an anthropological history of sugar and of its impact on the political economy and the social fabric of the British. In a similar though less ambitious manner, the multiple and meaningful implications of sweetness are explored here to illuminate how Mawri ground their understanding of their current predicament in a palatable grammar of signs and values.

5 Among some of the plants that are added to the cooking water are: *damaji* (*Chrozophora senegalensis*); *gujiya 'kasa* (commonly known as groundnut); *tserafako* (*Tribulus terrestris*); *anza* (*Boscia senegalensis*); *tsintsiya mararake* (type of thatching grass). As far as I know, the only thing these plants have in common is their ability to sweeten the water in which they soak.

6 The processes involved in childbearing and smithing also resonate with those of cooking. Cooking also involves the transformation of elements from one state (raw) into another (cooked). The resonance between these transformative activities is given more prominence in the region of Maradi (Niger) and in northern Nigeria, where the imagery of cooking informs the ritual process of initiation into the bori. During the *girka* (initiation) — which also means "cooking" — the neophyte is ritually "cooked" so that she may regain some of the heat she needs to bring a child into the world (see Masquelier 1987).

7 Note that the postpartum practices described here, along with their humoral basis, have accompanied Islam. Given the frequent inextricability of Muslim and indigenous ritual forms, it is particularly ironic that Islamic "custom" would come under fire for "wreaking havoc" in Mawri communities.

8 A woman I once spoke with told me that all of her sister's eight children had died because their births were not spaced out enough to insure the successful weaning of one child before the coming of another baby.

9 Unlike certain other spirits of the local pantheon, Maria is a relative newcomer to the bori scene. Perhaps this is why she bears a Muslim-sounding name, even though she is the antithesis of the proper Muslim wife; she is herself the expression of the multiple and often contradictory forces that have molded Mawri society and continue to do so. (Devotees also — but more rarely — refer to the spirit as Mangu.)

10 Harakwai is a powerful and revered spirit of Zarma origin who wears a white robe. His children are the spirits who are generally referred to as *babba'ku* (the "black ones"), though they do not all wear black robes. Kirai, for instance, wears a red hat and a red robe tied around the waist with a red sash, but some of his brothers, such as Souleymane, wear a black outfit. Thus Harakwai is associated with white while his children are known

as black spirits. Because of the contrasting colors that the spirits emblematize in the minds of 'yan bori, Harakwai is here set in opposition to the group formed by his children, and both are metaphorically equated with the two main Mawri meals, fura and tuwo: when milk is added to the ball of cooked millet flour, the resulting porridge (fura), which constitutes the midday meal, turns whitish, which is why it stands for the white spirit. Tuwo, a thick paste that has the consistency of polenta, has a white color when it is made with rice or millet flour and is slightly yellow when made from corn. However, it turns rather dark once the sauce (whose color varies depending on the ingredients—tomato paste, okra, sorrel, squash, pumpkin, and/or eggplant—and the combination of spices) has been added to it. Tuwo is the evening meal; leftovers are eaten for breakfast the following day. Mawri women lay the paste in a bowl or plate and then use a ladle to cover it with the sauce. That is why tuwo is considered black and can conceivably be an apt metaphor for the babba'ku spirits. Note that ba'ki, which is translated as "black," also means "dark green" and "dark blue" (ba'ki-ba'ki is the term for "dark").

11 Though, as I have shown briefly, bori is often equated with nurturance—both social and material—in the Mawri imagination, it is difficult to appraise the role played by the bori in times of hunger. I have no record of bori activity during the famines of the seventies and eighties, for instance. And though one would expect people to turn to the spirits and hold bori ceremonies in times of communal crises, many of the older 'yan bori I talked to would usually say that when there was hunger, no one had the energy—and presumably the resources—required to carry out a successful possession ritual.

12 Stoller (1989a) has described a set of spirits belonging to the Songhay pantheon that resemble Maria spirits in some ways. He links their appearance explicitly and directly to the increasing influence of neoconservative Islam in Niger. These figures of holey possession are known as Sasale and include both male and female spirits. They gamble and drink, engage in prostitution, and refuse to pray. In short, they do all the things a good Muslim should refrain from doing. According to believers in the spirits, the hegemonic practices of neoconservative Islam that the spirits ridicule are threatening the foundations of Songhay order, Stoller (1989a, 168) says.

13 The term karuwanci has often been translated into English as "courtesanship," to avoid the derogatory connotation associated with the concept of prostitution (Barkow 1971; Pittin 1983). A karuwa earns her keep through sexual favors by economic necessity, not by moral choice, it was surmised. While this was partly true in the late 1980s, in 1994, following the rise of orthodox Islam in Dogondoutchi, I found that both men and women had become more preoccupied with issues of marital and moral respect-

ability. By then, the term *karuwa,* when used to refer to certain unmarried women, had become much closer in meaning to the English word "prostitute"; there was moral opprobrium attached to the practice of karuwanci (see also Cooper 1997).

14 Gurmunya (the feminine form of gurmu) means "lame." Gurmunya is often believed to be Maria's mother. Her horse is thus immune to Maria's wrath, or at least it is assumed that Maria would never harm her mother's devotee.

15 During the initiation, whose purpose it is to allow the spirit to identify herself by name, Maria will not only publicly reveal her identity as a spirit; she will also tell "who she was before she died," that is, provide the name of a woman who died in pregnancy a while before. She will also reveal the names of this woman's parents and which village she was from.

16 The mortar and the pestle together symbolize the fruitful unity and complementarity between male and female principles, principles that provide the foundation for Mawri conceptions of the universe and its reproduction, from the most mundane processes such as cooking (see Last 1979, 307) to more global reproductive processes. Traditionally, at marriage, Mawri women brought the pestle while their new spouse came with the mortar (Piault 1963, 42). This gesture meaningfully reproduced the fecund union of complementary elements (mortar=womb/pestle=penis) so crucial to the viability of a marriage and the vitality of society because of what it produced (food=child). For a more extensive discussion of the parallels between alimentation and reproduction, see Darrah (1980). Nowadays, both the mortar and the pestle are purchased together at the market.

17 Intercourse requires the exchange of *manyi* (fluids) between sexual partners. The successful mixing of these sexual fluids will produce a fetus whose development and survival depends on the quantity and quality of the nutritious fluids provided by its mother. Because a good part of these fluids go to the woman's partner during intercourse, if this woman has sex during her pregnancy, she actually denies her fetus vital nutrients. The same logic requires that she avoid intercourse if she wants to have good milk for her baby.

18 In 1986 the infant mortality rate for Niger as a whole was 145 per 1,000 (République du Niger 1988, 53).

19 As already pointed out, Islam is often equated with salla (prayer); Muslims are referred to as "those who pray," in contrast to bori adepts, who are known as "those who sacrifice" (to the spirits).

20 A young friend of mine whose life, health, and happiness had been irremediably wrecked by Maria recalled for me that it had all started when her mother sent her with a girlfriend to a nearby village. She had felt someone behind her the whole way but had not been able to see anyone. She had a faint headache, and when she reached home, she felt as if her eyes were

going to fall out. She was very sick; her legs hurt and so did her ribs. When she recounted the incident to some girls who lived in the village she had visited, they said: "Why did you take that road? It is not a good road. Nobody takes it anymore, unless they have to go and bury a pregnant woman who has died."

21 As an icon of sterility, Maria may attack the parts of the female body that epitomize fertility and nurturance. A devotee of Maria once told me that a few months after she gave birth to a baby girl, her breasts started to swell horribly. They became huge. The blacksmith made incisions in the skin around the nipple with a red hot iron to let out the pus, but it did not help. She could not breast-feed her baby. After a year of intense suffering, she was diagnosed as being possessed by Maria. When she went to the dispensary, the doctor detected nothing abnormal because it was a spirit-induced illness, against which Western medicine is thought to be powerless.

22 One of my informants related the terrible circumstances of her father's death in the following terms:

> In our neighborhood, there is this beautiful woman who seduces men; she says, "Good evening, sir" at night, and then she follows them. They don't understand at first who she is. My father, one evening, stopped in front of the woman and she got in his car. As he was driving home, he turned to her, but there was nobody on the passenger seat anymore. He got scared and drove home to tell his younger brother about what had happened. His body was shaking like a leaf. He went straight to bed and in a matter of minutes, he was dead.

23 Maria bears intriguing similarities to 'Aisha Quandisha, a she-demon of Sudanese origin who has special devotees among the Hamadsha, the members of a loosely organized Islamic brotherhood in Morocco (see Crapanzano 1973). I am grateful to Paul Stoller for sharing this insight with me.

24 Spirits who take on a human appearance usually exhibit nonhuman traits such as animal feet. Male informants often pointed out to me that because feet are the last thing men will look at in a woman—they will first glance at her buttocks and the way she moves them, then examine her face—they easily fall prey to rapacious spirits who materialize as stunningly beautiful women.

25 These local conceptions of the symbolic, yet very tangible, dangers to which men expose themselves by having sex with prostitutes are very suggestive of other deadly threats, such as AIDS. Yet, at the time of my first fieldwork (1988–89), the disease was unknown in Arewa and had not made its way in the social imaginary, as it had in other parts of Africa (see Weiss 1996).

26 In itself, the act of shedding blood, especially if it is not induced for medici-

nal or ritual purposes by a specialist, is always potentially threatening (see Échard 1985).

27 These items were the only solid silver jewelry I saw during my stay in Arewa. Nowadays women tend to wear cheap, mass-produced plastic, gold- or silver-plated jewelry imported from Nigeria or southeast Asia.

28 There is an interesting twist to the commodity-bait complex in the context of missionary activity in Dogondoutchi. The first Christian missionaries (Redemptorists) to set foot in the area attracted children not with mirrors but with *candy*. Aside from "sweetening" the encounter between native and Christian subjects, the candy provided the children with a hint of the "pleasures" to come should they accept the missionaries' invitation to go live with them at the mission. By "taming" the children with sweets, the Redemptorists were attempting to recruit pupils for their newly opened mission school. The irony is that most, if not all, of the parents who agreed to send one or more of their sons to the mission school did it not because they believed in the putative benefits of education and literacy but because they knew that their children would be well fed. The anecdote about the missionary as a "candy man" was often offered to me as an explanation as to why Mawri children always rush toward Westerners while screaming "*Kado! kado!*" (from the French *cadeau:* gift). Of course, today the cadeau they expect from a foreigner is more often money than candy.

29 Because Zahoho is so lazy, he does not cultivate millet. That is why his mediums do not build him a house. "Whose millet would you take to feed the 'yan bori who are building the house?" asked old Na Hanci in response to my question about Zahoho's lack of a dwelling. His answer implied that the construction of a spirit house requires food and money (in addition to building materials) to "take care of" the masons and carpenters involved in the project. "Zahoho is simply looking for a place in the shade," Na Hanci further explained. "He does not want to work. It's the spirit's fault if his horse cannot work."

30 It is worth pointing out that such stable, personalized relationships are a characteristic feature of the commodity form itself.

31 Note the insulting content of the song. When she hears it, Maria may well decide to feel insulted and come possess her devotee.

8. Lightning, Death, and the Politics of Truth

1 See Échard (1991a) for a list of Muslim spirits in the neighboring Hausa communities of Ader.

2 As previously noted, tuwo is the basic evening meal that consists of a paste

of cooked millet, guinea corn, or rice flour onto which is tossed miya, a spicy sauce.

3   The spirits of lightning and rain bear uncanny similarities to Dahomean members of the thunder pantheon whom Herskovits describes in *Dahomey: An Ancient African Kingdom*: "If a person is killed by lightning, he too stands convicted by this fact of some grave crime which has incurred the displeasure of the gods of the Thunder pantheon" (1938, 398).

4   Witchcraft accusations, too, provide a way to strike back at prosperous Muslims who have become the symbols of the immoral economy from which they draw their riches (Masquelier 1993).

5   Thursday is the day that is associated with the Zarma spirits. Therefore ceremonies that are held especially for them almost always take place on that day of the week. Along with Sundays, Thursdays are the most propitious days of the week for holding a successful wasa.

6   In the opinion of the chief of bori who supervised the annual ceremony in Dogondoutchi, the watam bakwai was held to make sure the rain would come, to avoid snakes, and to prevent the coming of sorcerers who travel in the rain. This suggests that for some the threat of rain sorcerers has not been totally eliminated by the presence of the Zarma spirits.

7   *Faskare* (split firewood) is added to the milk offered to the spirits. Pounded into powder before it is poured in the calabash filled with milk, the wood is said to come from the remains of a tree that has been hit by lightning.

8   Dongo is the name given to the spirit Kirai in Zarma country.

9   In Songhayland, where the Zarma spirits come from, the stones are believed to be made from the saliva of Dongo (Kirai in Mawri society). This spirit is mean and cruel, and when he screams, he spits stones that kill people (Rouch 1989, 76).

10 According to Rouch (1989, 109), in the Zarma song performed for the spirit whom the Mawri name Kirai, the spirit is described as killing people with a needle.

11 Milk in this case has the property of cooling down the stone so that it will not harm anyone anymore. I have shown elsewhere that milk heals people and animals struck by lightning and also acts as preventative medicine against the threat of lightning (Masquelier 1994). According to Rouch (1989, 169), in Songhay society, when a thunderstone is found, it must be cooled off through immersion in a ritual pot filled with fresh milk. Finding a stone by chance is a particularly auspicious event, for, as noted, it can be used as a protective charm against lightning after being neutralized by the cooling action of milk.

12 Milk may also be poured on animals and people who have been hit by lightning but who are not dead. In a case a 'dan bori recalled for me, a cow,

her calf, and two sheep were struck by lightning in a field. They were alive but could not get up. A ceremony was held in the field, and devotees became possessed by the Zarma spirits who spoke. As soon as milk, mixed with medicines, was poured on their bodies, the wounded animals started moving. Before the ceremony was over, they were standing on their legs.

13 In their attempt to oppose the logic of the established order, bori practices lead to interesting inversions; when a person respectfully begs the Zarma spirits to reduce the fine they have imposed on him, the spirits increase, and sometimes double or triple, the amount of money owed. On the other hand, asking the spirits to increase the sum of money will bring about a reduction in the fine.

14 As Schmoll has noted, "While, in principle, the Hausa denounce the lie as bad, they also recognize it as a necessary part of survival. Indirectly, it also reinforces the strength and value of information that is the truth (*gaskiya*)" (1991, 59).

15 My efforts to elicit an exegesis for such a practice were vain. I could not find other instances in which the praying mantis's idiosyncracies were exploited.

16 At the turn of the century, Tremearne also noted that swearing on iron was more efficacious than taking an oath on the Koran: "Of old, oaths used to be taken on iron . . . even now many of the less civilized Hausa people are tested with this metal, a bayonet being passed across their throats, and then between their legs" (1913, 139).

17 The fines imposed by the spirits are quite high, often amounting to two or three months of a worker's salary. Because this money is then shared among the devotees of the Zarma spirits who participated in the ceremony held to hear the spirits' message, some Muslims argue that the practice of fining offenders is just a trick the 'yan bori use to get money.

18 Unlike the animals that are killed by lightning and that are interred after having been cooled off with milk, these "given" cattle were sacrificed to the spirits and their flesh eaten by 'yan bori, hence constituting yet another *tangible* appropriation of Muslim value.

19 In one case that was reported to me in 1988, the spirits not only killed three offenders with lightning but also the malamai who had prohibited a ceremony that was to be held on behalf of the deceased. A certain malam, Mai lahiya, and his colleague, Alou, notified the 'yan bori that they were to immediately put a stop to their preparations for a wasa. Those who had come all the way from Dogondoutchi to the village of the deceased to supervise the ceremony decided not to antagonize the representatives of Islam and to retreat peacefully. They were angry and offended by the intolerance and animosity of the two malamai but thought it best to let the spirits take action. Everyone, according to the narrator, was convinced that their

revenge was imminent. As soon as they left the village, the sky turned ink-black, and the wind started blowing as if it were going to rain. By the time the 'yan bori arrived home, the black clouds had vanished and the wind had died down. A few days later the 'yan bori got word that malam Mai lahiya had fallen ill. He was afflicted with rashes that itched terribly. A month later he was dead. His friend Alou started to scream night and day, but nobody could find out what was wrong with him. He was transferred from the village dispensary to the hospital of the nearest town and died there a few months later.

Bibliography

Abraham, R. C. 1962. *Dictionary of the Hausa Language.* London: University of London Press.

Abu-Lughod, Lila. 1986. *Veiled Sentiments: Honor and Poetry in a Bedouin Society.* Berkeley: University of California Press.

————. 1990. The Romance of Resistance: Tracing Transformations of Power through Bedouin Women. *American Ethnologist* 1 (17): 41–55.

Apter, Andrew. 1993. Attinga Revisited: Yoruba Witchcraft and the Cocoa Economy, 1950–1951. In *Modernity and Its Malcontents: Ritual and Power in Postcolonial Africa,* edited by Jean and John Comaroff, 111–28. Chicago: University of Chicago Press.

Ardener, Edwin. 1972. Belief and the Problem of Women. In *The Interpretation of Ritual,* edited by Jean S. La Fontaine, 135–58. London: Tavistock.

Ardener, Shirley, ed. 1975. *Perceiving Women.* New York: J. M. Dent.

Arens, William, and Ivan Karp. 1989. Introduction to *Creativity of Power: Cosmology and Action in African Societies,* edited by William Arens and Ivan Karp, xi–xxix. Washington, D.C.: Smithsonian Institution Press.

Arnaud, Robert. 1912. L'Islam et la politique musulmane française en Afrique occidentale française. *Renseignements Coloniaux* 3–20/116–27/142–56.

Arnould, Eric J. 1982. Regional Market System Development and Changes in Relations of Production in Three Communities in Zinder Province, the Niger Republic. Ph.D. diss., Department of Anthropology, University of Arizona.

————. 1984. Marketing and Social Reproduction in Zinder, Niger Republic. In *Households: Comparative and Historical Studies of the Domestic Group,* edited by Robert Mac Netting, Richard Wilk, and Eric J. Arnould, 130–62. Berkeley: University of California Press.

Auslander, Mark. 1993. Open the Wombs: The Symbolic Politics of Modern Ngoni Witchfinding. In *Modernity and Its Malcontents: Ritual and Power in Postcolonial Africa,* edited by Jean and John Comaroff, 167–192. Chicago: University of Chicago Press.

Austin, John L. 1962. *How to Do Things with Words.* Cambridge Harvard University Press.

Babcock, Barbara A. 1975. Mirrors, Masks, and Metafiction: Studies in Narrative Reflexivity. Ph.D. diss., University of Chicago.

Baier, Stephen. 1980. *An Economic History of Central Niger.* Oxford: Clarendon Press.

Balandier, Georges. 1957. *L'Afrique ambigüe.* Paris: Librairie Plon.

Barkow, Jerome. 1971. The Institution of Courtesanship in the Northern States of Nigeria. *Genève-Afrique* 10 (1): 1–16.

Barth, Henry. 1857. *Travels and Discoveries in North and Central Africa.* New York: Harper and Brothers.

Bastian, Misty L. 1992. The World as Marketplace: Historical, Cosmological, and Popular Constructions of the Onitsha Marketplace. Ph.D. diss., Department of Anthropology, University of Chicago.

———. 1998a. Mami Wata, Mr. White and the Sirens off Bar Beach: Spirits and Dangerous Consumption in the Nigerian Popular Press. In *Afrika und das Andere: Alterität und Innovation,* edited by Heike Schmidt and Albert Wirtz, 21–31. Hamburg: Lit Verlag.

———. 1998b. Fires, Tricksters and Poisoned Medicines: Popular Cultures of Rumor in Onitsha, Nigeria and Its Markets. *Etnofoor* 11 (2): 111–32.

Bastide, Roger. 1972. *Le rêve, la transe, et la folie.* Paris: Flammarion.

———. 1978. *The African Religions of Brazil.* Baltimore: Johns Hopkins University Press.

Bauman, Richard. 1977. *Verbal Art as Performance.* Prospect Heights, Ill.: Waveland Press.

Beattie, John, and John Middleton. 1969. Introduction to *Spirit Mediumship and Society in Africa,* edited by John Beattie and John Middleton, xvii–xxx. New York: Africana Publishing.

Belle. 1913. Monographie du secteur de Dogondoutchi. Document 6.1.2. Archives d'Outre Mer, Aix-en-Provence.

Bernus, Suzanne. 1969. *Particularisme ethnique en milieu urbain: L'exemple de Niamey.* Paris: Institut d'Ethnologie.

Besmer, Fremont. 1977. Initiation into the Bori Cult: A Case Study in Ningi Town. *Africa* 47 (1): 1–13.

———. 1983. *Horses, Musicians, and Gods: The Hausa Cult of Possession-Trance.* South Hadley, Mass.: Bergin and Garvey.

Boddy, Janice. 1989. *Wombs and Alien Spirits: Women, Men and the Zar Cult in Northern Sudan.* Bloomington: Indiana University Press.

———. 1992. Subversive Kinship: The Role of Spirit Possession in Negotiating Social Space in Rural Northern Sudan. Paper presented at the 91st American Anthropological Association Meeting, 3 December, San Francisco.

———. 1994. Spirit Possession Revisited: Beyond Instrumentality. *Annual Review of Anthropology* 23:407–34.

Bourdieu, Pierre. 1977. *Outline of a Theory of Practice,* translated by Richard Nice. Cambridge: Cambridge University Press.

Braudel, Fernand. 1980. *On History.* Chicago: University of Chicago Press.

Brink, Judy. 1997. Lost Rituals: Sunni Muslim Women in Rural Egypt. In

Mixed Blessings: Gender and Religious Fundamentalism Cross Culturally, edited by Judy Brink and Joan Mencher, 199–208. New York: Routledge.

Brodwin, Paul. 1996. *Medicine and Morality in Haiti: The Contest for Healing Power.* Cambridge: Cambridge University Press.

Brown, Karen McCarty. 1991. *Mama Lola: A Vodou Priestess in Brooklyn.* Berkeley: University of California Press.

Burke, Timothy. 1996. *Lifebuoy Men, Lux Women: Commodification, Consumption, and Cleanliness in Modern Zimbabwe.* Durham: Duke University Press.

Callaway, Barbara. 1984. Ambiguous Consequences of the Socialization and Seclusion of Hausa Women. *Journal of Modern African Studies* 22 (3): 429–50.

————. 1987. *Muslim Hausa Women in Nigeria: Tradition and Change.* Syracuse: Syracuse University Press.

Cartry, Michel. 1982. From the Village to the Bush: An Essay on the Gourmantche of Gobnangou (Upper Volta). In *Between Belief and Transgression: Structuralist Essays in Religion, History, and Myth,* translated by John Leavitt, 210–28. Chicago: University of Chicago Press.

Charlick, Robert. 1991. *Niger: Personal Rule and Survival in the Sahel.* Boulder: Westview Press.

Clarke, Peter B. 1982. *West Africa and Islam: A Study of Religious Development from the Eighth to the Twentieth Century.* London: Edward Arnold.

Cohen, Abner. 1969a. *Custom and Politics in Urban Africa: A Study of Hausa Migrants in Yoruba Towns.* London: Routledge and Kegan Paul.

————. 1969b. Political Anthropology: The Analysis of the Symbolism of Power Relations. *Man,* n.s., 4:215–35.

Cohen, William B. 1980. *The French Encounter with Africans: White Response to Blacks 1530–1880.* Bloomington: Indiana University Press.

Coles, Catherine, and Beverly Mack, ed. 1991. *Hausa Women in the Twentieth Century.* Madison: University of Wisconsin Press.

Collion, Marie-Hélène J. 1982. Colonial Rule and Changing Peasant Economy in Damagherim, Niger Republic. Ph.D. diss., Department of History, Cornell University.

Comaroff, Jean. 1981. Healing and Cultural Transformation: The Case of the Tswana of Southern Africa. *Social Science and Medicine* 15 (B): 367–78.

————. 1985. *Body of Power, Spirit of Resistance: The Culture and History of a South African People.* Chicago: University of Chicago Press.

Comaroff, Jean, and John L. Comaroff. 1990. Goodly Beasts, Beastly Goods: Cattle and Commodities in a South African Context. *American Ethnologist* 17 (2): 195–216.

————. 1991. *Of Revelation and Revolution: Christianity, Colonialism, and Consciousness in South Africa.* Vol. 1. Chicago: University of Chicago Press.

———. 1992. *Ethnography and the Historical Imagination.* Boulder: Westview Press.

———. 1993. Introduction to *Modernity and Its Malcontents: Ritual and Power in Postcolonial Africa,* edited by Jean and John L. Comaroff, xi–xxxvii. Chicago: University of Chicago Press.

———. 1997. *Of Revelation and Revolution: The Dialectics of Modernity on a South African Frontier.* Vol. 2. Chicago: University of Chicago Press.

Cooper, Barbara M. 1997. *Marriage in Maradi: Gender and Culture in a Hausa Society in Niger, 1900–1989.* Portsmouth, N.H.: Heinemann.

Counihan, Carole M. 1988. Female Identity, Food, and Power in Contemporary Florence. *Anthropological Quarterly* 62 (2): 51–62.

Crandon-Malamud, Libbet. 1991. *From the Fat of Our Souls: Social Change, Political Process, and Medical Pluralism in Bolivia.* Berkeley: University of California Press.

Crapanzano, Vincent. 1973. *The Hamadsha: A Study in Moroccan Ethnopsychiatry.* Berkeley: University of California Press.

———. 1977. Introduction to *Case Studies of Spirit Possession,* edited by Vincent Crapanzano and Vivian Garrison, 1–40. New York: John Wiley.

Crowder, Michael. 1968. *West Africa under Colonial Rule.* Evanston: Northwestern University Press.

Csordas, Thomas J. 1994. Introduction: The Body as Representation and Being-in-the-World. In *Embodiment and Experience: The Existential Ground for Culture and Self,* edited by Thomas J. Csordas. Cambridge: Cambridge University Press.

Darrah, Allan C. 1980. A Hermeneutic Approach to Hausa Therapeutics: The Allegory of the Living Fire. Ph.D. diss., Department of Anthropology, Northwestern University.

Davis, Natalie Zenon. 1990. The Shapes of Social History. *Storia della Storiografia* 17:28–34.

de Certeau, Michel. 1984. *The Practice of Everyday Life,* translated by Steven Rendall. Berkeley: University of California Press.

de Heusch, Luc. 1971. *Pourquoi l'épouser et autres essais.* Paris: Gallimard.

———. 1980. Heat, Physiology, and Cosmogony: *Rites de Passage* among the Thonga. In *Explorations in African Systems of Thought,* edited by Ivan Karp and Charles Birds, 27–43. Bloomington: Indiana University Press.

Delaney, Carol. 1991. *The Seed and the Soil: Gender and Cosmology in Turkish Village Society.* Berkeley: University of California Press.

de Latour Dejean, Eliane. 1975. La transformation du régime foncier: Appropriation des terres et formation de la classe dirigeante en pays Mawri (Niger). In *L'agriculture africaine et le capitalisme,* edited by Samir Amin, 185–231. Paris: Éditions Anthropos.

———. 1980. Shadows Nourished by the Sun: Rural Social Differentiation

BIBLIOGRAPHY 325

among the Mawri of Niger. In *Peasants in Africa: Historical and Contemporary Perspectives,* edited by Martin Klein, 104–41. Beverly Hills: Sage Publications.

de Latour, Eliane. 1982. La paix destructrice. In *Guerres de lignages et guerres d'états en Afrique,* edited by Jean Bazin and Emmanuel Terray, 237–66. Paris: Éditions des Archives Contemporaines.

———. 1984. Maîtres de la terre, maîtres de la guerre. *Cahiers d'Études Africaines* 95 (24): 273–97.

———. 1987. Le futur antérieur. In *La colonisation: Rupture ou parenthèse?* edited by Marc-Henri Piault, 123–76. Paris: Éditions L'Harmattan.

———. 1992. *Les temps du pouvoir.* Paris: Éditions de l'École des Hautes Études en Sciences Sociales.

Deren, Maya. [1953] 1991. *Divine Horsemen: The Living Gods of Haiti.* New York: McPherson and Company.

Deschamps, Hubert. 1963. Et maintenant, Lord Lugard? *Africa* 33(4): 293–306.

Desjarlais, Robert. 1992. *Body and Emotions: The Aesthetics of Illness and Healing in the Nepal Himalayas.* Philadelphia: University of Pennsylvania Press.

Devereux, Georges. 1970. *Essai d'éthnopsychiatrie générale.* Paris: Gallimard.

Devisch, Renaat. 1985. Symbol and Psychosomatic Symptom in Bodily Space-Time: The Case of the Yaka of Zaire. *International Journal of Psychology* 20:589–616.

———. 1993. *Weaving the Threads of Life: The Khita Gyn-Eco-Logical Healing Cult among the Yaka.* Chicago: University of Chicago Press.

Dewey, John. 1929. *Experience and Nature.* London: Allen and Unwin.

Douglas, Mary. 1970. *Natural Symbols: Explorations in Cosmology.* New York: Vintage Books.

Drewal, Margaret Thompson. 1992. *Yoruba Ritual: Performers, Play, Agency.* Bloomington: Indiana University Press.

Dunbar, Roberta Ann. 1991. Islamic Values, the State and the "Development of Women": The Case of Niger. In *Hausa Women in the Twentieth Century,* edited by Catherine Coles and Beverly Mack, 69–89. Madison: University of Wisconsin Press.

Durham, Deborah. 1995. Soliciting Gifts and Negotiating Agency: The Spirit of Asking in Botswana. *Journal of the Royal Anthropological Institute* 1 (1): 111–28.

Échard, Nicole. 1965. Note sur les forgerons de l'Ader (pays hausa, République du Niger). *Journal de la Société des Africanistes* 35 (2): 353–72.

———. 1978. Mais où sont les sorciers d'antan? Notes sur les sorciers hausa d'origine humaine en Ader. In *Systèmes de Signes,* 121–30. Paris: Hermann.

———. 1985. Même la viande est vendue avec le sang: De la sexualité des femmes, un exemple. In *L'arraisonnement des femmes: Essais en anthropologie des sexes,* edited by N. C. Mathieu, 37–60. Paris: Cahiers de l'Homme.

———. 1991a. The Hausa Bori Possession Cult in the Ader Region of Niger: Its Origins and Present-Day Function. In *Women's Medicine: The Zar-Bori Cult in Africa and Beyond,* edited by Ioan M. Lewis, Ahmed Al-Sari, and Sayyid Hurreiz, 64–80. Edinburgh: Edinburgh University Press.

———. 1991b. Gender Relationships and Religion: Women in the Hausa Bori of Ader. In *Hausa Women in the Twentieth Century,* edited by Catherine Coles and Beverly Mack, 207–20. Madison: University of Wisconsin Press.

———. 1992. Culte de possession et changement social: L'exemple du bori hausa de l'Ader et du Kurfey (Niger). *Archives de Sciences Sociales des Religions* 79 (2): 87–101.

Échard, Nicole, and Pierre Bonte. 1978. Anthropologie et sexualité: Les inégales. In *La condition féminine,* edited by CERM, 59–83. Paris: Éditions Sociales.

Egg, J., F. Levin, and M. Venin. 1975. Analyse descriptive de la famine des années 1931 au Niger et ses implications méthodologiques. Paris: Institut de Recherches des Nations Unies pour le Développement Social.

Erlmann, Veit, and Habou Magagi. 1989. *Girkaa: Une cérémonie d'initiation au culte de possession boorii des hausa de la région de Maradi (Niger).* Berlin: Dietrich Reimer Verlag.

Evans-Pritchard, Edward E. 1976. *Witchcraft, Oracles, and Magic among the Azande.* Oxford: Clarendon Press.

Fabian, Johannes. 1990. *Power and Performance: Ethnographic Explorations through Proverbial Wisdom and Theatre in Shaba, Zaire.* Madison: University of Wisconsin Press.

Fanon, Frantz. 1963. *The Wretched of the Earth,* translated by Constance Farrington. New York: Grove Press.

Faulkingham, Ralph. 1975. The Spirits and Their Cousins: Some Aspects of Belief, Ritual and Social Organization in a Rural Hausa Village in Niger. Research Report No. 15. University of Massachusetts, Amherst.

Fernandez, James W. 1982. *Bwiti: An Ethnography of the Religious Imagination in Africa.* Princeton: Princeton University Press.

———. 1986. *Persuasions and Performances: The Play of Tropes in Culture.* Bloomington: Indiana University Press.

Field, Margaret J. 1960. Search for Security: An Ethnopsychiatric Study of Rural Ghana. London: Faber and Faber.

Foucault, Michel. 1977. *Discipline and Punish.* New York: Pantheon Books.

———. 1980. *Power/Knowledge,* edited by Colin Gordon. New York: Pantheon.

Frishman, Alan. 1991. Hausa Women in the Urban Economy of Kano. In *Hausa Women in the Twentieth Century,* edited by Catherine Coles and Beverly Mack, 192–203. Madison: University of Wisconsin Press.

Frobenius, Leo. 1913. *The Voice of Africa: Being an Account of the Travels of the German Inner African Exploration Expedition in the Years 1910–1913*. London: Hutchinson.

Fry, Peter. 1976. *Spirits of Protest: Spirit-Mediums and the Articulation of Consensus among the Zezuru of Southern Rhodesia (Zimbabwe)*. New York: Cambridge University Press.

Fuglestad, Finn. 1975. Les haukas: Une interprétation historique. *Cahiers d'Études Africaines* 58 (15): 203–16.

———. 1983. *A History of Niger: 1850–1960*. New York: Cambridge University Press.

Gibbal, Jean-Marie. 1994. *Genii of the River Niger,* translated by Beth G. Raps. Chicago: University of Chicago Press.

Giles, Linda. 1987. Possession Cults on the Swahili Coast: A Re-examination of Theories of Marginality. *Africa* 57 (2): 234–58.

Gluckman, Max. 1970. *Customs and Conflicts in Africa.* Oxford: Blackwell.

Gomm, Roger. 1975. Bargaining from Weakness: Spirit Possession on the South Kenya Coast. *Man* 10 (4): 530–43.

Goody, Jack. 1971. The Impact of Islamic Writing on the Oral Cultures of West Africa. *Cahiers d'Études Africaines* 11 (43): 455–66.

Gottlieb, Alma. 1992. *Under the Kapok Tree: Identity and Difference in Beng Thought.* Bloomington: Indiana University Press.

Gouffé, Claude. 1966. "Manger" et "boire" en haoussa. *Revue de l'École Nationale des Langues Orientales* 3:77–111.

Gouilly, Alphonse. 1952. *L'Islam dans l'Afrique Occidentale.* Paris: Larose.

Greenberg, Joseph H. 1946. *The Influence of Islam on a Sudanese Religion.* New York: J. J. Augustin Publisher.

———. 1947. Some Aspects of Negro-Mohammedan Culture-Contact among the Hausa. *American Anthropologist* 43:51–61.

Grégoire, Emmanuel. 1992. *The Alhazai of Maradi: Traditional Hausa Merchants in a Changing Sahelian City,* translated by Benjamin Hardy. Boulder: Lynne Rienner Publishers.

———. 1993. Islam and the Identity of Merchants in Maradi (Niger). In *Muslim Identity and Social Change in Sub-Saharan Africa,* edited by Louis Brenner, 106–15. Bloomington: Indiana University Press.

Griaule, Marcel. 1965. *Conversations with Ogotemmeli: An Introduction to Dogon Religious Ideas.* New York: Oxford University Press.

Guillon, Jean Michel. 1967. Étude économique d'un milieu urbain sous-développé: Dogondoutchi, ville de la République du Niger. Grenoble: Institut de Géographie Alpine.

Gussler, Judith. 1973. Social Change, Ecology and Spirit Possession among South African Nguni. In *Religion, Altered States of Consciousness and Social*

Change, edited by Erika Bourguignon. Columbus: Ohio State University Press.

Hebdige, Dick. 1979. *Subculture: The Meaning of Style.* New York: Methuen.

Herbert, Eugenia. 1993. *Iron, Gender, and Power: Rituals of Transformation in African Societies.* Bloomington: Indiana University Press.

Herskovits, Melville. J. 1938. *Dahomey: An Ancient West African Kingdom.* Vol. 1 and 2. New York: J. J. Augustin Publisher.

Herzfeld, Michael. 1986. Closure as Cure: Tropes in the Exploration of Bodily and Social Disorder. *Current Anthropology* 27 (2): 107–20.

Higgott, Richard, and Finn Fuglestad. 1975. The 1974 Coup d'État in Niger: Toward an Explanation. *The Journal of Modern African Studies* 13 (3): 383–98.

Hill, Polly. 1969. Hidden Trade in Hausaland. *Man* 4 (3): 392–409.

Hiskett, Mervyn. 1984. *The Development of Islam in West Africa.* New York: Longman.

Horowitz, Michael M., et al. 1983. Niger: A Social and Institutional Profile. Binghamton, N.Y.: Institute for Development Anthropology.

Howes, David, ed. 1991. *The Varieties of Sensory Experience: A Sourcebook in the Anthropology of the Senses.* Toronto: University of Toronto Press.

Hugh-Jones, Christine. 1979. *From the Milk River: Spatial and Temporal Processes in Northwest Amazonia.* Cambridge: Cambridge University Press.

Huizinga, Johan. 1955. *Homo Ludens.* Boston: Beacon Press.

Hutchinson, Sharon. 1996. *Nuer Dilemmas: Coping with Money, War, and the State.* Berkeley: University of California Press.

Isichei, Elizabeth. 1987. The Maitatsine Risings in Nigeria 1980–85: A Revolt of the Disinherited. *Journal of Religion in Africa* 17: 194–208.

Jackson, Michael. 1983. Knowledge of the Body. *Man* 18: 237–45.

Janzen, John. 1978. *The Quest for Therapy in Lower Zaire.* Berkeley: University of California Press.

———. 1992. *Ngoma: Discourses of Healing in Central and Southern Africa.* Berkeley: University of California Press.

Jewsiewicki, Bogumil. 1996. Zairian Popular Painting as Commodity and as Communication. In *African Material Culture,* edited by Mary Jo Arnoldi, Christraud M. Geary, and Kris L. Hardin, 334–55. Bloomington: University of Indiana Press.

Johnson, G. Wesley. 1978. William Ponty and Republican Paternalism in French West Africa (1866–1915). In *African Proconsuls: European Governors in Africa,* edited by Lewis H. Gann and Peter Duignan, 127–56. New York: The Free Press.

Kane, Ousmane. 1994. "Izala: The Rise of Muslim Reformism in Northern Nigeria." In *Accounting for Fundamentalisms: The Dynamic Character of Religious Movements,* edited by Martin E. Marty and Scott Appleby. Chicago: The University of Chicago Press.

Kapferer, Bruce. 1983. *A Celebration of Demons: Exorcism and the Aesthetics of Healing in Sri Lanka.* Bloomington: Indiana University Press.

Kehoe, Alice B., and Dody H. Giletti. 1981. Women's Preponderance in Possession Cults: The Calcium-Deficiency Hypothesis Extended. *American Anthropologist* 83 (3): 549–61.

Kennedy, John G. 1967. Nubian Zar Ceremonies as Psychotherapy. *Human Organization* 26 (4): 185–94.

King, Anthony. 1966. A Bori Liturgy from Katsina. *African Language Studies* 7:105–25.

Kotoudi, Idimama. 1988a. Doutchi: La réussite de "l'école des blancs." *Nigérama* 3:51.

———. 1988b. Cannes à sucre de Fadama: les terres rétrécies. *Nigérama* 3:24.

Kramer, Fritz. 1993. *The Red Fez: Art and Spirit Possession in Africa,* translated by Malcolm R. Green. New York: Verso.

Kratz, Corinne A. 1994. *Affecting Performance: Meaning, Movement, and Experience in Okiek Women's Initiation.* Washington, D.C.: Smithsonian Institution Press.

Labouret, Henri. 1931. *À la recherche d'une politique coloniale dans l'Ouest africain.* Paris: Éditions du Comité de l'Afrique Française.

Laderman, Carol. 1991. *The Winds of Desire: Psychology, Medicine, and Aesthetics in Malay Shamanistic Performance.* Berkeley: University of California Press.

Lambek, Michael. 1981. *Human Spirits: A Cultural Account of Trance in Mayotte.* Cambridge: Cambridge University Press.

———. 1993. *Knowledge and Practice in Mayotte: Local Discourses of Islam, Sorcery, and Spirit Possession.* Toronto: Toronto University Press.

———. 1996. Afterword: Spirits and Their Histories. In *Spirits in Culture, History, and Mind,* edited by Jeannette M. Mageo and Alan Howard, 237–49. New York: Routledge.

Lan, David. 1985. *Guns and Rain: Guerrillas and Spirit Mediums in Zimbabwe.* Berkeley: University of California Press.

Larose, Serge. 1977. The Meaning of Africa in Haitian Vodou. In *Symbols and Sentiments: Cross-Cultural Studies in Symbolism,* edited by Ioan M. Lewis. London: Academic Press.

Last, Murray. 1976. The Presentation of Sickness in a Community of Non-Muslim Hausa. In *Social Anthropology and Medicine,* edited by Joseph B. Loudon. New York: Academic Press.

———. 1979. Strategies against Time. *Sociology of Health and Illness* 1 (3): 306–17.

———. 1981. The Importance of Knowing about Not Knowing. *Social Science and Medicine* 15B (3): 387–92.

———. 1991. Spirit Possession as Therapy: Bori among Non-Muslims in Nigeria. In *Women's Medicine: The Zar-Bori Cult in Africa and Beyond,* edited by Ioan M. Lewis, Ahmed Al-Sari, and Sayyid Hurreiz, 49–63. Edinburgh: Edinburgh University Press.

Le Chatelier, Alfred. 1899. *L'islam dans l'Afrique occidentale*. Paris: G. Steinheil Éditeur.

Leiris, Michel. 1958. *La Possession et ses aspects théâtraux chez les Éthiopiens de Gondar.* Paris: Plon.

Leroux, Henri. 1948. Animisme et islam dans la subdivision de Maradi (Niger). *Bulletin de l'IFAN* 10:595–695.

Leroy, Paul. 1934. Subdivision de Dogondoutchi, cercle de Dosso. Document 6.3.14. Niamey, Niger: Archives Nationales.

Lévi-Strauss, Claude. 1963. The Effectiveness of Symbols. In *Structural Anthropology,* translated by Claire Jacobson and Brooke Schoepf, 186–205. Vol 1. New York: Basic Books.

Levy, Robert I., Jeannette M. Mageo, and Alan Howard. 1996. Gods, Spirits, and History: A Theoretical Perspective. In *Spirits in Culture, History, and Mind,* edited by Jeannette M. Mageo and Alan Howard, 11–27. New York: Routledge.

Lewis, Ioan M. 1966. Spirit-Possession and Deprivation Cults. *Man* 1:307–29.

———. 1967. Spirits and the Sex War. *Man* 2 (4): 626–28.

———. 1986. *Religion in Context: Cults and Charisma.* Cambridge: Cambridge University Press.

———. 1989. *Ecstatic Religion: A Study of Shamanism and Spirit Possession.* 2d ed. New York: Routledge.

———. 1991. Introduction: Zar in Context: The Past, the Present and Future of an African Healing Cult. In *Women's Medicine: The Zar-Bori Cult in Africa and Beyond,* edited by Ioan M. Lewis, Ahmed Al-Sari, and Sayyid Hurreiz, 1–16. Edinburgh: Edinburgh University Press.

Lewis, Ioan M., ed. 1977. *Symbols and Sentiments: Cross-Cultural Studies in Symbolism.* London: Academic Press.

Lombard, J. 1967. Les cultes de possession en Afrique Noire et le *bori* hausa. *Psychopathologie africaine* 3 (3): 419–39.

Lovejoy, Paul E. 1971. Long Distance Trade and Islam: The Case of the Nineteenth Century Hausa Kola Trade. *Journal of the Historical Society of Nigeria* 5 (4): 537–47.

Malinowski, Bronislav. 1935. *Coral Gardens and Their Magic: A Study of the Methods of Tilling the Soil and of Agricultural Rites in the Trobriand Islands.* New York: American Book.

Manning, Frank, and Jean-Marc Philibert, eds. 1990. *Customs in Conflict: The Anthropology of a Changing World.* Lewiston, N.Y.: Broadview Press.

Marcus, George. 1986. Contemporary Problems of Ethnography in the Modern World System. In *Writing Culture: The Poetics and Politics of Ethnography,* edited by James Clifford and George Marcus, 165–93. Berkeley: University of California Press.

Marks, Shula, ed. 1987. *Not Either an Experimental Doll: The Separate Worlds of Three South African Women.* Bloomington: University of Indiana Press.

Masquelier, Adeline. 1987. Cooking the Bori Way: The Logic of Healing in the Hausa Cult of Possession. *Chicago Anthropology Exchange* 16:96–103.

———. 1992. Encounter with a Road Siren: Machines, Bodies, and Commodities in the Imagination of a Mawri Healer. *Visual Anthropology Review* 8 (1): 56–69.

———. 1993. Ritual Economies, Historical Mediations: The Power and Poetics of *Bori* among the Mawri of Niger. Ph.D. diss., Department of Anthropology, University of Chicago.

———. 1994. Lightning, Death, and the Avenging Spirits: *Bori* Values in a Muslim World. *Journal of Religion in Africa* 24 (1): 2–51.

———. 1996a. Mediating Threads: Clothing and the Texture of Spirit/Medium Relations in *Bori* (Southern Niger). In *Clothing and Difference: Embodied Identities in Colonial and Post-Colonial Africa,* edited by Hildi Hendrickson, 66–93. Durham: Duke University Press.

———. 1996b. Identity, Alterity and Ambiguity in a Nigerien Community: Competing Definitions of "True" Islam. In *Postcolonial Identities in Africa,* edited by Richard Werbner, 222–44. London: Zed Books.

———. 1997a. Vectors of Witchcraft: Spirit Transactions and the Materialization of Memory in Niger. *Anthropological Quarterly* 70 (4): 187–98.

———. 1997b. "When I Die, They Will Play the Drums at my Funeral": Death, Transition, and the Spirits in Niger. Paper presented at the annual meeting of the American Anthropological Association, November, San Francisco.

———. 1999a. "Money and Serpents, Their Remedy Is Killing": The Pathology of Consumption in Niger. *Research in Economic Anthropology* 20:97–115.

———. 1999b. Debating Muslims, Disputed Practices: Struggles for the Realization of an Alternative Moral Order in Niger. In *Civil Society and the Political Imagination in Africa: Critical Perspectives,* edited by John and Jean Comaroff, 219–50. Chicago: University of Chicago Press.

———. 1999c. The Invention of Anti-Tradition: Dodo Spirits in Southern Niger. In *Spirit Possession, Modernity, and Power in Africa,* edited by Heike Behrend and Ute Luig, 34–49. Madison: University of Wisconsin Press.

———. 2000. Of Headhunters and Cannibals: Migrancy, Labor, and Consumption in the Mawri Imagination. *Cultural Anthropology* 15 (1): 1–45.

Matory, James Lorand. 1994a. *Sex and the Empire That Is No More: Gender and the Politics of Metaphor in Oyo Yoruba Religion.* Minneapolis: University of Minnesota Press.

————. 1994b. Rival Empires: Islam and the Religions of Spirit Possession among the Oyo Yoruba. *American Ethnologist* 21 (3): 495–515.

Mauss, Marcel. 1936. *Les techniques du corps.* Paris: Presses Universitaires de France.

Mayer, Joel. 1999. "Tandja Mamadou Wins Presidential Elections." *Niger News: Kakaki.* 20 December. *http://www.texdirect.net/users/jmayer/kakaki/k000108.htm*

————. 2000. Hamadou Sworn in as PM. *Niger News: Kakaki.* 8 January. *http://www.texdirect.net/users/jmayer/kakai/k000108.htm*

Meigs, Anna S. 1984. *Food, Sex and Pollution: A New Guinea Religion.* New Brunswick, N.J.: Rutgers University Press.

Meillassoux, Claude. 1971. Introduction to *The Development of Indigenous Trade and Markets in West Africa,* edited by Claude Meillassoux. London: Oxford University Press.

Merleau-Ponty, Maurice. 1962. *The Phenomenology of Perception,* translated by Colin Smith. London: Routledge and Kegan Paul.

Mernissi, Fatima. 1987. *Beyond the Veil: Male-Female Dynamics in Modern Muslim Society.* Rev. ed. Bloomington: Indiana University Press.

Messing, Simon D. 1958. Group Therapy and Social Status in the Zar Cult of Ethiopia. *American Anthropologist* 60 (6): 1120–26.

Métraux, Alfred. 1958. *Le vaudou haitien.* Paris: Gallimard.

Miles, William F. S. 1994. *Hausaland Divided: Colonialism and Independence in Nigeria and Niger.* Ithaca, N.Y.: Cornell University Press.

Mintz, Sidney W. 1985. *Sweetness and Power: The Place of Sugar in Modern History.* New York: Viking.

Monfouga-Nicolas, Jacqueline. 1972. Ambivalence et culte de possession: Contribution à l'étude du bori hausa. Paris: Anthropos.

Muller, Carol Ann. 1999. *Rituals of Fertility and the Sacrifice of Desire: Nazarite Women's Performance in South Africa.* Chicago: University of Chicago Press.

Munn, Nancy. 1970. The Transformation of Subjects into Objects in Walbiri and Pitjantjajtara Myth. In *Australian Aboriginal Anthropology,* edited by Ronald M. Berndt, 141–63. Nedlands, Western Australia: University of Western Australia Press.

Nicolas, Guy. 1964. Étude de marchés en pays hausa (République du Niger). Documents ethnographiques, Université de Bordeaux.

————. 1966. Structures fondamentales de l'espace dans la cosmologie d'une société hausa. *Journal de la Société des Africanistes* 36 (2): 65–107.

————. 1968. Un système numérique symbolique: Le trois, le quatre et le sept dans la cosmologie d'une société hausa (vallée de Maradi). *Cahiers d'Études Africaines* 8 (4): 566–616.

————. 1969. Fondements magico-religieux du pouvoir politique au sein de la principauté hausa du Gobir. *Journal de la Société des Africanistes* 39 (2): 199–231.

———. 1971. Processus de résistance au "développement" au sein d'une société africaine. *Civilisations* 21 (1): 45–66.

———. 1975. *Dynamique sociale et appréhension du monde au sein d'une société hausa.* Paris: Institut d'Ethnologie.

———. 1979. Islam and Ethnicity South of the Sahara. *Cahiers d'Études Africaines* 18 (3): 347–77.

———. 1986. *Don rituel et échange marchand dans une société sahelienne.* Paris: Institut d'Ethnologie.

Nisula, Tapio. 1999. *Everyday Spirits and Medical Interventions: Ethnographic and Historical Notes on Therapeutic Conventions in Zanzibar Town.* Saarijärvi, Finland: Gummerus Kirjapaino.

O'Brien, Donald Cruise. 1967. Toward an 'Islamic Policy' in French West Africa 1854–1914. *Journal of African History* 8 (2): 303–16.

Ohnuki-Tierney, Emiko. 1993. *Rice as Self: Japanese Identities through Time.* Princeton, N.J.: Princeton University Press.

Olivier de Sardan, Jean-Pierre. 1992. Occultism and the Ethnographic 'I': The Exoticizing of Magic from Durkheim to "Postmodem" Anthropology. *Critique of Anthropology* 12 (1): 5–25.

———. 1993. La surinterprétation politique: Les cultes de possession hawka du Niger. In *Religion et modernité politique en Afrique noire,* edited by J.-F. Bayart, 163–213. Paris: Karthala.

Oloruntemehin, Olatunji. 1972. Theories and Realities in the Administration of Colonial French West Africa from 1890 to the First World War. *Journal of the Historical Society of Nigeria* 6 (3): 289–312.

Ong, Aihwa. 1987. *Spirits of Resistance and Capitalist Discipline: Factory Women in Malaysia.* Albany: State University of New York Press.

Onwuejeogwu, Michael. 1969. The Cult of Bori Spirits among the Hausa. In *Man in Africa,* edited by Mary Douglas and Phyllis Kaberry, 279–305. New York: Tavistock.

Ousmane, A. 1985. Le dieu du Baoura. *Sahel Dimanche,* 30 June.

———. 1988. Toungouma: La pierre qui rend justice. *Nigérama* 3:47–48.

Painter, Thomas M. 1986. In Search of the Peasant Connection: Spontaneous Cooperation, Introduced Cooperatives and Agricultural Development in Southwestern Niger. In *Anthropology and Rural Development in West Africa,* edited by Michael M. Horowitz and Thomas M. Painter, 195–219. Boulder: Westview Press.

Péhaut, Yves. 1970. L'arachide au Niger. *Études d'Économie Africaine.* Série Afrique Noire 1:11–103.

Piault, Colette. 1963. Contribution à l'étude de la vie quotidienne de la femme mawri. *Études Nigériennes* 10 IFAN-CNRS.

Piault, Marc-Henri. 1961. Populations de l'Arewa: Introduction à une étude régionale. *Études Nigériennes* 13 IFAN-CNRS.

———. 1970. *Histoire mawri: Introduction à l'étude des processus constitutifs d'un état.* Paris: Éditions du Centre National de la Recherche Scientifique.

———. 1971. Cycles de marché et "espaces" socio-politiques. In *The Development of Indigenous Trade and Markets in West Africa,* edited by Claude Meillassoux, 285–302. London: Oxford University Press.

———. 1975. Captifs du pouvoir et pouvoir des captifs. In *L'esclavage en Afrique précoloniale,* edited by Claude Meillassoux, 321–50. Paris: Maspero.

Piot, Charles. 1999. *Remotely Global: Village Modernity in West Africa.* Chicago: University of Chicago Press.

Pittin, Renée. 1983. Houses of Women: A Focus on Alternative Life-Styles in Katsina City. In *Female and Male in West Africa,* edited by Christine Oppong, 291–302. Boston: George Allen and Unwin.

Plagnol, Louis. 1947. Document 6.1.8. no. 2, Doutchi. Niamey: Archives Nationales du Niger.

Plato. [1929] 1981. Timaeus. In *Plato in Twelve Volumes.* Vol. 9, translated by Robert Gregg Bury. Cambridge: Harvard University Press.

Ponty, William. 1906. Circulaire à MM. *Les administrateurs et commandants de cercle de la colonie, au sujet du mouvement islamique.* Archives d'Outre Mer, Aix-en-Provence.

Popenoe, Rebecca. 1993. "Girl's Work is Stomach Work": Female Fatness as a Cultural Ideal among Sahelian Arabs. Unpublished manuscript.

Pratt, Mary Louise. 1992. *Imperial Eyes: Travel Writing and Transculturation.* New York: Routledge.

Prince, Raymond. 1968. *Trance and Possession States.* Montreal: RM Bucke Memorial Society.

Rabinow, Paul, and William M. Sullivan. 1987. The Interpretive Turn: A Second Look. In *Interpretive Social Science: A Second Look,* edited by Paul Rabinow and William M. Sullivan. Berkeley: University of California Press.

Ranger, Terence O. 1975. *Dance and Society in Eastern Africa 1890–1970: The Beni Ngoma.* Berkeley: University of California Press.

———. 1977. The People in African Resistance: A Review. *Journal of Southern African Studies* 4 (1): 125–46.

———. 1987. Taking Hold of the Land: Holy Places and Pilgrimages in Twentieth-Century Zimbabwe. *Past and Present* 117:158–94.

Ranger, Terence O., and Eric Hobsbawm, eds. 1984. *The Invention of Tradition.* New York: Cambridge University Press.

Rasmussen, Susan J. 1995. *Spirit Possession and Personhood among the Kel Ewey Tuareg.* Cambridge: Cambridge University Press.

Rattray, R. Sutherland. 1913. *Hausa Folklore: Customs, Proverbs, Etc.* Vol. 2. Oxford: The Clarendon Press.

Raulin, Henri. 1965. Travail et régimes fonciers au Niger. *Cahiers de l'Institut de Science Économique Appliquée. Série Ethnologie, Sociologie, Économie* 9 (166): 119–39.

Raybeck, Douglas, Judy Shoobe, and James Grauberg. 1989. Women, Stress, and Participation in Possession Cults: A Re-examination of the Calcium Deficiency Hypothesis. *Medical Anthropology Quarterly* 3 (2): 139–61.

Raynaut, Claude. 1976. Transformation du système de production et inégalité économique: Le cas d'un village haoussa (Niger). *Canadian Journal of African Studies* 2:279–306.

Reclus, Élysé. 1887. *L'Afrique occidentale.* Vol. 12. Paris: Librairie Hachette.

Regis, Helen A. 1997. Bad Sauce and the Withholding of the Rains: Medicine and Cultural Pluralism among the Fulbe of Northern Cameroon. Ph.D. diss., Department of Anthropology, Tulane University.

Reiter, Rayna R. 1975. Men and Women in the South of France: Public and Private Domain. In *Toward an Anthropology of Women,* edited by Rayna R. Reiter, 252–82. New York: Monthly Review Press.

République du Niger. n.d.(a). Calendrier historique de l'arrondissement de Doutchi. Document 6.1.11. Niamey: Archives Nationales.

———. n.d.(b). Monographie de la subdivision de Doutchi. Document 6.1.6 (c. 1936–40). Niamey: Archives Nationales.

———. 1912. Monographie du secteur de Dosso. Document 6.3.39. Niamey: Archives Nationales.

———. 1941. Monographie du secteur de Dosso. Document 5.1.8. Niamey: Archives Nationales.

———. 1947. Revue des évènements du deuxième trimestre, cercle de Dosso. Document 5.5.7. Niamey: Archives Nationales.

———. 1987. *Charte nationale.* Niamey: Secrétariat Général du Gouvernement.

———. 1988. *Annuaire statistique,* édition 1986–1987. Niamey: Ministère du Plan.

Rogers, Susan Carol. 1975. Female Forms of Power and the Myth of Male Dominance: Model of Female/Male Interaction in a Peasant Society. *American Ethnologist* 2 (4): 727–37.

Rosaldo, Michelle Z. 1974. "Women, Culture, and Society: A Theoretical Overview." In *Women, Culture, and Society,* ed. Michelle Z. Rosaldo and Louise Lamphere, 17–42. Stanford: Stanford University Press.

Rosenthal, Judy. 1998. *Possession, Ecstasy, and Law in Ewe Voodoo.* Charlottesville: University Press of Virginia.

Rouch, Jean. 1956. *Les maîtres fous* (film). Paris: Film de la Pléiade.

———. 1989. *La religion et la magie songhay.* 2d rev. ed. Brussels: Éditions de l'Université de Bruxelles.

Rouget, Gilbert. 1985. *Music and Trance: A Theory of the Relations between Music and Possession,* translated by Brunhilde Biebuyck and Gilbert Rouget. Chicago: University of Chicago Press.

Rowlands, Michael. 1996. The Consumption of an African Modernity. In *African Material Culture,* edited by Mary Jo Arnoldi, Christraud M. Geary, and Kris L. Hardin, 188–213. Bloomington: Indiana University Press.

Ryan, Pauline. 1976. Color Symbolism in Hausa Literature. *Journal of Anthropological Research* 32 (4): 141–60.

Sahlins, Marshall. 1985. *Islands of History.* Chicago: University of Chicago Press.

Salamone, Frank A. 1975. Religion as Play: A Friendly "Witchdoctor." *Journal of Religion in Africa* 3 (3): 201–11.

Saunders, Margaret O. 1978. Marriage and Divorce in a Muslim Hausa Town (Mirrya, Niger Republic). Ph.D. diss., Department of Anthropology, Indiana University.

Schaeffner, André. 1965. Rituel et pré-théâtre. In *Histoire des spectacles* (Encyclopédie de la Pléiade). Paris: Gallimard.

Schildkrout, Enid. 1983. Dependence and Autonomy: The Economic Activities of Secluded Hausa Women in Kano. In *Male and Female in West Africa,* edited by Christine Oppong, 107–26. Boston: George Allen and Unwin.

Schmoll, Pamela. 1991. Searching for Health in a World of Dis-ease: Affliction Management among Rural Hausa of the Maradi Valley. Ph.D. diss., Department of Anthropology, University of Chicago.

———. 1993. Black Stomach, Beautiful Stones: Soul-Eating among Hausa in Niger. In *Modernity and Its Malcontents: Ritual and Power in Postcolonial Africa,* edited by Jean and John Comaroff, 193–220. Chicago: University of Chicago Press.

Scott, James C. 1985. *Weapons of the Weak: Everyday Forms of Peasant Resistance.* New Haven: Yale University Press.

———. 1990. *Domination and the Arts of Resistance: Hidden Transcripts.* New Haven: Yale University Press.

Serée de Rivière, Edmond. 1946. Rapport de tournée effectuée par Serée de Rivière, chef de subdivision de Dogondoutchi. Document 6.3.38. Niamey: Archives Nationales du Niger.

Sharp, Lesley A. 1993. *The Possessed and the Dispossessed: Spirits, Identity, and Power in a Madagascar Migrant Town.* Berkeley: University of California Press.

Shaw, Rosalind. 1985. Gender and the Structuring of Reality in Temne Divination: An Interactive Study. *Africa* 55 (3): 286–303.

Shipton, Parker. 1989. *Bitter Money: Cultural Economy and Some African Mean-*

ings of Forbidden Commodities. American Ethnological Society Monograph, Number 1.

Sindzingre, Nicole. 1985. Healing Is as Healing Does: Pragmatic Resolution of Misfortune among the Senufo (Ivory Coast). *History and Anthropology* 2:33–57.

Smith, Mary F. 1955. Baba of Karo: A Woman of the Muslim Hausa. London: Faber and Faber.

Smith, Michael G. 1959. The Hausa System of Social Status. *Africa* 29 (3): 239–52.

———. 1962. Exchange and Marketing among the Hausa. In *Markets in Africa,* edited by Paul Bohannan and George Dalton. Evanston: Northwestern University Press.

———. 1965. The Hausa of Northern Nigeria. In *Peoples of Africa,* edited by James L. Gibbs Jr., 299–333. New York: Holt, Rinehart and Winston.

Stoller, Paul. 1984. Horrific Comedy: Cultural Resistance and the Hauka Movement in Niger. *Ethos* 12 (2): 165–88.

———. 1989a. *Fusion of the Worlds: An Ethnography of Possession among the Songhay of Niger.* Chicago: University of Chicago Press.

———. 1989b. *The Taste of Ethnographic Things: The Senses in Anthropology.* Philadelphia: University of Pennsylvania Press.

———. 1995. *Embodying Colonial Memories: Spirit Possession, Power, and the Hauka in West Africa.* New York: Routledge.

Stoller, Paul, and Cheryl Olkes. 1986. Bad Sauce, Good Ethnography. *Cultural Anthropology* 1 (3): 336–52.

———. 1987. *In Sorcery's Shadow.* Chicago: University of Chicago Press.

Sutter, John. 1979. Social Analysis of the Nigerien Rural Producer. Vol 2, Part D, of the Niger Agricultural Sector Assessment. Niamey: U. S. Agency for International Development.

Tambiah, Stanley J. 1985. *Culture, Thought and Social Action.* Cambridge: Harvard University Press.

Taussig, Michael. 1980. *The Devil and Commodity Fetishism in South America.* Chapel Hill: University of North Carolina Press.

———. 1984. History as Sorcery. *Representations* 7:87–109.

———. 1993. *Mimesis and Alterity: A Particular History of the Senses.* New York: Routledge.

Taylor, Christopher C. 1988. The Concept of Flow in Rwandan Popular Medicine. *Social Science and Medicine* 27 (12): 1343–48.

Tremearne, Arthur J. N. 1913. *Hausa Superstitions and Customs: An Introduction to the Folklore and the Folk.* Oxford: John Bale and Sons and Danielson.

———. 1914. *The Ban of the Bori: Demons and Demon Dancing in West and North Africa.* London: Heath, Cranton, and Ouseley.

Trevitt, Lorna. 1973. Attitudes and Customs in Childbirth amongst the Hausa Women in Zaria City. *Savanna* 2 (2): 223–26.

Triaud, Jean-Louis. 1974. La question musulmane en Côte d'Ivoire (1893–1939). *Revue Française d'Histoire d'Outre Mer* 61 (225): 542–71.

———. 1981. L'islam et l'état en République du Niger. *Le Mois en Afrique* 193:9–26.

———. 1982. L'islam et l'état en République du Niger. *Le Mois en Afrique* 194:35–48.

Trouillot, Michel-Rolph. 1995. *Silencing the Past: Power and the Production of History.* Boston: Beacon Press.

Turner, Victor W. 1957. *Schism and Continuity in an African Society.* Manchester: Manchester University Press.

———. 1968. *The Drums of Affliction: A Study of Religious Processes among the Ndembu of Zambia.* Oxford: Clarendon Press.

———. 1969. *The Ritual Process: Structure and Anti-Structure.* Chicago: Aldine.

Turner, Victor W., and Edward M. Bruner, eds. 1986. *The Anthropology of Experience.* Chicago: University of Illinois Press.

Umar, Muhammad Sani. 1993. Changing Islamic Identity in Nigeria from the 1960s to the 1980s: From Sufism to Anti-Sufism. In *Muslim Identity and Social Change in Sub-Saharan Africa,* edited by Louis Brenner, 154–78. Bloomington: Indiana University Press.

Vail, Leroy, and Landy White. 1978. Plantation Protest: The History of a Mozambican Song. *Journal of Southern African Studies* 5 (1): 1–25.

van Binsbergen, Wim M. J. 1976. Religious Innovation and Political Conflict in Zambia: A Contribution to the Interpretation of the Lumpa Rising. *African Perspectives* 2:101–35.

———. 1981. *Religious Change in Zambia: Exploratory Studies.* London: Kegan Paul International.

Van Onselin, Charles. 1973. Worker Consciousness in Black Miners: Southern Rhodesia, 1900–1920. *Journal of African History* 14:237–55.

Vaughan, Megan. 1991. *Curing Their Ills: Colonial Power and African Illness.* Stanford, Calif.: Stanford University Press.

Viellard, Gilbert. 1932. Coutumier du Cercle de Dosso. In *Coutumiers juridiques de l'Afrique occidentale française.* Vol. 3. Paris: Librairie Larose.

Wafer, Jim. 1991. *The Taste of Blood: Spirit Possession in Brazilian Candomblé.* Philadelphia: University of Pennsylvania Press.

Wall, Lewis L. 1988. *Hausa Medicine: Illness and Well-Being in a West African Culture.* Durham: Duke University Press.

Ward, C. 1980. Spirit Possession and Mental Health: A Psycho-Anthropological Perspective. *Human Relations* 33 (3): 149–63.

Weber, Max. 1964. *The Theory of Social and Economic Organization.* New York: Free Press.

Weiss, Brad. 1996. *The Making and Unmaking of the Haya Lived World: Consumption, Commoditization, and Everyday Practice.* Durham: Duke University Press.

Werbner, Richard. 1989. *Ritual Passage, Sacred Journey: The Process and Organization of Religious Movement.* Manchester, G.B.: Manchester University Press.

White, Luise. 1990. *The Comforts of Home: Prostitution in Colonial Nairobi.* Chicago: University of Chicago Press.

Whitting, Charles E. J. 1940. *Hausa and Fulani Proverbs.* Lagos, Nigeria: Government Printer.

Wilson, Peter J. 1967. Status Ambiguity and Spirit Possession. *Man* 2:366–78.

Wolf, Eric R. 1982. *Europe and the People without History.* Berkeley: University of California Press.

Works, John A. 1976. *Pilgrims in a Strange Land: Hausa Communities in Chad.* New York: Columbia University Press.

Worsley, Peter. 1982. Non-Western Medical Systems. *Annual Review of Anthropology* 11:315–48.

Index

Abraham, R. 209, 229, 233, 311 n.14

Abu-Lughod, 20, 21, 25, 170

AIDS, 315 n.25

Alhaji, 77, 85, 150, 200, 283, 311 n.16; spirit Malam, 51. *See also* Arziki; Mecca

Allah, 50, 70, 75, 78, 151, 160–61, 192, 195, 196, 222, 262, 266, 268, 278, 281; creator God, 303 n.1; God, 70, 78, 134. *See also* Islam; Satan

Altar(s) (hango), 54, 55, 57, 58, 65, 67, 71, 106, 111, 116, 218–19, 252, 293. *See also* Spirit houses

Anderson, Benedict, 215

Anthill(s), 112, 114, 118, 220

Apter, Andrew, 74

Arabic: language, 216, 263; script, 186. *See also* Koran

Ardener, Edwin, 18

Ardener, Shirley, 18

Arens, William, 21, 22

Arnaud, Robert, 38

Arnould, Eric, 196, 216

Arziki (wealth), 41, 56, 181, 184, 200, 204, 214, 309 n.5. *See also* Alhaji; Trade

Auslander, Mark, 74

Austin, John, 103

Azna: people, 32, 35, 37, 38, 41, 51, 125, 167, 301 n.3

Babba'ku spirits. *See* Zarma spirits

Babcock, Barbara, 254

Baboule mediums: clothing of, 162, 168–69, 177; imitating French military, 162, 164–69; money magic of, 179–82. *See also* Baboule spirits; Chibo; Medium(s)

Baboule spirits: and fire, 159–61, 164, 169, 176–77; strength of, 174–76

Baier, Stephen, 203

Balandier, Georges, 12

Barkow, Jerome, 305 n.6, 313 n.13

Barrenness, 90–91; associated with Maria, 245, 249, 250, 251

Barth, Henry, 301 n.4

Bastian, Misty, 74, 236, 309 n.3

Bastide, Roger, 11, 12

Bauman, Richard, 20

Baura, 167, 189

Beattie, John, 11

Belle, 204, 205, 230

Bernus, Suzanne, 263

Besmer, Fremont, 12, 26, 84, 95, 102, 103, 105

Boddy, Janice, 12, 13, 14, 15, 17, 21, 22, 30, 81, 83, 87, 91, 121, 122, 134, 135, 141, 146, 151, 235, 236, 260, 294

Bokaye (healers), 98–99, 198, 292; Koranic, 85; Muslim clothing of, 262

Bonte, Pierre, 233

Bori: as action upon the world, 124; auspicious days for, 100; boundaries, 8, 31; and change, 11, 22, 27, 43, 50, 62; and competition, 7, 268, 295; and food, 239–44, 313 n.11; and gender, 16, 18, 19, 28, 84, 95, 125, 237–40; heterogeneity of, 47, 91; and hierarchy, 96–99; history, 9, 10, 22, 26, 30, 31, 43, 162, 174, 190, 191, 226, 292, 298, 299; and marginality, 15–20, 26, 43, 201, 222; and marriage, 28, 85, 86, 237–40, 244; and Muslims, 6, 7, 8, 27, 42, 60, 84–87, 125, 151, 195–97, 200–204, 262–63, 267–68, 288–89, 298–99, 302 n.10, 318 n.17; persistence of, 29, 281, 298–99; as play, 125–26, 131–33; as resistance, 6, 23–29, 265, 295; as resource, 81, 298; and sacrifice, 314 n.19; as "women's business," 92–94. *See also* Pantheon; Possession; Sacrifice; Spirit house(s)

Bourdieu, Pierre, 15, 21, 22, 26, 55, 138

Braudel, Fernand, 292

Brink, Judy, 84
Brodwin, Paul, 17, 82, 92
Brown, Karen, 13, 17, 121, 122, 136, 148, 260
Burial: of lightning victims, 286–89; of pregnant women, 246–49
Burke, Timothy, 236
Bush (daji), 49, 53, 55, 61, 62–71, 73, 211, 213, 219, 295, 303 n.2, 304 n.8. See also Gyaran gari

Callaway, Barbara, 18, 26, 84, 244, 299
Capitalism. See Cash economy
Cartry, Michel, 49
Cash economy: Islam and, 203, 225; result of colonialism, 202–207, 225–26; as symbol of corruption of values, 208. See also Baboule mediums: money magic of; Cowries; Francs; French colonialism; Kasuwa; Trade
Census, 165, 182. See also French colonialism
Ceremonies and rituals: abandonment of pre-Islamic, 4, 9, 49, 50, 57–61, 64, 72–75, 195, 217, 225–26, 249, 266–67, 286, 293
Chair(s): as status symbol, 187
Charlick, Robert, 39, 230, 310 n.8
Chibo, 164–66, 169, 170, 175. See also Baboule mediums; Baboule spirits; Commandant Croccichia; French colonialism; Possession; Resistance
Chief. See Sarakuna
Christian(s), 42, 44, 271; colonizers, 37; missionaries, 254, 316 n.28; separate cemeteries of, 286
Clarke, Peter, 36
Clothing: as gift to spirits, 107–110, 304 n.1; as material expression of spirits, 178; of mediums, 162, 164, 168–69, 177, 186, 244, 250, 251, 252, 254, 296, 297; Muslim, 262–64, 269, 278, 280. See also Zarma spirits
Cohen, Abner, 24, 196, 215
Cohen, William, 36, 38
Coles, Catherine, 238
Collion, Marie-Hélène, 36, 182, 188

Colonialism. See French colonialism
Comaroff, Jean, xvi, 14, 16, 20, 21, 22, 25, 26, 30, 92, 122, 126, 128, 170, 171, 172, 173, 186, 236–37, 254, 283, 294
Comaroff, John, xvi, 22, 30, 92, 122, 126, 128, 172, 173, 236–37, 254, 294
Commandant Croccichia, 175, 308 n.2. See also Chibo; French colonialism; Komandan Mugu
Consciousness, 10–11, 29, 41, 170, 171, 172, 173, 183, 201, 215, 218, 226, 260
Cooper, Barbara, 21, 39, 84, 238, 275, 301 n.1, 305 n.6, 310 n.7, 314 n.13
Cosmetics and makeup: implies loose morals, 256; and Maria, 253–58. See also Maria; Perfume
Counihan, Carole, 228
Cowries, 182, 184; replaced by silver coins, 205; uses of, 309 n.7
Crandon-Malamud, Lisbet, 82, 92
Crapanzano, Vincent, 12, 17, 83, 315 n.23
Crowder, Michael, 188
Csordas, Thomas, 12, 183

Darrah, Allan, 84, 232, 233, 235, 238, 247, 248, 314 n.16
Davis, Natalie, 122
de Certeau, Michel, 68, 69
de Heusch, Luc, 11, 49
Delaney, Carol, 90
de Latour (Dejean), Éliane, 33, 34, 35, 36, 38, 39, 49, 59, 60, 202, 206, 207, 229, 294
Deren, Maya, 25, 87
Deschamps, Hubert, 302 n.5
Desjarlais, Robert, 44
Devereux, Georges, 11
Devisch, Renaat, 49, 184
Dewey, John, 183
Divination: to choose chief, 189; cowries and, 310 n.7; to determine place for market, 209
Doguwa, 46, 56, 59, 73, 102, 105, 111, 112, 118, 129, 130, 132, 133, 136, 139, 141, 142, 145, 148, 194, 195, 196, 197, 201, 217, 218, 226, 296, 305 n.9, 307 n.19, 309 n.2

Douglas, Mary, 183, 213
Drewal, Margaret, 126
Durham, Deborah, 236

Échard, Nicole, 9, 10, 26, 51, 90, 95, 168, 169, 233, 235, 270, 278, 279, 301 n.1, 316 n.1, 316 n.26
Empowerment: techniques of, 182–88, 201, 220–25
Erlmann, Veit, 103
Evans-Pritchard, Edward, 122, 124
Évolués, 41

Fabian, Johannes, 228
Fanon, Frantz, 24, 25
Faulkingham, Ralph, 84
Fernandez, James, 197
Field, Margaret, 12
Foucault, Michel, 15, 21, 22, 23, 201
Francs: devaluation of, 311 n.1; and spirits, 179–80; taxes to be paid in, 182
Frazer, James, 11
French colonialism: and Baboule, 162, 164–69, 174–78, 188–91; and cash economy, 36, 59, 202–7, 225–26; and chiefs, 188–89; and Islam, 36–38, 202, 215. See also Census; Chibo; Commandant Croccichia; Lightning; Niger: French administration of; Prison; Resistance; Taxation and taxes
Frishman, Alan, 305 n.6
Frobenius, Leo, 304 n.8
Fry, Peter, 25
Fuglestad, Finn, 36, 39, 163, 164, 165, 166, 167, 169, 170, 171, 176, 182, 270, 308 n.7

Gado. See Heritage
Gibbal, Jean-Marie, 12, 120, 123
Giles, Linda, 16
Giletti, Dody, 12
Gluckmann, Max, 24
Gomm, Roger, 12
Goody, Jack, 215
Gottlieb, Alma, 74, 236, 303 n.2

Gouffé, Claude, 259
Gouilly, Alphonse, 302 n.5
Gramsci, Antonio, 21
Grauberg, James, 12
Greenberg, Joseph, 84
Grégoire, Emmanuel, 43, 196, 199, 215, 309 n.5
Griaule, Marcel, 112
Guillas, Elian, 203
Guillon, Jean-Michel, 193, 198
Gumba (uncooked millet), 71, 247–48
Gussler, Judith, 12
Gyaran gari, 30, 49–53, 63, 64, 67–72; abandonment of, 49–50, 64, 72; and illness, 49, 71–72; timing of, 64

Hauka spirits. See Baboule spirits
Healers, 92–93, 95. See also Bokaye
Healing, 23, 65, 78–79, 83, 125, 126, 130, 157, 294
Health (lahiya), 63, 68, 71, 74, 142, 143, 150, 151, 154; and biomedicine, 80, 92; and diagnosis-making, 82–86; as dimension of possession, 79; and exorcism, 82; and pregnancy, 80, 232–235; and spirits, 77–78, 82, 85, 106–7, 110–11, 306 n.15
Hebdige, Dick, 170, 202
Herbert, Eugenia, 278
Heritage, 32, 33, 56, 57, 58, 60, 61, 203, 244, 281
Herskovits, Melville, 265, 271, 317 n.3
Herzfeld, Michael, 82
Higgott, Richard, 39
Hill, Polly, 196, 238
Hiskett, Mervyn, 215
Hobsbawm, Eric, 246
Holey, 13, 121, 269, 308 n.5
Horowitz, Michael, 216, 217
Horse. See Medium(s)
Households: changing configuration, 36, 59, 60; as icon of past, 60; Muslim, 42, 44, 94, 127; precolonial 33; ritual contribution from, 64, 71; women's positions in, 18, 28
Howard, Alan, 130, 228
Howes, David, 228

Hugh-Jones, Christine, 228
Huizinga, Johan, 126
Hutchinson, Karen, 236

Ileto, Reynaldo, 171
Illness, 105; associated with sugar, 232;
  skin color as sign of, 143; spirits as
  agents of, 48, 65, 79, 80, 81, 84–86,
  105; 152
Imperialism. See French colonialism
Initiation, 46, 97, 111–18
Irvine, Judith, 101
Isichei, Elizabeth, 43
Islam: in association with power, 41,
  200; colonial attitudes toward, 36–
  38, 202, 215; equated with prayer, 4,
  28, 314 n.19; expansion of, 9, 10, 28,
  32, 37, 41, 42, 201–3; and greed, 45,
  60; hegemony of, 4, 8, 30, 74, 203,
  223–24, 283, 289, 298–99, 313 n.12; as
  loss, 208; and trade, 5, 42, 75, 200–
  1, 214–17; universality of, 75; and
  women, 85–86, 93, 237–38, 245, 281,
  313 n.13. See also Allah; Arabic; Bori:
  and Muslims; Cash economy: Islam
  and; Kasuwa: as Muslim institution;
  Koran; Malamai (Muslim clerics);
  Mecca; Seclusion; Spirit house(s):
  and mosques; Umma
Izala, 43, 299, 302 n.9

Jackson, Michael, 183, 184, 185
Janzen, John, 14, 49, 92, 126
Jewsiewicki, Bogumil, 236
Johnson, G. Wesley, 38

Kane, Ousmane, 302 n.9
Kankara. See Thunderstone(s)
Kapferer, Bruce, 13, 14, 24
'Karfi (strength), 181, 188
Karp, Ivan, 21, 22
Karuwa. See Prostitute (karuwa) and
  prostitution
Kasuwa (market): 46, 80, 100, 127, 128,
  130; dangers of, 192–94, 211–13, 309
  n.3; Doguwa of, 194–97, 217, 226,
  296, 309 n.2; establishment of, 62,

67, 194; as fundamental institution of
  Mawri society, 204; as Muslim insti-
  tution, 214–17; mystical geography
  and, 218; organization of, 198–99;
  world, 39. See also Cash economy;
  Trade
Kehoe, Alice, 12
Kennedy, John, 12
King, Anthony, 133
Kinship: Mawri, 33, 136–44; spirit,
  136–44
Kola nut(s), 99, 159, 198, 199, 205, 208,
  241, 250
Komandan Mugu, 160, 164, 175, 308 n.2.
  See also Baboule spirits; Comman-
  dant Crocchicha; Pantheon
Koran, 7, 17, 28, 43, 45, 78, 84, 203, 204,
  222, 263, 278, 279, 280, 288, 318 n.16;
  Koranic injunctions, 43; Koranic
  message, 36, 60; Koranic orientations,
  27; Koranic prayers, 263; Koranic
  scholar, 78; Koranic verses, 151
Kotoudi, Idimama, 230
Krammer, Fritz, 14, 26, 163, 184
Kratz, Corinne, 49

Labouret, Henri, 38
Laderman, Carol, 104
Lahiya. See Health
Lambek, Michael, 13, 14, 121, 122, 125,
  135, 136, 138, 153, 158, 183, 291
Lan, David, 14, 21, 25, 74, 122, 170, 171,
  236
Larose, Serge, 13
Last, Murray, 49, 92, 133, 233, 314 n.16
Le Chatelier, Alfred, 302 n.5
Leiris, Michel, 12, 87, 120, 147, 303 n.1
Leroy, Paul, 167
Lévi-Strauss, Claude, 82, 228
Levy, Robert, 130, 228
Lewis, Ioan, 7, 12, 15, 16, 20, 170, 192,
  292, 294
Lightning, 10; as means of resisting
  French, 177–78; as means of resist-
  ing Islam, 265, 269, 318 n.19; Muslim
  concept of, 266–267. See also Zarma
  spirits

Literacy, 31, 186–87, 308 n.5, 316 n.28
Lougou, 33, 34, 35, 51, 167, 190, 301 n.3
Lovejoy, Paul, 214, 215
Luck. *See* sa'a

Mack, Beverly, 238
Magagi, Habou, 103
Mageo, Jeannette, 130, 228
Makeup. *See* Cosmetics and makeup
Malamai (Muslim clerics), 195, 262, 263, 279, 283, 284, 288, 289, 292, 311 n.18, 318 n.19. *See also* Bori: and Muslims; Islam; Spirit house(s): destruction of
Malinowski, Bronislav, 66, 103
Mango(es): metaphor for life, 259
Manning, Frank, 24
Marcus, George, 170
Maria, 5, 6, 144, 149, 153; and consumer culture, 231, 244–46, 253–55, 260; and destructive sexuality, 244–46, 252–53; dislikes children, 247, 250–52; as incarnation of dead pregnant women, 249, 314 nn.15, 20; and polygamy, 257; wanton nature of, 147–48; wife of Zahoho, 152, 153, 227–28, 257–59, 316 n.29. *See also* Cosmetics and makeup; Mirror(s); Perfume; Possession; Prostitute (karuwa) and prostitution; Sexuality; Zaki (sweetness)
Market. *See* Kasuwa
Marks, Shula, 170
Masquelier, Adeline, 30, 40, 43, 59, 73, 75, 90, 98, 105, 107, 110, 128, 130, 178, 188, 208, 218, 228, 234, 264, 265, 267, 302 n.9, 303 n.5, 304 n.1, 305 n.9, 306 n.15, 309 n.2, 317 n.4, 317 n.11
Matankari, 34, 35, 167, 177, 301 n.3, 312 n.6
Matory, James, 14, 87, 265, 292, 304 n.4
Mauss, Marcel, 185
Mayer, Joel, 40, 302 n.8
Mayu. *See* Sorcerer
Mecca: and Medina, 275, 283; pilgrimage to, 8, 22, 77, 85, 150, 168, 200, 216, 262, 281. *See also* Alhaji; Islam
Medicine(s), 77, 83, 93, 95, 252, 266;

herbal, 99, 305 n.10; in initiation, 97; and market, 212; and milk, 273, 318 n.12; Muslim, 307 n.21; practice of, 98; preparation of, 96, 305 n.8; and prosperity, 114; sale of, 81, 243; and spirits, 98; Western, 79, 315 n.21
Medium(s): referred to as horse, 161, 176–77, 314 n.14, 316 n.29. *See also* Baboule mediums; Possession
Meigs, Anna, 228
Meillassoux, Claude, 311 n.15
Merleau-Ponty, Maurice, 159, 183, 185
Mernissi, Fatima, 84
Messing, Simon, 12
Métraux, Alfred, 12, 13
Middleton, John, 11
Migration, 3, 40, 60
Miles, William, 41, 275
Milk: and lightning, 271, 317 n.11, 317 n.12, 318 n.18; and medicine, 273, 318 n.12
Millet, 1, 3, 55, 144, 308 n.4; bed of, 57; day laborers paid in, 207; as food staple, 206; as gift, 137
Mintz, Sidney, 230, 231, 312 n.4
Mirror(s): and Maria, 254; and Westerners, 254
Money. *See* Cash economy
Monfouga-Nicolas, Jacqueline, 8, 49, 84, 87, 88, 90, 95, 125, 169
Muller, Carol, 48
Munn, Nancy, 55
Music and musicians, 3, 7, 100–105, 138, 159–60, 177, 196, 227, 228, 241–42, 272, 305 n.12, 306 nn.13, 14
"Muted group" theory, 18–19

Nicolas, Guy, 9, 33, 34, 39, 42, 55, 62, 63, 65, 66, 68, 71, 84, 102, 196, 200, 204, 209, 212, 213, 263
Niger: foreign aid, 40; French administration of, 164–67, 275, 285; and Islam, 41–42; at independence, 38–39, 41, 77, 203; Republic of, 162; Zarma government of, 270. *See also* French colonialism
Nisula, Tapio, 92, 294

O'Brien, Donald, 38
Ohnuki-Tierney, Emiko, 228
Olivier de Sardan, Jean-Pierre, 122, 123, 124, 163
Olkes, Cheryl, 123, 228
Oloruntemehin, Olatunji, 36
Ong, Aihwa, 14, 21, 25, 170, 260
Onwuejeogwu, Michael, 12, 26
Ox: sacrificial, 194–95, 283, 293. See also Sacrifice

Pantheon: Baboule, 175; Bori, 5, 88, 96, 103, 105, 110, 111, 125, 130, 137, 143, 155, 253, 255, 262, 271, 289, 291, 312 n.9; Gubawa, 63; personal, 151; Songhay, 169, 313 n.12, 317 n.10; thunder, 317 n.3; Zar, 151
Péhaut, Yves, 59, 203
Perfume, 245, 250, 253–57; drank by Maria, 256, 261. See also Cosmetics and makeup; Maria
Philibert, Jean-Marc, 24
Piault, Colette, 233, 314 n.16
Piault, Marc-Henri, 32, 33, 34, 37, 51, 196, 199, 294, 301 nn.3, 4
Piot, Charles, 74, 236
Pittin, Renée, 238, 305 n.6, 313 n.13
Plagnol, Louis, 63
Plato, 11
Ponty, William, 37, 38
Popenoe, Rebecca, 228
Possession: as bodily practice, 185–87; equestrian metaphor of, 87; fake, 132–33; feminizing effect of, 89; as hard work, 305 n.7; as history, 9–10; latent dimension of, 122, 133, 148; as madness, 11–12; and marriage, 89, 304 n.4; multidimensionality of, 124; and otherness, 155; and receptivity, 87–90, 154; and resistance, 25–31, 162–67, 265, 294; spontaneous, 128–30; as theater, 12–13, 132; trivialization of, 133. See also Baboule mediums; Baboule spirits; Bori; Maria; Medium(s); Wasa
Power, 20–23, 169–74, 226; of bori, 200, 201, 208; center of, 197, 200,
202; and mundane practices, 22; reduction of devotees', 217, 208; of the spirits, 196, 199, 209, 213. See also Bori; Resistance
Pratt, Mary Luise, 21
Prince, Raymond, 12
Prison, 175–76, 181, 308 n.2. See also French colonialism
Prostitute (karuwa) and prostitution: and bori, 6, 43, 46, 83, 89, 91, 94, 131, 237, 305 n.6; and Islam, 313 n.13; and Maria, 106, 144, 148, 149, 155, 244–46, 257; musicians as, 102. See also Sexuality

Rabinow, Paul, 14
Ranger, Terence, 21, 25, 26, 170, 218, 222, 246
Rasmussen, Susan, 13, 265
Rattray, R. Sutherland, 234
Raybeck, Douglas, 12
Raynaut, Claude, 60
Reclus, Élysé, 1
Regis, Helen, 92
Reiter, Rayna, 18
Resistance, 23–31; Baboule movement as, 172–73; and possession, 162–67, 265; as ritualized mode of action, 170. See also Bori; Power
Ricoeur, Paul, 14
Rogers, Susan, 18
Rosalso, Michele, 18
Rosenthal, Judy, 12, 13, 14
Rouch, Jean, 11, 12, 163, 168, 169, 174, 175, 185, 263, 269, 275, 307 n.18, 308 nn.3, 6, 317 n.9, 10, 11
Rouget, Gilbert, 12, 104
Rowlands, Michael, 261
Ryan, Pauline, 279

Sa'a (luck), 56, 130, 166, 181, 204, 214, 308 n.7
Sacrifice, 8, 33, 34, 53, 54, 56–57, 58, 61, 62, 63, 64, 67, 68–71, 98, 111, 113, 116, 194–95, 196, 216, 221, 271, 293, 304 n.8; sacrificial knife, 56, 57, 58
Sahlins, Marshall, 294

Salamone, Frank, 126
Sarakuna (chiefs), 188; chosen by divination, 189; chosen by French, 188–89. *See also* Sarki
Sarauniya, 33, 51, 167, 188, 189, 190
Sarki, 34, 89, 175, 189; sarkin Arewa, 35, 164, 167, 177, 188, 190, 194; sarkin bori, 96, 97, 142, 177, 179, 282, 303 n.6; sarkin gaugawa, 272; warriors of, 35
Satan, 78, 84, 279–81
Saunders, Margaret, 239
Schaeffner, André, 12
Schildkrout, Enid, 238
Schmoll, Pamela, 8, 60, 84, 88, 92, 95, 169, 181, 196, 199, 209, 210, 236, 246, 255, 274, 318 n.14
Scott, James, 21, 25, 26, 171, 173
Seclusion: of Muslim women, 6, 18, 209, 310 n.9. *See also* Islam: and women
Self: conception of, 87–89; and body, 87–89, 157, 285; soul, 88–89, 285, 304 n.5
Serée de Rivière, Edmond, 32
Sexuality: dangers of, 252–53, 315 n.25. *See also* AIDS; Maria; Prostitution
Sharp, Lesley, 4, 14, 16
Shaw, Rosalind, 26
Shipton, Parker, 74
Shoobe, Judy, 12
Sindzingre, Nicole, 49
Slavery, 35, 201, 301 n.4; and sacrifice, 194
Smith, Mary, 91, 210, 211, 234
Smith, Michael, 196, 197, 198, 248
Sorcerer (maye), 177, 265–67, 269–70, 272, 279, 303 n.5, 317 n.6. *See also* Witchcraft and witches
Spirit(s): and dreams, 6, 127, 130, 243, 253; evil, 73, 75, 128; existence, 7; and human settlements, 51, 52, 55, 56, 57; invisible, 134; land, 33, 51, 55, 58, 64; negotiation with, 127; new, 10; obligations to, 92; origin of, 52–53; and peace, 58–59; tutelary, 7; as violent, 10, 133; and wind, 64–65, 88, 100, 269, 306 n.15

Spirit house(s): destruction of, 311 n.18; and Maria, 255; and moral topography, 222; and mosques, 222–24, 296; presents to, 221–22, 224; of Zarma spirits, 218–20, 276. *See also* Altar(s) (hango)
Spirit world: families of, 135, 139–41; overlapping with human world, 141–44; parallels with human worlds, 143; rivalries in, 136–38
Stoller, Paul, 13, 66, 101, 103, 120, 123, 135, 163, 165, 168, 169, 174, 228, 229, 269, 308 n.5, 312 n.12, 315 n.23
Sugar, 10, as embodiment of zaki, 229, 312 n.4; fura enhanced by, 231, 311 n.2; importation of, 230, 256; and Maria, 255–56; and pregnancy, 232–33
Sullivan, William, 14
Sutter, John, 202
Sweetness, 6, 10. *See* Sugar; Zaki

Tambiah, Stanley, 66
Tarkama (judgment by ordeal), 56–57
Taussig, Michael, 163, 173
Taxation and taxes, 36, 165, 181–82, 188, 201, 203, 209, 309 nn.1, 4; resistance to taxes, 165, 169, 181, 182. *See also* French colonialism
Taylor, Christopher, 49
Thunderstones, 272, 278, 317 n.11
Trade: as only avenue to arziki, 200. *See also* Arziki (wealth); Cash economy; Islam; Kasuwa
Tremearne, Arthur, 84, 234, 318 n.16
Trevitt, Lorna, 234
Triaud, Jean-Louis, 38, 41
Trouillot, Michel-Rolph, 174, 190, 191
Turner, Victor, 13, 16, 19, 20, 24, 49, 166
Twins: mythical, 52–53

Umar, Muhammad, 43, 302 n.9
Umma, 50, 263

Vail, Leroy, 21
van Binsbergen, Wim, 21, 25, 26, 174
Van Onselin, Charles, 25

Vaughan, Megan, 80
Viellard, Gilbert, 262
Vodou, 17, 25, 133, 136, 148

Wafer, Jim, 14, 121, 122
Wall, Lewis, 49, 84, 112, 198, 234, 279
War, 32, 34, 35, 38, 40, 56, 60, 189, 202, 301 n.3; holy wars, 29, 37; World War II, 38
Wasa, 159, 169, 176, 241, 243, 244, 250, 251, 258, 270, 280–83, 308 n.1, 317 n.5, 318 n.19
Weber, Max, 20, 21
Weiss, Brad, 49, 67, 92, 149, 228, 236, 237, 315 n.25
Werbner, Richard, 74
White, Landeg, 21
White, Luise, 259

Whitting, Charles, 213
Wilson, Peter, 12
Witchcraft and witches, 164, 168, 267, 275, 301 n.2. *See also* Sorcerer (maye)
Wolf, Eric, 170
Works, John, 196, 214
Worsley, Peter, 92

Zaki (sweetness): 10, multiple meanings of, 228–29; and pregnancy, 232–33, 247; and sexuality, 232, 247
Zar, 13, 15, 17, 30, 81, 91, 120, 122, 141, 146, 147, 151, 303 n.1
Zarma people, 38, 39, 95, 177–78
Zarma spirits, 10, 96, 100, 107, 111, 114, 169, 246, 304 n.8, 306 n.14, 307 nn.18, 19; and justice, 275–79, 318 n.13; lightning and, 177–78, 269–72

Adeline Masquelier is Associate Professor
in the department of anthropology
at Tulane University.

Library of Congress Cataloging-in-Publication Data

Masquelier, Adeline Marie
Prayer has spoiled everything : possession, power,
and identity in an Islamic town of Niger /
Adeline Masquelier.
p. cm. — (Body, commodity, text)
Includes bibliographical references and index.
ISBN 0-8223-2633-7 (cloth : alk. paper) —
ISBN 0-8223-2639-6 (pbk. : alk. paper)
1. Mawri (African people)—Niger—Dogondoutchi—
Religion.   2. Bori (Cult)—Niger—Dogondoutchi.
3. Dogondoutchi (Niger)—Religion.   I. Title.
II. Series.
BL2480.M32 M37 2001
299'.37—dc21   00-047696